BRIDGING CULTURAL AND DEVELOPMENTAL
APPROACHES TO PSYCHOLOGY

Bridging Cultural and Developmental Approaches to Psychology

New Syntheses in Theory, Research, and Policy

EDITED BY

LENE ARNETT JENSEN

OXFORD
UNIVERSITY PRESS
2011

OXFORD
UNIVERSITY PRESS

Oxford University Press, Inc., publishes works that further
Oxford University's objective of excellence
in research, scholarship, and education.

Oxford   New York
Auckland   Cape Town   Dar es Salaam   Hong Kong   Karachi
Kuala Lumpur   Madrid   Melbourne   Mexico City   Nairobi
New Delhi   Shanghai   Taipei   Toronto

With offices in
Argentina   Austria   Brazil   Chile   Czech Republic   France   Greece
Guatemala   Hungary   Italy   Japan   Poland   Portugal   Singapore
South Korea   Switzerland   Thailand   Turkey   Ukraine   Vietnam

Published by Oxford University Press, Inc.
198 Madison Avenue, New York, New York 10016

www.oup.com

Oxford is a registered trademark of Oxford University Press, Inc.

Library of Congress Cataloging-in-Publication Data
Bridging cultural and developmental approaches to psychology: new syntheses
in theory, research, and policy / edited by Lene Arnett Jensen.
    p. cm.
Includes bibliographical references and index.
ISBN 978-0-19-538343-0
1. Developmental psychology.   2. Developmental psychology—Social aspects.
I. Jensen, Lene Arnett.
BF713.B75 2010
155—dc22
2010009153

9 8 7 6 5 4 3 2

Printed in the United States of America
on acid-free paper

To my parents, whose many travels and moves have
given me more than one place to call home.

"We build too many walls and not enough bridges"

—Isaac Newton

CONTENTS

About the Editor   xi

Contributors   xiii

Foreword
William Damon   xvii

Introduction: Changing Our Scholarship for a Changing World
Lene Arnett Jensen   xxi

PART I.   DEVELOPMENTAL PROCESSES AND CULTURE

Chapter 1.   The Cultural-Developmental Theory of Moral Psychology:
A New Synthesis
Lene Arnett Jensen   3

Chapter 2.   Cultural Frames of Children's Learning Beliefs
Jin Li   26

Chapter 3.   A Global Window on Memory Development
Michelle D. Leichtman   49

PART II.   DEVELOPMENTAL CONTEXTS AND CULTURE

Chapter 4.   Merging Cultural and Psychological Accounts
of Family Contexts
Jacqueline J. Goodnow   73

Chapter 5.   Culture, Peer Relationships, and Human Development
Xinyin Chen   92

Chapter 6.   Civil Societies as Cultural and Developmental Contexts
for Civic Identity Formation
Constance Flanagan, M. Loreto Martínez, & Patricio Cumsille   113

Chapter 7.   Adolescent Ties to Adult Communities: The Intersection
of Culture and Development
Alice Schlegel   138

PART III.   DEVELOPMENTAL SELVES AND CULTURE

Chapter 8.   Identity Development in Multiple Cultural Contexts
Jean S. Phinney & Oscar A. Baldelomar   161

Chapter 9.   Cultural and Developmental Pathways to Acceptance
of Self and Acceptance of the World
Fred Rothbaum & Yan Z. Wang   187

Chapter 10.   The Development of Individual Purposes: Creating
Actuality Through Novelty
Jaan Valsiner   212

PART IV.   DEVELOPMENTAL PHASES AND CULTURE

Chapter 11.   The Culturalization of Developmental Trajectories:
A Perspective on African Childhoods and Adolescences
A. Bame Nsamenang   235

Chapter 12.   Emerging Adulthood(s): The Cultural Psychology
of a New Life Stage
Jeffrey Jensen Arnett   255

Chapter 13.   Reconceptualizing Lifespan Development Through
a Hindu Perspective
T.S. Saraswathi, Jayanthi Mistry, & Ranjana Dutta   276

COMMENTARY

Chapter 14.   Commentary: Ontogenetic Cultural Psychology
Richard A. Shweder   303

Index   311

ABOUT THE EDITOR

Lene Arnett Jensen is Associate Professor of Psychology at Clark University, USA, where she holds the Oliver and Dorothy Hayden Junior Faculty Fellowship. She received her Ph.D. from the University of Chicago. Her writings address cultural identity, moral development, and civic engagement. Her research focuses on immigrants and groups that are culturally and religiously diverse. Dr. Jensen's publications include *Immigrant Civic Engagement: New Translations* (2008, with C. A. Flanagan, Taylor, & Francis) and *New Horizons in Developmental Theory and Research* (2005, with R. W. Larson, Jossey-Bass/ Wiley). She is Editor-in-Chief of *New Directions for Child and Adolescent Development*, and a member of the editorial board of the Journal of Research on Adolescence. She also serves on the board of directors of two community organizations, Liberty's Promise in Washington, D.C. and Children's Friend in Worcester, MA. A native of Denmark, Dr. Jensen has resided in a number of countries, including Belgium, India and France. She lives in Massachusetts, USA, with her husband and twin children.

CONTRIBUTORS

Jeffrey Jensen Arnett is Research Professor in the Department of Psychology at Clark University, USA. His main scholarly interests involve emerging adults (ages 18–29). His books include *Emerging Adulthood: The Winding Road from the Late Teens Through the Twenties* (2004, Oxford University Press), and the two-volume *International Encyclopedia of Adolescence* (2007, Routledge). Dr. Arnett is also Editor of the *Journal of Adolescent Research.*

Oscar A. Baldelomar is a doctoral candidate in developmental psychology at the University of California, Los Angeles, USA. He conducts research on ethnic identity development in Costa Rica and the United States. He uses psychological and anthropological methodologies, and has created new measures of identity development in children and adolescents. His research has been published in *Child Development.*

Xinyin Chen is Professor of Psychology at University of Western Ontario, Canada. He has received a William T. Grant Scholars Award and several other awards. He is interested in children's socioemotional functioning and relationships, with a focus on cross-cultural issues. He has edited several books, including *Peer Relationships in Cultural Context* and *Socioemotional Development in Cultural Context*. Dr. Chen has also published over 100 articles and chapters about culture and development.

Patricio Cumsille is Associate Profesor of Psychology and Vice-Chair for Research and Graduate Studies in Psychology at Pontificia Universidad Católica de Chile. His research addresses adolescent autonomy development and quantitative methods. Dr. Cumsille is Editor of *Psykhe*, a leading psychological journal in Latin America.

William Damon is Professor of Education and Director of the Center on Adolescence at Stanford University, USA. Dr. Damon has written about moral character and commitment at all ages of life. His books include *The Moral Child* (1990), *Some Do Care* (1992) (with Anne Colby*)*, *Greater Expectations* (1995), *The Youth Charter* (1997), *Good Work* (2001) (with Howard Gardner and Mihaly Csikszentmihalyi), *Noble Purpose* (2003), *The Moral Advantage* (2004), and *The Path to Purpose* (2008).

Ranjana Dutta is Professor of Psychology at Saginaw Valley State University, USA. She holds a MS in child development and family studies from Maharaja Sayajirao University, India, and a Ph.D. in individual and family studies from Pennsylvania State University, USA. Dr. Dutta's scholarly interests include socialization in India and lifespan implications such as perceived control, goals, and wisdom.

Constance Flanagan is Professor in the School of Human Ecology at the University of Wisconsin-Madison, USA. Her research concerns adolescents' theories of the 'social contract' and the role of mediating institutions as spaces where youth negotiate the social contract. Dr. Flanagan is co-editor of the new Wiley *Handbook of Research and Policy on Youth Civic Engagement.*

Jacqueline J. Goodnow is Research Professor at the Institute of Early Childhood at Macquarie University, Australia. She addresses how cultural contexts enrich our understanding of what development covers, and how individuals develop different skills and values. Dr. Goodnow's books include *Cultural Practices as Contexts for Development* (with Miller & Kessel, 1995, Jossey-Bass).

Michelle D. Leichtman is Associate Professor of Psychology and Lamberton Chair in the Study of Criminal Justice and Society at the University of New Hampshire in Durham, USA. Dr. Leichtman holds a B.A. from Wellesley College and an MA and Ph.D. from Cornell University. She is a developmental psychologist who has published widely on issues surrounding children's memory development.

Jin Li is Associate Professor at Brown University, USA. Originally from China, she received her doctorate in human development from Harvard University. She studies how children of different cultures and ethnicities, particularly immigrant groups, develop learning beliefs and how they achieve. She also studies self-conscious emotions such as respect, pride, shame and guilt across cultures. She has received funding from a number of foundations and has published widely in professional journals and books.

M. Loreto Martínez is Associate Profesor of Psychology at Pontificia Universidad Católica de Chile. Her research focuses on the development civic competencies and commitments in adolescence, in particular, as they relate to opportunities for social involvement in school, community, and youth organizations. Dr. Martínez is also conducting longitudinal research on adolescent autonomy in Chilean youth.

Jayanthi Mistry is Associate Professor in the Eliot-Pearson Department of Child Development at Tufts University, USA. Originally from India, she received her doctorate from Purdue University, and then completed a two year NIMH Postdoctoral Fellowship in the Department of Psychology at the University of Utah. Her scholarship takes a socio-cultural approach, addressing the processes whereby children from ethnic minority and immigrant families develop and negotiate multiple cultural orientations and identities.

A. Bame Nsamenang is Associate Professor of Psychology and Learning Science at the University of Yaoundé 1 (ENS) and Director of Human Development Resource Centre in Bamenda, Cameroon. His research explores local understandings of child and youth development in African cultural circumstances. Dr. Nsamenang's publications include *Human Development in Cultural Context: A Third World Perspective* (1992, Sage), and *Cultures of Human Development and Education: Challenge to Growing up in Africa* (2004, Nova).

Jean Phinney is Emeritus Professor of Psychology from California State University, Los Angeles, and currently a visiting scholar at the University of California, Berkeley, USA. For 20 years, her research has focused on identity formation, particularly ethnic and cultural identity among adolescents and emerging adults. Dr. Phinney developed the widely used Multigroup Ethnic Identity Measure. Her books include *Immigrant Youth in Cultural Transition* (2006, with Berry, Sam, & Vedder, Erlbaum).

Fred Rothbaum is Professor and Director of Graduate Studies at the Eliot-Pearson Department of Child Development at Tufts University, USA. He has published widely on socialization and cultural processes as they relate to children's perceived control, behavior problems, attachment and emotion regulation. Dr. Rothbaum is also President of the Child & Family WebGuide, a web portal providing research to parents, professionals and students.

T. S. Saraswathi is retired Senior Professor in Human Development and Family Studies from the Maharaja Sayajirao University of Baroda, India. Dr. Saraswathi is co-editor of the *Handbook of Cross-Cultural Psychology* (1997, vol.2), *The International Encyclopedia of Adolescence* (2007), *and World Youth: Adolescence in Eight Regions of the Globe* (2003). She has also edited *Cross-Cultural Perspectives in Human Development* (2003) and *Culture, Socialization, and Human Development* (1999).

Alice Schlegel is Professor Emerita of Anthropology and Research Associate at the McClelland Institute for Children, Youth and Families at the University of Arizona, USA. Her fieldwork has addressed the Hopi in the U.S., and adolescent industrial apprenticeship and civic participation in Germany and Italy. Her numerous publications include the worldwide survey, *Adolescence: An Anthropological Inquiry* (1991, with Barry, Free Press).

Richard A. Shweder is a cultural anthropologist and the William Claude Reavis Distinguished Service Professor of Human Development at the University of Chicago, USA. His research addresses moral reasoning, emotional functioning, gender roles, and explanations of illness. Dr. Shweder's books include *The Child* (2009, University of Chicago Press), *Why Do Men Barbecue?* (2003, Harvard University Press), and *Thinking Through Cultures* (1991, Harvard University Press).

Jaan Valsiner is Professor of Psychology at Clark University, USA. He brings a developmental axiomatic base to cultural analyses of psychological phenomena. Dr. Valsiner is Founding Editor of the journal *Culture & Psychology* (1995, Sage), and Editor-in-Chief of *Integrative Psychological and Behavioral Sciences* (Springer). His books include *The Guided Mind* (1998, Harvard University Press), *Culture and Human Development* (2000, Sage), and the *Cambridge Handbook of Socio-Cultural Psychology* (2007, with Rosa, Cambridge University Press).

Yan Z. Wang is Assistant Professor at the School of Family, Consumer and Nutrition Sciences at Northern Illinois University, USA. Dr. Wang received her M.A. from East China Normal University, and her Ph.D. from the University of Illinois at Urbana-Champaign. Her research addresses the influence of cultural frameworks on individual development and family dynamics. Dr. Wang has published on methodological issues in culture studies, dinnertime family interactions, and immigrant parenting.

FOREWORD

WILLIAM DAMON

Social science is replete with parallel speech. In fact, the more fundamental a problem—that is, the more central it is to basic human concerns—the more likely it is that it will be treated with multiple social-scientific analyses that are difficult to connect. Among the more notorious examples of this are the four ideas at the heart of this book: culture, development, morality, and self. These immensely important concepts have been dealt with in so many different ways across so many incongruent frames of analysis that attempts at discussion often slip away with a frustrating sense that the parties have done little more than talked past one another with separate word meanings.

Is culture a matter of belief, practice, history, geography, or populace? Does development imply a special kind of change, or is it synonymous with learning? Is morality a matter of justice, social rules, personal sentiment, intention, routine conduct, or dramatic life-and-death decisions in lifeboats and trolley cars? Is the locus of self to be found in individual or collective identity? These divisions are definitional and more: they reflect divergent visions of human nature that often have proven irreconcilable in both scholarly and popular debate. For the mission of building knowledge about crucial human phenomena, this obviously is an unfortunate state of affairs.

The present book attacks this problem by building bridges among perspectives on culture and human development—perspectives that in prior work have sometimes stood in opposition and sometimes ignored one another entirely. Bringing together disparate frames of analysis is always a worthwhile endeavor, for the simple reason that it opens the way to insights that are inaccessible to either frame alone. Neither the cultural nor the developmental perspective in itself can offer a complete vision of human life. This is because, taken to their logical conclusions, both have blind spots: the cultural perspective has little interest in commonalities among people from dissimilar backgrounds; the developmental perspective favors generalities that can disregard or distort particular life experiences. What could be more fruitful than combining the two perspectives into an inclusive account of human behavior as it plays out across time and circumstance?

Yet the two perspectives are not easy to reconcile. Points of resistance have ranged from the definitional that I mentioned above, to the ideological, to the conceptual. On the ideological front, cultural and developmental views often have been separated by longstanding oppositions between universalism and contextualism, absolutism and relativism, uniformity and diversity, and even the historically charged conflict of nativism versus imperialism. Such oppositions extend well beyond the circles of academic debate: one of the burning political questions of our time is how much solidarity in cultural values and practices a society should aim for when it inducts new members through socialization or immigration. On the conceptual front, scholars have bumped up against the familiar problem of finding a language that captures both cultural and developmental concerns. The concepts that help us understand individual change and continuity across life settings do not often serve to respect the existence of contextually induced variations, nor do they express the power that collective representations may have to shape an individual's psychological destiny. A true synthesis of the two perspectives requires concepts that advance both agendas together.

The success of the present book is that it has rendered obsolete many of these disabling points of resistance, and it has made significant progress in resolving those that remain. The book covers a full assortment of contentious social-science topics—moral values, civic society, political action, religious faith, family structure, youth attitudes and behavior—and examines each issue with a spirit of open-minded inquiry. The scholarly discourse is constructive rather than argumentative throughout the volume, clearing away the distracting clutter of ideological dispute. This allows the authors freedom to explore topics of mutual interest to cultural and developmental psychologists with reference to theory and findings from both traditions. The result is a collection of essays that do more than sum up what is already known about culture and human development. The chapters, and the collection as a whole, point the way to a new understanding of how people find direction and meaning in their lives over the course of their never-ending cultural experiences.

Such an inquiry requires integrative thinking, joining rather than juxtaposing the two frames of analysis. It reminds me of the phase that Arthur Koestler coined when writing about the act of creation in science: "bisociation," or the capacity to bring two planes of reasoning together to draw a new conclusion. This volume is full of bisociative reasoning. Consequently, the volume's discourse goes beyond the constructive to the creative. Both of these attributes are welcome, refreshing, and noteworthy in any scholarly compendium.

Virtually every chapter bears this bisociative quality. One author, for example writes that "identity development and culture do not constitute separate topics with differing implications for psychology. Rather, they are inextricably linked. . ." And another writes that "human beings create signs and let these signs regulate their behavior." In both remarks, and in many other instances in the volume, a remarkable claim is being made: constructs that traditionally have been separated as distinct factors for the sake of analysis (identity status, cultural background, language, behavior) are *in psychological and social reality* not distinct at all but actually constitute one another, both experientially and during formation.

This is not, of course, the first time social scientists have made such remarks; but reading this volume, one comes away with the feeling that these social scientists really mean it—that they indeed are serious about pursuing the very challenging aim of understanding the dynamic mix of individual and social processes that shape both culture and human development. Each chapter in the volume takes a notable step toward achieving this aim.

In its aim, and in its achievements, the volume is a victory against reductionism, which has felt like a rising tide recently (although I imagine that, in the history of ideas, it always has felt that way). The quest to understand the full complexity of human life flies in the face of accounts that promote single-factor explanations, by genes, memes, or whatever. Because reductionist accounts are so seductive in their rhetorical power, they are more marketable; no doubt they will always be with us. But almost everyone knows better. One pleasure of this volume is that the authors act accordingly.

A common theme in writings about cultural psychology—and one of the concerns that stimulated this book—is that most human development studies to date have been done by, with, and for Americans. The concern, of course, is that such studies cannot inform us of what it is like to grow up and live through the variety of the world's non-American cultural experiences. I share this concern. But I would add to it a reciprocal concern one hears less frequently. How can we know what it means to be an American without an appreciation of that worldly variety? I think here of a friend who many years ago immigrated to this country from Europe as a young man, later to rise to a position of eminence in our society. I asked him when in his life he felt that he had become an American. He answered that it happened after he made a trip back to Europe, well over a decade after he first arrived here. It was only then that he could see clearly what he had left behind and how he had changed. His cultural identity was sharpened by an improved awareness of the contrast between the old and the new, and it then became part of his understanding of his own development. This struck me as a common and significant experience—especially in today's world—that has been too little examined through either cultural or developmental analysis. The kind of scholarship represented in this volume is exactly what we need to provide full accounts of how key cultural-developmental transformations of this sort come about.

Introduction

Changing Our Scholarship for a Changing World

LENE ARNETT JENSEN

Today the world's population is close to 7 billion. At about 300 million, the population of the United States is less than 5% of the total. Looking at developmental science, however, one might think that a very large proportion of the world's population was American. It is not only that a large proportion of developmental research includes American participants and is published by American scholars (e.g., Arnett, 2008). It is also that the research questions often are posed in light of the American context with little attention to what it is like to live in other cultures. There is a need to seriously broaden this theoretical and research approach to address the life-courses of diverse peoples. And this need will only continue to grow. By 2050, the prediction is that the global population will be 9 billion, with nearly all of the growth occurring in developing countries.

Not only is the global population growing but there is also an unprecedented flow across cultures of people, ideas, and goods. With increasing migrations, worldwide media, and international trade, diverse peoples interact with one another more than ever. With these interactions come changes to cultures and the psychological development of their members (Jensen, in press; Jensen, Arnett, & McKenzie, in press).

A few snapshots are illustrative. In Chile, urban teenagers congregate en masse at parties, where they flout the traditional sexual mores of what once was one of the most conservative countries in Latin America. At the parties, promoted through Fotologs and MSN Messenger, adolescents meet up with fleeting partners to dance and make out with abandon (Barrionuevo, 2008). In China, "factory girls" in their late teens to mid-twenties stream from rural villages to cities to work. In the process, their lives are changed in myriad ways as some attend English classes, some become escorts to wealthy business men, and many increasingly emphasize self-reliance while also sending hard-earned money back home (Chang, 2008). In Holland, ethnic Dutch college students have started camel farms to sell camel's milk to Moroccan and Somali immigrants, a career path greeted with puzzlement by their college professors and prohibitions by the Dutch agricultural authorities and the European Union (Heingartner, 2009).

In a world of changing demographics and increasingly interconnected cultures, scholarship and policy approaches also need to change. The aim of this book is to take up this challenge and opportunity by bridging cultural and developmental approaches to human psychology. The book brings together a group of experts from diverse disciplines and diverse parts of the world, who have taken on the task of integrating findings on human development with cultural findings. The experts present new theoretical and research syntheses for their areas of scholarship, and they discuss implications for public policy.

Bridging Cultural and Developmental Approaches to Psychology

During the last couple of decades, a number of scholars have created a distinct area of "cultural psychology" (e.g., Cole, 1996; Miller, 1999; Rogoff, 2003; Shore, 1996; Shweder, 2003; Valsiner, 2000). This includes scholars from fields such as anthropology, communication, education, linguistics, psychology, social work, and neuroscience. Many of their efforts have gone into defining a discipline and distinguishing it from others, such as cross-cultural psychology, which at least according to some cultural psychologists for a considerable time had focused primarily on how people's thoughts and behaviors are fundamentally the same across cultures (Stigler, Shweder, & Herdt, 1990). By now a sufficiently broad and deep corpus of cultural psychology research exists that a cultural psychology handbook has been published (Kitayama & Cohen, 2007).

Looking at developmental science, there is clear interest in cultural issues. For example, the latest Handbook of Child Psychology (Damon & Lerner, 2006) includes a chapter on cultural psychology, and a number of the other chapters address cultural issues or state that future research must address cultural diversity. This interest in culture is also evident in developmental conferences, developmental job postings, and new and upcoming developmental textbooks. Although culture will not become the single-most important construct of research in developmental science (as it is in cultural psychology), addressing how culture intersects with development is the next frontier (Jensen & Larson, 2005).

Three Questions

To bridge developmental and cultural approaches and arrive at new syntheses, the present authors address three specific sets of questions for their areas of expertise:

1. On the one hand, developmental approaches to psychology typically provide one-size-fits-all theories. One-size-fits-all does not really work well for simple things, like bathrobes. Nor does it seem to work any better for something as complex as human development. On the other hand, cultural psychology provides detailed conceptions of diverse cultural groups. This potentially suggests a need for a-theory-for-every-culture, raising the specter of theoretical pandemonium. Bridging the two approaches, what are new syntheses that offer a more appealing alternative to one-size-fits-all and one-for-every-culture?

2. One attempt to reconcile developmental and cultural approaches to psychology has been the suggestion that the former addresses the "structure" of human thought and behavior, whereas the latter addresses "content." Structure pertains to things that purportedly are psychologically deep, such as fear of punishment or attachment between children and caregivers. Content constitutes much more specific aspects of thought and behavior, the kinds of things on which structure operates, such as whether or not one is fearful of deceased ancestors and whether or not children attach to one or more caregivers. To what extent does the distinction between structure and content adequately capture the insights from both developmental and cultural approaches to psychology? To what extent do findings suggest that developmental structures, such as how to segment the life-course, how to conceptualize identity, and how to represent the self and the world vary across cultures? If the structure–content distinction is inadequate, what are plausible alternatives?

3. Turning to policy, some have claimed that developmental approaches to psychology can lead to a kind of colonialism (*see* Chapter 11). The argument is that theories purported to be universal and their policy implications are exported to other cultures, although these theories are typically based in work with American middle-class research participants. Others have claimed that cultural psychology can lead to a kind of rosy romanticism or all-out relativism where diverse cultural practices are regarded exclusively in a positive light and potential clashes between cultures and their practices are ignored. Does bridging developmental and cultural approaches to psychology offer new and helpful alternatives to these old but persistent issues of universalism and relativism?

Topics and Organization

In this book, the three sets of questions are addressed in a total of 13 chapters. The chapters are divided into four sections. Part I addresses "Psychological Processes and Culture," with chapters on moral reasoning and development (Jensen), children's learning beliefs (Li), and memory development (Leichtman).

Part II on "Developmental Contexts and Culture" focuses on family (Goodnow), peers (Chen), civic organizations (Flanagan, Martínez, and Cumsille), and adult communities (Schlegel). In Part III on "Developmental Selves and Culture," the authors attend to identity development (Phinney and Baldelomar), acceptance of self and the world (Rothbaum and Wang), and individual purposes (Valsiner). The last section, Part IV, on "Developmental Phases and Culture," addresses how the life-course is divided or partitioned in diverse cultures with a focus on childhood and adolescence (Nsamenang), emerging adulthood (Arnett), and phases across the lifespan (Saraswathi, Mistry, and Dutta).

It is important to note that the order of sections and of chapters within sections does not imply that some topics or areas are developmentally "prior" or "deeper," as compared to others. In fact, as noted above, this book and its authors revisit the question of what is psychologically deep and *a priori*, as well as the very meaning of notions of the psychologically deep and *a priori*. For example, as Jacqueline Goodnow discusses in her chapter on family, developmental approaches often place the family at the inner contextual core of a child's development. Yet, in many respects, other contexts such as legal systems and cultural norms are no less basic or primary. Among other things, laws and norms define who are considered to be family members, the domain of family influence, and what are taken to be moral and "natural" goals of family life. Thus Goodnow puts forth a new theoretical alternative to nested models of concentric circles with family at the developmental core. Goodnow's chapter is the first of four in the section on developmental contexts. As should now be evident, however, this does not signify that family comes first or is psychologically deeper than other contexts. Rather the chapter challenges the conventional wisdom from the start. Similarly, each of the chapters in the first section of the book on "developmental processes" reconsiders common differentiations between structure and content in regards to reasoning, learning, and memory.

It is also important to point out that this book aims to revisit common developmental science conventions of how the life-course is structured and segmented. Developmental science courses, textbooks, journals, professional organizations, and so forth frequently divide "childhood" from "adolescence," which in turn seems to be followed by a lengthy lump of "adulthood." Here, reconsideration of this structure takes place on a number of levels. First, the present book brings together scholars who specialize in diverse phases of the life-course, and whose professional paths also take them to different professional meetings and outlets. Second, the section of the book on developmental phases includes three chapters that offer new ways to conceptualize the life-course on the basis of cultural findings. The authors of these three chapters also deliberate the extent to which certain life-course phases are best conceptualized in the singular, such as childhood and emerging adulthood, or the plural, that is childhoods and emerging adulthoods. Third, the segmenting of the life-course that is done by developmental science is related to the segmenting that occurs in society, and some of the present chapters address the implications of this.

For example, in her chapter on the extent of adolescents' involvement in adult communities, Alice Schlegel elaborates on unintended but nevertheless disconcerting psychological and social consequences of separating adolescents from adults. Meanwhile, Connie Flanagan and her colleagues point to developmental opportunities for peer groups of adolescents who form youth-based cultural and civic organizations. Also, Jean Phinney and Oscar Baldelomar consider the implications for adolescents' identity development and well-being in light of the extent to which they are in sync with the expectations for independence and interdependence of their culture. In short, the life-course is examined here from both a developmental and cultural perspective and with an eye to both scientific theory and social policy implications.

With its inclusion of diverse life phases, diverse topics, and experts from diverse cultures (about 60% of the authors are of cultural backgrounds that are not American), the present book aims to speak to a broad range of developmental and cultural issues. Even for topics not addressed in this volume, the syntheses between universalistic, one-size-fits-all approaches and particularistic, one-theory-for-every-culture approaches offered across chapters may be interesting and useful.

Finally, in the spirit of bridging, William Damon (a developmental scientist) and Richard Shweder (a cultural anthropologist) have authored a foreword and commentary, respectively.

Acknowledgments

I would like gratefully to acknowledge the support by the Society for Research in Child Development and the Department of Psychology at Clark University for a 3-day conference that brought together the present authors at Clark University in Worcester, Massachusetts, USA in October 2008. The conference promoted exceptionally constructive dialogue, collective feedback on drafts of every chapter, and common commitment to bridging cultural and developmental approaches. I also thank Kelly Boulay, Angela De Dios, Ayfer Dost, Theresa Jackson, Jessica McKenzie, Peggy Moskowitz, Joanna Wu, and Juan Zhong for their skilled, unflappable, and cheerful assistance with the organization of the conference.

I very much appreciate the support of Lori Handelman, Senior Editor at Oxford University Press. Her professional and affable advice throughout the writing and production of the book has been very helpful.

There are a number of persons whose blend of collegiality, friendship, and mentorship is a longstanding source of support to me. I deeply value our conversations, ranging from the future of our disciplines to the pragmatics of editing. My thanks go to William Damon, Reed Larson, Richard Lerner, Richard Shweder, Niobe Way, and James Youniss.

Special thanks to my husband, Jeffrey Arnett, who always is willing to read another draft, answer another question, discuss another idea, and pour another glass of wine when all else fails.

Finally, I am deeply indebted to every author who contributed a chapter to this book. It is a group of authors who are exceptionally creative, thoughtful, and generous.

References

Arnett, J. J. (2008). The neglected 95%: Why American psychology needs to become less American. *American Psychologist, 63,* 602–614.

Barrionuevo, A. (2008, September 12). In Tangle of Young Lips, a Sex Rebellion in Chile. *New York Times*, pp. A1, A8–9.

Cole, M. (1996). *Cultural Psychology: A Once and Future Discipline*. Harvard University Press.

Chang, L. (2008). *Factory girls: From village to city in a changing China*. New York: Spiegel & Grau.

Damon, W., & Lerner, R. (2006), *Handbook of child psychology* (6th edition). New York: Wiley.

Heingartner, D. (2009, September 15). The Camel as Cow, a Cautionary Tale. *New York Times*, p. A6.

Jensen, L. A. (in press). Immigrant youth in the United States: Coming of age among diverse civic cultures. In Sherrod, L. R., Torney-Purta, J., & Flanagan, C. A. (Eds.), *Handbook of research and policy on civic engagement in youth*. Hoboken, NJ: Wiley.

Jensen, L. A., Arnett, J. J., & McKenzie, J. (in press). Globalization and cultural identity developments in adolescence and emerging adulthood. In Schwartz, S. J., Luyckx, K., & Vignoles, V. L. (Eds.), *Handbook of identity theory and research*. New York: Springer Publishing Company.

Jensen L. A., & Larson, R. W. (Eds.). (2005). New horizons in developmental theory and research. *New Directions for Child and Adolescent Development, 109.*

Kitayama, S., & Cohen, D. (2007). *Handbook of cultural psychology*. New York, NY: Guilford.

Miller, J. G. (1999). Cultural psychology: Implications for basic psychological theory. *American Psychological Society, 10,* 85–91.

Rogoff, B. (2003). *The Cultural Nature of Human Development*. Oxford University Press.

Shore, B. (1996). *Culture in Mind: Cognition, Culture and the Problem of Meaning*. Oxford University Press.

Shweder, R. A. (2003). *Why Do Men Barbecue? Recipes for Cultural Psychology*. Harvard University Press.

Stigler, J. W., Shweder, R. A., & Herdt, G. H. (1990). *Cultural psychology: Essays on comparative human development*. New York: Cambridge University Press.

Valsiner, J. (2000). *Culture and Human Development*. Sage Publications.

PART I

DEVELOPMENTAL PROCESSES AND CULTURE

CHAPTER 1

The Cultural-Developmental Theory of Moral Psychology

A New Synthesis

LENE ARNETT JENSEN

At a time when people increasingly grow up and live in a globalized world with exposure to multiple cultures, we are challenged to conduct research that captures both the developmental and cultural sides of people's psychology (Arnett, 2002; Jensen, 2003; Jensen, Arnett and McKenzie, in press; Larson, 2002; Nsamenang, 1992; Phinney, 2000; Valsiner, 2007). Across diverse research areas, scholars more and more recognize culture and psychological development as intertwined (Cole, 1996; French, Schneider, and Chen, 2006; Leichtman, 2006; Rothbaum et al., 2000; Shweder et al., 2005; Sternberg, 2004). Here my aim is to present a theoretical synthesis that takes both culture and development into account with respect to moral psychology. I term this new conceptualization a *cultural-developmental template* (*see also* Jensen, 2008a).

The template charts developmental patterns across the life-course for moral reasoning in terms of the three Ethics of Autonomy, Community, and Divinity (e.g., Jensen, 1991, Shweder, 1990). In this chapter, I thus start by providing a brief background on the three ethics approach. Then, I describe how the cultural-developmental template model builds on findings utilizing the three ethics as well as a substantial body of developmental and cultural findings on morality from other research traditions. Next, I illustrate how the cultural-developmental template is not a one-size-fits-all model. I give two examples of how its general developmental patterns accommodate to the different constellations of Ethics held by culturally diverse peoples. The chapter then turns to specific research expectations as well as broader research implications that follow from the present theoretical proposal. Finally, I discuss how the cultural-developmental template model entails suggestions for policy consideration.

Here, development is defined as psychological change that occurs in human beings as they age. Developmental change may involve increase or decrease; it may be quantitative or qualitative; and it may be gradual or stage-like. Culture is defined as symbolic and behavioral inheritances shared and co-constructed by members of a community (Shweder et al., 2006). Symbolic inheritances are conceptions of divinity, nature, society, and persons, and behavioral inheritances consist of common or habitual familial and social practices. Culture, then, is *not* synonymous with country or ethnicity but rather describes communities whose members share key beliefs and behaviors. For example, the present chapter includes discussion of religiously conservative and liberal cultural communities. It bears mention, too, that there is variation among individuals within cultural communities, and variation exists among cultures in their degree of ideological and behavioral heterogeneity.

Although the focus here is on moral psychology, the present cultural-developmental template conceptualization might be useful for other research areas as well. Thus it provides a way to strike a balance between universalistic, one-size-fits-all approaches and particularistic, one-theory-for-every-culture approaches.

Beyond a Single Moral Structure: The Three Ethics Approach

During the 1980s and 1990s, a number of researchers made the case that existing theories of moral development, such as the cognitive-developmental and domain theories (Kohlberg, 1981; Turiel, 1983), highlighted moral conceptions pertaining to the welfare and rights of individuals but that insufficient consideration was being paid to an array of other moral conceptions important to people across diverse cultures (e.g., Colby and Damon, 1992; Dien, 1982; Edwards, 1987; Gilligan, 1982; Jensen, 1997a; Ma, 1988; Miller, 1989; Nisan, 1987; Shweder, 1982a, 1982b, 1990; Zimba, 1994). For example, researchers noted that concepts pertaining to community, collectivity, and interdependence were in need of additional attention, as were concepts pertaining to religion and spirituality.

During this time, many researchers also came to the conclusion that community-and divinity-oriented moral concepts, such as the Chinese concept of filial piety or the Buddhist concept of Nibbana or self-liberation, cannot simply be classified as "content" rather than "structure" of moral reasoning. First, the criteria by which such concepts constituted content rather than structure were not articulated in a convincing and compelling way (c.f., Brainerd, 1978, on criteria for structure to serve as an explanatory device). Second, it became increasingly clear that relegating a wide variety of community- and divinity-oriented reasons to a "content" heap of research oblivion was tant-amount to dismissing key conceptions of morality that exist within a variety of cultures.

Aiming to encompass highly diverse moral conceptions, Shweder and colleagues proposed a tripartite distinction between Ethics of Autonomy, Community, and Divinity (Jensen, 1991; Shweder, 1990; Shweder et al., 1997). These three ethics involve different notions of what is at the heart of person-hood and, consequently, different moral reasons.

The Ethic of Autonomy—to which developmental moral psychology has long paid the most attention, according to Shweder—involves a focus on people as individuals who have needs, desires, and preferences. The moral goal is to recognize the right to the fulfillment of these needs and desires and to strive to make available the means to satisfy them. Whereas an autonomous self is free to make many choices, the self is restricted by concerns with inflict-ing harm on other individuals, encroaching on their rights, and consideration for their needs. Thus, in terms of moral reasoning, the Ethic of Autonomy centers on moral concepts that address the interests, well-being, and rights of individuals (self or other) as well as fairness between individuals. It also includes the notion of taking responsibility for oneself and autonomy-oriented virtues such as self-esteem, self-expression, and independence.

The Ethic of Community addresses how people are members of social groups such as family, school, and nation and how they occupy various roles and positions within these groups. The moral goal of this social self is the fulfillment of role-based duties to others as well as protecting and ensuring the positive functioning of social groups. Accordingly, the Ethic of Community includes moral concepts pertaining to persons' duties to others, and concern with the customs, interests, and welfare of groups. This ethic also comprises community-oriented virtues such as self-moderation and loyalty toward social groups and their members.

The Ethic of Divinity focuses on people as spiritual or religious entities. Here the moral goal is for the self to become increasingly connected to that which is pure or divine. The central moral conceptions of the Ethic of Divinity pertain to divine and natural law, injunctions and lessons found in sacred texts, and the striving to avoid spiritual degradation and come closer to moral purity. This ethic also taps divinity-oriented virtues such as awe, faith-fulness, and humility.

Research has shown the presence of all three ethics in diverse cultures (e.g., Arnett, Ramos, and Jensen, 2001; Buchanan, 2003; Haidt, Koller, and Dias, 1993; Jensen, 1995, 1997b, 1998a, 1998b, 2008b, 2008c; Rozin, Lowery, Imada, and Haidt, 1999; Vainio, 2003; Vasquez et al., 2001). Furthermore, research has indicated cultural differences across and within countries. Across countries, findings suggest that American participants use Ethic of Autonomy concepts more than participants in countries such as Brazil, India, and the Philippines (Haidt et al. 1993; Jensen, 1998a; Vasquez et al., 2001). Research within India, Finland, and the United States has also indicated a difference between religious groups, with religiously liberal persons reasoning more in terms of Autonomy and less in terms of Divinity than religiously conservative persons (Jensen, 1997b, 1998a; Vainio, 2003). Moral motives pertaining to Autonomy, Community, and Divinity, then, are widespread across cultures.

A New Cultural-Developmental Synthesis

Research with the three ethics provides for a way to capture highly diverse moral concepts used by different cultural groups. Up until now, however, research with the three ethics addressing development has been limited. To address the intersection of culture and development, it may thus be helpful to consider how Shweder's cultural approach can be extended by accounting for developmental findings and concepts.

In considering how the three ethics vary developmentally, it is necessary to address two issues: *(1)* the *degree* to which an ethic is used at different ages (e.g., Does use of the Ethic of Community go down, remain stable, or go up with age?) and *(2)* the specific *types* of moral concepts that persons of various ages use within an ethic (e.g., Does a child reason in terms of different kinds of Ethic of Community concepts as compared to an adolescent or an adult?).

Much of the research that has analyzed people's moral reasoning in terms of the three ethics has used a coding system developed and revised by Jensen (1991, 1996, 2004). In this system, each moral reason a person provides is coded into one ethic (i.e., Autonomy, Community, or Divinity), allowing for an assessment of the *degree* to which a person uses each of the three ethics.

Furthermore, each of a person's moral reasons is coded into one of numerous subcategories (each ethic includes 13–16 subcategories, e.g., "Self's Psychological Well-Being" and "Rights" for Autonomy, "Duty to Others" and "Social Order or Harmony Goals" for Community, and "Scriptural Authority" and "God-Given Conscience" for Divinity), allowing for an assessment of the specific *type* of moral concept used within an ethic. Distinguishing not only among the three ethics but also among types of moral concepts within each ethic means that highly diverse concepts can be taken into account. For example, both the Chinese concept of shame (Fung, 1999) and the Indian concept of role-based obligations (e.g., Miller, 1994) would be coded into the Ethic of Community. However, they would most likely be coded into the different subcategories of "Community-Oriented Virtues" and "Duty to Others," respectively.

In the following, I will first propose a model for how degree and type of use of the three ethics is related to development. This model builds on a substantial body of developmental and cultural research to be described below. The model as a whole is thus based on extensive empirical work, but for some of its elements the available evidence is more limited. Where this is the case, it will be noted. The description of the model will be followed by an explanation of how my intent is for it to be used as a *cultural-developmental template* for research with different age groups within diverse cultures. The model, then, is not one-size-fits-all but, rather, accommodates the prevailing ethics of diverse peoples.

In other words, the template model takes different forms in different cultures. Examples of this will be shown.

Development and the Three Ethics

The model in Figure 1–1 illustrates the present proposal for how the three ethics are used across childhood, adolescence, and adulthood. In other words, the three lines show a developmental pattern for the Ethics of Autonomy, Community, and Divinity. The positions of the lines, however, do *not* indicate their relative frequency in relation to one another (e.g., use of Autonomy being more frequent than use of Community and Divinity).

With respect to the Ethic of Autonomy, the proposition is that reasons within this ethic emerge early and that the *degree* to which persons use this ethic stays *relatively* stable across adolescence and into adulthood. However, the *types* of Autonomy concepts that persons use are likely to change, in part, with age.

Support for this proposition comes from the consistent finding across the research approaches of Kohlberg, Turiel, and Gilligan that children in different cultures speak early about harm to the self and the interests of the self (Colby et al., 1983; Gilligan, 1982; Kohlberg, 1984; Snarey, 1985; Turiel, 2002; Walker, 1989; *see also* Eisenberg et al., 1995). Furthermore, as domain work by Turiel and colleagues has shown, children in quite diverse cultures also reason about harm to other individuals and their needs or interests (Turiel, 2002). This finding has also been found in studies from different cultures using a variety of other theoretical approaches (Gilligan, 1982; Haidt et al., 1993; Miller, 1994).

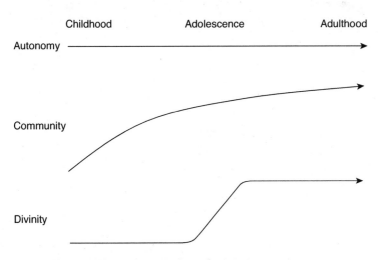

FIGURE 1.1 The cultural–developmental template.
Note. Each of the lines shows developmental patterns across the life span, from childhood to adulthood. The positions of the lines do *not* indicate their relative frequency in relation to one another (e.g., use of Autonomy being more frequent than use of Community and Divinity).

As persons in different cultures grow into adolescence and adulthood, research has shown that some reasoning pertaining to the welfare of the self and other individuals remains (Eisenberg et al., 1995; Gilligan, 1982; Haidt et al., 1993; Jensen, 1995, 1998a; Turiel, 2002; Vasquez et al. 2001; Walker et al., 1995; Zimba, 1994). Adolescents and adults continue to reason in terms of these concepts for diverse issues and perhaps especially for issues of relevance to their own lives (Buchanan, 2003; Walker et al., 1995). And it is likely that many or even most of the moral issues that people contemplate (outside of a research setting) are indeed of personal relevance.

Yet, in the course of adolescence and adulthood, other types of Ethic of Autonomy reasoning also become increasingly used, even if they are unlikely to become the most common types of Autonomy reasoning. Research with European and American participants, including the moral development work by Piaget (1932/1965), has indicated that adolescents and adults are more likely than children to speak of concepts such as individual rights and equity in a consistent manner (Killen, 2002; Walker, 1989). Although these concepts do not prevail in the reasoning of adults across cultures (Snarey, 1985), research has indicated that adolescents and adults in cultures such as India and Zambia give consideration to equity and justice (Miller and Luthar, 1989; Zimba, 1994).

The proposal here, then, is that the degree of Autonomy reasoning stays relatively stable across the lifespan but with some changes in types of Autonomy reasoning. However, it also needs to be noted that in cultures where there is a very strong push for collectivity or submission to divinity, there may be somewhat of a decline over time in Autonomy reasoning. In such cultures, considerations of the needs, desires, and interests of individuals (especially the self) are seen as either irrelevant or morally objectionable, and hence, by or into adulthood, such moral considerations might go down.

Turning to the Ethic of Community, the proposal is that both the *degree* of usage and the diversity of *types* of concepts rise throughout childhood and into adolescence and adulthood. As shown in developmental research by Kohlberg and colleagues (Kohlberg, 1984) as well as cultural research by Shweder and colleagues (1990), younger children in diverse cultures invoke some Community concepts, such as those relating to the interests of one's family and familial customs. Cross-cultural research with the domain approach also shows this, even as domain researchers have regarded the reasoning as "conventional" rather than moral (Turiel, 1983, 2002). Moral reasoning related to the family finds continued expression past childhood and probably even more so in the course of adolescence and adulthood as a person's awareness of diverse types of family considerations increases (e.g., duty to family in addition to family interests and customs; e.g., Miller, Bersoff, and Harwood, 1990). Also, in the course of adolescence and with the transition into adulthood, people take on an increasing number of adult family roles and responsibilities.

By late childhood and adolescence, a person is likely also to add community concepts that pertain to social groups other than the family. Thus, research across many cultures has found that children's social circle widens as they reach late childhood and grow into adolescence (Whiting and Edwards, 1988). For example, by late childhood and early adolescence, the salience of friends and peers rises (*see* Chen, 2011; Hurrelmann, 1996; Rubin, Bukowski, and Parker, 1998; Schlegel and Barry, 1991; Youniss and Smollar, 1985). Other collective contexts, too, gain in importance across cultures, including school and workplace (*see* Schlegel, 2011). Thus, compared to younger children, the expectation reflected in Figure 1–1 is that older children and adolescents use more Community concepts pertaining to nonfamilial groups.

By the time a person reaches late adolescence or adulthood, moral concepts that pertain to even broader social entities such as society as a whole become used in a more frequent and consistent manner. Thus, longitudinal research has shown how persons in their late teens and adulthood reason more about matters pertaining to societal organization (e.g., utilitarian considerations), as compared to children and younger adolescents (Eisenberg et al., 1995; Walker, 1989; *see also* Flanagan, Martínez, & Cumsille, 2011). Although this longitudinal research has been carried out in North America, the findings are likely to generalize. A variety of cultural research with adults, including in India, Israel, and Zambia, has shown how they give consideration to what is best for society as a whole (Jensen, 1998a; Nisan, 1987; Zimba, 1994).

With respect to the Ethic of Divinity, there is less research available, and hence, the proposal here has a more restricted empirical basis. In cultures that emphasize scriptural authority or where people conceive of supernatural entities (such as God) as largely distinct from humans (e.g., as omniscient and omnipotent), the present suggestion is that the *degree* of use of the Ethic of Divinity will be low among children but will then rise in adolescence and become similar to adult use of this ethic. The reason is that in such communities, the culturally articulated concepts pertaining to supernatural entities are of such an abstract nature that they may be readily translated into moral reasoning only by adolescents whose cognitive skills allow for more abstraction than those of younger children (Adelson, 1971; Keating, 1990; Kohlberg, 1976; Piaget, 1972). It should be noted that research indicates that children growing up in cultures with a predominance of abstract conceptions of the supernatural can express conceptions of these supernatural entities (Jensen, 2009a; Oser, Scarlett, and Bucher, 2005). The suggestion here is that these conceptions do not get applied to moral reasoning until adolescence. Additionally, the present proposal is that the *types* of Divinity concepts used by older adolescents will be largely similar to those used by adults. Older adolescents are likely to be as capable as adults of using diverse Divinity concepts such as those referencing scriptural authority, God's authority, and spiritual virtues.

Preliminary research support for this pattern derives from in-depth interviews with children (ages 7–12 years), adolescents (ages 13–18 years), and adults (ages 36–57 years) who formed part of an American religiously conservative congregation (Jensen and McKenzie, in preparation). In their conservative Protestant religion, God is omniscient and omnipotent. In response to six different moral issues, the adolescents and adults used significantly more Ethic of Divinity reasons than the children, and the children used very few Divinity reasons. Furthermore, adolescents and adults did not differ in the number or types of Divinity concepts that they used.

Support for the pattern is also suggested by the fact that a number of religious traditions have ceremonies and celebrations in early or mid-adolescence that explicitly confer moral responsibility on the adolescents and link that responsibility to knowledge of religious teachings (Mahoney et al., 2003; Sita, 1999). Within Catholicism, for example, adolescents who take part in the Confirmation ceremony promise to live by the teachings of the Catholic Church, and they show that they are ready to be responsible for their actions. Within Judaism, when an adolescent boy becomes Bar Mitzvah or an adolescent girl becomes Bat Mitzvah, they assume responsibility for obeying the laws of Judaism and the Jewish people. Thus, Bar Mitzvah and Bat Mitzvah are Hebrew for "son of the commandments" and "daughter of the commandments," respectively. The presence of these rituals in diverse religions begins to point to adolescence as a key time for the explicit expression of moral reasons within an Ethic of Divinity.

The age pattern for the Ethic of Divinity proposed above, however, may only apply to some religious cultures. In cultures where scriptural accounts of supernatural or transcendent entities are less salient or where people regard such entities as less distinct from humans, it is possible that Divinity concepts are more accessible to, and hence used more by, children in their moral reasoning (Saraswathi, 2005). In some Hindu communities, for example, religious devotion finds expression in tangible and recurrent activities (e.g., bathing, dressing, and feeding the gods); there are many places within and outside the home for worship (e.g., household shrines, temples, roadside shrines); and there are a variety of persons seen to have god-like status or special connections with the gods (e.g., gurus, sadhus [renouncers], temple priests) (Jensen, 1998a; Shweder et al., 1990). In such cultures, children may reason about moral issues in terms of Ethic of Divinity concepts from fairly early on because these concepts are tied repeatedly to specific everyday activities and objects. Then, in the course of adolescence and adulthood, additional Divinity concepts may become part of a person's moral reasoning.

As Figure 1–1 shows, the present proposal is that use of each of the three ethics generally either stays relatively stable or increases. With age, there is likely to be increasing cognitive complexity (Csikszentmihalyi, 1993; Lerner, 2002), which would allow for increased use of diverse moral concepts. Research on moral reasoning also shows that the number of moral reasons provided by participants goes up with age (Jensen and McKenzie, in preparation; Walker et al., 1995).

The Cultural-Developmental Template

As mentioned above, my intent is for Figure 1–1 to serve as a *cultural-developmental template* for research with different age groups within diverse cultures. This means that the developmental patterns in Figure 1–1 are accommodated to the constellation of ethics that prevail within different cultures.

Thus people of different cultures vary on the extent to which they emphasize the three ethics.

To give an example, research in a number of countries has shown that in some religiously liberal cultures, adult members frequently use the Ethics of Autonomy and Community and quite rarely use the Ethic of Divinity (Buchanan, 2003; Jensen, 1997a, 1997b, 1998a, 1998b; Vainio, 2003). Given this finding, it is possible to make predictions for the expression of the cultural-developmental template in these kinds of religiously liberal cultures. As seen in Figure 1–2, the expectation would be that children, adolescents, and adults will make frequent use of Autonomy concepts, although as described earlier, the type used may well change with age. Community concepts will be rarer among younger children but will then become quite common among adolescents and adults. (It is possible that the Ethic of Community will rise more quickly among religiously liberal children in relatively interdependence-oriented societies such as India, as compared to children growing up in religiously liberal communities in relatively independence-oriented societies such as the United States; *see also* Phinney & Baldelomar, 2011). With respect to the Ethic of Divinity, the expectation is that it will be used infrequently at all ages, and if it emerges, this will only occur in the course of adolescence.

To give another example, in some religiously conservative cultures, adults frequently reason in terms of the Ethics of Community and Divinity and infrequently in terms of the Ethic of Autonomy (Buchanan, 2003; Jensen, 1997a, 1997b, 1998a, 1998b; Vainio, 2003). Accommodating the cultural-developmental template to this finding, Figure 1–3 shows the predicted cultural-developmental patterns for religiously conservative groups. Here, children, adolescents, and adults will infrequently use the Ethic of Autonomy. In fact,

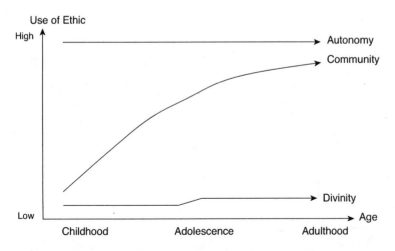

FIGURE 1.2 Expression of the cultural–developmental template among religious liberals

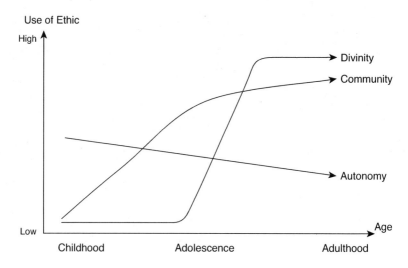

FIGURE 1.3 Expression of the cultural–developmental template among religious conservatives

as noted earlier, there may even be some decrease in this ethic over the lifespan because of the emphasis on renouncing self-interest that characterizes some religiously conservative communities. With respect to the Ethic of Community, the expectation would be that its prevalence will be fairly low among younger children, higher among children in late childhood and early adolescence, and high among late adolescents and adults. Use of the Ethic of Divinity will be low among children (at least for religiously conservative communities with abstract conceptions of the supernatural, as explained earlier) but will then rise markedly in adolescence and remain high throughout adulthood.

In summary, the *cultural-developmental template* allows for a way to conceptualize moral development in children, adolescents, and adults who form part of diverse cultural communities. The template incorporates highly diverse moral concepts that culturally diverse peoples use to explain and guide their behaviors. The template incorporates complexity by accounting for multiple dimensions; specifically, it allows us to see people's moral lives through the lenses of *both* culture and development (Jensen, 2008a). The template also allows for flexibility in that it allows for consideration of the interaction of development and culture. The present theoretical synthesis, then, strikes a middle ground between having a single model for people everywhere and the prospect of having one model for every culture.

Prospects for New Research: Specific Expectations

Like all theoretical proposals, the present one entails specific research expectations. The present proposal, however, also has some broader implications for how to conduct research on moral psychology. This is because it synthesizes two research paradigms with different conceptions and traditions of how to study morality. I will discuss the specific research expectations first and then turn to the broader research implications.

The Template Thesis

The cultural-developmental template described above lays out expectations for developmental changes in use of the Ethics of Autonomy, Community, and Divinity in the context of cultural variation. As described, the proposed developmental changes in *degree* of usage of the Ethics of Autonomy and Community are supported by a substantial body of research, and the expectation would be that they would find continued support.

We know somewhat less about some of the lifespan developmental changes in *types* of Autonomy and Community reasoning used within various cultures. Here there is a need for more research to test and elaborate on the present proposal.

We know relatively little about lifespan changes for the Ethic of Divinity. It is an emerging area of research. The present template suggests how changes in Divinity reasoning may occur developmentally (with adolescence being an important period), as well as how this developmental pattern may depend on both the extent of Divinity reasoning used within a culture and the kind of conceptualizations of the supernatural that prevail within a culture. These specific suggestions require additional testing.

The Definition of Morality Thesis

The present cultural-developmental proposal entails a broad definition of morality that includes Autonomy, Community, and Divinity reasoning. The present model also details how cultures differ on their constellation of ethics (e.g., in some cultures there is a general preference for Community over Autonomy, whereas in other cultures it is the other way around). Consequently, one expectation is that people from different cultures, to some extent, will vary in the kinds of behaviors they include within the moral domain. For example, people who reason in terms of Ethic of Divinity concepts such as God's will or the human body being God's temple are likely to regard a number of behaviors as moral that people who do not use this kind of reasoning will imbue with little or no moral significance. Research has shown support for this thesis with respect to behaviors such as suicide in the case of terminal illness and alcohol use (Jensen, 1995). For example, to some people who consider their body to be God's temple, any alcohol use is regarded as a moral offense because it adulterates that which is part of God. More research is needed on how different constellations of ethics (at various ages and in various cultures) are related to different definitions of what is moral and what is not.

Another expectation is that people from different cultures may vary on the kinds of criteria they have for regarding behaviors as moral. In some theories of moral development, especially in domain and cognitive-developmental theory, the criteria of universalizability has been prominent. This criterion means that in order for a rule to be moral, it must apply to everyone. The universalizability criterion, however, may not be universal. For example, research has indicated that religiously conservative cultures have a hierarchical worldview (Ammerman, 1987; Jensen, 1997a, 2006). In this view, God is above humans. Among humans, differences exist between various groups, including believers and nonbelievers. Based on such a worldview along with Ethic of Divinity reasoning, a conservative Christian can maintain that one may require more morally of a Christian than a non-Christian (such as sexual abstinence prior to marriage, modesty in dress, and tithing). An orthodox Jew can hold that moral expectations for Jews are different from those for non-Jews (such as keeping kosher and circumcision).

It would seem that a large number of peoples do not share the universalizability criterion that came out of Western rationalist philosophy (Wilson, 1993), or at least it is not their only or foremost criterion. As noted by Blasi (1987, 1990), we need more research on people's indigenous criteria rather than presupposing criteria coming out of particular philosophical traditions. The present proposal is that it would be fruitful to examine the kinds of criteria held by people with different constellations of the three ethics.

The Constellation of Ethics Thesis

As described earlier, the proposal here is that cultures are characterized by distinct constellations of ethics (such as Autonomy and Community above Divinity). Furthermore, the present expectation is that individuals, too, reason about different moral issues in terms of particular constellation of ethics and that these constellations change with development. In other words, the expectation is not what we might term a toolbox approach to moral reasoning, which would predict that an individual uses one kind of reasoning (or tool) for one issue, a different kind for another issue, and so forth. Instead, the present expectation is in harmony with recent identity work on moral reasoning and behavior that also emphasizes a certain measure of moral reasoning coherence within the self (Blasi, 1994; Colby and Damon, 1992; Lapsley and Narvaez, 2004; Youniss and Yates, 1997). As described by Blasi (1994), for example, a person will reason in terms of certain moral concepts across diverse issues. As a person comes to identify strongly with these concepts, they become a core part of the person's sense of self that will habitually guide behavior. In turn, the behaviors may reinforce and refine the moral identity.

The present thesis, however, does not entail that an individual's constellation of ethics is impervious to some variation across moral issues. Research has suggested that people, to some extent, reason differently about researcher-generated vignettes than participant-generated personal moral experiences. This has been found both for research with Kohlberg's stages (Walker et al. 1995) and the three ethics (Buchanan, 2003; Jensen and McKenzie, in preparation).

Research with the three ethics has also suggested that individuals' reasoning about some issues may be influenced by public debate. For example, across highly varied moral issues, religiously conservative American adults almost never reason in terms of the Ethic of Autonomy concept of individual rights. A clear exception, however, occurs for the issue of abortion, where they often invoke the rights of the fetus. Here, their reasoning seems influenced by recognition of the popularity and persuasiveness of rights language in the American public forum (Jensen, 1998b).

Also, it may be that there is some cultural variation on the extent to which people aim for a stable constellation of ethics to apply across moral issues. For example, research with Chinese participants has noted a proclivity to reason about moral issues on the basis of the specifics of the situation and their reluctance to formulate highly general moral principles (Dien, 1982; Walker and Moran, 1991).

Research, then, is needed on how development and culture influence individuals' constellation of ethics. Merging the above findings with the identity work, we might expect that persons would be particularly likely to experience fluctuation or inconsistency in their constellation of ethics during periods of developmental change (e.g., moving from one phase of the life course to another) and during periods of cultural change (e.g., within a culture as a whole or for a person moving from one culture to another).

The Moral Emotion Question

The proposed cultural-developmental template is mainly based on a large body of available research focusing on reasoning. Some work, including recent findings, has highlighted moral emotions (e.g., Eisenberg, 1992; Haidt, 2001; Kagan, 1987). Here, some questions for research on moral emotions from a cultural-developmental perspective will be put forth: Could developmental templates be proposed for various moral emotions, such as guilt, shame, or gratitude? How might such templates vary across cultures? How might development and/or culture relate to what is defined as moral rather than non-moral emotions? How might development and/or culture influence the extent to which people's moral behaviors are based on emotions or reasoning? How might development and/or culture even influence how this distinction between reasoning and emotions is understood and experienced?

To the extent that some moral emotions map onto the three ethics, it is possible that the present template is applicable to these emotions. In a series of studies, Rozin and colleagues (1999) found that anger, contempt, and disgust were strongly related to the Ethics of Autonomy, Community, and Divinity, respectively. If more research were to show such relations for a number of other emotions, it might be that specific cultural-developmental expectations could be proposed for the *degree* to which people experience Autonomy, Community, and Divinity emotions as well as for the specific *types* of Autonomy, Community, and Divinity emotions that they experience.

Prospects for New Research: Broader Implications

Cultural Variations in the Life-Course

Turning to broader research implications of synthesizing developmental and cultural perspectives, one of those is the need to consider that cultural variations in the life-course itself may influence moral development. For example, recent research indicates that a new phase of the life-course has become normative in the United States and other post-industrial societies. Spanning the late teens through the mid-to-late twenties, researchers term this period *emerging adulthood* (Arnett, 1998, 2000, 2004, 2011). Emerging adulthood has been found to be distinct from both adolescence and adulthood behaviorally, demographically, and subjectively. It is a "self-focused age" (Arnett, 2004), with emerging adults aiming to form independent beliefs, establish financial autonomy from parents, and take responsibility for the consequences of their own actions. As noted, emerging adulthood is not a period of life that is present in all cultures. Researchers see it as a period that has become notable in societies where educational training has become extended and marriage and family obligations often are postponed (Mayseless and Scharf, 2003; Nelson, 2009).

In cultures where there is an emerging adulthood phase, one might expect this phase to be characterized by substantial Ethic of Autonomy reasoning. There might even be a temporary uptick in the Autonomy pattern described in Figure 1–1. Several studies with the three ethics has indeed shown a pronounced, if not exclusive, use of the Ethic of Autonomy among American emerging adults (Arnett et al. 2001; Jensen, 1995; Jensen, Arnett, Feldman, and Cauffman, 2002, 2004).

To give another example of the significance of cultural variations in the life-course, the indigenous Indian conception of the life-course includes a final "Sanyasa" phase, where older persons are supposed to renounce their ties to community to focus on their connection with the spiritual notion of Atman. As described by Saraswathi and colleagues (2005, 2011), the Sanyasa ideal is to lead a life as water on a lotus leaf—on the leaf but not of it. For Indians who adhere to this life-course conception, one might expect a final decrease in the otherwise common Ethic Community pattern described in Figure 1–1.

Cultural Variations and Developmental Contexts

Taking a cultural-developmental approach also entails addressing how the contexts that influence moral development will vary across cultures. Over the course of the early 20th century—as mass education in Europe and the United States became common and compulsory—Piaget (1932/1965) emphasized the peer context. Kohlberg (1984) continued the emphasis on peers. There also appears to be an implicit focus on peers in domain research (Turiel, 2002). The moral vignettes that domain researchers use in their research typically involve interactions between peers (e.g., hitting an age mate, pushing a playground peer off a swing, failing to share with a classmate, teasing a peer). Recent research on morality has addressed other contexts—especially family (e.g., Smetana, 2000; Walker, 1989) but also civic organizations (e.g., Flanagan, 2003; Jensen, 2009b, in press; Youniss and Yates, 1997).

Today's children and adolescents growing up in urban areas all over the world are exposed to moral messages from many other sources too: after-school counselors, extracurricular activity coaches, television, magazines, websites, and so forth. What is the influence on moral development of these other contexts? Meanwhile, in a number of areas of the world (especially rural and poor ones), the moral contexts surrounding children and adolescents are different. Children's daily access to mass media, such as television and the Internet, is much more restricted. Adolescents—especially girls—are far less likely to attend secondary educational institutions. Both children and adolescents spend more time in the contexts of family and small communities. What are the implications for the moral development of these children and adolescents? Because the contexts of moral significance are likely to vary not only across age but also across cultures, an implication of taking a cultural-developmental approach is the need to consider more contexts than typically have received research attention (Jensen and Larson, 2005).

The Cultural-Developmental Approach and Policy Considerations

In this final section, I turn to policy considerations. I briefly discuss how social policies and moral development research share common foci, and then I turn to some suggestions for how the present cultural-developmental approach to morality has implications for social policies.

Like moral development research, social policies are centrally focused on moral values and goals. Social policies consistently aim to promote that which is deemed morally desirable and decrease that which is deemed morally deficient. For example, social policies often involve weighing of moral goals such as individual rights, the duties of individuals or societies who are well-off toward individuals or societies who are less well-off, and how to optimize a variety of psychological and physical benefits for various members of society.

Like moral developmental research, social policies also often address the development of children or youth. Social policies influence children, either directly as in educational programs or more indirectly as in policies that affect families and other contexts of importance to children. Social policies also often go beyond the short run and have as their purview the society that youth will inherit and of which they will take leadership. In other words, policy is often made not only with an eye to today's societal members but also tomorrow's generation.

The fact that social policies and moral development research both address moral goals, moral development, and posterity make it clear that the two areas can inform one another. In light of the focus of this chapter and the present book, I will specifically discuss how the cultural-developmental approach to morality has implications for social policy aimed at culturally diverse groups.

The cultural-developmental template indicates that moral development across cultures takes both common and variable forms. There is not one and only one moral developmental trajectory, but nor are all moral goals and trajectories across cultures incommensurable and incompatible. One general implication is that social policies should be able to bridge between cultures.

More specifically, such bridging might more often than not be most successful if it builds on a willingness to examine where there are points of commonality between cultures while simultaneously allowing for some cultural variation. For example, recent research with immigrants in the United States indicates that they judge civic involvement to be important (Jensen, 2008b), and they are about as civically involved as non-immigrants (Huddy and Khatib, 2007; Jensen, in press; Lopez and Marcelo, 2008; Stepick, Stepick, and Labissiere, 2008). Here, then, is a moral value and behavior shared across cultural groups. However, immigrants' moral motives for civic involvement are not identical to those of non-immigrant. Immigrants' civic involvement is rooted, in part, in values of their cultures and religions of origin, as well as their distinctive bicultural experiences (Jensen, 2008b).

Looking at immigrants, it might be easy to see cultural differences, to infer that such differences preclude positive involvement in American society, and to urge social policies aimed at comprehensive changes to the cultures of immigrants. And indeed, prominent scientists and public policy pundits have done just that (e.g., Huntington, 2004). In contrast, the cultural-developmental template approach presented here suggests that it might be worthwhile for policymakers (and researchers) to recognize cultures as multifaceted, to ascertain and build on moral goals shared between cultures, and to be open to the possibility that some cultural differences can co-exist. In fact, some cultural differences can be a conduit rather than an encumbrance to shared goals, the way that immigrants and non-immigrants are motivated by somewhat different cultural values to be civically engaged.

Although the cultural-developmental template points to a social policy approach to bridging between cultures, it may also be useful in identifying circumstances where bridging will be difficult and even fraught with conflict. More often than not, bridging will be most challenging where cultural groups apply different Ethics to reach opposing moral judgments or to reach different views of the extent to which issues fall within the moral domain. For example, as described earlier, religiously liberal and conservative cultural groups are markedly different in their use of the Ethics of Autonomy and Divinity. This difference underpins how the two groups reach opposing moral judgments on a substantial number of issues (Jensen, 1997a, 1997b, 1998a, 1998b, 2000, 2006, 2008a). Many religious conservatives, for example, apply an Ethic of Divinity to a variety of life-and-death issues (i.e., abortion and terminal illness), reasoning that decisions about these issues ought to be left to God. Many religious liberals, in sharp contrast, apply an Ethic of Autonomy to these issues invoking the right of individuals to make decisions on their own behalf.

The difference in the two groups' use of the Ethics of Autonomy and Divinity also underpins differences on the extent to which an issue is deemed moral. As described earlier, to religious conservatives who regard the human body as God's temple, some issues such as alcohol use may be viewed as moral to an extent that is not shared by liberals. In sum, finding a consensus on social policy will be particularly difficult on issues where cultural groups use different ethics to reach opposing moral judgments or divergent assessments of their moral significance.

In the case of the opposition between religious liberals and conservatives in the United States, this difficulty has been captured by the application of the term *culture wars* (Hunter, 1991). The term recognizes deep and real divisions between the groups in terms of morality and worldviews. Yet, perhaps here, too, it might be worthwhile to return to the suggestion above of remembering that cultures are multifaceted and to aim to ascertain and build on moral values and goals shared between cultures.

Conclusion

The cultural-developmental template and the research that undergirds it make it clear that morality is fundamental to the human condition. Across cultures and across essentially all phases of the life-course, we ascribe moral meaning to behaviors and experiences.

At the same time, people increasingly live in a globalized and multicultural world, and it is time to see people's moral lives in light of both developmental and cultural psychology. Persons ages 7, 17, and 47 years to some extent differ in their moral reasoning, even if they share a common culture. Persons from diverse cultures such as India, Kenya, and the United States to some extent differ in their moral concepts, even if they are the same age. The present cultural-developmental synthesis offers the possibility of integrating both of these valuable insights in future theoretical and methodological work in moral psychology. The synthesis also points to implications for social policy consideration.

Note

I would like to thank the Society for Research in Child Development for its support of the conference on Bridging Developmental and Cultural Psychology that preceded the writing of this chapter.

References

Adelson, J. (1971). The political imagination of the young adolescent. *Daedalus,* 100: 1013–1050.

Ammerman, N. T. (1987). *Bible believers.* New Brunswick, NJ: Rutgers University Press.

Arnett, J. J. (1998). Learning to stand alone: The contemporary American transition to adulthood in cultural and historical context. *Human Development*, 41: 295–315.

Arnett, J. J. (2000). Emerging adulthood: A theory of development from the late teens through the twenties. *American Psychologist*, 55: 469–480.

Arnett, J. J. (2002). The psychology of globalization. *American Psychologist*, 57: 774–783.

Arnett, J. J. (2004). *Emerging adulthood: The winding road from the late teens through the twenties*. New York: Oxford University Press.

Arnett, J. J. (2011). Emerging adulthood(s): The cultural psychology of a new life stage. In L. A. Jensen (Ed.), *Bridging cultural and developmental psychology: New syntheses in theory, research and policy* (pp. 255–275). New York: Oxford University Press.

Arnett, J. J., Ramos, K. D., & Jensen, L. A. (2001). Ideological views in emerging adulthood: Balancing autonomy and community. *Journal of Adult Development*, 8: 69–79.

Blasi, A. (1987). Comment: The psychological definition of morality. In J. Kagan, & S. Lamb (Eds.), *The emergence of morality in young children* (pp. 83–90). Chicago, IL: The University of Chicago Press.

Blasi, A. (1990). How should psychologists define morality? Or, the negative side effects of philosophy's influence on psychology. In T. Wren (Ed.), *The moral domain: Essays on the ongoing discussion between philosophy and the social sciences* (pp. 38–70). Cambridge, MA: The MIT Press.

Blasi, A. (1994). Moral identity: Its role in moral functioning (pp. 168–178). In B. Puka (Ed.), *Fundamental research in moral development*. New York: Garland Publishing.

Brainerd, C. J. (1978). The stage question in cognitive-developmental theory. *Behavioral and Brain Sciences*, 2: 173–213.

Buchanan, T. (2003). *Keeping the world together: Investigating the moral discourse of three generations of American evangelicals*. Unpublished manuscript, Wheaton College, Illinois.

Chen, X. (2011). Culture, peer relationships, and human development. In L. A. Jensen (Ed.), *Bridging cultural and developmental psychology: New syntheses in theory, research and policy.* (pp. 92–112). New York: Oxford University Press.

Colby, A., & Damon, W. (1992). *Some do care: Contemporary lives of moral commitment*. New York: The Free Press.

Colby, A., Kohlberg, L, Gibbs, J., & Lieberman, M. (1983). A longitudinal study of moral judgment. *Monographs of the Society for Research in Child Development*, 48.

Cole, M. (1996). *Cultural psychology: A once and future discipline*. Cambridge, MA: The Belknap Press of Harvard University Press.

Csikszentmihalyi, M. (1993). *The evolving self: A psychology for the third millennium*. New York: HarperCollins.

Dien, D. S. (1982). A Chinese perspective on Kohlberg's theory of moral development. *Developmental Review*, 2: 331–341.

Edwards, C. P. (1987). Culture and the construction of moral values: A comparative ethnography of moral encounters in two cultural settings. In J. Kagan & S. Lamb (Eds.), *The emergence of morality in young children*. Chicago, IL: University of Chicago Press.

Eisenberg, N. (1992). *The caring child*. Cambridge, MA: Harvard University Press.

Eisenberg, N., Carlo, G., Murphy, B., & Van Court, P. (1995). Prosocial development in late adolescence. *Child Development*, 66: 1179–1197.

Flanagan, C. A. (2003). Trust, identity, and civic hope. *Applied Developmental Science,* 7: 165–171.

Flanagan, C., Martínez, M. L., & Cumsille P. (2011). Civil societies as cultural and developmental contexts for civic identity formation. In L. A. Jensen (Ed.), *Bridging developmental approaches to psychology: New syntheses in theory, research and policy* (pp. 113–137). New York: Oxford University Press.

French, D. C., Schneider, B. H., & Chen, X. (2006). *Peer relationships in cultural context.* New York: Cambridge University Press.

Fung, H. (1999). Becoming a moral child: The socialization of shame among young Chinese children. *Ethos,* 27: 180–209.

Gilligan, C. F. (1982). *In a different voice: Psychological theory and women's development.* Cambridge, MA: Harvard University Press.

Haidt, J. (2001). The emotional dog and its rational tail: A social intuitionist approach to moral judgment. *Psychological Review,* 108: 814–834.

Haidt, J., Koller, S. H., & Dias, M. G. (1993). Affect, culture, and morality, or, Is it wrong to eat your dog? *Journal of Personality and Social Psychology,* 65: 613–628.

Huddy, L., & Khatib, N. (2007). American patriotism, national identity, and political involvement. *American Journal of Political Science,* 51: 63–77.

Hunter, J. D. (1991). *Culture wars: The struggle to define America.* New York: BasicBooks.

Hurrelmann, K. (1996). The social world of adolescents: A sociological perspective. In K. Hurrelmann & S. Hamilton (Eds.), *Social problems and social contexts in adolescence: Perspectives across boundaries* (pp. 39–62). Hawthorne, NY: Aldine de Gruyter.

Jensen, L. A. (1991). *Coding Manual: Ethics of Autonomy, Community, and Divinity.* Unpublished manuscript, University of Chicago.

Jensen, L. A. (1995). Habits of the heart revisited: Ethics of autonomy, community and divinity in adults' moral language. *Qualitative Sociology,* 18: 71–86.

Jensen, L. A. (1996). *Different habits, different hearts: Orthodoxy and progressivism in the United States and India.* Unpublished doctoral dissertation, The University of Chicago.

Jensen, L. A. (1997a). Different worldviews, different morals: America's culture war divide. *Human Development,* 40: 325–344.

Jensen, L. A. (1997b). Culture wars: American moral divisions across the adult lifespan. *Journal of Adult Development,* 4: 107–121.

Jensen, L. A. (1998a). Moral divisions within countries between orthodoxy and progressivism: India and the United States. *Journal for the Scientific Study of Religion,* 37: 90–107.

Jensen, L. A. (1998b). Different habits, different hearts: The moral languages of the culture war. *The American Sociologist,* 29: 83–101.

Jensen, L. A. (2000). Conversions across the culture war divide: Two case studies. In M. E. Miller & A. N. West (Eds.), *Spirituality, ethics, and relationship in adulthood: Clinical and theoretical explorations.* International University Press/Psychosocial Press.

Jensen, L. A. (2003). Coming of age in a multicultural world: Adolescent cultural identity formation and globalization. *Applied Developmental Science,* 7: 188–195.

Jensen, L. A. (2004). *Coding Manual: Ethics of Autonomy, Community, and Divinity* (Revised). www.LeneArnettJensen.com. Last accessed on April 20, 2010.

Jensen, L. A. (2006). Liberal and conservative conceptions of family: A cultural-developmental study. *The International Journal for the Psychology of Religion,* 16: 253–269.

Jensen, L. A. (2008a). Through two lenses: A cultural-developmental approach to moral psychology. *Developmental Review,* 28: 289–315.

Jensen, L. A. (2008b). Immigrants' cultural identities as sources of civic engagement. In L. A. Jensen, & C. A. Flanagan. (Eds.). *Immigrant civic engagement. Applied Developmental Science.*

Jensen, L. A. (2008c). Immigrant civic engagement and religion: The paradoxical roles of religious motives and organizations. In R. Lerner, R. Roeser, & E. Phelps (Eds.), *Positive youth development and spirituality: From theory to research.* West Conshohocken, PA: Templeton Foundation Press.

Jensen, L. A. (2009a). Conceptions of God and the Devil: A cultural-developmental study. *Journal for the Scientific Study of Religion,* 48: 121–145.

Jensen, L. A. (2009b). *To Do or Not To Do: Immigrant civic and political involvement.* Unpublished manuscript, Clark University.

Jensen, L. A. (in press). Immigrant youth in the United States: Coming of age among diverse civic cultures. In Sherrod, L. R., Torney-Purta, J., & Flanagan, C. A. (Eds.), *Handbook of Research and Policy on Civic Engagement in Youth.* Hoboken, NJ: Wiley.

Jensen, L. A., Arnett, J. J., Feldman, S. S., & Cauffman, E. (2002). It's wrong, but everybody does it: Academic dishonesty among high school and college students. *Contemporary Educational Psychology,* 27: 209–228.

Jensen, L. A., Arnett, J. J., Feldman, S. S., & Cauffman, E. (2004). The right to do wrong: Lying to parents among adolescents and emerging adults. *Journal of Youth and Adolescence,* 33: 101–112.

Jensen, L. A., Arnett, J. J., & McKenzie, J. (in press). Globalization and cultural identity developments in adolescence and emerging adulthood. In Schwartz, S. J., Luyckx, K., & Vignoles, V. L. (Eds.), *Handbook of Identity Theory and Research.* New York, NY: Springer Publishing Company.

Jensen, L. A., & Larson, R. W. (2005). Developmental horizons: Legacies and prospects in child and adolescent development. In L. A. Jensen & R. Larson (Eds.), *New horizons in developmental theory and research. New Directions for Child and Adolescent Development,* 109: 5–13.

Jensen, L. A., & McKenzie, J. (in preparation). *Moral reasoning among religiously liberal and conservative Americans: A cultural-developmental approach.* Unpublished manuscript, Clark University.

Kagan, J. (1987). Introduction. In J. Kagan & S. Lamb, *The emergence of morality in young children.* Chicago, IL: The University of Chicago Press.

Keating, D. (1990). Adolescent thinking. In S. S. Feldman, & G. Elliott (Eds.), *At the threshold: The developing adolescent* (pp. 54–89). Cambridge, MA: Harvard University Press.

Killen, M. (2002). Early deliberations: A developmental psychologist investigates how children think about fairness and exclusion. *Teaching Tolerance,* 22: 44–49.

Kohlberg, L. (1976). Moral stages and moralization: The cognitive-developmental approach. In T. Lickona (Ed.), *Moral development and behavior.* New York: Holt, Rinehart and Winston.

Kohlberg, L. (1981). *The philosophy of moral development.* San Francisco, CA: Harper & Row.

Kohlberg, L. (1984). *The psychology of moral development.* San Francisco, CA: Harper & Row.

Lapsley, D. K., & Narvaez, D. (2004). A social cognitive approach to the moral personality. In D. K. Lapsley & D. Narvaez (Eds.), *Moral development, self, and identity: essays in honor of Augusto Blasi* (pp. 189–212). Mahwah, NJ: Lawrence Erlbaum Associates.

Larson, R. (2002). Globalization, societal change, and new technologies: What they mean for the future of adolescence. *Journal of Research on Adolescence,* 12: 1–30.

Lei, T. (1994). Being and becoming moral in Chinese culture: Unique or universal? *Cross-Cultural Research,* 28: 58–91.

Leichtman, M. D. (2006). Cultural and maturational influences on long-term event memory. In C. Tamis-LeMonda, & L. Balter (Eds.), *Child psychology: A handbook of contemporary issues (second edition).* Philadelphia, PA: Psychology Press.

Lerner, R. (2002, February). *The five C's: Developmental complexity.* Paper presented at "Beyond the Self: Perspectives on Transcendence and Identity Development" meeting, Pasadena, CA.

Lopez, M. H., & Marcelo, K. B. (2008). The civic engagement of immigrant youth: New evidence from the 2006 Civic and Political Health of the Nation Survey. In L. A. Jensen & C. A. Flanagan (Eds.), *Immigrant Civic Engagement: New Translation,* Special issue of *Applied Developmental Science,* 12: 66–73.

Ma, H. K. (1988). The Chinese perspectives on moral judgment development. *International Journal of Psychology,* 23: 201–227.

Mahoney, A., Pargament, K. I., Murray-Swank, A, & Murray-Swank, N. (2003). Religion and the sanctification of family relationships. *Review of Religious Research,* 44: 220–236.

Mayseless, O., & Scharf, M. (2003). What does it mean to be an adult? The Israeli experience. In J. J. Arnett, & N. Galambos (Eds.), *New Directions in Child Development,* 100: 5–20.

Miller, J. G. (1989). A cultural perspective on the morality of beneficence and interpersonal responsibility. In S. Ting-Tomey, & F. Korzenny (Eds.), *International and intercultural communication annual, Vol. 15* (pp. 11–27). Newbury Park, CA: Sage Publications.

Miller, J. G. (1994). Cultural diversity in the morality of caring: Individually oriented versus duty-based interpersonal moral codes. *Cross-Cultural Research,* 28: 3–39.

Miller, J. G., Bersoff, D. M., & Harwood, R. L. (1990). Perceptions of social responsibility in India and in the United States: Moral imperatives or personal decisions? *Journal of Personality and Social Personality,* 58: 33–47.

Miller, J. G., & Luthar, S. (1989). Issues of interpersonal responsibility and accountability: A comparison of Indians' and Americans' moral judgment. *Social Cognition,* 7: 237–261.

Nelson, L. J. (2009). An examination of emerging adulthood in Romanian college students. *International Journal of Behavioral Development,* 33: 402–411.

Nisan, M. (1987). Moral norms and social conventions: A cross-cultural study. *Developmental Psychology,* 23: 719–725.

Nsamenang, A. B. (1992). *Human development in cultural context.* Newbury Park, CA: Sage Publications.

Oser, F. K., Scarlett, G., & Bucher, A. (2005). Religious and spiritual development throughout the lifespan. In W. Damon & R. M. Lerner (Eds.), *Handbook of child psychology.* New York: Wiley.

Phinney, J. S. (2000). Identity formation across cultures: The interaction of personal, societal, and historical change. *Human Development,* 43: 27–31.

Phinney, J. S., & Baldelomar, O. A. (2011). Identity development in multiple cultural contexts. In L. A. Jensen (Ed.), *Bridging cultural and developmental psychology: New syntheses in theory, research and policy* (pp. 161–186). New York: Oxford University Press.

Piaget, J. (1965). *The moral judgment of the child.* New York: The Free Press. (Original work published 1932).

Piaget, J. (1972). Intellectual evolution from adolescence to adulthood. *Human Development,* 15: 1–12.

Rogoff, B. (2003). *The cultural nature of human development.* Oxford, UK: Oxford University Press.

Rothbaum, F., Weisz, J., Pott, M., Miyake, K., & Morelli, G. (2000). Attachment and culture. *American Psychologist,* 55: 1093–1104.

Rozin, P., Lowery, L., Imada, S., & Haidt, J. (1999). The CAD triad hypothesis: A mapping between three moral emotions (contempt, anger, disgust) and three moral codes (community, autonomy, divinity). *Journal of Personality and Social Psychology,* 76: 574–586.

Rubin, K., Bukowski, W., & Parker, J. (1998). Peer interactions, relationships and groups. In W. Damon (Series Ed.) and N. Eisenberg (Volume Ed.), *Handbook of child psychology, Volume 3: Social, emotional, and personality development* (5th ed.). New York: Wiley.

Saraswathi, T. S. (2005). Hindu worldview in the development of selfways: The "Atman" as the real self. In L. A. Jensen & R. Larson (Eds.), New horizons in developmental theory and research. *New Directions for Child and Adolescent Development,* 109: 43–50.

Saraswathi, T. S., Mistry, J., & Dutta, R. (2011). Reconceptualizing lifespan development through a Hindu perspective. In L. A. Jensen (Ed.), *Bridging cultural and developmental psychology: New syntheses in theory, research and policy* (pp. 276–299). New York: Oxford University Press.

Schlegel, A., & Barry, H. (1991). *Adolescence: An anthropological inquiry.* New York: Free Press.

Schlegel, A. (2011). Adolescent ties to adult communities: the intersection of culture and development. In L. A. Jensen (Ed.), *Bridging cultural and developmental psychology: New syntheses in theory, research and policy* (pp. 138–158). New York: Oxford University Press.

Shweder, R. A. (1982a). Liberalism as destiny. *Contemporary Psychology,* 27: 421–424.

Shweder, R. A. (1982b). Beyond self-constructed knowledge: The study of culture and morality. *Merrill-Palmer Quarterly,* 28: 41–69.

Shweder, R. A. (1990). In defense of moral realism: Reply to Gabennesch. *Child Development,* 61: 2060–2067.

Shweder, R. A., Goodnow, J., Hatano, G., LeVine, R., Markus, H., & Miller, P. (2006). The cultural psychology of development: One mind, many mentalities. In W. Damon & R. M. Lerner (Eds.), *Handbook of child development* (pp. 716–792). New York: Wiley.

Shweder, R. A., Mahapatra, M., & Miller, J. G. (1990). Culture and moral development. In J. W. Stigler, R. A. Shweder, & G. Herdt (Eds.), *Cultural psychology* (pp. 130–204). Cambridge, UK: Cambridge University Press.

Shweder, R. A., Much, N. C., Mahapatra, M., & Park, L. (1997). The "big three" of morality (autonomy, community, divinity), and the "big three" explanations of suffering. In A. Brandt, & P. Rozin (Eds.), *Morality and Health.* New York: Routledge.

Sita, L. (1999). *Coming of age.* Woodbridge, CT: Blackbirch Press.

Smetana, J. G. (2000). Middle-class African American adolescents' and parents' conceptions of parental authority and parenting practices: A longitudinal investigation. *Child Development,* 71: 1672–1686.

Snarey, J. R. (1985). Cross-cultural universality of socio-moral development: A critical review of Kohlbergian research. *Psychological Bulletin,* 97: 202–232.

Stepick, A., Stepick, C. D., Labissirere, Y. (2008). South Florida's immigrant youth and civic engagement: Major engagement, minor differences. In L. A. Jensen & C. A. Flanagan (Eds.), *Immigrant Civic Engagement: New Translation,* Special issue of *Applied Developmental Science,* 12: 57–65.

Sternberg, R. J. (2004). Culture and intelligence. *American Psychologist,* 59: 325–338.

Turiel, E. (1983). *The development of social knowledge: Morality and convention.* Cambridge, UK: Cambridge University Press.

Turiel, E. (2002). *The culture of morality.* Cambridge, UK: Cambridge University Press.

Vainio, A. (2003). *One morality—Or multiple moralities?* Unpublished doctoral dissertation, University of Helsinki, Finland.

Valsiner, J. (2007). *Culture in minds and societies.* Los Angeles: Sage Publications.

Vasquez, K., Keltner, D., Ebenbach, D. H., & Banaszynski, T. L. (2001). Cultural variation and similarity in moral rhetorics: Voices from the Philippines and the United States. *Journal of Cross-Cultural Research,* 32: 93–120.

Walker, L. J. (1989). A longitudinal study of moral reasoning. *Child Development,* 51: 131–139.

Walker, L. J., & Moran, T. J. (1991). Moral reasoning in a communist Chinese society. *Journal of Moral Education,* 20: 139–155.

Walker, L. J., Pitts, R. C., Hennig, K. H., & Matsuba, M. K. (1995). Reasoning about morality and real-life moral problems. In M. Killen, & D. Hart (Eds.), *Morality in everyday life: Developmental perspectives* (pp. 371–407). New York: Cambridge University Press.

Whiting, B. B., & Edwards, C. P. (1988). *Children of different worlds: The formation of social behavior.* Cambridge, MA: Harvard University Press.

Wilson, J. Q. (1993). *The moral sense.* New York: Free Press.

Youniss, J., & Smollar, J. (1985). *Adolescent relations with mothers, fathers, and friends.* Chicago, IL: University of Chicago Press.

Youniss, J., & Yates, M. (1997). *Community service and social responsibility in youth.* Chicago, IL: University of Chicago Press.

Zimba, R. F. (1994). The understanding of morality, convention, and personal preference in an African setting: Findings from Zambia. *Journal of Cross-Cultural Psychology,* 25: 369–393.

CHAPTER 2

Cultural Frames of Children's Learning Beliefs

JIN LI

According to Bertrand Russell (1945), during the amazing 400 years of Greek Antiquity, Greek philosophers laid down virtually all philosophical topics for later generations in the West to contemplate. Zeno was one of the Greek philosophers who flourished during the 5th century B.C.A. He is well-known for his argument that an arrow in flight is at each moment simply where it is; it is therefore always at rest. He held that there is no motion and no change in the world. In the subsequent debate about whether the world is always in flux, as put forth by Heraclitus, or it does not change, as contended by Parmanides, Zeno's idea was evoked. The fact that Russell and other later thinkers continue to discuss Zeno's argument is testimony to the unabated fascination Western thinkers exhibit about nature.

Zeno's brilliant mind feat is just a part of a vast edifice of Western intellectual history. His way of thinking exemplifies the Western approach that sets the external world as the target of thinking and analysis (Rothbaum & Wang, 2011). Essential questions for human beings of what to know, how we know it, and how certain our knowledge is demarcate the frames of contemplation. This approach has been foundational to Western civilization, particularly to scientific thinking. It also underlies much of Western beliefs about learning.

The Chinese approach to knowing and learning also dates back to a comparable time. Consider the following exchange:

> Ranyou complained to his teacher Confucius that it is not that he did not like
> Confucius teaching about self-perfecting to become the most sincere, genuine,

and humane person, but that he did not have enough strength to follow through with this process. Confucius replied: "Those who do not have the strength for it collapse somewhere along the way. But with you, you have drawn your own line before you start" (Ames & Rosemont, 1998, p.106).

The phrase "plenty of enthusiasm but not enough strength to follow through," which is still used in daily Chinese today, originated from the dialogue between Ranyou and Confucius.

This kind of discussion about understanding a life purpose and following through with action turned out to be central to an approach to learning that sets one's self—not the external world—as the target of contemplation and personal transformation (*see also* Rothbaum & Wang, 2011). This intellectual tradition, too, marked the philosophical terrain for questions of how to be, how to live, and how to grow as a human being. Its enduring influence is still powerfully reflected in present-day Chinese and many East Asian people's thinking, feeling, and behavior in learning, despite all the changes since ancient times.

In this chapter, I argue that cultural learning models exist. I review research on the different learning models in two large groups of cultures, European/ European American versus Chinese/Asian. I use the terms *West* and *European* to denote the common intellectual heritage that developed in Europe over the last 2500 years. Similarly, I use *East Asia/Asian* to refer the Confucian tradition that has influenced Japan, Korea, and Vietnam (Kim & Park, 2008), as well as the more direct Confucian heritage societies of China, Taiwan, Hong Kong, and Singapore. Next, I discuss how cultural insights gained into this topic can be usefully integrated with developmental psychology. In doing so, I also look at how the traditionally opposing sides of structure versus content might both be needed for research. I conclude the chapter with some thoughts on how such research may help us understand learning beliefs in today's fast-changing and globalized world.

Cultural Learning Models

The capacity for higher-order learning is the reason we are able to create, keep, and continue to advance our cultural heritage, whereas very smart primates cannot (Tomasello, 1999). Human learning as a vast topic has been approached by many researchers across many disciplinary fields. Much of this research has focused on individual learners' learning capacity, processes, motivation, achievement, and pedagogy in formal education. Research did not begin attending to socio-cultural factors that shape people's learning beliefs until recent decades. Research on individual learners is important, but it does not explain why cultural groups, above and beyond individual differences, display different patterns of thoughts, affect, and behavior in learning (Chan & Rao, 2009; Gallimore & Goldenberg, 2001; Hufton & Elliott, 2000; Serpell, 1993; Stevenson & Stigler, 1992).

Since the 1980s, culturally oriented research has generated clear evidence that human learning, formal or informal, is influenced by the values and orientations of the culture or ethnic community in which individuals develop. For example, the notion of intelligence, lying at the core of many learning theories, was found to differ across cultures. Europeans and European Americans view intelligence more as an innate capacity, manifested in speed of processing information, verbal expressivity, and analytical reasoning (Sternberg, 1985). In contrast, African conceptions of intelligence focus on wisdom, trustworthiness, and social attentiveness (Dasen, 1984; Serpell, 1993; Nsamenang, 2011). Japanese conceptions also elaborate on the social dimension but differs between kinds of social competence, such as one's sociability and ability to sympathize with others (Azuma & Kashiwagi, 1987).

With regard to other personal characteristics in learning, Western students emphasize individual qualities such as independence, task efficiency, competition (Hess & Azuma, 1991), self-esteem, and social competence (Chao, 1996; Wentzel & Caldwell, 1997). But Japanese students display a strong group orientation and thoroughness in their approaches to tasks (Hess & Azuma, 1991; Lewis, 1995). Similarly, Western learners attribute achievement to ability, whereas their Asian peers do so to effort (Hau & Salili, 1991; Stevenson & Stigler, 1992). Yet Russian students' motivation for learning anchors differently around the unique concepts of *dusha* (soul) and *kulturny* (culture) (Hufton & Elliott, 2000).

This informative research led me (Li, 2001) to term culturally developed learning values and orientations as *cultural learning models* based on anthropological theories (D'Andrade, 1995; Harkness & Super, 1996; Shweder, 1991). Accordingly, cultural learning models refer to culturally constructed, shared views of learning—that is, beliefs that serve to structure and constrain people's learning experiences and interpretations as well as to inform their goals for action (Quinn & Holland, 1987). They are the frames of the members' thinking, feeling, and behavior in learning. However, it is erroneous to assume that members of a given culture are mere mirror copies of their cultural learning models. Instead, they appropriate the models based on their individual life aspirations and preferences. Individuals may negotiate with, and sometimes even reject, certain aspects of their cultural models (*see* Goodnow, 2011; Flanagan, Martínez, & Cumsille, 2011; Strauss, 1992).

Two Cultures' Learning Models

To document cultural learning models, I conducted several studies on European American and Chinese conceptions of learning (Li, 2001, 2002a, 2003). These two cultures were chosen for their very different intellectual traditions despite their shared emphasis on learning. One way to access culture-level conceptions of learning is to analyze daily language that refers to learning in each culture. Accordingly, European American and Chinese college students (who were preferred because of the higher demand on their ability to differentiate fine meanings of words) free-associated with the English term *learn/learning* and its Chinese equivalent *xuexi* (学习) (Li, 2003, for details). This procedure produced nearly 500 terms from each culture, which were further reduced with a rating procedure to 205 English and 225 Chinese terms representing core cultural terms, respectively. These core terms were sorted into groups by respective college students based on similarity in meaning. With cluster analyses, the sorted groups resulted in each culture's conceptual map of learning.

Next, I (Li, 2002a) asked European American and Chinese college students in China to describe their ideal learners to obtain accounts of learning images as embodied in real people beyond the learning lexicon in my first study. Ideal learner images are assumed to exist in people's minds through the process of enculturation. As such, members of the culture use these images consciously or unconsciously to guide their own learning and to socialize their own children (Bruner, 1986). Participants wrote about four dimensions: *(1)* ideal learners' thinking on their purposes and processes of learning; *(2)* their views of the relationship between learning and one's moral development; *(3)* their learning behaviors in routine situations such as facing high achievement, failure, and boredom; and *(4)* their emotional patterns associated with good or poor learning. Analyses of these written descriptions yielded four profiles corresponding to the four sets of probes for each culture (Li, 2002a, for details).

The basic findings from the two studies converge to two comprehensive pictures of the two cultures' learning models. Table 2–1 summarizes the four large common components for both cultures: purpose, agentic process, achievement, and affect.

European American Model

The European American model (Table 2–1) centers around a set of purposes that focus on the finely differentiated functions of the mind to understand the world. As an essential part of the Western intellectual tradition, also clearly shown in Zeno's argument, the mind assumes most importance in human learning. Recent research on Western European university students also supports this basic finding (Kühnen et al., 2009). Furthermore, the European American model stresses developing personal ability and skills and realizing personal goals.

To pursue these purposes, learners display their agency in four kinds of learning processes. First, they are actively engaged in a broad range of activities and experiences, using both their minds as well as bodies (e.g., hands-on learning) to learn whatever they deem important and are fascinated about. Second, learners do what their minds do best in learning: think. Thinking in all forms (e.g., quantitative or visual), levels (e.g., differentiating vs. synthesizing), and dimensions (deductive logic or imagination) is supreme in Western learning. Third, inquiry guides learners to examine and question the known and to explore and discover the new. Fourth, communication—particularly verbal communication—is crucial because communication is both a manifestation of one's intelligence and at the same time a means to achieve one's learning (Kim, 2002).

With regard to affect, personal curiosity about, and interest in, the world are very much part of the learning purposes (Hidi & Renninger, 2006). Intrinsic enjoyment (Deci & Ryan, 2000) and challenging attitudes also accompany

Table 2.1 Components and Dimensions of European American and Chinese
Learning Models

European American	Chinese
Purpose of Learning	
Cultivate mind/understand world	Perfect self morally/socially
Develop ability/skill	Acquire knowledge/skills for self
Reach personal goals	Contribute to society
Agentic Process of Learning	
Active engagement	Diligence
Thinking	Self-exertion
Inquiry	Endurance of hardship
Communication	Perseverance
	Concentration
Kinds of Achievement	
Understanding of essentials/expertise	Breadth-depth/mastery of knowledge
Personal insights/creativity	Application of knowledge
Being the best one can be	Unity of knowledge and moral character
Affect	
Positive	
Curiosity/interest	Commitment ("establish one's will")
Intrinsic enjoyment	Love/passion/thirst
Challenging attitudes	Respect/receptivity
Pride for achievement	Humility for achievement
Negative	
Indifference/boredom	Lack of desire
Extrinsic motivation	Arrogance
Disappointment/low self-esteem for failure	Shame/guilt for failure

Adapted from Table 14–1, Li, J. & Fischer, K. W. (2004). Thoughts and emotions in American and Chinese
cultural beliefs about learning. In D. Y. Dai & R. Sternberg (Eds.), *Motivation, emotion, and cognition:
Integrative perspectives on intellectual functioning and development* (pp. 385–418). Mahwah, NJ: Erlbaum.

learners throughout these processes. Such learning leads to developing expertise in a field, personal insights and creative problem solving in real life, and
being the best one can be. When these goals are realized, learners feel proud of
themselves. However, when experiencing failure, they feel disappointment and
low self-esteem.

Chinese Learning Model

The most salient purpose of Chinese learners is perfecting themselves morally
and socially as opposed to understanding the world (Table 2–1)—that is, the
self is the project of one's learning. This finding corresponds to the literature

on Confucian thought (Tu, 1979). The tenet of the conversation between Ranyou and Confucius was about this very process. Moreover, learners also aim at acquiring knowledge/skill for themselves, stressing mastery before engaging in inquiry and discovery. Learners express their desire to make contributions to society, a larger social purpose that has been advocated by Confucian teaching (Wu & Lai, 1992). It also corresponds to the ethic of community, as one of the three major human ethics that Shweder theorized (Shweder et al., 1997; also Jensen, 2011).

Embedded in these purposes are commitment and passion, which may or may not be intrinsic in origin as understood in the West. To pursue those purposes, learners need to develop the so-called learning virtues of diligence, self-exertion, endurance of hardship, perseverance, and concentration. These virtues are seen as more essential than actual learning activities such as reading or thinking. These learning virtues are believed applicable to any learning activity. Family and school actively engage the child in establishing a larger purpose to pursue for life. This process has also been found to guide children toward a meaningful life across cultures and ethnic groups (Damon, 2003).

An important difference in learning-related affect between the two cultural models is that the Chinese emphasizes respect/receptivity to teaching, as opposed to Western challenging attitude toward existing knowledge and authority. However, it is also erroneous to assume that because of respect/receptivity, Chinese/East Asian learners are only passive and obedient learners who lack independent thinking (e.g., Tweed & Lehman, 2002). Research by Pratt et al. (1999) shows that Asian students prefer to memorize, understand, and apply the material under study first before questioning the authority and modifying the original knowledge. They also are reluctant to challenge teachers in public, even when they have questions in class. The preferred style is to listen attentively and to absorb the information being taught by the teacher first. Then they seek the teachers out after class to ask questions or to clarify confusion. Part of their reluctance also results from their consideration of other students in class because asking many questions may "interfere with" their peers' learning (Li, 2009a). Asian students appear to be highly sensitive to others' needs (Cohen & Gunz, 2002; Heine et al., 2008; Rothbaum & Wang, 2011). Finally, their reluctance to be vocal in class stems also from their concern that challenging teachers in class may "break the teaching performance" of the teacher, a central cultural activity that is taken very seriously by the teacher, students, and the culture at large (Li, 2009a). This teacher–student cooperation has been called a virtuoso style in Asian classrooms (Paine, 1990), much like a conductor conducting a symphony in Western music. The respect that the audience grants to the performing orchestra is analogous to the class attending a teacher's teaching that displays his or her moral embodiment, virtue, care, dedication, and artistry.

Such learning aims at breadth and depth, mastery of knowledge, application to real-life situations, and unity of one's knowledge and moral character. It is worth noting that this moral theme lies at the heart of the Chinese learning model. However, compared with the European American model, Chinese respondents referred much less to exploration, inquiry, and thinking.

When achieving learning, learners remain calm and humble, unlike their European American peers who feel pride. Chinese learners also watch out for complacency to continue self-perfecting. When facing poor learning, they feel shame/guilt not only for themselves but also in reference to those who nurtured them. Interestingly, not only does failure not reduce Asian learners' motivation, it actually increases their motivation to self-improve. This tendency was also supported by research: when failing a task, European Canadians were more likely to give up, but the Japanese students persisted longer (Heine et al., 2001).

Despite these differences, some similarities between the two cultural learning models also emerged. For example, high competence matters to both cultures' learners for a successful life. Chinese learners also aim at understanding of the material, much like their European American peers (Sacks & Chan, 2003), although they may go about achieving understanding differently (Marton, Dall'Alba, & Beaty, 1993). Whereas European American learners verbalize their thoughts and ask questions in class, East Asian learners prefer to work on the material over a long time, committing all parts to memory and digesting them before questioning. Nevertheless, they have similar aims of understanding. Finally, many European American respondents also described making a difference in the world, alleviating suffering, and correcting injustice. However, these moral purposes were not expressed as prevalently as by Chinese learners.

How Children Develop Learning Beliefs in these Cultures

Thus far, I have presented the two cultural learning models based on empirical research. It is clear that culture plays an important role in framing learning models, which should influence how children develop their own learning beliefs (BLs). Yet, developmental research as whole has not paid sufficient attention to how children develop BLs under the influence of their cultural learning models. We know very little of how children *come to hold* different beliefs that are found among adults across cultures. In other words, there exists a disconnect between the well-documented cultural learning models (at least with regard to Western and East Asian cultures) and developmental psychology on this topic.

Below I consider two related lines of research to bridge the disconnect. The first is children's BLs themselves and the related developmental trajectories. This development may be posited as a combined function of general cognitive development and cultural influence. Because children's BLs could be treated as both a structural and content topic, I consider both. The second area is the socialization process that underlies children's developing BLs. Here, I focus on parental socialization but point out the need to study school socialization. I show empirical efforts first, followed by a discussion of age-based trajectories whenever sufficient research merits such a conjecture.

As shown previously, children's BLs cover a large terrain. Research that addresses both development and cultural psychology is limited. Available research concerns three general sets of BLs between the two cultures under discussion: beliefs about the learning process, beliefs about learning purposes, and perceptions of achieving peers. These attempts shed light on how bridging developmental and cultural psychology can lead to better understanding of this topic.

Children's Beliefs of the Learning Process

Although learning is a central pan-human activity, thinking about learning is not something that occupies young children's minds (Bartsch, Horvath, & Estes, 2003). There are two general reasons for why children are limited in this regard. First, most children younger than 4 years may not have the cognitive sophistication to fully comprehend the abstract notion of learning, despite their own rapid learning. Second, children younger than 4 years have been shown to lack a fully developed theory of mind (ToM), which is the understanding that others have minds with desires, knowledge, and beliefs that may be independent of one's own. ToM is foundational to human social cognition. Learning in the human world usually occurs in a social setting where one person does not know something but another does, and the first person can get the knowledge from the second person, which is the essence of purposeful learning as a function of another's purposeful teaching. To understand such socially coordinated learning requires an appreciation of both persons' minds in the learning/teaching process, which may indeed require ToM. Research shows that Western children as young as 2.5 years have a bourgeoning sense that if they do not know something (e.g., words), they can get it from someone who does (Strauss, 2005).

However, children do not have sophisticated understanding of *how* learning takes place until they are 5 or 6 years old, quite possibly older. Longitudinal language data show that European American children younger than 4 years do not spontaneously talk about learning much. Whenever they do, they talk mostly about *what* is learned but not *why, where,* and *how* learning takes place—that is, the learning process (Bartsch et al., 2003). Sobel, Li, & Corriveau (2007) conducted a more fine-tuned analysis of the language data and confirmed the findings of Bartsch et al. However, they also found that as they grew older, children talked more about the learning process.

Sobel and colleagues (2007) also studied European American 4- and 6-year-olds in a laboratory setting and found that 4-year-olds' conception of learning is based primarily on the learner's desire. In other words, learning will happen if the learner *wants* to learn, and nothing else matters. This finding coheres with the general literature of ToM on desire being understood by young children first before the notions of knowledge, belief, and the intricate relationships between these two mental states in another's mind (Bartsch & Wellman, 1995; Flavell, Green, & Flavell, 1995). By age 6 years, most children understood that the learner also needs to pay attention to and actually receive the information before he/she can learn something; desire alone does not suffice. Moreover, 6- and 7-year-olds begin to understand that both desire and attention may not guarantee success of learning—one also needs to *do* something (e.g., practice) to get the knowledge/skill. Another study (Li, Sobel, & Corriveau, 2005) showed that children may need to grow several years older to appreciate the idea that one's learning capacity might be finite (e.g., one cannot learn all the songs in the world) and that one's learning capacity might be constrained by time and difficulty of the knowledge (e.g., the multiplication tables may not be learned in 5 minutes).

These findings based on European American children may serve as a starting point for researchers to examine how cultural influences can be integrated. Two considerations may be of particular relevance: structure versus content and age-based trajectory. With regard to the former, developmental researchers have identified the notion of capacity as a structural element (*see* Leichtman, 2011). Capacity conceived of as a structure both enables and limits what the child can do. Therefore, capacity usually refers to universal human endowment regarded as necessary before other mental processes are possible. For example, object permanence at the end of infancy, as Piaget discovered it, is regarded as a universal achievement of all human infants. Without it, human cognition would not develop further. Because of the clear boundary between what the child cannot do without ToM and then can do with ToM, it is regarded as a universal mental structure that is foundational to human social cognition. ToM, as documented by research, emerges in all human children around age 4 years (Perner, Leekam, & Wimmer, 1987).

The notion of *content* is the specific incidences to which children apply their capacity. For example, children can use their ToM to think about someone else wanting a cookie or a ball or the person's mistaken belief versus knowledge of where the cookie/ball is. Understanding another's desire, belief, and knowledge here are treated as structural elements, but the cookie, ball, and any other object of one's thought are content elements. In the ToM literature, structural elements matter more because, as has been argued, they underly content and may be less variable, whereas content can vary much more widely.

However, the emergence of ToM as a new capacity in children may give rise to many divergent types of thinking, each of which could be further divided into structure and content—for example, children's understanding of social norms versus the specific social rules (Rakoczy, Warneken, & Tomasello, 2008). It is likely that these further areas of cognition are subject to cultural influence. Children's conceptions of learning may be one of these areas. Juxtaposing the basic distinction between structure and content, learning conceptions may be more profitably studied as a structural topic. Thus, we may ask if East Asian children also understand desire before attention and intention in the same sequence and timing as Western children. Research indeed shows that Chinese children understand desire, similarly to English-speaking children, before the mental states of belief and knowledge (Tardif & Wellman, 2000; Wellman et al., 2006). However, given that the East Asian learning model emphasizes virtues rather than mind, it is reasonable to expect that their preschoolers may become more sensitive to the learning virtues of diligence, persistence, and concentration as requisites to learning than Western children. Similarly, Western children should display a greater sensitivity to ability, exploration, and creativity relative to East Asian children because of their cultural preference.

A study that I conducted (Li, 2004a) for European American and Chinese preschoolers ages 4 to 6 years tested these hypotheses with story beginnings to elicit children's responses to learning scenarios. Specifically, we showed each child a hardworking bird, who tried hard to learn how to fly and succeeded, as opposed to a bear who tried to learn how to catch fish but gave up in the end. Children were asked to complete the stories. We found that European American children talked more about ability (e.g., "the bear is too young to catch fish"), exploration (e.g., "the bear should keep trying different things to see if he can catch a fish"), and creative strategies (e.g., "the bear can use a noodle to wrap around his waist in the swimming pool first"). In comparison, Chinese children mentioned more how much the bird practiced (diligence/self-exertion), how the bird was not afraid of falling down and making mistakes (endurance of hardship/persistence), and how the bear's divided attention prevented him/her from learning well (lack of concentration). These divergent trends became more consistent in each group's older age, respectively.

The focus on attentiveness as a structural element for learning conceptions by Chinese children was particularly instructive in light of bridging culture and developmental perspectives. Among 5- and 6-year-olds, 30% of Chinese children talked about the bear's concentration problem as a cause of his/her failure, but no European American agemates did so. Despite the finding by Sobel et al. on European American children's emergent understanding of attention in learning, European American children did not mention concentration in my study. A plausible reason was that concentration/attentiveness is a more sophisticated notion than just exposure to the song to be learned. Understanding concentration/attentiveness requires that the child know how the mind should zero in to a learning task, how one should proceed, and the consequences the lack of it may entail. Because Chinese children are likely to be immersed more with virtue socialization in their home and school, it was not surprising that they ascribed the bear's failure to lack of the concentration among other virtues. These Chinese preschoolers seemed to achieve an earlier awareness of attentiveness, presumably because they had been taught the pros and cons of concentration and to behave accordingly. It is thus reasonable to assume that both cultures' children eventually understand concentration, but whether they may achieve this understanding earlier or later depends on whether their culture emphasizes it.

Similarly, we can generate more relevant hypotheses for further research on other structural elements in this topic. Thus, we may expect that East Asian children will show more heightened awareness of intention (effort), an expanded view of capacity (although one cannot learn all the songs in the world, one can still learn a lot more if one works hard), understanding that learning takes time (although one can't learn the multiplication tables in 5 minutes, one can learn them with persistence). Moreover, these children should also display an earlier awareness of other related virtues such as the learner's need to overcome difficulties, humility, and respect for teachers (*see* Rothbaum & Wang, 2011).

Similarly, further down, Western children may develop finer understanding of how the mind works along the well-studied domains of knowledge (truth) versus belief and self-world relationships displayed in exploration, inquiry, and creativity. With regard to the former domain, Wellman et al. (2006) documented that Western preschoolers showed an earlier awareness of various belief states than Chinese children (e.g., someone has knowledge/truth vs. a false belief of a situation). But Chinese children showed an earlier awareness of knowledge (e.g., someone is knowledgeable vs. ignorant of a given situation). With regard to the latter domain, European American children elaborated more on exploration, inquiry, and creativity than Chinese preschoolers in my narrative study (Li, 2004a).

Further developmental trajectories should be studied as a continuation of these early divergent pathways. A focus on the timing of children achieving various key understandings will undoubtedly inform childrearing and education practice. There is evidence that the East Asian children undergo an intensifying trend in their development of learning virtues and associated behavior and reach maturity in adolescence (Li, 2006). However, comparable research on Western children's development is lacking.

Children's Beliefs About Learning Purposes

A large body of research exists on achievement motivation in the field of educational psychology. The concept of achievement goals has been studied extensively (Cury et al., 2006). Yet, most research in this area takes neither a developmental nor a cultural perspective. As a result, we read that a learner should have either an entity theory (either a person has or does not have intelligence) or incremental (a person can become smart) theory of intelligence (Dweck, 1999) as if the learner were a culture-free being. Or a learner has either performance goals (to show how smart he or she is) or mastery goals (to learn). All these goal theories focus on dichotomous concepts that also correspond to another long-standing dichotomous distinction between intrinsic versus extrinsic motivation (Deci & Ryan, 2000). Recent theories further differentiated performance goals into another dichotomy: approach versus avoidance performance goals. The former predicts willingness and work by a learner to get good grades despite lack of true mastery goals. But avoidance performance goals are serious problems in a learner's achievement orientation because the person tries to avoid work (Elliot & Harackiewicz, 1996). Most recently, goal theorists introduced various social goals in service of learners' achievement (Urdan & Maehr, 1995).

As noted earlier, cultural analysis of learning has opened up a larger realm for goals in people's learning. Therefore, it is more sensible to view learning goals as a matter of content rather than structure. Accordingly, we may expect learning goals to vary widely across cultures and ethnic groups. For East

Asians, academic goals may be secondary to some other higher purposes that are part and parcel of their learning. For example, the idea of intelligence may not even be a strong concern for Asian children (e.g., Japanese educators downplay individual children's intelligence to foster children's social development; Tobin, Wu, & Davidson, 1989). Research also shows that intrinsic motivation may not matter as much to East Asian (Iyengar & Lepper, 1999) as well as other low-income ethnic minority children (as it does to middle-class European American children; Bempachetet al., 2009).

I (2003, 2006) used the term *learning purposes* to expand the scope of the traditional definition of achievement goals. The main difference is to consider the question of what benefits the learner sees learning brings to him/her, rather than relying on the *a priori* assumptions of intelligence and achievement being central attributes of people's learning goals. I found that Chinese learners expressed moral, cognitive, and future-projective goals as well as goals of love/enjoyment, improving socioeconomic status, lifelong learning, honoring parents, harmony, developing social relationships, catching up with others, and keeping up with societal development. In other words, Chinese adolescents expressed not a dichotomous set, but a multitude of purposes for learning. Moreover, except the cognitive purposes, the majority of their purposes did not fit squarely with the intelligence/ability-based achievement goals, as studied in the field. It is thus quite likely that traditional theories of achievement goals may have neglected many important purposes of learning in the world's people.

There is even less research on how children in different cultures develop learning purposes/goals. We are left with much research on school-aged children, particularly adolescents, but very little on the developmental origin and pathways from early ages. This is to say that there is a greater disconnect between cultural analysis and developmental psychology. To bridge this gap, I conducted two studies.

We interviewed middle-class European American and Chinese preschool children ages 3 to 6 years (four age groups) with two sets of story beginnings. The first set depicted a child who liked to go to school and another child who did not (Li, 2002b, 2004b). The second set of stories showed a child caught between doing homework and wanting to play with children outside (Li, 2009b). The first set elicited children's perceptions of learning purposes, whereas the second set probed children's understanding of the conflict between their need to learn and their desire to play.

We found that even 3-year-olds in both cultures could articulate learning purposes. Common with both groups was much talk about intellectual benefits of learning different things, becoming smart, and literacy (e.g., "you will know how to read"). They also shared social purposes such as making friends, being liked by others, and helping people with their knowledge. Cultural differences appeared in the degree of emphasis. Accordingly, European American children expressed more the ideas that attending school is an obligation (e.g., "you have to go to school"), making friends, importance of reading/writing, and enjoyment/fun (e.g., playing) at school. Chinese children stressed mastery of knowledge, learning–growing connection, social reward/respect learning that brings them, economic benefit, and help for others.

Children younger than age 4 years had a hard time responding to the study–play conflict story; hence, we collected data from 5- and 6-year-olds. Upon entry into formal schooling, every child must come to terms with the dilemma between the demand for them to learn and their desire to play. Our goal was to understand how the two groups of children viewed the conflict and how they went abut resolving it. Because of the moral orientation toward learning, the need to learn in Confucian heritage cultures is not something subject to children's questioning and negotiation. We term this awareness as *non-questionable* and *non-negotiable* sense of learning (Li et al., 2008). We expected Chinese children to display an early awareness of the moral message that regards learning as a personal obligation and commitment. Similarly, we anticipated that European American children would weigh schoolwork and play more or less equally. Hence, European American children would view resolution of this dilemma as lying in the process of balancing the two and through negotiation with the adult world that put the learning demand on children.

Analysis of their narratives showed that Chinese children insisted more on what we call "must finish work" first before they could play. In comparison, European American children expressed a view that work and play are equally important and that they could negotiate which one should be done first with adults. These findings support our hypothesis that children in these cultures develop different learning purposes. By ages 5 and 6 years, Chinese children already expressed a stronger orientation toward the non-questionable and non-negotiation purpose of learning, which may lead to their commitment to study. Comparatively, European American children held the view that study and play had equal weight in their lives. Which one to do first depends on the learner's personal interest and his/her negotiation with the social world.

Research indicates that older East Asian children continue to develop in the direction shown by preschoolers (e.g., Korean children, Kim & Park, 2008). I (2006) examined early, middle, and late Chinese adolescents and found no increase in the kinds of learning purposes as noted previously. It is thus likely that East Asian children's learning purposes may be cemented during elementary school. Although comparable developmental data are not clear on Western children, it would be reasonable to assume that Western children, too, may internalize their learning purposes by late elementary school. However, because Western learning emphasizes understanding of the world through exploration and inquiry, children may change quite a bit during adolescence, when they engage in intense self-exploration and struggle with identity development. Their new understanding of the world may alter their learning purposes more than those of East Asian adolescents.

Children's Perceptions of Achieving Peers

Modern formal learning occurs with age-graded peers. Peers, therefore, are a significant social context for child development (*see* Chen, 2011). Research on

Western children has shown that because of their limited capacity (therefore a structural element) to process self-other comparative information, preschoolers tend to overestimate their competence/achievement (Ruble, Eisenberg, & Higgins, 1994; Stipek & Mac Iver, 1989). For example, they tend to announce their achievement openly without regard for how such announcement may make their peers feel (e.g., "my picture is pretty, and yours is ugly!"). As they enter school, children become aware that such open self-praise at the expense of others may have negative social consequences. Brickman and Bulman (1977) documented the double-sided nature of high achievement in the West. Accordingly, high achievers felt proud and happy about themselves, but they also felt guilty about their peers' lesser achievement. Two plausible explanations have been offered to account for this ambivalence. First, as Ruble et al. (1994) and also Rothbaum and Yan (2011) quite convincingly show, extensive research indicates that Western people hold a fixed view of the self. As such, people feel positively about themselves when they achieve well. However, when not achieving well, the self is inevitably implicated as lacking something inherent, usually intelligence in academic learning. This realization can be devastating to the person's self-worth. The second useful account is that the West—particularly the United States—is an intensely competitive culture, but what makes matters more challenging to individuals is that competition is viewed as a zero-sum game by school children (e.g., Fülöp, 2004). This cultural overtone in conjunction with the fixed view of the self makes Western children more vulnerable to negativity that is rather a common result of the highly evaluative process of Western academic learning.

In contrast, the self in East Asian cultures is not viewed as fixed but instead as malleable to personal effort and social influence. If a person does well on a task, the self is not implicated wholly positive; rather the self is regarded as still changeable in any direction. Similarly, if the person fails, it does not implicate anything inherently negative in the person. Because lifelong learning is taken as a fundamental life-course for anyone by Confucian teaching, the self is expected and encouraged to improve regardless of how much one has achieved or failed. Of utmost importance is that the person is willing and actually makes an effort to self-improve (Li, 2002a; Rothbaum & Wang, 2011). Thus, it is not surprising that Japanese schoolchildren viewed the notion of competition as an opportunity to help each other so that both can improve in the end rather than a zero-sum game (Fülöp, 2004).

Research tracing the developmental origin of children's social perception in learning as a function of cultural differences is scarce. My colleague and I (Li & Wang, 2004) conducted two studies to address this research gap. We were particularly interested in seeing how young children perceived their achieving peers. We predicted that European American children would feel more negatively about high-achieving peers, but Chinese children would express liking and emulation toward such peers instead. In the first study, we presented European American and Chinese 4- to 6-year-olds a story where a protagonist child brought a drawing to the teacher, which the teacher openly praised as the best in class. In the second study, we told each child another story: a child in class was the only one who correctly wrote all the words that were given by the teacher. Children were asked to complete these stories. Analyses supported our prediction that European American children acknowledged the happy achiever and the proud teacher/parents, but they also expressed more rejection and isolation against the achiever. By contrast, Chinese children expressed more liking and emulation toward the high achiever (e.g., "I want to be like her"). Chinese children mentioned one negative reaction, which we termed *arrogance concern*: they were worried that the high achiever may be vulnerable to being too full of him-/herself to continue self-improving.

Recent research on how older elementary schoolchildren disclosed their achievement to peers provides further support for charting the diverse development in this area. Heymanet al. (2008) found that European American schoolchildren would only disclose their achievement to peers who had similar achievement levels, but they would not disclose their achievement to peers with higher or lower levels in fear that they would be regarded as bragging (if disclosed to lower achiever) or revealing one's low ability (if disclosed to higher achiever). However, Chinese schoolchildren would disclose their own achievement to all peers regardless of their levels. If disclosed to a higher achiever, the disclosing peer is regarded as eliciting help from the higher achiever, and help is on the way. If it is disclosed to a lower achiever, the disclosing peer is regarded as offering help, and the lower achiever would be grateful for such help. These findings cohere with the Japanese conception of competition and the general Confucian emphasis on the self as malleable and learning as a process of self-improvement. However, research on how the fixed self-view develops in the West is scarce. More developmental research is needed to map out the full developmental trajectories of this important area.

Capturing Socialization at Home and School as Displaying Culture at Work

Much less research is available on the direct influence of socialization of young children's BLs despite the extensive research on *what* children learn (but not their BLs) under various types of socialization (Hart & Risley, 1995). Although young children receive stimulation from many sources, the main source, as much developmental research confirms, is parental socialization as a main disseminator of culture (Chao, 1996; Fung, 1999; Wang, 2001). Because the actual values may differ widely across culture, this parental socialization process may be more profitably studied as a content process.

To document parental socialization, my colleague and I collected mother–child conversations about learning (Li et al., 2008) because talking to children is a powerful form of socialization (Wang, 2001). We asked 90 European American and 92 Taiwanese mothers of early elementary schoolchildren to identify two real incidents where the mother thought that her child showed a good versus a poor learning attitude/behavior. The mother was then asked to talk to her child about each incident. These conversations were audio-taped and transcribed for analysis. We used sequential analysis to trace which partner led in expressing what idea across at least four turns within each topic.

Below I discuss only the results pertaining to good learning attitude/ behavior because of space limit. European American mothers probed more than Taiwanese mothers about their children's affect, such as interest, curiosity, and pride. They also talked more about learning activities, mental processes, and learning strategies than Taiwanese mothers. However, Taiwanese mothers probed more for learning virtues. Sequential results showed that European American mothers began by mentioning their children's good learning incidents. They next engaged their children in savoring their positive affects as noted previously. This was followed by maternal probing for good learning activities that caused the good learning behavior. After this, mothers returned to more savoring of positive affect. Taiwanese mothers showed some similarities but also differences. Whereas the first two steps were similar, they probed learning virtues after savoring positive affect. Then they linked the experience to good learning activities and finally returned to more learning virtues. The two examples below illustrate the typical mother–child conversation from each culture:

European American mother (hereafter M): Honey, I heard that the principal praised you for something you did last week.

Child (hereafter C): Oh, yeah! Every time she came to my class, she saw me work. . . . Then she praised me on the load speaker. . . . Everyone heard it.

M: How did that make you feel?

C: Okay.

M: Just Okay?

C: I guess I was happy.

M: How else did it make you feel?

C: Excited.

M: Hmm, hmm, . . .

C: I was proud of myself.

M: There you go! What work were you doing when she came to your class?

C: We were writing. . . .

M: I am proud of you, too.

Taiwanese mother (hereafter M): Jiajia, I heard that you were number 1 in swimming.

Taiwanese child (hereafter C): No. I was only number 2!

M: Number 2 is just as good. I bet that made you feel good.

C: Hmm. . .

M: Hey, I remember that you were afraid of the water in the beginning. How did you overcome your fear?

C: I asked my coach to teach me how to hold breath. I practiced a lot.

M: Yes, that is a way to go . . . you need to practice a lot, persist through. So if I bring a kid who doesn't know how to swim, could you explain to him how to hold breath and how to practice?

C: Yes, I can.

M: Remember, practice and persistence through difficulties are the real key.

These real-time socialization data support our hypotheses that cultural models of learning underlie what parents do to socialize their children—a developmental process. However, such research trying to bridge cultural insight with developmental psychology is generally lacking. It is important to document how parental socialization continues and how parents adjust their socialization strategies as a function of their developing children. Moreover, the process of how school socializes children in this process is largely unknown. But school's role is powerful. The aforementioned research on cultural understanding of competition is an example of the type of research that could shed importance light on school's role in shaping children's BLs.

Conclusion

In this chapter, I have presented research on cultural diversity in BLs exists. I have also pointed out the specific gaps between cultural psychology and related developmental research and have shown examples of efforts that tried to bridge the gaps. Whenever appropriate, I discussed the remaining large disconnects that have yet to be bridged.

To conclude this chapter, I highlight some general but relevant points about the need to bridge these two sides of research. As Jensen's (2011) introduction states, the pulling forces by these two distinct research traditions may be deepseated. We are faced with the inevitable dilemma: should we embrace either a one-size-fits-all, or are we better off developing a psychology for each culture or, for that matter, for each ethnic group or even a subgroup within an ethnic group? My response to these questions is it depends. Studying more general aspects of BLs can shed light on human capacity that is needed for children to construct BLs in any culture. As discussed previously, ToM may indeed be important before we could expect children to develop both general and culture-specific BLs further.

Today's world is also becoming more streamlined with regard to education. Compulsory education looks more similar across cultures because they model predominantly after the Western style of formal education. Given this increasing reality, certain uniformity of learning and resultant BLs within the formal system is expected. Both the learning outcome and the process are quite subject to standardized measures of achievement. To the extent that parents and society desire these standardized outcomes, general theories of learning that promote such outcomes may be useful to diverse cultures as well as individuals.

Is there a distinct learning model for each culture? My response is that it depends on whether the conceptions and behaviors in learning, socialization, and affect can be empirically observed as distinct. If, for example, Koreans, Japanese, and Chinese are found to have sufficiently different BLs that are linked to their differential learning outcomes, then it is more sensible to study these BLs as separate systems. However, if they are not very different, which the existing research seems to suggest, then it is more advantageous to study them together. The same argument can be made about any cultural groups. If there are common BLs, which research also seems to confirm (e.g., intellectual benefits from learning), then these general trends also need to be understood.

The fact that different learning models exist against the backdrop of the increasingly more uniform formal education begs the inevitable issue as to whether some models are better than others, or these should be assumed to be equally good? If we choose some or, more extremely, only one over the others, are we not disregarding cultural diversity and, worse yet, dismissing the others? I offer a twofold response. On the one hand, to the extent that parents, learners themselves, and their own societies desire a particular outcome of learning— say, science learning—then whatever learning model seems to lead more readily to these desired ends may be preferred by the very people involved in teaching, learning, and socializing. However, for learning other subjects— particularly culturally unique knowledge/skills—a uniform way of learning may not be helpful. People are likely to resume their traditional learning processes and styles. On the other hand, I do not see that only one model will be chosen by all peoples for any single subject, even science. Many Asian students prefer to memorize things first before questioning. They prefer much practice for mastery before truly inquiring. But many also learn science very well. If people have access to different models (e.g., today's immigrants), they may choose the ideas and practices that suit their needs. There is no reason to believe that people will not adopt different elements from different models. Understanding and making more learning models available to all learners may help them adapt in a given developmental context.

However, cultural learning models are not free-standing models like commodities on the market, but they are deeply tied to people's cultural and ethnic identity and therefore to their deep emotions regarding their very sense of self and existence. I frequently hear my Asian American students say "We are Asians; we are supposed to get all As" (as urged by their parents). Perhaps such expressions contain a grain of sarcasm, but the serious reference to their identity of their acknowledged need to self-perfect is also clear. Therefore, those who attach their identity to a given learning model are unlikely to jettison the model. They are more likely to embrace their own model and socialize their own children accordingly, despite their bilingual and bicultural challenges. Individual people are the ones to decide what to accept, what to negotiate with, and what to ultimately reject.

In today's fast changing and globalized world, there is a greater need to study cultural learning models and related development. More and more children are raised in more than one culture. Fewer and fewer children are truly isolated from the rest of the worlds. These global trends require that we endeavor to understand learning models from many more cultures and the processes by which children develop their own BLs. In turn, parents, schools, communities, and cultures themselves can be better informed for their decisions and practices.

References

Azuma, H., & Kashiwagi, K. (1987). Descriptors for an intelligent person: A Japanese study. *Japanese Psychological Research, 29*: 17–26.

Bartsch, K, & Wellman, H. M. (1995). *Children talk about the mind.* New York: Oxford University Press.

Bartsch, K., Horvath, K., & Estes, D. (2003). Young children's talk about learning events. *Cognitive Development, 18*: 177–193.

Bempechat, J., Li, J., Wenk, K. A., & Holloway, S. (2009). Learning beliefs of low-income students: A qualitative study of adolescent meaning making. Manuscript under review.

Brickman, P., & Bulman, R. J. (1977). Pleasure and pain in social comparison. In J. M. Suls & R. L. Miller (Eds.), *Social comparison processes: Theoretical and empirical perspectives* (pp. 149–186). Washington, DC: Hemishpere.

Bruner, J. S. (1986). Value presupposition of developmental theory. In L. Cirillo & S. Wapner (Eds.), *Value presuppositions in theories of human development* (pp. 19–28). Hillsdale, NJ: Erlbaum.

Chan, C., & Rao, N. (Eds.). (2009). *Revisiting the Chinese learner: Psychological and pedagogical perspectives.* Comparative Education Research Centre (CERC), University of Hong Kong and Springer Press.

Chao, R. K. (1996). Chinese and European American mothers' views about the role of parenting in children's school success. *Journal of Cross-Cultural Psychology, 27*: 403–423.

Chen, X. (2011). Culture, peer relationships, and human development. In L. A. Jensen (Ed.), *Bridging cultural and developmental psychology: New syntheses in theory, research and policy* (pp. 92–112). New York: Oxford University Press.

Cohen, D., & Gunz, A. (2002). As seen by the other . . .: Perspectives on the self in the memories and emotional perceptions of Easterners and Westerners. *Psychological Science, 13*: 55–59.

Cury, F., Elliot, A. J., Da Fonseca, D., & Moller, A. C. (2006). The social-cognitive model of achievement motivation and the 2×2 achievement goal framework. *Journal of Personality and Social Psychology, 90*(4): 666–679.

D'Andrade, R. G. (1995). *The development of cognitive anthropology.* New York: Cambridge University Press.

Damon, W. (2003). *Noble purpose: The joy of living a meaningful life.* Philadelphia, PA: Templeton Foundation Press.

Dasen, P. R. (1984). The cross-cultural study of intelligence: Piaget and the Baoulé. *International Journal of Psychology, 19*: 407–434.

Deci, E. L., & Ryan, R. M. (2000). The "what" and "why" of goal pursuits: Human needs and the self-determination of behavior. *Psychological Inquiry, 11*(4): 227–268.

Dweck, C. S. (1999). *Self-theories.* Philadelphia, PA: Psychology Press.

Elliot, A. J., & Harackiewicz, J. M. (1996). Approach and avoidance achievement goals and intrinsic motivation: A mediational analysis. *Journal of Personality and Social Psychology, 70*(3): 461–475.

Flanagan, C., Martínez, M. L., & Cumsille P. (2011). Civil societies as cultural and developmental contexts for civic identity formation. In L. A. Jensen (Ed.), *Bridging developmental approaches to psychology: New syntheses in theory, research and policy* (pp. 113–137). New York: Oxford University Press.

Flavell, J. H., Green, F. L., & Flavell, E. R. (1995). *Young children's knowledge about thinking.* Monographs of the Society for Research in Child Development, 60, *(1, Series No. 243).*

Fülöp, M. (2004). Competition as a culturally constructed concept. In: C. Baillie; E. Dunn, & Y. Zheng. (Eds.) *Travelling facts. The social construction, distribution, and accumulation of knowledge* (pp. 124–148). Frankfurt/New York: Campus Verlag.

Fung, H. (1999). Becoming a moral child: The socialization of shame among young Chinese children. *Ethos, 27:* 180–209.

Gallimore, R., & Goldenberg, C. (2001). Analyzing cultural models and settings to connect minority achievement and school improvement research. *Educational Psychologist, 36*(1): 45–65.

Goodnow, J. J. (2011). Merging cultural and psychological accounts of family contexts. In L. A. Jensen (Ed.), *Bridging cultural and developmental psychology: New syntheses in theory, research and policy* (pp. 73–91). New York: Oxford University Press.

Harkness, S., & Super, C. M. (Eds.). (1996). *Parents' cultural belief systems: Their origins, expressions, and consequences.* New York: Guilford.

Hart, B., & Risley, T. R. (1995). *Meaningful differences in the everyday experience of young American children.* Baltimore, MD: Brookes.

Hau, K. T., & Salili, F. (1991). Structure and semantic differential placement of specific causes: Academic causal attributions by Chinese students in Hong Kong. *International Journal of Psychology, 26:* 175–193.

Heine, S. J., Kitayama, S., & Lehman, D. R. (2001). Divergent consequences of success and failure in Japan and North America: An investigation of self-improving motivations and malleable selves. *Journal of Personality and Social Psychology, 81:* 599–615.

Heine, S. J., Takemoto, T, Moskalenko, S., Lasaleta, J., & Henrich, J. (2008). Mirrors in the head: Cultural variation in objective self-awareness. *Personality and Social Psychology Bulletin,* 34(7): 879–887.

Hess, R. D., & Azuma, M. (1991). Cultural support for schooling: Contrasts between Japan and the United States. *Educational Researcher,* 20(9): 2–8.

Heyman, G. D., Fu, G.-Y., & Lee, K. (2008). Reasoning about the disclosure of success and failure to friends among children in the United States and China. *Developmental Psychology,* 44(4): 908–918.

Hidi, S., & Renninger, K. A. (2006). The four-phase model of interest development. *Educational Psychologist,* 41(2): 111–127.

Hufton, N., & Elloitt, J. (2000). Motivation to learn: The pedagogical nexus in the Russian school: Some implications for transnational research and policy borrowing. *Educational Studies,* 26: 115–122.

Iyengar, S. S., & Lepper, M. R. (1999). Rethinking the value of choice: A cultural perspective on intrinsic motivation. *Journal of Personality and Social Psychology,* 76: 349–366.

Jensen, L. A. (2011). The cultural-developmental theory of moral psychology: A new synthesis. In L. A. Jensen (Ed.), *Bridging developmental approaches to psychology: New syntheses in theory, research, and policy* (pp. 3–25). New York: Oxford University Press.

Kim, H. S. (2002). We talk, therefore we think? A Cultural analysis of the effect of talking on thinking. *Journal of Personality and Social Psychology,* 83: 828–842.

Kim, U., & Park, Y. S. (2008). Cognitive, relational and social basis of academic
achievement in Confucian cultures: Psychological, indigenous and cultural perspectives. In R. Sorrentino and S. Yamaguchi (Eds.), *Handbook of motivation and
cognition across cultures* (pp. 491–515). New York: Elsevier.

Kühnen, U., van Egmond, M., Haber, F., Kuschel, S., Özelsel, A. & Rossi, A. (2009). Mind
and virtue: The meaning of learning across cultures. In J. Berninghausen & G. Gunderson,
Kammler, U. Kühnen & R. Schönhagen (Eds.), *Lost in TransNation: Towards an intercultural dimension in higher education* (pp. 27–40). Kellner Verlag, Bremen.

Leichtman, M. (2011). A global window on memory development. In L. A. Jensen (Ed.),
*Bridging cultural and developmental psychology: New syntheses in theory, research and
policy* (pp. 49–70). New York: Oxford University Press.

Lewis, C. C. (1995). *Educating hearts and minds: Reflections on Japanese preschool
and elementary education.* New York: Cambridge University Press.

Li, J. (2001). Chinese conceptualization of learning. *Ethos,* 29: 111–137.

Li, J. (2002a). A cultural model of learning: Chinese "heart and mind for wanting to
learn." *Journal of Cross-Cultural Psychology,* 33(3): 248–269.

Li, J. (2002b). Models of learning in different cultures. In J. Bempechat & J. Elliott
(Eds.), *Achievement motivation in culture and context: Understanding children's
learning experiences, New Directions in Child and Adolescent Development*
(pp. 45–63). San Francisco, CA: Jossey-Bass.

Li, J. (2003). U.S. and Chinese cultural beliefs about learning. *Journal of Educational
Psychology,* 95(2): 258–267.

Li, J. (2004a). Learning as a task and a virtue: U.S. and Chinese preschoolers explain
learning. *Developmental Psychology,* 40(4): 595–605.

Li, J. (2004b). "I learn and I grow big:" Chinese preschoolers' purposes for learning.
International Journal of Behavioral Development, 28(2): 116–128.

Li, J. (2006). Self in learning: Chinese adolescents' goals and sense of agency. *Child
Development,* 77(2): 482–501.

Li, J. (2009a). To speak or not to speak: European American keenness versus Chinese
reluctance. Manuscript under preparation.

Li, J. (2009b). Negotiable or non-negotiable: U.S. and Chinese kindergartners' views
about the conflict between study and play. Manuscript under preparation.

Li, J., & Wang, Q. (2004). Perceptions of achievement and achieving peers in U.S. and
Chinese kindergartners. *Social Development,* 13(3): 413–436.

Li, J., & Sobel, D. M., Corriveau, K. (2005). *Children's developing conceptions of
learning.* Poster presented at the Biannual Meetings of Society for Research in Child
Development, Atlanta, GA.

Li, J., Holloway, S. D., Bempechat, J., & Loh, E. (2008). Building and using a social
network: Nurture for low-income Chinese American adolescents' learning. In H.
Yoshikawa & N. Way (Eds.), *Beyond families and schools: How broader social con-
texts shape the adjustment of children and youth in immigrant families* (pp. 7–25).
New Directions in Child and Adolescent Development Series. R. W. Larson &
L. A. Jensen (Series Eds.). San Francisco, CA: Jossey-Bass.

Li, J., Fung, H., Liang, C.-H., Resch, J., & Luo, L. (2008, July). Guiding for self-discovery
or self-betterment: European American and Taiwanese mothers talking to their children
about learning. In A. Bernardo (Chair), *Achievement motivation and achievement attribution among Asian students: Insights from qualitative data.* Invited paper symposium
by the International Congress of Psychology, Berlin, Germany.

Marton, F., Dall'Alba, G., & Beaty, E. (1993). Conceptions of learning. *International Journal of Educational Research,* 19: 277–300.

Nsamenang, A. B. (2011). The culturalization of developmental trajectories: A perspective on African childhoods and adolescences. In L. A. Jensen (Ed.), *Bridging cultural and developmental psychology: New syntheses in theory, research and policy* (pp. 235–254). New York: Oxford University Press.

Paine, L. W. (1990). The teacher as virtuoso: A Chinese model for teaching. *The Teachers College Record,* 92(1): 49–81.

Perner, J., Leekam, S. R., & Wimmer, H. (1987). Three-year olds difficulty with false belief: The case for a conceptual deficit. *British Journal of Developmental Psychology,* 5(2): 125–137.

Pratt, D. D., Kelly, M., & Wong, K. M. (1999). Chinese conceptions of "effective teaching" in Hong Kong: Towards culturally sensitive evaluation of teaching. *International Journal of Lifelong Learning,* 18: 241–258.

Quinn, N., & Holland, D. (1987). Introduction. In D. Holland & N. Quinn (Eds.), *Cultural models in language and thought* (pp. 3–40). New York: Cambridge University Press.

Rakoczy, H., Warneken, F., Tomasello, M. (2008). The sources of normativity: Young children's awareness of the normative structure of games. *Developmental Psychology,* 44(3): 875–881.

Rosemont, H. Jr. (1992). Rights-bearing individuals and role-bearing persons. In Bockover, M. I. (Ed.), *Rules, rituals, and responsibility: Essays dedicated to Herbert Fingarette* (pp. 71–101). La Sale, IL: Open Court.

Rothbaum, F., & Wang, Y. Z. (2011). Cultural and developmental pathways to acceptance of self and acceptance of the world. In L. A. Jensen (Ed.), *Bridging cultural and developmental psychology: New syntheses in theory, research and policy* (pp. 187–211). New York: Oxford University Press.

Ruble, D. N., Eisenberg, R., Higgins, E. T. (1994). Developmental changes in achievement evaluations: Motivational implications of self-other differences. *Child Development,* 65: 1095–1110.

Russell, B. (1945). *A history of Western philosophy.* New York: Simon & Schuster.

Sacks, J., & Chan, C. (2003). Dual scaling analysis of Chinese students' conception of learning. *Educational Psychology,* 23(2): 181–193.

Serpell, R. (1993). *The significance of schooling: Life journeys in an African society.* New York: Cambridge University Press.

Shweder, R. A. (1991). *Thinking through cultures.* Cambridge, MA: Harvard University Press.

Shweder, R. A., Much, N. C., Mahapatra, M., & Park, L. (1997). The "big three" of morality (autonomy, community, divinity), and the "big three" explanations of suffering. In A. Brandt, & P. Rozin (Eds.), *Morality and Health.* New York: Routledge.

Sobel, D., Li, J., & Corriveau, K. (2007). "It danced around in my head and I learned it:" What children know about learning. *Journal of Cognition and Development,* 8(3): 1–25.

Sternberg, R. J. (1985). Implicit theories of intelligence, creativity, and wisdom. *Journal of Personality and Social Psychology,* 49: 607–627.

Stevenson, H. W., & Stigler, J. W. (1992). *The learning gap.* New York: Simon & Schuster.

Stipek, D., & Mac Iver, D. (1989). Developmental change in children's assessment of intellectual competence. *Child Development,* 60: 521–538.

Strauss, C. (1992). Models of motives. In R. G. D'Andrade & C. Strauss (eds.), *Human motives and cultural models* (pp. 1–20). New York: Cambridge University Press.

Strauss, S. (2005). Teaching as a natural cognitive ability: Implications for classroom practice and teacher education. In D. B. Pillemer & Sheldon, W., *Developmental psychology and social change: Research, history and policy* (pp. 368–388). New York: Cambridge University Press.

Tardif, T., & Wellman, H. M. (2000). Acquisition of mental state language in Mandarin- and Cantonese-speaking children. *Developmental Psychology*, 36: 25–43.

Tomasello, M. (1999). *The cultural origins of human cognition.* Cambridge, MA: Harvard University Press.

Tu, W. M. (1979). *Humanity and self-cultivation: Essays in Confucian thought.* Berkeley, CA: Asian Humanities Press.

Tweed, R. G., & Lehman, D. R. (2002). Learning considered within a cultural context: Confucian and Socratic approaches. *American Psychologist,* 57(2): 89–99.

Urdan, T. C., & Maehr, M. L. (1995). Beyond a two-goal theory of motivation and achievement: A case for social goals. *Review of Educational Research,* 65: 213–243.

Wang, Q. (2001). "Did you have fun?" American and Chinese mother-child conversations about shared emotional experiences. *Cognitive Development,* 16: 693–715.

Wellman, H. M, Fang, F.-X., Liu, D., Zhu, L.-Q., & Liu, G.-X. (2006). Scaling of theory-of-mind understandings in Chinese children. *Psychological Science,* 17(12): 1075–1081.

Wentzel, K. R., & Caldwell, K. (1997). Friendships, peer acceptance, and group membership: Relations to academic achievement in middle school. *Child Development,* 68: 1198–1209.

Wu, S.-P., & Lai, C.-Y. (1992). *Complete text of the four books and five classics in modern Chinese* [in Chinese]. Beijing, China: International Culture Press.

CHAPTER 3

A Global Window on Memory Development

MICHELLE D. LEICHTMAN

Memory development has a long and celebrated history in developmental psychology. For more than 100 years, the dramatic changes in memory that take place across the life-course have generated interest from researchers, theorists, and practitioners (e.g., Freud, 1905, 1953; Stern & Stern, 1919, 1989; Montessori, 1949, 1989). Such early and sustained interest seems easily justified. After all, as Montessori noted, "in order to gain something from life, we must retain traces of experiences undergone, and here memory comes to our aid." (Montessori, 1949, 1989, p. 13)

Despite the obvious potential for wide variation in the nature of human experience across the world, only recently have memory researchers begun to recognize the power and scope of cultural differences in memory. As in many other areas of developmental psychology, historically most studies of memory development have focused on White, middle-class American or European children and have attempted to plot developmental trends presumed, at least implicitly, to be universal (Graham, 1992; Ceci & Leichtman, 1992). Yet recent investigations have provided a new, global window on memory, forcing researchers to revisit assumptions about the nature and range of factors that influence how memory unfolds across the life-course. This state of the field makes memory development a perfect case study for reflection on broader questions of how development and culture should be integrated, in both theoretical and practical terms.

In the following chapter, I consider the relationship between culture and development from the vantage point of memory research. The chapter is organized around three broad questions that current literature has begun to address. First, *where should we look for cultural effects on memory?* To place this question in perspective, I first describe the shift in contemporary developmental research away from traditional acontextual studies of memory toward those that feature context and individual differences. Next, I describe five functionally distinct memory systems identified in the cognitive neuroscience literature (working, episodic, semantic, procedural, and perceptual representation memory systems). Borrowing conceptually from theories of intelligence that categorize tasks in terms of their reliance on acquired knowledge, I consider how likely performance in each area of memory is to be influenced by cultural variables. Second, *what is the empirical evidence for cultural effects on memory?* Here, I provide a selective review of recent research in cognitive and developmental psychology that illustrates the nature of cultural differences in memory. I discuss cultural differences in episodic memory, which have received the brunt of researchers' attention, as well as other forms of memory. Third, *by what mechanisms are cultural effects on memory transmitted?* Here, I review environmental factors that may affect memory across cultures, emphasizing its close relationship with other culture-dependent developmental processes. I follow with a section on research implications.

Where Should We Look for Cultural Effects on Memory?

Traditional Perspectives and Individual Differences

Researchers have long been concerned with describing human memory in functional terms that map onto performance at the behavioral level and, more recently, at the level of the brain (e.g., Eichenbaum, 2002; Eichenbaum & Fortin, 2005; Squire & Schacter, 2002). In a tradition dating back to Ebbinghaus' (1885) seminal experiments using nonsense syllables, work in both cognitive and developmental psychology has sought to describe a set of basic, universal processes that guide human memory across situations and across the world. For example, systems and processing approaches, two divergent approaches that have dominated contemporary research on adult memory, both reflect this goal (Deluca & Chiaravalloti, 2004). These approaches have generated a rich theoretical and empirical backdrop for understanding memory that is largely consistent with neuropsychological evidence and useful for cognitive and developmental psychologists alike (Deluca & Chiaravalloti, 2004; Eichenbaum, 2002; Schacter, Wagner, & Buckner, 2000).

Similarly to studies conducted earlier in the century, significant empirical work in the modern history of memory research has focused on elucidating universal memory structures and processes, giving limited attention to plausible individual and contextual differences in performance (e.g., Eichenbaum, 2002; Klatzky, 1980). Thus, the majority of memory studies in both the first and second half of the 20th century treated variables associated with participant gender, socio-economic status, and cultural background as noise to be eliminated by design or controlled in analyses. Other, less obvious individual differences with implications for memory, such as prior training or cognitive and personality characteristics, were not traditionally the focus of significant empirical study. Like the characteristics of individuals, characteristics of the settings in which memory tasks occur have taken a back seat, including inherent social demand characteristics and the meaning of the setting for participants (Ceci & Leichtman, 1992).

In developmental research on memory, this situation began to change dramatically about 25 years ago, assisted by several factors. Across the field of developmental psychology, concerns about ecological validity inspired researchers to scrutinize the contribution of context to a host of well-researched developmental processes, and memory development was no exception (Brofenbrenner, 1979; Neisser & Hyman, 1982, 2000). In the field of psychology as a whole, the newfound integration of social psychological questions and cognitive methods under the auspices of social cognition also directed attention to the potential influence of social psychological variables on basic cognitive processes, including memory (e.g., Sutin, 2008). At the same time, concerns about the memory performance of children in real-world contexts—most notably courtrooms—were generated by a confluence of legal and social factors in the United States (e.g., McGough, 1997; Ceci, Kulkofsky, Klemfuss, Sweeney, & Bruck, 2007). It became paramount for researchers to consider how laboratory studies applied when children experienced, witnessed, and recalled crimes. In educational settings as well, researchers sought to maximize memory performance for students with different developmental and cognitive profiles (e.g., Levine, 2002; Pressley, Cariglia-Bull, Deane, & Schneider, 1987; Skowronek, Leichtman, & Pillemer, 2008).

Outside of mainstream memory research, cultural theorists have long ascribed a central and enduring role to contextual influences on development (e.g., Vygotsky, 1978). However, as Rogoff and Chavajay (1995) have pointed out, prior to the 1980s the majority of empirical studies of memory across cultures focused on broad differences in ability between populations, often on "school-like" free recall tasks for unrelated pieces of information. Typically, target populations from developing countries in Africa and Central or South America exhibited relatively poor performance on these tasks in contrast to North Americans and Europeans (Rogoff & Chavajay, 1995; *see also* Nsamenang, 2011). However, as research in the area advanced, it became clear that other kinds of memory tasks, such as tests of spatial or prose memory, did not show the same cultural differences, nor did free recall tasks for lists of related items. The revelation that schooling was closely tied to performance on many of the original, academic-style recall tasks that had been used to assess memory prompted a more nuanced way of thinking about contextual factors that might underlie cultural differences (Rogoff & Mistry, 1985; Mistry, Rogoff, & Herman, 2001).

The theoretical shift toward closer consideration of context prompted studies of a broad spectrum of contextual influences on memory development (Ceci & Leichtman, 1992). Researchers explored how performance on analogous memory tasks changed with a small revision in the nature of the target items (e.g., Ceci, 2003), the familiarity of locations in which the tasks took place (e.g., Ceci & Bronfenbrenner, 1985), or the domain of to-be-remembered text (e.g., Schneider, Bjorklund, & Maier-Bruckner, 1996). As part of this consideration of context, attention also turned to individual differences between participants, with striking results. For example, a seminal series of studies demonstrated that expertise in the domain of a memory task could overturn well-established developmental effects, such as when children with chess expertise were asked to memorize meaningfully organized arrays on a chess board and outperformed naïve adults (Chi, 1978; Schneider, Gruper, Gold, & Opwis, 1993). Similarly, memory was explored in a variety of natural contexts. Researchers targeted everyday events alongside unusual or traumatic ones, exploring parameters associated with memory duration, perspective, and accuracy (Neisser & Hyman, 1982, 2000; Pillemer, 1998). In other domains, such as memory for procedures or spatial information, performance of the same population was contrasted on analogous tasks presented in abstract contexts versus familiar ones. For example, Ceci & Roazzi (1994) demonstrated that Brazilian street children could recall and work fluently with mathematical concepts necessary to their trade while showing impoverished performance on analogous tasks in abstract academic contexts. This work on memory paralleled, in spirit, anthropologically inspired studies in other domains of cognition such as mathematics and everyday reasoning, which revealed similarly striking context effects (Lave, 1988).

The upshot of this recent, diverse body of memory research is the revelation that small, even seemingly innocuous, differences in the context in which information is presented or retrieved, including those associated with the state of mind of the rememberer, can significantly affect memory performance. From this perspective, the potential for differences in memory across cultures looms large. Across cultures, the entire external, social, linguistic, and cognitive context in which memory is acquired and expressed by mature individuals has the potential to vary significantly. Moreover, differences in memory across cultures may be exaggerated by continual exposure to contextual differences across the life-course.

The Likely Influence of Culture on Five Kinds of Memory

Extensive behavioral and neuroscientific evidence suggests that rather than representing a unitary construct, "memory" consists of multiple, functionally disparate systems (Eustache & Desgranges, 2008; Tulving, 1985). Although discussion continues regarding the ideal way to describe the number and unique properties of these systems, several well-supported dissociations are apropos. Seeking to integrate diverse approaches to modeling memory, including the seminal theories of Baddley (2003) and Tulving (1985, 1993), Eustache and Desgranges (2008) have recently presented a summary of conceptual dissociations in memory that have been well-supported by clinical studies of individuals experiencing selective brain damage, along with other cognitive and neuropsychological work. They have identified five separate memory systems, described in more detail in the discussion that follows. These include: *(1)* working memory implicated in short-term tasks, *(2)* episodic memory for personally experienced events, *(3)* semantic memory for general factual information, *(4)* procedural memory for retention of skills or routines, and *(5)* the perceptual representation system (PRS) used in perceptual identification and priming tasks.

These five distinct systems offer a useful point of departure for characterizing the kinds of memory tasks that are likely to be sensitive to cultural effects. The distinction between working, or short-term, memory and long-term memory is relevant[1] (Atkinson & Shiffrin, 1968). Working memory is a limited-capacity system that holds information for a period of up to only several seconds and involves separable subcomponents (e.g., phonological loop, visuospatial sketchpad). In contrast, the four remaining systems involve long-term memory (Eustache & Desgranges, 2008). Modern literature on memory and culture has concentrated overwhelmingly on long-term rather than working memory processes, and the most striking documentation of cultural differences has been in the domain of episodic memory, particularly for autobiographical events.

Why should this be the case? First, a heightened interest in personal event memory has arisen among developmentalists in the last 20 years, and explorations of culture have been part of this broader research program (e.g., Leichtman & Wang, 2005; Pillemer, 1998; Schneider & Pressley, 1997). A more compelling point is that logically, the most obvious place to look for differences between cultures is on tasks that reflect those memory systems with the greatest sensitivity to the effects of experience. Episodic memory represents one such system. Although the concept of episodic memory has undergone refinement, by any definition it involves exposure to single, one-point-in-time events that are retained across time. Episodic memory is accompanied by autonoetic consciousness, or a conscious realization of one's experience, and is often recollected verbally (Tulving, 1993). Episodic memory tasks include those that tap autobiographical memories for major, meaningful life events, and everyday experiences. They also include tests of impersonal information acquired during a single exposure, on tasks such as the Wechsler Memory Scale, the California Verbal Learning Test, Baddley's Doors and People Task, and commonly used Remember/Know paradigms (Eustache & Desgranges, 2008; Tulving, 1985).

A relevant construct for predicting which memory tasks are likely to show the most dramatic cultural influences can be borrowed from the psychometric literature on human intelligence. Catell (1963, 1971) identified the central distinction between "fluid" and "crystallized" intelligence, two orthogonal factors in intellectual functioning. Fluid intelligence involves the ability to reason under novel conditions (e.g., recognize patterns, understand abstract relationships between concepts, draw inferences, and solve problems), independently of prior knowledge that has been accumulated across the course of experience (Catell, 1971; Swanson, 2008). In this sense, fluid intelligence reflects fundamental, biologically endowed abilities that are closely tied to basic central nervous system functioning and impervious to selective brain injuries (Cattell, 1963). In contrast, crystallized intelligence refers to the ability to use skills, knowledge, and experiences that are deeply embedded in the context of culture. Crystallized intelligence is implicated in academic achievement and relies on exposure to and retention of specific, task-relevant information (Catell, 1963, 1971; Swanson, 2008). In general, verbal and mathematical abilities load onto crystallized intelligence scores. As Catell originally noted, during childhood crystallized intelligence is "powered by time and interest within the culturally set framework of the school experience" (Catell, 1963, p. 9), and in adulthood it reflects the more advanced development of whichever skills receive the most extensive time and interest (Catell, 1963). Although crystallized intelligence involves much more than memory, it relies heavily on the ability to retain and access information from long-term storage.

Like tasks of intellectual functioning that involve other aspects of cognition, memory tasks can be classified according to their reliance on accumulated knowledge or experience, which can only be obtained in a cultural context. From this perspective, performance on episodic, semantic, and procedural memory tasks can be thought of as crystallized, in that performance relies on the ability to tap into a particular pool of acquired knowledge. Working memory tasks and those that tap the perceptual representation system can be conceptualized as more fluid in nature.

To elaborate, episodic tasks are explicit memory tasks that require individuals to consciously call past experience to mind (Tulving & Schacter, 1990). Such tasks map well onto the construct of crystallized ability because performance relies on conscious retrieval and use of particular information acquired over time. In addition, explicit memory tasks often have a verbal component in which individuals identify or describe past experience in words. For example, measures of personal event memory often verbally prompt participants to recall past experiences and then to communicate those experiences using verbal narratives. The verbal skills required for such tasks, along with the ability to remember and share relevant event features within a culturally embedded framework, are shaped by incremental experience.

Similarly, semantic memory, which refers to memory for factual information and other forms of general world knowledge, can be conceptualized as crystallized in that performance relies on specific acquired experience. A blatant example is vocabulary, which is part of the semantic knowledge base. Mastery of vocabulary depends on the languages to which a child is exposed and to specific features of the home environment, most notably the characteristics of parents' speech (e.g., Hoff-Ginsberg & Schatz, 1982). The widely used Wechsler Adult Intelligence Scale (WAIS) features vocabulary questions as part of a battery of verbal subtests designed to measure crystallized intelligence. Sample questions from this section include: "What does "desultory" mean?" and "What does "retain" mean?"[2] Prior exposure to these words or their linguistic roots would clearly boost performance on such a task.

Several other verbal subtests of the WAIS targeting crystallized intelligence also rely on semantic memory. The information subtest focuses on factual knowledge. In this section, participants answer factual information questions such as "Who wrote Tom Sawyer?" and "How many nickels make a dime?" The comprehension subtest assesses practical knowledge and understanding of social rules. Sample questions include "What is the advantage of keeping money in a bank?" and "What should you do if you see someone forget his book when he leaves a restaurant?" Finally, the similarities subtest assesses logical or abstract thinking. Participants are asked to reflect on similarities between two different entities—for example, "In what way are a lion and a tiger alike?" Although these diverse verbal subsections invoke a variety of other intellectual skills related to categorization, thinking, and reasoning, they all require retrieval from semantic memory. Thus, along with native ability, the degree to which individuals have been exposed to particular information in the domains of language, factual knowledge, and social experience determines proficiency. Although the WAIS and similar IQ tests are predicated on the notion that the majority of individuals taking them will have the necessary baseline level of exposure in these domains, it is easy to imagine that across diverse cultures, such exposure would be uneven. This point, which is relevant to the present discussion because it underscores potential cultural influences on semantic memory, has been raised in the context of worries about the culture fairness of intelligence tests (e.g., Catell, 1963; Fagan & Holland, 2007).

In contrast to semantic and episodic memory, procedural memory involves the retrieval of routines or habits that become highly automated across time, such as those that apply when playing a musical instrument, weaving on a loom, shooting a bow and arrow, or riding horseback. Procedural memory is considered to be a form of implicit memory, in that it can function largely without deliberate retrieval efforts or conscious awareness (Tulving & Schacter, 1990). For example, once a skill such as trotting on horseback has been mastered, activating procedural memory does not require verbalizing the subcomponents ("sponge the reigns with a light connection to the bit, vocalize the command "trot up," post up as the horse's front outside leg moves forward. . .") or even bringing them into conscious awareness. Nonetheless, procedural memories can be construed as crystallized in that they rely extensively on acquired experience. Theoretically, procedural memory performance is a function of culture, in that culture determines whether a person is likely to be exposed to and acquire any given set of to-be-remembered skills (Super & Harkness, 2002).

Although memory is fundamentally about how the brain processes experience, not all memory tasks reflect abilities that crystallize with experience. Classic working memory tasks such as forward verbal span (reflecting the phonological loop), forward visual span (reflecting the visuospatial sketchpad), and backward digit span (reflecting central executive function) are traditionally associated with fluid intelligence, a view that is supported by correlational and factor analytic studies (Engle, Tuholski, Laughlin, & Conway, 1999; Swanson, 2008). Speculatively, this means that relative to their episodic, semantic, and procedural counterparts, such tasks more closely reflect biologically endowed characteristics such as speed of processing, short-term storage capacity, and general central nervous system integrity that are relatively impervious to the effects of experience (Catell, 1971; 1980; Schnyer, Allen, & Forster, 1997). Accordingly, normative differences in performance on working memory tasks exist between populations of typically developing children and those with genetically rooted learning disabilities such as Attention Deficit Hyperactivity Disorder (Barkley, 2001; Skowronek, Leichtman, & Pillemer, 2008). Working memory tasks are commonly administered as part of neurocognitive or intelligence test batteries with the assumption that they are culture-free (Ostrosky-Solis & Oberg, 2006). Recent work directly comparing performance of populations in diverse countries (e.g., on digit span) indicates that this may not be entirely the case, since performance varies somewhat across the world. However, rather than overarching cultural differences, linguistic effects on speed of task completion and the opportunity for literacy appear to be responsible for country-to-country variation (Ostrosky-Solis & Lozano, 2006; Ostrosky-Solis & Oberg, 2006).

A final memory system, the PRS, involves the processing of abstract and specific perceptual information, including words and objects. The PRS is involved in many implicit tasks in which memory operates outside conscious awareness, including most priming tasks (Tulving & Schacter, 1990; Schnyer et al., 1997). For example, in word-priming tasks, seeing a particular word on a list (e.g., "calcium") increases that chances that people will access it later in response to a prompt (e.g., when asked to write a word starting with "CAL"), even when they have no awareness of having seen it before. Similarly, subtly reminding people of a gender stereotype has been shown to influence their stereotype-relevant behavior, even when the stereotype remains outside awareness. The PRS is a low-level, cortically based memory system which, like fluid processes in intelligence, operates as a function of stable, biologically endowed proclivities that have little to do with the conscious application of acquired knowledge. The basic operation of the PRS, like the operation of working memory, should be minimally affected by differences in culture and environment. Nonetheless, the specific information to which a particular individual is exposed will go a long way toward determining performance on tasks that rely on the PRS. For example, the implicit priming effects that emerge when racial or gender stereotypes are activated depend on previous immersion in a culture in which those stereotypes are prevalent (e.g., Shih, Pittinsky, & Ambady, 1999).

Logically, "crystallized" episodic tasks that are affected by many aspects of experience would seem the most likely memory tasks to show dramatic cultural variations. Indeed, a burgeoning literature over the past decade bears this out. The primary focus has been on memory for personally experienced past events, which has been shown to reflect cultural variations in social, cognitive, and linguistic domains. Considerably less research has been directed at assessing cultural differences on tasks that reflect other forms of memory, although, as already noted, these differences are likely to exist. After reviewing cultural differences in episodic memory, I return to this point below.

What is the Evidence for Cultural Effects on Memory?

Culture and Episodic Memory

Several strands of research on episodic memory across cultures are apparent in the contemporary landscape of memory development. Among the earliest and best-developed group of studies on this topic are those that have contrasted Asian and North American populations. Much of this work departs from the notion that individuals in Asian cultures (e.g., China, Korea, and India) tend to espouse an interdependent social orientation in which an emphasis is placed on interpersonal harmony, common goals, and shared social identities (Markus & Kitayama, 1991; Wang & Leichtman, 2000). In contrast, individuals in North American cultures tend to espouse an independent social orientation, emphasizing personal autonomy, self-expression, and unique personal characteristics (Markus & Kitayama, 1991). Such general statements about the social orientation of particular cultures are necessarily incomplete and occasionally misleading, as extensive variation in the nature of social orientation exists within as well as between cultures (Fiske, 2002; Leichtman & Wang, 2005; Oyserman, Kuhn, & Kemmelmeier, 2002). Nonetheless, these broad conceptualizations have been useful for thinking about potential diversity in the value and practice of autobiographical memory (e.g., Leichtman & Wang. 2005b; Leichtman, Wang, & Pillemer, 2003) along with other domains of social and cognitive development. (*See* Nsamenang, 2011; Li, 2011) In cultures where most individuals are independently oriented, remembering, evaluating, and communicating information about personally meaningful past experiences assists in the goal of defining one's unique and well-bounded self (Leichtman & Wang, 2005, 2005b; Pillemer, 1998). In contrast, in cultures in which individuals are more interdependently oriented, using memory in this way may not be as frequent, valued, or adaptive (Leichtman & Wang, 2005, 2005b; Leichtman, Wang, & Pillemer, 2003). Instead, culture-specific practices outside the arena of memory (e.g., fulfillment of social roles and duties, day-to-day proximate interactions) may serve similar goals.

Consistent with this prediction, researchers have discovered striking differences between cultures in a host of factors related to autobiographical memory, including the timing of earliest memories, the professed value placed on personal remembering, the characteristics of conversations about memory, and the structure and style of personal memory narratives (e.g., Leichtman, 2006; Wang, 2007). Research indicates that these differences appear early in childhood and extend into adulthood (e.g., Han, Leichtman, & Wang, 1998; Wang, 2007).

By way of illustration, studies targeting adults' earliest childhood memories have achieved intriguing results. In seminal work on this topic, Mullen (1994) conducted a questionnaire study with Asian, Asian American, and European American adults. When European Americans were contrasted with the other two groups combined, analyses indicated that European Americans' earliest reported memories were 6 months earlier. When contrasted with results from the group that included only native Korean-Americans, European American's memories were 16.7 months earlier. In addition, European American adults provided more detailed and self-focused reports.

Wang (2001) conducted a similar questionnaire study contrasting the childhood memory reports of urban college students in China and the United States. This work documented a 6-month difference in age of earliest memory in the same direction as Mullen's (1994) findings. American adults reported earliest memories from an average age of 3 years 3 months, whereas Chinese adults reported earliest memories from 3 years 9 months. In terms of content, Americans' memories were longer, more specific, and more emotionally expressive. In a laboratory study of participants from the United States, England, and China, Wang, Conway, and Hou (2007) further supported these differences in access to and age of earliest childhood memories. Participants attempted to recount as many memories as possible that had occurred before the age of 5 years within a 5-minute period. Chinese participants recalled fewer childhood memories than the two Western groups, and their earliest memories were 6 months later.

Moving away from East Asia, Leichtman, Bhogle, Sankaranarayanan, and Hobeika (2003) examined the memories of rural and urban Southern Indians and Americans. One hundred eleven participants took part in verbal memory interviews in their native language (i.e., Kannada or English). The goal was to compare memory reports in cultural groups for whom the entire context of childhood and adulthood varied dramatically in ways that might be related to the eventual retention of autobiographical memories (e.g., language, religion, social hierarchy, occupation). Thus, the two groups of Indian participants came from low socio-economic populations, whereas Americans came from middle- and upper-middle-class urban and suburban populations. Notably, the rural Indian participants were primarily goat herders living in villages, and approximately half did not know their exact date of birth. The interviewers prompted participants to provide memories of childhood along with memories of more recent events.

Consistent with expectations, across the course of an interview that probed for childhood memories in several different ways, significantly fewer rural Indian participants (43%) reported retaining any childhood memories at all in comparison with urban Indians (74%) and Americans (97%). The contrast among groups was even more striking when all reported memories were coded as referring to either specific, one-moment-in-time events ("I remember one day when the peppers were stolen from the field") or more general, ongoing childhood routines (e.g., "playing in the mud") in a coding scheme originally developed by Pillemer and colleagues (Pillemer, Goldsmith, Panter, & White, 1988). Only 14% of rural Indians reported one-point-in-time events, whereas slightly more urban Indians (22%) and many more Americans (52%) did so. The interviews did not require participants to date their memories, but approximately 50% of Americans did so, with estimates ranging between 3 and 12 years. A small number of participants (6) in the urban Indian sample dated their memories, with estimates ranging from 6 to 11 years, whereas no rural

Indians did so. In terms of the qualities of the narratives, Americans' narratives about specific past events were longer, more descriptive, and judged by independent raters to be richer and less skeletal than those of both Indian groups. The majority of Americans (90%) and the majority of urban Indians (71%) indicated that they talked about the past in daily life, and Americans often added that this was an important aspect of their routine (e.g., "What else would I talk about at dinner with my family?"). In contrast, only 12% of rural Indian participants indicated that they talked about the past in daily life, and their answers suggested that such talk was superfluous (e.g., "Why would I talk about the past? The past is just as the future.") Thus, these data supported the notion that access to and timing of early event memories, and the nature and meaning of these memories may vary widely across diverse populations.

Outside the Asian/North American context, Hayne and McDonald (2003) probed the memories of indigenous Maori and White, or Pakeha, New Zealanders' with written questionnaires. Their studies indicated that the timing of earliest memory varied across these diverse cultural groups co-existing in the same country. The earliest memories of the Maori, who come from a culture that emphasizes the importance of oral traditions, dated from a mean age of 33 months—10 months earlier than the memories of Pakeha participants. In a separate study of mothers from the same populations (Reese, Hayne, & MacDonald, 2008), researchers analyzed the content of narrative memories of their children's births. Consistent with the earlier timing of memories among Maori that had previously been established, these birth stories reflected cultural differences in memory content. Maori mothers provided more elaborate memory narratives and more references to relational time and internal states.

Sahin and Mebert (2008) focused on the memories of young adults in the United States and Turkey, a culture that has been characterized as generally collectivist but with many similarities to European and American cultures in terms of lifestyle and achievement orientation (Imamoglu, 1998). Using a written questionnaire, the researchers collected earliest memories of more than 400 American and Turkish young adults. Consistent with the pattern of findings from studies conducted in Korea, China, and India, Turkish participants dated their earliest memories at a mean age of just over 4 years—6 months later than those of Americans. When prompted to rate the importance of their personal memories on a scale of 1 to 10, American participants also rated their memories as significantly more important to them than did Turkish participants.

These findings of differences in the nature of memory among populations of adults have been shown to extend to children at the point in life when they are first learning to talk about past experiences. (e.g., Han, Leichtman, & Wang, 1998; Wang, 2007) In a groundbreaking study, Mullen and Yi (1995) recorded Canadian and Korean mothers in conversation with their preschool children across the course of a day. Korean mothers spoke much less often with their children about past events than did Canadian mothers, and their accounts were shorter, less elaborative, less laden with emotional terms, and more factually oriented. Similarly, Leichtman, et al. (2003) filmed 4-year-old rural Indian and American children during 3 hours of daily life. Although the activities children participated in were similar (working, playing), the amount of discussion they heard about the past was markedly different. American mothers used about 20 sentences per hour that referred to the past (4% of speech), whereas Indian mothers used only 2 sentences (1% of all speech). When American mothers referred to the past, they did so in more detailed, elaborate ways.

How might such differences in what children hear about past events correspond to their own talk about the personal past? In a study of Korean, Chinese, and American children, Han, Leichtman, and Wang (1998) addressed this question. Researchers interviewed 4- and 6-year-olds about a variety of past events (e.g., "Tell me everything that happened at bedtime last night."). American and Chinese children provided longer narratives than Koreans, measured in words and sentences. On other key variables, however, the two Asian samples were similar and significantly different from Americans. American children's memory narratives were more often focused on specific, one-point-in-time past events and were more descriptive and more self-focused and contained more references to judgments, predilections, and internal cognitive states.

Several studies of children's memories elicited in other contexts have documented a similar pattern of results. For example, Wang, Leichtman, & Davies (2000) and Wang (2007) focused on samples of Chinese and American mother–child dyads. In both studies, parents and children discussed memories together in their natural style. In each case, American mothers were more high-elaborative and child-focused, asking many open-ended questions and scaffolding children's memory reports, and mothers' interrogative styles corresponded to children's. (See Fivush, Haden, & Reese, 2006, for a review of elaboration in mother–child memory talk.) In both studies, American children provided more information about the personal past in response to mothers' questions, and Wang (2007) demonstrated that this effect endured over time.

Returning to adults, several recent cross-cultural studies on the distribution of memories across the life-course are noteworthy. One of the most robust effects in memory research is the reminiscence bump, or the tendency for personal event memories from age 10 to 30 years to be retrieved at disproportionately higher rates than one would expect from a normal retention function (Berntsen & Rubin, 2002). Conway, Wang, Hanyu, and Haque (2005) compared the retrieval curve for autobiographical memories prompted with cue words in samples from the United States, United Kingdom, Japan, Bangladesh, and China. Their research documented an almost identical pattern of distribution across these diverse cultures, all of which showed a marked reminiscence bump. Erdogan, Baran, Avlar, Tas, and Tekcan (2008) documented a similar reminiscence bump in Turkey, which they reported was comparable to data collected earlier in Denmark. These findings add an important perspective to the present discussion, because they indicate that some areas of memory performance that one might expect to vary across cultures appear strikingly universal. Researchers have suggested that a "life script" with elements common to individuals across many cultures (e.g., beginning school, marriage, birth of children) may guide memory retrieval for events across the life-course (Conway et al., 2005; Pillemer & Dickson, in press).

Culture and Non-Episodic Forms of Memory

As noted earlier, although a significant portion of modern research on memory across cultures has focused on episodic memory, several other forms of memory also have the potential to vary across cultures. In surveying work in the area, it seems possible that cultural variations in some kinds of memory tasks have not been studied for the simple reason that they are so obvious. For example, normative differences in the content of the semantic knowledge base are almost certain to exist among people who speak different languages, study different holy scriptures, partake in different oral traditions, hold different ethnotheories (e.g., Super & Harkness, 2001), and engage in different cultural practices. As a case in point, even individuals from relatively similar cultures such as Germany and the United States are likely to demonstrate significantly different semantic memory when asked questions targeting specific vocabulary (e.g., What is the meaning of "Geschwindigkeitsgrenze?" ". . . meatloaf?") or culture-specific information (e.g., "What was the name of the middle girl on the Brady Bunch?" or "What were the major contributions of Helmut Kohl's administration?"). Naturally, documenting knowledge differences of this kind has been relatively uninteresting to memory researchers because, rather than reflecting any underlying differences across populations, such differences are completely reliant on exposure to particular kinds of information in the environment. Nonetheless, from the vantage point of memory development, the knowledge base is a fundamental part of what develops, and it makes an important contribution to memory performance across the life-course (Brown, 1975). Thus, although obvious, sweeping cultural differences in the content of the knowledge base are important to acknowledge.

What about more fundamental differences in memory that are not linked to obvious cultural differences in exposure? A most intriguing set of findings has emerged from recent laboratory work in cognition, where studies have indicated that the distribution of attention tends to be different among individuals from independently oriented North American and interdependently oriented Asian cultures. A potential explanation for such differences is that in interdependently oriented Asian cultures, a premium is placed on attending to others as well as the self, and thus over time individuals develop cognitive styles in which attention is divided across the self and others or, more broadly, across a target and its context (e.g., Masuda & Nisbett, 2001). Thus, in a pair of studies of Japanese and American adults, Duffy and Kitayama (2007) investigated whether perception of the location of a simple object presented on a computer screen would be differentially biased across cultures by exposure to previous context information. Japanese participants were more likely than Americans to show a mnemonic context effect, using previously presented context information to guide their judgments about the location of a target on a computer screen. This work further supported the interpretation that cultural differences in the mnemonic context effect were a function of participants' beliefs. Across the sample as a whole, beliefs about heterogeneity were positively correlated to the application of context information to the judgment task.

From the perspective of memory development, these findings indicate that low-level, implicit cognitive processes that are part of the domain of the PRS may vary across cultures in ways that profoundly affect memory. Although these processes may have a critical impact, they may not be obvious to the naked eye of those interested in cultural differences in memory. Recent methodological advances in cognitive, social, and neuro-psychology that have helped reveal the implicit processes underlying much of memory performance promise to be useful in further excavating cultural differences in memory.

By What Mechanisms Does Culture Influence Memory?

Culture and the Socio-Cultural Contexts of Childhood

The review above illustrates the potential for cultural variations to emerge in a number of different kinds of memory. From a developmental perspective, cultural differences that appear in adulthood are likely to be shaped by the meaning of particular forms of remembering within a culture and by continual exposure across the life-course to situations in which specific forms of cognition and social behavior are adaptive.

Socio-cultural perspectives emphasize the emergence of autobiographical memory in the context of children's early social environments (e.g., Nelson, 2007). Research over the past decade has demonstrated that one of the most powerful tools in shaping personal event memory is the dialogue that children have with their caregivers on a regular basis (e.g., Fivush, Haden, & Reese, 2006; Leichtman, Pillemer, Wang, Koreishi, & Han, 2000). The style of memory talk to which a child is exposed, repeated over the course of days, weeks, and years, has a critical impact on how children themselves talk about the past and, perhaps more importantly, how they think about it (Leichtman & Wang, 2005; Han, Leichtman, & Wang, 1998). This finding has now been demonstrated empirically in numerous laboratory and naturalistic studies of children's memory (e.g., Fivush, Haden, & Reese, 2006; Leichtman, Wang, Koreishi, & Han, 1998; Pillemer, 1998).

As noted, researchers have discovered marked differences in the ways that parents in independently and interdependently oriented cultures talk with their children about the personal past. In independently oriented cultures, parents are likely to encourage elaborated, self-focused memory sharing that emphasizes the autonomy and unique qualities of the individual. In contrast, in interdependently oriented cultures, parents are less likely to talk about the personal past. When memory conversations occur in these cultures, they tend to take a less elaborative, more paradigmatic form that emphasizes factual information and didactic teaching (e.g., Mullen & Yi, 1995; Wang, 2007). These different memory styles are consistent with broad cultural differences in the nature of self-construal and other social factors, such as the degree of social hierarchy a society prescribes between parents and children. Along with these factors, the functions of memory talk vary across cultures in systematic ways (Leichtman & Wang, 2005; Wang & Ross, 2007). For example, in many independently oriented cultures such as the United States, detailed, elaborate discussions about the past are a critical part of social bonding and creating a social identity. Living in a social milieu in which examples of elaborated memory talk are both readily available and highly valued as a social tool increases the chances that children will attend to and engage in this kind of conversation. Thus, although children in all cultures are born with the capacity to process factual event details and can do so when given the chance on equivalent factual tasks (Han, Leichtman, & Wang, 1998), those who live in cultures where elaborated memory talk is prevalent will simply remember more about the socially valued elements of personal event memory (Leichtman, Wang, Koreishi, & Han, 1998).

This socio-cultural perspective has been more extensively articulated in the domain of autobiographical memory development than in other areas, such as the development of semantic or procedural memory (Leichtman & Wang, 2005b; Nelson, 2007). Autobiographical memory is more obviously and closely tied to thematic information about the self than other domains of memory, and in fact, measures of autobiographical memory have been shown to correlate with independent measures of self-construal in several cultures (e.g., Leichtman & Wang, 2005b; Sahin & Mebert, 2008) as well as associated conversational practices. However, in theory, other domains of memory performance can be equally affected by differences in the overarching value systems of diverse cultures and by the nature of the learning opportunities those cultures provide for their children (Rogoff & Chavajay, 1995). Cultures that value the study of factual information in particular domains (mathematics, gardening, religion) and those that provide opportunities for children to master particular kinds of procedural learning (weaving, skiing) shape the constellation of children's knowledge and also unwittingly shape likely performance on a variety of novel tasks. The strongest evidence for this comes from the studies of context conducted within single cultures that were described earlier in this paper (e.g., Ceci & Roazzi, 1994; Schneider et al., 1993). Both the knowledge base and implicit, procedural memories change how individuals approach novel, relevant information. Further, constant exposure to situations that call for attention and other kinds of cognitive resources to be allocated in particular ways can have far-reaching effects on cognition, as Duffy and Kitayama's (2007) work on mnemonic context has illustrated.

Elsewhere, colleagues and I have made that argument that socio-cultural factors at many levels of the environment have the potential to produce cultural differences in memory, sometimes in surprising ways (*see* Leichtman & Wang, 2005, for a review.) The cultural messages about memory that echo through children's environments in the form of the psychology of caregivers, the customs of childrearing, and the physical and social settings in which children live (Super & Harkness, 2002) are reflected in children's memory performance

(Leichtman & Wang, 2005b). In the coming years, researchers may uncover more specific cultural variations in memory that reflect these different messages and practices. From the broader perspective of history, it is interesting to note that factors associated with particular socio-historical contexts and government policies have occasionally also wielded an influence on the uses of memory by a population of individuals. An example of this is the government-directed autobiographical writing practices that surfaced during the Russian Revolution and had the widespread effect of bolstering particular forms of autobiographical memory in Russia (Hellbeck, 2001; Wang & Leichtman, 2005). Another example is the one-child policy in China. By creating a nontraditional social environment in Chinese families in which single children were the focus of concentrated attention, the policy had the effect of producing patterns of autobiographical memory more typical of children in United States and other Western cultures (Wang, Leichtman, & White, 1998).

Implications for Research and Theory

Future Directions

Contemporary research on cultural differences in memory has been largely concentrated on episodic memory for meaningful events. Although we have good evidence that the environment of childhood helps shape the form and content of such memory, important questions remain about the assortment of culture-specific variables that may affect its encoding and expression. Perhaps most complex and promising is the question of what potential functions episodic memory serves across developmental stages and cultures. A critical question that is beyond the scope of any single memory study is how these functions interact with and are supplanted by other social behaviors and cognitions in ways that are adaptive to the goals of each culture in which they appear.

Scrutiny of Eustache and Desgranges' (2008) five memory systems makes clear that cultural differences in tasks that tap non-episodic memory systems may also warrant attention. In particular, cultural differences in semantic and procedural memory and some aspects of the perceptual representation system may be interesting to explore, because performance on these tasks relies heavily on the particulars of experience. Cultural differences in both kinds of memory may be especially important in terms of their broader implications for cognitive and social functioning. Just as cultural differences in the division of attention (e.g., Mistry et al., 2001) have implications for many interactions in daily life, so do differences in the knowledge base associated with semantic memory and the routines associated with procedural memory. It is becoming clear that differences in quotidian experience across cultures have nuanced effects on memory that we are only beginning to understand. At the very least, analysis of cultural differences in terms of the five memory systems suggests that a systematic approach toward delineating where culture is likely to wield the biggest influence on memory is now possible and appropriate.

Structure versus Content in Memory Development

A critical assumption of virtually all current memory models is that the basic operations, or "hardware," of the memory system should be universal. For example, visual recognition memory does not operate on different principles for babies born into different social contexts, although they might learn to recognize different items more readily based on exposure. Semantic memory is fundamental to all children learning vocabulary words or accumulating factual information about the world, although these words or facts may be different for different children. The same is true for the myriad memory processes that function as part of the five memory systems described above. Although the basic principles, or structures, of memory are part of the human birthright and remain consistent across cultures, the content of memory has the potential to vary considerably. Based on culture-dependent differences in the material, social, and cognitive contexts that surround them, growing children retain different sets of remembered experiences, different stores of factual knowledge, and fluent, automatic recall of different kinds of procedures. Even within the same culture, where much of the surrounding context is socially shared, both systematic and idiosyncratic individual differences in what children value, attend to, and process has the potential to create extensive individual differences in the content of memory.

A compelling message that has emerged from contemporary memory research is that the contents of memory drive how the system operates. The parameters of performance on any given memory task are always determined in part by the content that is being processed, in connection with the previously acquired contents of memory. Thus, fundamental differences in what particular cultures call on people to regularly remember for optimal functioning (e.g., the physical gesture of a superior other vs. the nuances of one's own emotional state) determine how memory processes from the lowest to highest levels of analysis are likely to play out (i.e., where attention will be allocated, what information will be transferred to long-term memory, how quickly and under what circumstances visual recognition will occur, how long particular information will remain accessible). In this sense, although it is strictly true that the structure of memory is universal and the content is not, it is not true that the content is less important to memory performance. Content is not a "surface" variable that is superfluous to understanding more elemental processes—it is critical in its own right. After all, content drives not only how memory functions at the level of research descriptions, it drives the phenomenology of human experience.

Conclusions

The contemporary shift in the field of memory development toward focusing on context and individual differences has provided a fertile background for thinking about memory across cultures. Research on memory and culture conducted over the past 10 years has been particularly productive in terms of documenting cultural differences in episodic memory processes, especially in the realm of autobiographical memory. However, other critical memory systems identified in cognitive and neuropsychological work also have the potential to vary across cultures as a function of social values and practices. As noted, semantic memory, procedural memory, and even implicit processes associated with the perceptual representation system can be construed as crystallized abilities. Thus, these forms of memory may also find unique expression across dramatically varying cultural environments. Although these aspects of memory are less obviously linked with the measures of self-construal and mother–child conversation that have been heavily implicated in cultural variations in autobiographical memory, they also function as a reflection of the cognitive and social contexts of the people who use them.

This is an exciting time to study culture and memory development. Researchers have just begun to understand the power and scope of cultural effects, and a fuller picture of how the distinct systems that make up human memory unfold and interact in cultural context seems to be just around the corner.

Notes

1. Although conceptually distinct and empirically separable in some contexts, "short-term" and "working" memory are significantly overlapping constructs that will be used synonymously in this discussion (Swanson, 2008).

2. All reported sample test items have been taken from The Psychological Corporation (1997).

References

Atkinson, R. C., & Shiffrin, R. M. (1968). Human Memory: A proposed system and its control processes. In K. W. Spence and J. T. Spence (Eds.) *The Psychology of Learning and Motivation: Advances in Research and Theory, volume 29* (pp. 89–195). New York: Academic Press.

Baddley, A. D. (2003). Working memory: Looking back and looking forward. *Nature Reviews Neuroscience, 4,* 829–839.

Barkley, R. A. (2001). Executive functions and self regulation: An evolutionary neuropsychological perspective. *Neuropsychology Review, 11,* 1–29.

Berntsen, D., & Rubin, D. C. (2002). Emotionally charged autobiographical memories across the life-span: The recall of happy, sad, traumatic and involuntary memories. *Psychology & Aging, 17,* 636–652.

Bronfenbrenner, U. (1979). *The ecology of human development.* Cambridge, MA: Harvard University Press.

Brown, A. (1975). The development of memory: Knowing, knowing about knowing and knowing how to know. In H. Reese (Ed.) *Advances in child development and behavior (vol. 10).* New York: Academic Press.

Catell, R. B. (1963). Theory of fluid and crystallized intelligence: A critical experiment. *Journal of Educational Psychology, 54* (1), 1–22.

Catell, R. B. (1971). *Abilities: Their structure, growth and action.* Boston, MA: Houghton Mifflin.

Ceci, S. J. (2003). Cast in six ponds and you'll reel in something: Looking back on 25 years of research. *American Psychologist, 58* (11), 864–873.

Ceci, S. J. & Bronfenbrenner, U. (1985). Don't forget to take the cupcakes out of the oven: Prospective memory, time monitoring and context. *Child Development, 56,* 152–164.

Ceci, S. J.; Kulkofsky, S., Klemfuss, J. Z., Sweeney, C. D. & Bruck, M. (2007). Unwarranted assumptions about children's testimonial accuracy. *Annual Review of Clinical Psychology, 3,* 311–328.

Ceci, S. J. & Leichtman, M. D. (1992). Memory, cognition and learning: Developmental and ecological considerations. In S. J. Segalowitz & I. Rapin, (Eds.) *Handbook of neuropsychology, Vol. 7* (pp. 223–239). New York: Elsevier Science.

Ceci, S. J. & Roazzi, A. (1994). The effects of context on cognition: Postcards from Brazil. In Sternberg, R. J. &Wagner, R. K. (Eds.), *Mind in context: Interactionist perspective on human intelligence* (pp. 74–101). New York: Cambridge University Press.

Chi, M. T. H. (1978). Knowledge structures and memory development. In R. S. Siegler (Ed.), *Children's thinking: What develops?* Hillsdale, NJ: Lawrence Erlbaum Associates.

Conway, M. A., Wang, Q., Hanyu, K. & Haque, S. (2005). A cross-cultural investigation of autobiographical memory: On the universality and cultural variation of the reminiscence bump. *Journal of Cross-Cultural Psychology, 36,* 739–749.

Deluca, J. & Chiaravalloti, N. D. (2004). Memory and learning in adults. *Comprehensive handbook of psychological assessment: Intellectual and Neuropsychological Assessment, Volume 1* (Chapter 14, pp. 217–241). New York: Wiley.

Duffy, S. & Kitayama, S. (2007). Mnemonic context effect in two cultures: Attention to memory representations? *Cognitive Science: A Multidisciplinary Journal, 31*(6), 1009–1020.

Ebbinghaus, H. (1885). *Memory: A contribution to experimental psychology.* (H. A. Ruger & C. E. Bussenius, Translators). New York: Dover.

Eichenbaum, H. (2002*). The cognitive neuroscience of memory.* New York: Oxford University Press.

Eichenbaum, H. & Fortin, N. J. (2005). Bridging the gap between brain and behavior. *Journal of the Experimental Analysis of Behavior, 84*(3), 619–629.

Engle, R. W., Tuholski, S. W., Laughlin, J. E. & Conway, A. R. (1999). Working memory, short-term memory, and general fluid intelligence: A latent-variable approach. *Journal of Experimental Psychology: General, 128,* 309–331.

Erdogan, A., Baran, B., Avlar, B., Tas, A. C. & Tekcan, A. I. (2008). The persistence of positive events in life scripts. *Applied Cognitive Psychology, 22,* 95–111.

Eustache, F. & Desgranges, B. (2008). MNESIS: Towards the integration of current multisystem models of memory. *Neuropsychology Review, 18,* 53–69.

Fagan, J. F. & Holland, C. R. (2007). Racial equality in intelligence: Predictions from a theory of intelligence as processing. *Intelligence, 35*(4), 319–334.

Fiske, A. P. (2002). Using individualism and collectivism to compare cultures-A critique of the validity and measurement of the constructs: Comment on Oyserman et al. (2002). *Psychological Bulletin, 128*(1), 78–88.

Fivush, R., Haden, C. A., & Reese, E. (2006). Elaborating on elaborations: Role of maternal reminiscing style in cognitive and socioemotional development. *Child Development, 77,* 1568–1588.

Freud, S. (1920/1953). *A general introduction to psychoanalysis.* New York: Simon & Schuster.

Graham, S. (1992). Most of the subjects were white and middle class: Trends in published research on African Americans in selected APA journals, 1970–1989. *American Psychologist, 47* (5), 629–639.

Han, J. J., Leichtman, M. D. & Wang, Q. (1998). Autobiographical memory in Korean, Chinese and American children. *Developmental Psychology, 34*(4), 701–713.

Hayne, H. & MacDonald, S. (2003). The socialization of autobiographical memory in children and adults: The roles of culture and gender. In R. Fivush and C. A. Haden (Eds.), *Autobiographical memory and the construction of the narrative self: Developmental and cultural perspectives* (pp. 99–120). Mahwah, NJ: Lawrence Erlbaum Associates.

Hoff- Ginsberg, E. & Schatz, M. (1982). Linguistic input and the child's acquisition of language. *Psychological Bulletin, 92*(1), 3–26.

Imamoglu, E. O. (2003). Individuation and relatedness: Not opposing but distinct and complementary. *Genetic, Social, and General Society Monographs, 129*(4), 367–402.

Klatzky, R. L. (1980). *Human memory structures and processes.* San Francisco, CA: WH Freeman and Company.

Lave, J. (1988). *Cognition in practice: Mind, mathematics and culture in everyday life.* Cambridge, UK: Cambridge University Press.

Leichtman, M. D. (2006). Cultural and maturational influences on long-term event memory. In L. Balter & C. Tamis-Lemonda (Eds.), *Child psychology: A handbook of contemporary issues (2nd ed.).* New York: Psychology Press.

Leichtman, M. D., Bhogle, S., Sankaranarayanan, A. & Hobeika, D. (2003). *Autobiographical memory and children's narrative environments in Southern India and the Northern United States.* Unpublished manuscript.

Leichtman, M. D., Pillemer, D. B., Wang, Q., Koreishi, A., & Han, J. J. (2000). When baby Maisy came to school: Mothers' interview styles and preschoolers' event memories. *Cognitive Development, 15,* 1–16.

Leichtman, M. D. & Wang, Q. (2005). A socio-historical perspective on autobiographical memory development. In D. B. Pillemer & S. H. White (Eds.), *Developmental Psychology and Social Change: Research, History and Policy.* New York: Cambridge University Press.

Leichtman, M. D. & Wang, Q. (2005b). Autobiographical memory in the developmental niche: A cross-cultural perspective. In B. D. Homer and C. S. Tamis-LeMonda (Eds.), *The Development of Social Cognition and Communication* (pp. 337–360). Mahwah, NJ: Lawrence Erlbaum Associates.

Leichtman, M. D., Wang, Q. & Pillemer, D. B. (2003). Cultural variations in interdependence and autobiographical memory: Lessons from Korea, China, India and the United States. In R. Fivush & C. Haden (Eds.), *Autobiographical memory and the construction of the narrative self.* Mahwah, NJ: Lawrence Erlbaum Associates.

Levine, M. (2002). *A mind at a time.* New York: Simon & Schuster.

Li, J. (2011). Cultural frames of children's learning beliefs. In L. A. Jensen (Ed.), *Bridging cultural and developmental psychology: New syntheses in theory, research and policy* (pp. 26–48). New York: Oxford University Press.

Markus, H. R. & Kitayama, S. (1991). Culture and the self: Implications for cognition, emotion and motivation. *Psychological Review, 98*(2), 224–253.

Masuda, T. & Nisbett, R. E. (2001). Attending holistically versus analytically: Comparing the context sensitivity of Japanese and Americans. *Journal of Personality and Social Psychology, 81,* 922–934.

Mistry, J., Rogoff, B. & Herman, H. (2001). What is the meaning of meaningful purpose in children's remembering? Istomina revisited. *Mind, Culture and Activity, 8*(1), 28–41.

McGough, L. (1997). Stretching the blanket: Legal reforms affecting the child witness. *Learning and Individual Differences, 9*(4), 317–340.

Montessori, M. (1948/1989). *To educate the human potential.* Oxford, UK: Clio Press.

Mullen, M. K. (1994). Earliest recollections of childhood: A demographic analysis. *Cognition, 52,* 55–79.

Mullen, M. K. & Yi, S. (1995). The cultural context of talk about the past: Implications for the development of autobiographical memory. *Cognitive Development, 10,* 407–419.

Neisser, U. & Hyman, I. (Eds.) (1982/2000). *Remembering in natural contexts.* New York: Worth Publishers.

Nelson, K. (2007). *Young minds in social worlds.* Cambridge, MA: Harvard University Press.

Nsamenang, A. B. (2011). The culturalization of developmental trajectories: A perspective on African childhoods and adolescences. In L. A. Jensen (Ed.), *Bridging cultural and developmental psychology: New syntheses in theory, research and policy* (pp. 235–254). New York: Oxford University Press.

Ostrosky-Solis, F. & Lozano, A. (2006). Digit span: Effect of education and culture. *International Journal of Psychology, 41*(5), 333–341.

Ostrosky-Solis, F., & Oberg, G. (2006). Neuropsychological functions across the world-common and different features: From digit span to moral judgment. *International Journal of Psychology, 41*(5), 321–323.

Oyserman, D., Kuhn, H. M. & Kemmelmeier, M. (2002). Rethinking individualism and collectivism: Evaluation of theoretical assumptions and meta-analyses. *Psychological Bulletin, 128,* 3–72.

Pillemer, D. B. (1998). *Momentous Events, Vivid Memories.* Cambridge: Harvard University Press.

Pillemer, D. B. & Dickson, R. (in press). Adults' memories of their own childhoods. To appear in A. Ben-Arieh, J. Cashmore, G. Goodman, J. Kampmann, & G. B. Melton (Eds.), *The Handbook of Child Research,* Sage Publications.

Pillemer, D. B., Goldsmith, L. R., Panter, A. T., & White, S. H. (1988). Very long-term memories of the first year in college. *Journal of Experimental Psychology: Learning, Memory and Cognition, 14*(4), 709–715.

Pressley, M., Cariglia-Bull, T., Deane, S., & Schneider, W. (1987). Short-term memory, verbal competence, and age as predictors of imagery instructional effectiveness. *Journal of Experimental Child Psychology, 43*(2), 194–211.

Reese, E. Hayne, H., & MacDonald, S. (2008). Looking back to the future: Maori and Pakeha mother-child birth stories. *Child Development, 79*(1), 114–125.

Rogoff, B., & Chavajay, P. (1995). What's become of research on the cultural basis of cognitive development. *American Psychologist, 50*(10), 859–877.

Rogoff, B., & Mistry, J. (1985). Memory development on cultural context. In M. Pressley, & C. Brainerd (Eds.), *Cognitive learning and memory in children* (pp. 117–142). New York: Springer-Verlag.

Sahin, B., & Mebert, C. (2008, March). *Autobiographical memory and cultural self-construals in US and Turkish adolescents.* Poster presented at the Society for Research in Adolescence. Chicago, IL.

Schacter, D. L. (1990). Perceptual representation systems and implicit memory: Towards a resolution of the multiple memory systems debate. *Annals of the New York Academy of Sciences, 608,* 543–571.

Schacter, D. L., Wagner, A. D., & Buckner, R. L. (2000). Memory systems of 1999. In E. Tulving, & F. Craik (Eds.), *The Oxford handbook of memory* (pp. 627–643). New York: Oxford University Press.

Schneider, W., Bjorklund, D., & Maier-Bruckner, W. (1996). The effects of expertise and IQ on chidren's memory: When knowledge is, and when it is not enough. *International Journal of Behavioral Development, 19*(4), 773–796.

Schneider, W., Gruper, H., Gold, A., & Opwis, K. (1993). Chess expertise and memory for chess positions in children and adults. *Journal of Experimental Child Psychology, 56*(3), 328–349.

Schneider, W., & Pressley, M. (1997). *Memory development between two and twenty.* Mahwah, NJ: Erlbaum.

Schnyer, D. M., Allen, J. J. B., & Forster, K. I. (1997). Event-related brain potential examination of implicit processes: Masked and unmasked repetition priming. *Neuropsychology, 11*(2), 243–260.

Shih, M., Pittinsky, T. L., & Ambady, N. (1999). Stereotype susceptibility: Identity salience and shifts in quantitative performance. *Psychological Science, 10,* 81–84.

Skowronek, J. S.; Leichtman, M. D., & Pillemer, D. B. (2008). Long-term episodic memory in children with attention-deficit/hyperactivity disorders. *Learning Disabilities Research & Practice, 23*(1), 25–35.

Squire, L. R., & Schacter, D. L. (2002). *Neuropsychology of memory* (3rd ed.). New York: Guilford Press.

Stern, W., & Stern, C. (1909/1999). *Recollection, testimony and lying in early childhood.* (J. T. Lamiell, Translator). Washington, D.C.: American Psychological Association.

Super, C. M., & Harkness, S. (2002). Culture structures the environment for development. *Human Development, 45*(4), 270–274.

Sutin, A. R. (2008). Autobiographical memory as a dynamic process: Autobiographical memory mediates basic tendencies and characteristic adaptations. *Journal of Research on Personality, 42*(4), 1060–1066.

Swanson, H. L. (2008). Working memory and intelligence in children: What develops? *Journal of Educational Psychology, 100*(3), 581–602.

The Psychological Corporation (1997). *Simulated items similar to those on the Wechsler Adult Intelligence Scale: Third Edition.*

Tulving, E. (1985). How many memory systems are there? *American Psychologist, 4,* 385–398.

Tulving, E. (1985b). Memory and consciousness. *Canadian Psychologist, 26,* 1–12.

Tulving, E. (1993). What is episodic memory? *Current Directions in Psychological Science, 2,* 67–70.

Tulving, E., & Schacter, D. L. (1990). Priming and human memory systems. *Science, 247,* 301–306.

Vygotsky, L. S. (1978). *Mind in Society.* Cambridge, MA: Harvard University Press.

Wang, Q. (2001). Cultural effects on adults' earliest childhood recollections and self-description: Implications for the relation between memory and the self. *Journal of Personality and Social Psychology, 81*(2), 220–233.

Wang, Q. (2007). "Remember when you got the big, big bulldozer?" Mother-child reminiscing across time and across cultures. *Social Cognition, 25*(4), 455–471.

Wang, Q., Conway, M., & Hou, Y. (2007). Infantile amnesia: A cross-cultural investigation. In M. Sun (Ed), *New research in cognitive sciences* (pp. 95–104). New York: Nova Scientific Publishers.

Wang, Q., & Leichtman, M. D. (2000). Same beginnings, different stories: A comparison of American and Chinese children's narratives. *Child Development, 71*(5), 1329–1346.

Wang, Q., Leichtman, M. D., & Davies, K. (2000). Sharing memories and telling stories: American and Chinese mothers and their 3-year-olds. *Memory, 8*(3), 159–177.

Wang, Q., Leichtman, M. D., & White, S. H. (1998). Childhood memory and self-description: The impact of growing up an only child. *Cognition, 69*(1), 73–103.

Wang, Q., & Ross, M. (2007). Culture and memory. In S. Kitayama & D. Cohen (Eds.). *Handbook of cultural psychology* (pp. 645–667). New York: Guilford.

PART II

DEVELOPMENTAL CONTEXTS AND CULTURE

CHAPTER 4

Merging Cultural and Psychological Accounts of Family Contexts

JACQUELINE J. GOODNOW

This chapter, like others in this volume, addresses how we can effectively build and use bridges between cultural and psychological analyses of development. Doing so would yield a fresh look at the nature of development and the settings in which it occurs, lead to new questions, and suggest ways to link research on development to social policies.

How do we achieve those benefits? All bridge-building, I suggest, needs to start with a search for matching points, avoiding "bridges to nowhere." One general matching point is the shared view that development occurs within contexts (contexts such as family, school, community, or society). Cultural analyses of development often phrase this interest in terms of bringing together "micro" and "macro" contexts. Psychologists increasingly use phrases such as developmental contextualism (Lerner et al., 2006) or environment-fit (Eccles, Wigfield, & Byrnes, 2003).

That matching point offers a way of seeing how cultural and psychological analyses overlap, differ, and can be brought together. The benefits lie in an increased understanding of the forms that development takes and its course. The benefits lie also in an increased understanding of social policies. Policies often reflect, for example, different approaches to what represents an ideal context and to the ways in which families can make effective transitions from one context to another. In effect, we can use the one set of concepts to consider both an understanding of development and an understanding of policies and to link the two.

The challenge now is one of going beyond that broad match, locating some specific points for useful bridging. As a step toward meeting that challenge,

I shall focus on ways of specifying and differentiating among contexts. Three approaches are singled out. These emphasize the nature of activities and participation, the presence of shared or unshared ways of thinking and acting, and the nature of interconnections among people and across contexts. The first three sections of the chapter describe these approaches and what they add to developmental theory and research. The final section takes up the additions they suggest to our understanding of social policies.

The bias throughout is toward outlining first how each of the three approaches to development in context appears in psychological theory and research and then asking what expansions are added by cultural analyses using the same kind of approach. That way of proceeding falls short of a two-way ideal, one of which asks also how psychological analyses can add to cultural analyses. It may also seem to imply that psychology has the greater need for enrichment. That is certainly not my view. It reflects instead my sense that the majority of readers of this volume will start, as I did, from a psychological base. The expansions offered by cultural analyses will then be the more novel and useful. The emphasis will also be on family contexts. The expansions suggested could apply to other contexts as well. Family contexts, however, have long been a strong concern in psychological analyses of development, making them a prime focus.

Relevant to all parts of the chapter are two general points. The first of these has to do with the terms we use to refer to the areas for bridging. Calling one side *psychological* and one side *cultural* may seem to imply some complete separation across disciplines. There are, however, psychologists with a strong interest in the perspectives of anthropologists, and anthropologists with a strong interest in the perspectives of psychologists. In a similar fashion, the terms *cultural psychology* and *developmental psychology* may seem to imply that only psychologists have an interest in the nature of development. This, again, is certainly not the case. There is a common interest in development, seen from different perspectives.

The other general point has to do with dichotomies that are often part of a cultural/psychological divide. Lene Jensen, in her role as editor, has asked for comment in each chapter regarding two of these.

One is the line often drawn between "universalist" perspectives (we need to discover the aspects of development that are common to all cultures, disregarding the variations) and "separatist" perspectives (we need to discover and respect the uniqueness of each culture; a search only for "universals" misses the important phenomena). The best way forward may be a combination of both perspectives. A combination of both, for example, is contained in descriptions of cultural variations as a case of "one mind, many mentalities" (Shweder et al., 2006) or a case of there always being social contracts among various social groups, with the nature of these contracts varying from one cultural group to another (*see* Flanagan, Martínez, & Cumsille, 2011). We now need to be alert to other possible ways of avoiding the universal/separatist divide.

The other dichotomy singled out is a distinction between *structure* and *content*, with structure seen as the emergence of capacities that are largely independent of experience, and content referring to what is thought about or used as a base for the development of skills. Sharp divides of this kind have been eroded by an increasing recognition of the significance of specific areas of expertise, experience, and practice. Still present, however, are some related sharp divides: a divide, for example, between *cognitive* development and *social* development and a divide between *the family* and *the outside world*. Cultural analyses of development in context, I suggest, are of particular value when it comes to bringing out the drawbacks to these several dichotomies or sharp divisions and to suggesting alternatives.

Describing Contexts: The Nature of Activities and Practices

For the description of any context and its effects, both psychological and cultural analyses find it useful to ask what usually happens there. The activities carried out at home, in school, or in the company of peers, for example, often differ from one setting to another. Questions about who takes part in various activities and how they do so are also common. Rogoff's work on cultural variations in the nature of children's participation in various activities (especially adult activities) is a prime example (e.g., Rogoff, 2003).

A particular interest in activities carried out in a routine, everyday fashion, and in their consequences is also common. These may take a variety of forms, ranging from ways of talking or story-telling to ways of sharing food or space, styles of dress, and divisions by age or gender (Goodnow, Miller, & Kessel, 1995, provide a review).

Within psychological analyses of families, these repeated actions have been described as routines or rituals (e.g., Fiese et al.,1993; Serpell et al., 2002). Within cultural analyses, the term used to describe activities is more often *practices*. Practices are not only routine—they are also usually accompanied by a sense of their being "natural" or "proper" (Miller & Goodnow, 1995). They are also ways of acting that are followed by all or most of the people in one's own social group (they are in this sense "cultural practices"): a feature that cements still further the sense that these are natural or proper ways of behaving.

The sense that these activities are natural or proper is one proposed consequence from routines or practices. We take for granted, for example, local practices that have to do with what children eat, wear, are named, and where and when they should sleep (e.g., Shweder, Jensen, & Goldstein, 1995).

Highlighted as a consequence is also the maintenance of a sense of structure or order in one's life: a sense that can be lost or undermined when the usual routines or practices are disrupted. A sudden drop in income, for example, can disrupt a family's established use of childcare, with flow-on effects to patterns of parenting and of occupation. It has been proposed that analyses of family life need to take a closer look at disruptions such as these, noting especially the skills and strategies that parents use to sustain a sense of structure and order or to recover from its loss (Love et al., 2005).

A further proposed consequence has to do with our understanding of the world around us. Meanings and views of the world are seen as flowing out of practices. It is from accepted practices, it has been argued, that we form any concept such as "childhood" or "maturity" or any general image of "parenting." The developmental flow is then not from concepts or beliefs to the actions people take. Instead, the flow is from what people do to the views they hold and to their feelings about what should occur.

From practices also flow our evaluative judgments. We use the extent to which the usual practices have been followed, for example, as a basis for assessing our own performance as parents or for judging others as good, careless, neglectful, strict, conservative, authoritarian, abusive, enmeshed, or dysfunctional: adjectives we often apply both in everyday life and in decisions about protective care or custody. We have a great deal to learn about links between particular activities and particular judgments. What specifically is a parent doing or not doing, for example, that gives rise to a judgment such as "neglectful"? Exploring these links would be one further way of expanding psychological analyses of family life and development.

Describing Contexts: The Presence of Shared and Unshared Views

Psychological analyses of family life often consider the extent to which parents, siblings, or generations hold the same views or follow similar paths. Cultural analyses first add an expansion in terms of people. Now the concern is with the extent to which members of a cultural group agree. In terms such as *cultural models* or *cultural practices*, for example, "cultural" refers to widely shared views or activities.

That broader way of looking at shared views may seem remote from psychological analyses of families. Psychologists, however, might well take further a few studies that link the two. Romney and colleagues, for example, have explored the impact of whether individuals occupy a central or a marginal position in relation to the larger group. People who hold views similar to those of most others in their group turn out to be more often regarded as reliable (Romney, Weller, & Batchelder, 1986). Their children are also more likely to be regarded by teachers as doing well, as having "fewer problems" (Deal, Halvorson, & Wampler, 1989).

A second useful expansion asks about the areas in which shared or unshared views are regarded as acceptable or even promoted. For example, "modern" societies have been described as approving of individuality or "creativity" when it comes to activities such as the internal decoration of a home. Some touches of personal taste are almost required. In contrast, whether one engages in some form of work or not is far less likely to be seen as a matter of personal taste (Berger, 1977).

That emphasis on tolerated or disapproved areas of difference flows usefully over to analyses of families. Differences between parents and children, for example, are often regarded only as occasions of conflict. However, there are also areas of acceptable disagreement—areas of difference that parents easily tolerate or even approve of (Goodnow, 1994) or that children find tolerable rather than embarrassing when they consider parents' actions or ideas.

The third and last line of expansion is the broadest. It has to do with what is regarded as the normative state for any society. From cultural analyses comes the argument that the normative state is not a single set of beliefs or values: a single view, for example, of "good parenting." It consists instead of differences and attempts to have one's own view or one's own practice prevail. In effect, "multiplicity and contest" is the normative state (e.g., Strauss, 1992). Interest turns then to the ways in which people seek to have their view become the prevailing or hegemonic view, ideally coming to be regarded by people as their own, even when it is to their disadvantage (Gramsci, 1971). One of those ways consists of making some concepts or some versions of events so "natural" that second thoughts and dissent rarely occur. How "naturalization" occurs in large social groups has been especially well-explored in analyses of news events (e.g., Fishman, 1980; Hallin, 1986). We might now give more attention to the ways in which families do so. For example, how do families promote a view of some beliefs and practices as so "natural" that questions never arise or are felt to be a sign of error, lack of faith, or problematic development? The presence of routines seems likely to be only one such step.

"Contest" and "naturalization" may also not cover all that may happen. Some cultural analyses have added the occurrence of "negotiations" between those who take one view and those who hold another (e.g., Gledhill, 1988). Negotiation now becomes a normative state, prompting questions about the forms it takes and its outcomes.

These several analyses of society have particular promise as a way of expanding psychological analyses of families. Some use of them has, in fact, already begun. Research on negotiations provides a good example. Families, at least in European countries, have been described as changing from "command households" to "negotiation households" (Du-Bois Raymond, 2001). That shift is seen as reflecting an increasing emphasis on individuals—in a world of increasing options and uncertain futures—as expected to carve out their own ways forward, to work at creating their own future (e.g., Beck, 1997).

A second example of use is a view of identity as negotiated, with negotiations occurring both within and outside the family. When Moroccan girls live in the Netherlands, for instance, they negotiate with parents on issues such as appropriate dress and appropriate friendships. At the same time, both they and their parents need to reach some common ground with the non-Islamic society that surrounds them. The outcome is the emergence of something new. The views of self that these girls develop are in no sense an abandonment of Islamic identity. They are, however, a changed version of what it means to be "Islamic" (Ketner, Butelaar, & Bosma, 2004).

The third and last example has to do with shifts in the way differences among members of the family are regarded. Ram and Ross (2008) have noted that studies of sibling conflicts have concentrated on negative forms of disagreement and negative consequences. There has been less exploration of constructive negotiations and when they occur. They are more likely to occur when a conflict of interests is not accompanied by aggression or a sense of past wrongs, there has been some interval of time since the original disagreement, and there is some prior understanding of what each party is seeking. Needed now, Ram and Ross (2008) propose, is further research on the forms that constructive negotiation takes and the circumstances that make it likely to be attempted and to succeed.

A similar kind of shift marks an emerging approach to differences between parents and children. Kuczynski and Parkin (2007) note that psychological analyses of disagreement between parents and children typically concentrate on whether the outcome is one of compliance. They propose that closer attention to the nature of negotiations is needed—attention to who takes the lead (noted is Bandura's interest in occasions when people recruit others rather than negotiating in solo fashion), who is negotiated with (e. g., children negotiate more with mothers than with fathers), the meanings parents give to challenges or differences in viewpoint, and the areas in which negotiation is seen as tolerable or not. Children may learn, for example, that haggling over the price of goods in the market is an expected sign of competence. Haggling over parents' instructions or one's pocket money may be a different matter. We might now ask how children acquire negotiation competence, how families mark some views or practices as more or less negotiable, how children respond to areas marked by parents as non-negotiable, and the ways in which negotiations within families are like or unlike those that occur in other settings.

In short, the analysis of shared and unshared views is again an approach to specifying the nature of contexts that brings out points where psychologically and culturallyoriented analyses are beginning to merge or may usefully be brought together. As was the case for the first approach—the exploration of activities and practices—that interweaving can highlight gaps in our understanding and suggest new directions in our studies of the nature of development and of family life.

Describing Contexts: Interconnections Among People and Across Contexts

Both psychological and cultural analyses of contexts often start from the view that one way to describe settings is in terms of links between the people present: their relationships and obligations to one another and their interactions on special occasions or in the course of everyday life.

Both also often start from the view that settings or contexts are linked to one another. On the cultural side, that view is often expressed in terms of the need to bring together "micro" and "macro" settings. On the psychological side, for example, the family may be seen as at the center of a "nested" set, surrounded by contexts (e.g., school, neighborhood, community) that become increasingly "distal" from direct interpersonal contact and the family center (Bronfenbrenner, 1979, 1995).

Where then are the differences between psychological and cultural analyses? Where are the expansions or points of convergence that we could profitably take further? With those questions again in mind, I turn first to proposals about interconnections among people and then to proposals related to interconnections across contexts.

Interconnections Among People

Analyses of interconnections often ask about the ways in which people form alliances or support one another, the extent to which they understand one another and feel some sensitivity or empathy toward one another, and the extent to which they feel some sense of belonging to the group and of safety or security within it.

In psychological research, those issues are most often considered in terms of family dyads (e.g., a parent and child) or triads (e.g., two parents and a child, a parent and two children, two siblings). Cultural perspectives widen that frame. Now, for example, questions about alliances appear more often in the form of asking about support networks. The sense of belonging and identity also receives a larger frame, nicely expressed in the title of John Whiting's (1941) classic analysis of development: "*Becoming a Kwoma*" (*see also* Nsamenang, 2011). There may still be studies that focus on small groups—for example, studies of family divisions of labor. These studies often start, however, from interest in what happens within the wider group. Interest in children's gendered divisions of household work, for example, often starts from a perception of household divisions as a way of encouraging children to accept as natural the gendered division of work outside the family.

Cultural analyses also underline the value of placing individual development in a frame of connections to others. Concepts of identity provide one example. To concerns with the development of a sense of personal identity, we are now beginning to add a stronger interest in *social identity* (a term borrowed from social psychology, e.g., Tajfel, 1982) and in the ways children acquire a sense of "us" or as well as a sense of "me" (e.g., Ruble, Alvarez et al., 2004; Fuligni, 2005, *see also* Phinney & Baldelomar, 2011).

Views of cognitive development supply another example. Cultural analyses have helped psychological studies to move toward increased attention to joint participation in various tasks and to questions about "distributed cognition." In a team, for example, no one person needs to develop all skills; it is essential, however, to divide up the work and to know who has what skill. Attention to the significance of others as audiences has also increased. We seldom act or learn without some sense of what others do or how others will perceive what we do. In the terms of Hatano and Wertsch (2001), we need to think not only about the physical presence of others but also about the audiences we expect to encounter and the audiences we value: in their terms, "culture in mind."

Despite those moves toward convergence, there are still provocative differences between cultural and psychological analyses of how people are related to one another. In psychological analyses of relationships, the emphasis often falls on the uniqueness of relationships. Each, for example, is "unique because it is constructed from the mutual contributions of each partner over time" (Laible & Thompson, 2007, p. 181). Cultural analyses more often place their emphasis on types of relationships—on categories that can be used to cut across situations or across cultures.

Proposals from an anthropologist (Fiske, 1991,1992) provide a rewarding example. Fiske starts from an interest in distinctions among relationships that are constant across cultural groups but can also be used to distinguish among them. His four types are communal (we are primarily concerned with each other's well-being), hierarchical ranking, equality matching (e.g. in return for what you have given me, I give something equal in value but not identical in kind), and market pricing (e.g., my return for your labor is its money market value). Each type, he proposes, carries with it particular obligations and particular expectations about how people *should* behave. Fiske sees the four types as constant across cultural groups. What varies is the placement of particular relationships into the four categories. In some social groups, for example, the relationship with a grandfather may be communal in type. In another, the expected placement is hierarchical ranking. What varies may also be the mixing of types that can occur. In one culture, for example, a parent–child relationship may be primarily communal, with touches of hierarchical ranking. In another, that mix may be reversed.

Fiske's model has already attracted attention from a number of psychologists—predominantly social psychologists (Haslam, 2004, provides a wide-ranging overview). Bugental (2000) has also used it as one base for a theory of "social domains." Especially appealing to scholars with an interest in development, however, are Fiske's (1991) questions: What needs to be learned and how does that learning proceed?

Fiske (1991) proposes that the accurate placement of people in particular categories needs to be learned. The new questions then have to do with the kinds of errors that are more or less likely to occur (e.g., Haslam, 1994) and the ways in which people go about repairing them (e.g., Harach & Kuscynski, 2005—a study focused on repair actions by children and parents). Questions about how we come to know which errors matter most are also prompted. Fiske (1991) proposes that, among adults, the errors that give rise to the strongest feelings are those that confuse communal and market pricing relationships (e.g., I expect the governing principle to be "for love," you expect it to be "for money," as able to be bought and as reasonably rewarded by money). Errors at the very end of what is felt to be tolerable are also particularly interesting. They are "outrageous," "heretical," "taboo," or "unthinkable" (e.g., Fiske & Tetlock, 1997; Tetlock, McGraw, & Kristel, 2004).

What do analyses such as these have to do with family life and family contexts? On all sides, the view taken is that learning starts early in life, in "family lessons." It is in the course of family life, for example, that we first acquire a sense that others regard some skills as significant whereas others are trivial (D'Andrade, 1981; Goodnow, 1990; Gauvain & Perez, 2007). It is in family contexts also that we first learn that some ways of speaking and story-telling are appropriate for this audience but not for another (Miller & Mangelsdorf, 2005), that there is a difference between behaviors at home and behaviors "in public," and that some displays of competence will be regarded by others as "showing off." At least in some families, we also learn that not doing well in school will violate an obligation to our families and may bring shame on them (Fuligni, 2001).

It is in family contexts that we may also first learn what counts as a relationship error and which errors matter most. It is from household tasks, for example, that children may first learn to be careful about the place of money. You should not, for example, offer to pay a sibling to do what are called "your jobs." You should not ask what you will be paid when asked to do something and you should certainly not make a work contribution and then ask for a money reward (Goodnow, 2004). In more formal terms, this is one way by which children are introduced to the view that you should be cautious about bringing a market-pricing element into what is expected to be a communal relationship.

In short, we are prompted now to ask questions that hold promise as a way to increase our understanding of the nature of relationship learning and social development and of the ways in which learning is initially family-based and then, in ways still not well-understood, carried over to other contexts or modified by them.

Interconnections Across Contexts

A view of development as taking place within a set of inter-related contexts is common to both cultural and psychological analyses (Goodnow, 2010). As a starting-point, I take the model presented by Bronfenbrenner (1979, 1995). His model is not the only one offered. It is, however, the one most often used by psychologists when they wish to start with the family circle and also go beyond it. I shall then use it as the basis for asking: What can culturally oriented analyses offer in the way of changes or additions to psychological analyses of links across contexts?

One of those additions takes the form of noting that some contexts are being given little or no attention. Bronfenbrenner's model, for example, covers contexts such as school, friends, community, and economic/political frames. Not on the list are churches or other religious centers, which are often ignored in essentially secular accounts of contexts but of great importance to many people and their views about development (Haight, 2002, Jensen, 2008 & 2011).

A larger set of additions and questions has to do with the ways in which contexts are inter-related. Bronfenbrenner has offered two descriptions. A graphic version, often reproduced, takes the form of concentric circles, arranged in layers with the family at the core. That graphic version shows no interactions among contexts. The verbal description, however, includes an emphasis on contexts as influencing one another, often in bidirectional fashion—an emphasis nicely concretized in the concept of "spillover" between the worlds of work and family (Crouter, 1984, 2006).

To this part of the model, culturally oriented analyses suggest several changes and additions. I shall group these into *(1)* the part played by parents and children and *(2)* the placement of family at the center and as distinct from "the outside world."

THE PART PLAYED BY PARENTS AND BY CHILDREN

In most psychological analyses, parents are seen as offering a protective barrier between children and the "outside world": filtering, buffering, shielding. Culturally oriented perspectives point to further roles. In one of these, parents actively prepare their children for the negative experiences they may meet: for encounters, for example, with various kinds of discrimination (e.g., Hughes & Chen, 1997; Carranza, 2007). In another, parents effectively locate and manage community resources that are likely to be beneficial to the family (Furstenberg et al., 1999). What matters are parents' knowledge of how various systems "work" (their *cultural capital*; Bourdieu & Passeron, 1977) and the ways in which they pass this knowledge on to other members of the family.

In both of those additions, children still emerge in limited roles. They are seen, for example, as making only a late entry into the larger world. By way of channels such as television, however, children do have early encounters with various parts of the outside world. Late entry may also be an ethnocentric view. Children in many countries are expected to enter paid work and contribute to the family income, at an age that many outsiders would regard as "too young" and as undermining the status of parents (Nsamenang, 2011; Weisner, 2001). In many families, children also play an active and independent part in connecting one context with another. Especially in immigrant families, for example, children learn—without being taught by parents—how to "navigate" across the several worlds of family, friends, and school (Phelan, Davidson, & Cao, 1991). They also often act as interpreters for parents. Now children introduce parents to an "outside world" and open up new paths.

THE PLACEMENT OF FAMILIES IN THE "NESTED" SET

One proposed departure from Bronfenbrenner's model keeps the notion of "nested" contexts but alters their positions. As a particular example, I single out proposals from Raffaelli et al. (2005; their paper also includes a review of related proposals). They note that among ethnic minority youth, children and adults have an early and a sharp awareness of "outside" conditions and the impact of these on what is open to them. We might well reverse the usual arrangement of layers, they argue, placing the "outside world" at the center and asking how effects radiate out to family life.

Change to the original model also takes the form of rethinking the divide between the family and "outside worlds." The "outside world" may in fact be part of family life from its very beginning. When we begin a task such as parenting, for example, we start with views that are already in place in our cultural group: views of childhood, of parenting, and of what mothers and fathers do. We begin also with practices that are already in place: practices ranging from ways of naming and dressing children to the differential involvements of mothers and fathers (*see also* Tharakad, Mistry, & Dutta, 2011). These handed-down views and practices may change somewhat over time, but they are present from the start of any parental action.

In effect, families are not some isolated, private world. The "external world" is already part of any family interaction and the divide between family and the "outside world" needs to be rethought.

Social Policies

One aim of this book has to do with understanding not only the general nature of development but also the nature of social policies—understanding the shapes they take and the shapes they might take. There already exist several analyses of links between developmental research and social policies (e.g., Huston, 2006; Shonkoff & Phillips, 2000). The additions now suggested have to do with specifying what makes some policies "social," identifying a problem, and deciding on an approach to it. For each of those steps we can build on proposals that come from culturally oriented analyses of what "development in context" may mean.

What Makes Some Policies "Social?" How Do They Vary?

From culturally oriented analyses of contexts as marked by activities of various kinds, we can usefully take one way of differentiating among activities, asking: Who plays what part? In general, that kind of approach suggests that policies are called "social" when the state plays some part—that is, the state is involved in framing, funding, monitoring, or enforcing various ways of proceeding.

The nature of the state's involvement also offers a way to differentiate among social policies. For example, there is a difference between the state making a service available and requiring its use. There is a difference between encouraging parents to minimize their use of physical forms of control or discipline and making those forms illegal or making it mandatory for teachers or physicians to report what they see as possible parental abuse. Now the state actively constrains the actions of others.

The state's exercise of power can also change the options open to parents. When it specifies some form of "parent education," for example, parents still have the option of ignoring what is said to them. When the state can remove children from parental care, parents have little or no power over the actions of the state. They may then see their only option as one of keeping themselves or their children invisible to the state's regulatory bodies: from schools, health services, the police, or welfare agencies.

In another form of constraint, the state can make the gate to change so narrow that parents and children need to make special efforts to pass through it.

When the state gives extra funding for resources and special classes for children diagnosed as having attention deficit disorder or dyslexia, for example, parents work at achieving this diagnosis for their child. Narrower still is the gate for entry into a country by people who are refugees, displaced, or asylum-seekers. Passing through that gate may only be possible if asylum seekers adopt, at least publicly, descriptions of themselves that fit the official criteria (e.g., the criterion of having a "well-founded fear" of persecution if one is returned, often based on past involvement in disapproved political activity). When children arrive without parents (their numbers are now increasing considerably), they can rarely meet those criteria. Instead, they must present a story of being without parents or other family and of being in need of protection. In effect, the narrow gate forces the presentation of a new version of oneself and one's history. The old version and any dissent from the existing rules then come to be expressed only in private or in underground fashion (Goodnow, in press). In short, considering the specific part played by the state helps clarify the special nature of social policies and the differences among them.

Identifying Problems

Any step toward improving development—by parents or by the state—starts from the sense that there is a problem. Involved also is the perception of a problem as impossible to ignore, as able to be changed, as part of one's responsibility, and as likely to get worse if no action is taken.

What do culturally oriented analyses of contexts and development suggest on this score? A first comment is that the identification of problems is likely to reflect one's own interests and social position. The state, for example, is more likely to emphasize and to direct its funding toward weaknesses and difficulties, rather than strengths. In a sense, virtue or success is expected to be its own reward. The state appears also to especially influenced by arguments to the effect that the cost of inaction—to the state—will be higher than the costs of action.

From culturally oriented analyses comes also a concern with perceptions of a problem as general (e.g., this child is stupid, this family is totally dysfunctional) rather than perceiving any problem as situated, as occurring in some situations or settings but not in others. Research on the verbal fluency of children in some minority groups has provided a sharp example of this kind of bias. Originally assessed as generally limited, it has turned out to vary with the setting—for example, often low in classrooms but high outside it. The assessment of parenting skills calls for the same awareness. Easily assessed as high or low, these skills can vary from one place to another, one age group to another, one challenge to another. Policies that recognize the extent to which what people do or appear able to do is "situated" are then preferred. Problem identifications based only on one setting can often yield little beyond that setting. Programs that allow some flexibility from one setting to another are also preferred, with some variation by community rather than fixed statewide or nationwide programs.

The Nature of Actions

Analyses of practices—one of the ways described earlier as marking culturally oriented analyses of development in context—suggest first that we ask whether the emphasis will be on changes in ideas or in everyday practices. Changes in practices are the steps recommended as the places to start. Changes in concepts may flow from these. For example, from changes in practices related to gender (e.g., changes in the use of terms such as *everyman* or *mankind*), there can emerge changes in the views held about gender. Even without that flow, changes in practice may be the more easily achieved aspects of change. The state can, for example, make schooling up to a certain age mandatory for all children living within the state's borders, with no attempt at changing parents' general views about gender. To take another example, the state can also prohibit marriage before a certain age, with no attempt at changing parents' general views of marriage and parental control.

From culturally oriented analyses comes also the suggestion that we ask whether the emphasis will be on changes in individuals, in settings, or in the interconnections between people and the worlds they encounter. Policies directed toward changes in the skills and styles of parents, for example, come predominantly from a focus on individuals. Changes in the settings children encounter (e.g., changes in the stereotyping encountered or in the accessibility of routes to a better future) stem predominantly from a focus on the impact of contexts other than the family. Policies directed toward helping people move from one context to another (e.g., from home to school or from school into paid work) stem predominantly from a focus on interconnections between contexts.

Interconnections between contexts have attracted particular attention, in the form of questions about the kinds of paths that are available, known about, and seen as able to be accessed. Work by Cooper and colleagues provides an example (e.g., Cooper, Dominquez, & Rosas, 2006). The groups of major interest in that work are adolescents with Asian or Latino background within the setting of schools in California. For these children to achieve what they might achieve, or hope to achieve, two approaches to change are seen as useful. One is an increase in an aspect of settings: in this case, the flexibility of routes toward a hoped-for goal (e.g., entry into particular occupations or particular kinds of tertiary education). The other approach is an increased knowledge of what those goals require and of the choices that need to be made at several points along the way through high school. This is the approach to change that Cooper and colleagues have emphasized. It exemplifies especially well approaches to change in the form of increasing parents' and children's ability to locate in their environments useful resources or alternative ways forward.

A Further Way Forward: The Significance of Shared Views

Noted up to this point have been actions of several kinds: changing practices, for example, or altering the availability and the knowledge people have of paths that link one context to another. Cultural analyses draw our attention also to the value of going beyond the recognition that views are likely to differ. Added also is the value of coming to know where differences lie and how some common ground can be established. That emphasis can be usefully extended to the understanding of social policies.

Worth asking at the start, for example, are questions about differences in the views held about the aims and the rationales for social policies. The arguments offered for the introduction and evaluation of policies, for instance, are often couched in terms of economic costs and benefits (e.g., early childhood education is seen as an economic "investment"). That kind of rationale is inevitably attractive. Funding and the state's budget are always part of political decisions. However, reservations have come from developmentalists about the extent to which an emphasis only on that kind of rationale brings a loss of concern for children's welfare, rights, or quality of life (e.g., Huston, 2006; Phillips, 2006).

Developmentalists may also differ from one another and from politicians in their views of the course of change and the timing of intervention by the state. Policies are usually based on the hope that they will bring about both immediate and future changes. At issue then are the assumed links between the present and the future. On this score, the view held by many is that policies directed toward young children will continue and will shape the future. That may indeed be all that is seen as needed. Contextually oriented analysts, however, are wary of any policy that assumes a nicely straight line between what happens at one time and what happens at another. The more appropriate view of development is one that allows for both drops and recoveries as resources and settings change (e.g., Shonkoff & Phillips, 2000). Policies that focus only on the early phases of development are then not sufficient. The direction of resources toward help at later times of difficulty or transition is also needed: for example, transitions at various points in the school system or into paid work or disruptions in family life.

What part do shared and unshared views between the family and the state play? The areas where differences occur, with effects on the effectiveness of social policies, are likely to be of several kinds. Parents, for example, hold a variety of expectations about the state's several agencies: "the welfare," "the government," "the schools," "the police." They also have varying degrees of trust in these (*see also* Flanagan, Martínez, & Cumsille, 2011). In turn, the state and its agencies have varying expectations and degrees of trust when it comes to parents in general or, as emphasized by culturally- oriented analyses, to parents in particular social groups. We are some distance from understanding how the expectations of parents and of the state come about. Coming to know the views held on both sides, however, is critical. Without that, no policy is likely to be effective.

How then are we likely to learn where differences occur and to move toward establishing some common ground? Attracting increasing attention is the step of including any "target" group—the group expected to benefit—in the design, implementation, and evaluation of any policy or program. That recommendation has been made for children or young people as well as for adults. It has also been seen as particularly important when the "target" group is culturally different from the groups that design or implement policies and is then all the more likely to hold different views of a problem, of the nature of development, and of a possible or ideal future (e.g., Goodnow, 2008). We now need to move more readily toward such inclusive and collaborative steps, using them to learn where differences lie, which ones matter most to the goals we seek to achieve, and how we can design, implement, and evaluate policies that will not be seen by others as alien, as an imposition, or as simply missing the point in their identification of problems or their proposals for change.

Conclusion

We all recognize that policies are based on underlying views of development, of the possibilities for change, and of the ways to achieve change. Less easily recognized are gaps and biases within our own underlying views. No approach to development will be without these. We can, however, use the perspectives of others as ways to become aware of them. For example, we can turn to the perspectives of people with social or cultural backgrounds that are different from our own. We can also turn to the perspectives of social scientists who start from the need to understand contexts and perspectives that differ from our own. This book is one example of that approach. A book edited by Cooper et al. (2005) is another major example. The perspectives that come from other disciplines are also likely to be marked by gaps and biases. The difference in viewpoints, however, can in itself prompt us to take a second look at our own views of development and at the way these flow on to social policies.

Useful also is attention to the ways in which psychologically oriented analyses of development have changed over time. Psychology has moved, for example, in the views once held of the intellectual capacities and styles of people in other cultures or minority groups. We also have come to recognize limitations in our usual sampling, starting with the sampling of gender and, increasingly, the sampling of groups with backgrounds and interests that often differ from those of the children or parents who are the easiest to access or the most likely to agree to participate in our studies.

In effect, the analysis of policies directed toward improvement in the positions of others and an understanding of their perspectives underlines a message that has appeared several times throughout this chapter and provides a fitting conclusion to it and perhaps to the book as a whole. In the course of our efforts to bridge cultural and psychological analyses of development, we may gain a better understanding of the views of development held by the people we see as "others" We are also likely to emerge with what may be a greater benefit: a better understanding of our own views.

References

Beck, U. (1997). Democratization of the family. *Childhood, 4*, 151–168.
Berger, P. (1977). *Facing up to modernity*. New York: Basic Books.

Bourdieu, P., & Passeron, C. (1977). *Reproduction in education, society and culture*. London: Sage.

Bronfenbrenner, U. (1979). *The ecology of human development*. Cambridge MA: Cambridge University Press.

Bronfenbrenner, U. (1995). Developmental ecology through space and time. In P. Moen, G. H. Elder Jr., & K. Lüscher (Eds.), *Examining lives in context: Perspectives on the ecology of human development* (pp. 619–648). Washington DC: American Psychological Association.

Bugental, D. B. (2000). Acquisition of the algorithms of social life: a domain-based approach. *Psychological Bulletin, 26*, 187–209.

Carranza, M. E. (2007). Building resilience and resistance against racism and discrimination among Salvadorian female youth in Canada. *Child and Family Social Work, 12*, 390–398.

Cooper, C. R., García Coll, C. T., Bartko, W. T., Davis, H. & Chatman, C. (Eds.) (2006). *Developmental pathways through middle childhood: Rethinking contexts and diversity as resources*. Mahwah, NJ: Erlbaum.

Cooper, C. R., Dominquez, E., & Rosas, S. (2006). Soledad's dream: Diversity, children's worlds, and pathways to college in democracies. In C. R. Cooper, C. García Coll, T. Bartko, H. Davis, & C. Chatman (Eds.), *Developmental pathways through middle childhood* (pp. 235–260). Mahwah, NJ: Erlbaum.

Crouter, A. C. (1984). Spillover from family to work: the neglected side of the work-family interface. *Human Relations, 37*, 425–442.

Crouter, A. C. (2006). Mothers and fathers at work: Implications for families and children. In A. Clarke-Stewart & J. Dunn (Eds.), *Families count: Effects on child and adolescent development* (pp. 135–154). Cambridge NY: Cambridge University Press.

D'Andrade, R. G. (1981). The cultural part of cognition. *Cognitive Science, 5*, 179–195.

Deal, J. E., Halvorson, C. F., & Wampler, K. S. (1989). Parental agreement on child-rearing orientations: Relations to parental, marital and child characteristics. *Child Development, 60*, 925–934.

Du Bois-Reymond, M. (2001). Negotiation families. In M. Du Bois-Reymond, H. Süncker, & H. H. Kruger (Eds.), *Childhood in Europe* (pp. 63–90). New York: Peter Lang.

Eccles, J., J. S. Wigfield, A., & Byrnes, J. (2003). Cognitive development in adolescence. In R. M. Lerner, M. A. Easterbrooks, & J. Mistry (Eds.), *Handbook of psychology: Developmental psychology* (Vol. 6, pp. 325–350). New York: Wiley.

Fiese, B., Hooker, K., Kotrary, L. M., & Schwagler, J. (1993). Family rituals in the early stages of parenthood. *Journal of Marriage and the Family, 57*, 633–642.

Fishman, M. (1986). *Manufacturing the news*. Austin, TX: University of Texas Press.

Fiske, A. P. (1991). *Structures of social life: The four elementary forms of human relations*. New York: Free Press.

Fiske, A. P. (1992). The four elementary forms of sociality: Framework for a unified theory of social relations. *Psychological Review, 99*, 689–723.

Fiske, A. P., & Tetlock, P. (1997). Taboo trade-offs: Reactions to transactions that transgress spheres of justice. *Political Psychology, 18*, 255–297.

Flanagan, C., Martínez, M. L., & Cumsille P. (2011). Civil societies as cultural and developmental contexts for civic identity formation. In L. A. Jensen (Ed.), *Bridging developmental approaches to psychology: New syntheses in theory, research and policy* (pp. 113–137). New York: Oxford University Press.

Fuligni, A. (2001). Family obligation and the academic motivation of adolescents from Asian, Latin American, and European backgrounds. In A. Fuligni (Ed.), *Family obligation and assistance during adolescence* (pp. 61–76). San Francisco: Jossey-Bass.

Fuligni, A. (2005). *Contesting stereotypes, creating identities: Social categories, social identities, and educational participation.* New York: Russell Sage Foundation.

Furstenberg, F. F., Jr., Cook, F. D., Eccles, J., Elder, G. H., & Sameroff, A. (1999). *Managing to make it: Urban families and adolescent success.* Chicago, IL: University of Chicago Press.

Gauvain, M. & Perez, S. M. (2007). The socialization of cognition. In J. Grusec & P. Hastings (Eds.), *Handbook of socialization: Theory and research* (pp. 588–613). New York: Guilford Press.

Gledhill C. (1988). Pleasurable negotiations. In D. Pribham (Ed.), *Female spectators looking at film and television.* London: Verso.

Goodnow, J. J. (1990). The socialization of cognition: What's involved? In J. W. Stigler, R. Shweder, & G. Herdt (Eds.), *Cultural Psychology* (pp. 259–286). Cambridge: Cambridge University Press.

Goodnow, J. J. (1994). Acceptable disagreement across generations. In J. Smetana (Ed.), *Beliefs about parenting* (pp. 51–64). San Francisco: Jossey-Bass.

Goodnow, J. J. (2004). The domain of work in households: A relational models approach. In N. Haslam (Ed.), *Relational models theory: a contemporary overview* (pp. 167–195). Mahwah NJ: Erlbaum.

Goodnow, J. J. (2008). Research and action: Challenges, moves forward and unfinished Tasks. In G. Robinson, U. Eickelkamp, J. Goodnow, & I. Katz, *Contexts of child development: Culture, policy and intervention* (pp.79–89). Darwin: University of Darwin Press.

Goodnow, J. J. (2010). Cultural contexts: Ways of specifying and linking to development. In M. Bornstein (Ed.) *Handbook of cultural developmental science.* (pp. 3–20). Mahwah, NJ: Erlbaum.

Goodnow, J. J. (in press). Refugees, asylum-seekers, displaced persons: children in precarious positions. In A. Ben-Arieh, J. Cashmore, G. Goodman, & G. Melton (Eds.), *Handbook for research with children.* New York: Sage.

Goodnow, J. J., Miller, P. J., & Kessel, F. (Eds.) (1995). *Cultural practices as contexts for development.* San Francisco, CA: Jossey-Bass.

Gramsci, A. (1971). *Selections from the prison notebooks.* New York: International Press.

Haight, W. L. (2002). *African-American children at church.* Cambridge, UK: Cambridge University Press.

Hallin, D. C. (1986). *"The uncensored war": The media and Vietnam.* New York: Oxford University Press.

Harach, L., & Kuczynski, L. (2005). Construction and maintenance of parent-child relationships: Bidirectional contributions from the perspective of parents. *Infant and Child Development, 14,* 327–343.

Haslam, N. (2004). *Relational models theory: A contemporary overview.* Mahwah, NJ: Erlbaum.

Haslam, N. (1994). Categories of social relationships. *Cognition, 63,* 59–90.

Hatano, G., & Wertsch, J. (2001). Sociocultural approaches to cognitive development: The constitutions of culture in mind. *Human Development, 44,* 77–83.

Hughes, D., & Chen, L. (1997). What and when parents tell their children about race: An examination of race-related socialization in African-American families. *Applied Developmental Science, 1,* 120–214.

Huston, A. C. (2006). Connecting the science of child development to public policy. *Social Policy Report,* 19(4), 3–18. Ann Arbor, MI: Society for Research in child Development.

Jensen, L. A. (2008). Through two lenses: A cultural-developmental approach to moral psychology. *Developmental Review, 28,* 289–315.

Jensen, L. A. (2011). The cultural-developmental theory of moral psychology: A new syntheses. In L. A. Jensen (Ed.), *Bridging developmental approaches to psychology: New syntheses in theory, research, and policy* (pp. 3–25). New York: Oxford University Press.

Ketner, S. L., Buitelaar, M. W., & Bosma, H. A. (2004). Identity strategies among adolescent girls of Moroccan descent in the Netherlands. *Identity: An International Journal of Theory and Research, 4,* 145–169.

Kuscynski, L., & Parkin, C. M. (2007). Agency and bidirectionality in socialization: Interactions, transactions and relational dialectics. In J. Grusec & P. Hastings (Eds.), *Handbook of socialization: Theory and research* (pp. 259–283). New York: Guilford Press.

Laible, D., & Thompson, R. A. (2007). Early socialization: a relational perspective. In J. Grusec & P. Hastings (Eds.), *Handbook of socialization: Theory and research* (pp. 181–207). New York: Guilford Press.

Lerner, R. M., Lerner, J. V., Almerigi, J., & Theokas, C. (2006). Dynamics of individual ←→ context relations in human development. In J. C. Thomas, D. Segal & M. Herson (Eds.), *Comprehensive handbook of personality and psychopathology:* Vol. 1 (pp. 23–43). London: Sage.

Love, E. D., Weisner, T. S., Geis, S., & Huston, A. C. (2005). Child care instability and the effort to sustain a working daily routine. In C. R. Cooper, C. T. García Coll, W. T. Bartko, H. Davis, & C. Chatman (Eds.), *Developmental pathways through middle childhood: Rethinking contexts and diversity as resources* (pp. 121–144). Mahwah NJ: Erlbaum.

Miller, P. J., & Goodnow, J. J. (1995). Cultural practices: Toward an integration of culture and development. In J. J. Goodnow, P. J. Miller, & F. Kessel (Eds.), *Cultural practices as contexts for development* (pp. 5–16). San Francisco, CA: Jossey-Bass.

Miller, P. J., & Mangelsdorf, S. C. (2005). Developing selves are meaning-making selves: Recouping the social in social development. In Jensen, L. A. & R. W. Larson (Eds.), *New horizons in developmental theory and research* (pp. 23–32). San Francisco, CA: Jossey-Bass.

Nsamenang, A. B. (2011). The culturalization of developmental trajectories: A perspective on African childhoods and adolescences. In L. A. Jensen (Ed.), *Bridging cultural and developmental psychology: New syntheses in theory, research and policy* (pp. 235–254). New York: Oxford University Press.

Phelan, P., Davidson, A. L., & Cao, H. T. (1991). Students' multiple worlds: Negotiating the boundaries of family, peer, and school cultures. *Anthropology and Education Quarterly, 22,* 224–250.

Phinney, J. S., & Baldelomar, O. A. (2011). Identity development in multiple cultural contexts. In L. A. Jensen (Ed.), *Bridging cultural and developmental psychology: New syntheses in theory, research and policy* (pp. 161–186). New York: Oxford University Press.

Raffaelli, M., Carlo, G., Carranza, M. A., & Gonzales-Kruger, G. E. (2005). Understanding Latino children and adolescents in the mainstream: Placing culture at the center of developmental models. In Jensen, L. A. & R. W. Larson (Eds.), *New horizons in developmental theory and research* (pp. 23–32). San Francisco, CA: Jossey-Bass.

Ram, A., & Ross, H (2008). "We got to figure it out": Information-sharing and siblings' negotiations of conflicts of interest. *Social Development, 17*, 512–527.

Rogoff, B. (2003). *The cultural nature of human development.* Oxford, UK: Oxford University Press.

Romney, K. A., Weller, S. C., & Batchelder, E. H. (1986). Culture as consensus: a theory of culture and informant accuracy. *American Anthropologist, 88*, 313–332.

Ruble, D. N., Alvarez, J., Bachman, M., Cameron, J., Fuligni, A., García Coll, C., & Rhee, E. (2004). The development of a sense of "we": The emergence and implications of children's collective identity. In M. A. Bennett & F. Sani (Eds.), *The development of the social self* (pp. 29–76). New York: Psychology Press.

Saraswathi, T. S., Mistry, J., & Dutta, R. (2011). Reconceptualizing lifespan development through a Hindu perspective. In L. A. Jensen (Ed.), *Bridging cultural and developmental psychology: New syntheses in theory, research and policy* (pp. 276–299). New York: Oxford University Press.

Schieffelin, B., & Ochs, E. (Eds.) (1986). *Language socialization across cultures.* New York: Cambridge University Press.

Serpell, R., Sonnenschein, S., Baker, L., & Gapanathy, H. (2002). The intimate culture of families in the early socialization of literacy. *Journal of Family Psychology, 16*, 391–405.

Shonkoff, J. P., & Phillips, D. A. (Eds.) (2000). *From neurons to neighborhoods: The science of early childhood development.* Washington DC: National Academy Press.

Shweder R. A., Jensen, L. A., & Goldstein, W. M. (1995). Who sleeps by whom revisited: A method for extracting the moral goods in practices. In J. J. Goodnow, P. J. Miller, & F. Kessel (Eds.), *Cultural practices as contexts for development* (pp. 21–40). San Francisco, CA: Jossey-Bass.

Shweder, R. A., Goodnow, J. J., Hatano, G., LeVine, R. A., Markus, H. R., & Miller, P. J. (2006). The cultural psychology of development: One mind, many mentalities. In R. A. Lerner & W. Damon (Eds.), *Handbook of child psychology* (Vol. 1, pp. 716–792). Hoboken, NJ: Wiley.

Strauss C. (1992). Models and motives. In R. G. D'Andrade & C. Strauss (Eds.) (1992), *Human motivation and cultural models* (pp. 1–20). New York: Cambridge University Press.

Tajfel, H. (1982). *Social identity and intergroup relations.* Cambridge, UK: Cambridge University Press.

Tetlock, P., McGraw, A. P., & Kristel, O. V. (2004). Proscribed forms of social cognition: Taboo trade-offs, blocked exchanges, forbidden base rates, and heretical counterfactuals. In N. Haslam (Ed.), *Relational models theory: A contemporary overview* (pp. 247–262). Mahwah, NJ: Erlbaum.

Turner, J. C. (1987). *Rediscovering the social group: A self-categorization theory.* Oxford, UK: Blackwell.

Weisner, T. (2001). Children investing in their families: the importance of child obligation for successful development. In A. Fuligni (Ed.), *Family obligation and assistance during adolescence* (pp. 77–83). San Francisco, CA: Jossey-Bass.

Whiting J. W. M. (1941). *Becoming a Kwoma; Teaching and learning in a New Guinea tribe.* New Haven, CT: Yale University Press.

CHAPTER 5

Culture, Peer Relationships, and Human Development

XINYIN CHEN

Since the early 1930s, theorists and researchers in psychology and other social sciences have recognized the role of peer relationships in human development (Piaget, 1932; Sullivan, 1953). Peer relationships are considered an important context for children and adolescents to learn social and cognitive skills (Hartup, 1992). Moreover, being associated with peers may provide a sense of belongingness, security, and self-validation (e.g., Sullivan, 1953). Findings from various research programs have supported these arguments. Children who engage in active social interactions and maintain positive peer relationships have more opportunities than others to obtain assistance from peers and develop confidence in exploring the world (Nsamenang, 2011; Rubin, Bukowski, & Parker, 2006). In contrast, children who experience difficulties in peer relationships are likely to develop social and psychological problems such as academic failure, juvenile delinquency, and psychopathological symptoms (e.g., Coie, Terry, Lenox, Lochman, & Hyman, 1995; DeRosier, Kupersmidt, & Patterson, 1994; Ladd & Troop-Gordon, 2003).

Hinde (1987) has argued that different levels of social experiences are embedded within an all-reaching cultural system. Similarly, Harris (1995) has suggested that cultural norms, either adopted from existing cultural systems or created by children themselves, provide a basis for children's peer interactions and mutual socialization. Research on children's peer relationships has been conducted mostly in Western—particularly North American—societies. Over the past two decades, however, there has been increased interest in peer relationships in different cultures. The results of empirical studies indicate that children's peer experiences vary considerably across cultures.

The main theme of this chapter is the understanding of peer experiences from a cultural perspective and the role of peer interactions and relationships in bridging culture and human development. I first describe the research on children's peer relationships and their contributions to developmental outcomes. Then, I review the literature on children's peer interactions in different societies and discuss cultural variations in the structural and functional features of friendships and peer groups. In the following section, I provide a contextual–developmental perspective on cultural values, peer relationships, and individual development. My chapter concludes with a discussion of future directions in the study of culture, peer relationships, and development.

Peer Relationships and Human Development

Children's peer experiences mainly include *(1)* peer interactions, *(2)* dyadic relationships with friends, *(3)* peer groups, and *(4)* overall peer acceptance and rejection. Peer interaction, as the social exchange in which each participant's behavior is both a response to, and stimulus for, other participants' behavior, provides a rich and complex context for children to communicate with and influence each other (Rubin et al., 2006). During interaction, children cooperate, fight, withdraw, and engage in rough-and-tumble, socio-dramatic, and other activities. There is evidence that both the prevalence (the extent to which children engage in interaction) and the nature (e.g., cooperative vs. antisocial–disruptive) of peer interaction are related to developmental outcomes (e.g., Dodge, Pettit, McClaskey, & Brown, 1986). Active social participation and cooperative and low-power interaction styles tend to be associated with adaptive socio-emotional and cognitive development. In contrast, inability to get involved in peer interaction or participation in deviant peer activities is likely to predict social and school problems (e.g., Dishon, Nelson, & Bullock, 2004; Dodge et al., 2008; Wentzel, 2003).

The main aspects of friendship include having a friend, characteristics of friends, and friendship quality (Hartup & Stevens, 1999). Most children from the preschool age are involved in mutual friendships. Although causal directions are often unclear, it has been found that the possession of friendships is responsible for some of the adjustment outcomes such as perceived well-being and self-esteem, behavioral and emotional problems, school performance, and overall social acceptance (e.g., Ladd, 1990). Nevertheless, how friends contribute to children's development depends largely on who the friends are. Affiliations with socially competent and antisocial-deviant friends have dramatically different effects (e.g., Dishion et al., 2004). Finally, the quality of friendship is associated with social and psychological adjustment in children and adolescents (Berndt, 2002; Ladd, Kochenderfer, & Coleman, 1996). Children and adolescents who report high levels of intimacy and support in friendship tend to adjust better in social and emotional areas than those who have conflict-ridden and contentious relationships (Hartup, 1999).

The peer group represents a salient social phenomenon from middle childhood to adolescence (Brown & Klute, 2003). Natural peer groups, often formed spontaneously out of common interests, are networks of interacting individuals who spend time together and share activities. Children with similar qualities tend to attract each other and, after getting together, start to socialize each other (Cairns & Cairns, 1994). Some of the processes of peer group influence, such as social learning and mutual support, are similar to those in dyadic relationships between friends. Peer groups may also influence individuals through norm-based group processes such as mutual regulation and within-group assimilation and group reputational effects (Cairns & Cairns, 1994). Peer groups have been found to contribute to social, school, and psychological adjustment such as academic motivation, school dropout, early pregnancy, and substance use (e.g., Espelage, Holt, & Henkel, 2003; Kinderman, McCollom, & Gibson, 1995).

Finally, overall peer acceptance refers to the child's experience of being liked or disliked by others in larger social settings such as the classroom or school. Using the sociometric techniques developed by Moreno (1934) and Coie, Dodge, and Coppotelli (1982), researchers can identify children with different types of social status (popular, rejected, controversial, neglected, and average) associated with peer acceptance and rejection. Peer acceptance and rejection appear to predict a variety of developmental outcomes. Whereas children who are accepted by peers tend to be well-adjusted socially and psychologically, children who are rejected or neglected by peers are likely to display school problems such as academic failure and school drop-out, juvenile delinquency, conduct disorder, and mental health problems (*see* Rubin et al., 2006, for a comprehensive review).

In short, children's peer relationships play an important role in shaping the patterns of socio-emotional and cognitive development. Moreover, the different aspects of peer relationships (peer interactions, friendships, groups, and overall peer acceptance) may make common as well as unique contributions to adaptive and maladaptive development (e.g., Hoza, Molina, Bukowski, & Sippola, 1995).

Culture and Peer Interactions

Children living in different cultural conditions may differ in the occurrence and quality of peer interactions. Specific cultural beliefs and values may be related to the experiences in peer interactions and the developmental trajectories of children with certain behavioral characteristics and interaction styles. The role of culture often emerges in children's engagement in play and individual and group behaviors in peer interactions.

Play and Playfulness in Peer Interactions

Developmental researchers have investigated children's peer interactions across cultures by observing children's play. Substantial variations have been found in the amount of time that children spend in play in different societies. According to Larson and Verma (1999), children in pre-industrialized societies tend to spend less time playing with peers than their counterparts in Western post-industrialized societies. Compared with children in Japan and the United States, children in rural Kenya and India had significantly less playing time because they had to help with household responsibilities (Whiting & Edwards, 1988; *see also* Nsamenang, 2011). Children in some East Asian countries, such as China and Korea, often have to concentrate on schoolwork and thus spend less time playing than North American children (Larson & Verman, 1999; Stevenson et al., 1990). The amount of time that children spend in play may be related to socialization beliefs about the role of play in development. Parents in many African, Asian, and Latin American societies have traditionally seen little value of children's play for learning social norms and developing social and cognitive skills (Parmar, Harkness, & Super, 2004; Rogoff, Mistry, Goncu, & Mosier, 1993). As a result, children in these societies are provided fewer opportunities to play with peers than their Western counterparts.

There are also cross-cultural differences in the characteristics of children's play. Little, Brendgen, Wanner, and Krappmann (1999) found that compared with children in West Berlin, children in former East Berlin experienced less fun and enjoyment with their peers, largely because of the adult control of children's peer interaction. With the changes in the education system after the German unification, peer interactions among children in East Berlin have been based more on personal choices and less controlled by adults. As a result, children in Eastern Berlin seem to engage in more playful and intimate interactions with friends, express more personal likings, and experience higher enjoyment in their peer interactions.

Self-Expression in Peer Interactions: Socio-Dramatic Behavior

Another qualitative feature of peer interaction that varies across cultures is socio-dramatic activity in children's play. According to Farver, Kim, and Lee (1995) and Edwards (2000), socio-dramatic behavior and pretense require children to control their social-evaluative anxiety and to express their inner interests and personal styles. In Western societies, children are socialized to behave in an assertive manner and are encouraged to exhibit personal styles (e.g., Smetana, 2002; Triandis, 1995). Accordingly, the social and ecological environment (e.g., the structuring of activities, physical settings) is set up to facilitate the development of self-directive and expressive skills. As a result, Western children tend to engage in more socio-dramatic behaviors than children in many other—particularly group-oriented—cultures. It has been found that children in Maya (Gaskins, 2000), Bedouin Arab (Ariel & Sever, 1980), Kenya, Mexico, and India (Edwards, 2000) engage in little socio-dramatic activity. Farver et al. (1995) also found that Korean-American preschool children displayed less social and pretend play than Anglo-American children. Moreover, when Korean-American children engaged in pretend play, it contained more everyday and family role activities and less fantastic themes (e.g., actions related to legend or fairy tale characters that did not exist) (Farver & Shin, 1997). Similar results were found in studies conducted with preschool children in Korea and China (Parmar et al., 2004; Tieszen, 1979).

Cultural differences in children's socio-dramatic behaviors may reflect Westernization or urbanization of the society or community. For example, Gosso Lima, Morais, and Otta (2007) examined the play behaviors of children from three different places in Brazil: an Indian village (Paranowaona), a small coastal town (Seashore in Sao Paulo state), and urban Sao Paulo. The researchers found that the urban children, especially from high socioeconomic status (SES) families, displayed significantly more pretend or socio-dramatic behaviors. Moreover, urban children's socio-dramatic activities involved more fantastic characters or themes. Interestingly, relatively high-prevalent characters in the pretend play of Seashore children were domestic animals (dogs and horses), which, according to Gosso et al. (2007), resulted from the close contact of the children with them in daily life. Therefore, the extent to which children engage in socio-dramatic activities and their content are influenced by social and cultural conditions.

Social Evaluations and Responses in Peer Interactions

Cultural norms and values with regard to particular behavioral characteristics are reflected in social evaluations and responses in peer interactions. This is illustrated in different experiences of shy children in peer interactions in China and North America. Shyness, a behavioral manifestation of internal anxiety in challenging social situations, is regarded as incompetent and immature in Western cultures (e.g., Coplan & Armer, 2007). As a result, when shy children initiate a social interaction, which is often passive (e.g., hovering, waiting, and nonverbal behaviors), peers tend to respond with overt rejection or intentional ignoring (Rubin, Burgess, & Coplan, 2002). Unlike Western culture, shyness and social restraint are considered an indication of mastery and accomplishment in traditional Chinese culture (Liang, 1987). The cultural endorsement leads to different peer attitudes toward children who display shy, wary, and inhibited behaviors.

Chen, DeSouza, Chen, and Wang (2006a) investigated how shy children engaged in peer interactions in samples of Chinese and Canadian children. Four same-sex children at age 4 years were observed in free-play sessions in the laboratory. Shyness was assessed based on children's onlooker (watching the activities of others but not entering the activity) and unoccupied (an absence of focus or intent, wandering aimlessly or staring blankly into space) behaviors. The results first indicated that shy Chinese and Canadian children were less likely than their non-shy counterparts to make active initiations. Thus, in both cultures, shy children's internal anxiety, vigilance, and wariness may prevent them from initiating social contact in an assertive manner (e.g., Asendorpf, 1991; Rubin et al., 2002). There were significant differences between the samples in the responses that shy children received from peers and the initiations that peers made voluntarily to shy children. When shy Canadian children made social initiations, peers were more likely to make negative responses, such as overt refusal, disagreement, and intentional ignoring of an initiation (e.g., "No!" and "I won't do it."). However, peers responded in a more positive manner in China by controlling their negative actions and by showing approval, cooperation, and support (e.g., "I really like your drawing!"). There were also differences between the samples in peer voluntary initiations to shy children. In Canada, relative to initiations made to non-shy children, initiations made to shy children were more likely to be coercive (e.g., a direct demand such as "Gimme that," or verbal teasing), and less likely to be cooperative (e.g., "Can I play with you?"). This was not the case within the Chinese sample, where peer voluntary initiations to shy and non-shy children did not differ. Finally, when peers made social initiations, shy children in Canada were more likely to respond negatively than their counterparts in China.

Taken together, the results suggest that there are evident cross-cultural differences in peer responses to shy children's initiations and in peer voluntary initiations to shy children. Whereas peers are generally antagonistic, forceful, and non-responsive in their interactions with shy children in Canada, peers appear more supportive and cooperative toward shy children in China. The different experiences of shy children may result in their different attitudes and behaviors toward others. Social support that shy children in China receive may help them engage in positive peer interactions, which are important for learning social skills and appropriate behaviors. However, the difficulties and frustrations that Canadian shy children experience may facilitate the formation of negative attitudes toward others and the development of maladaptive behaviors.

Culture and Friendship and the Peer Group

Establishing specific friendships with others and becoming integrated into social networks are main indexes of success with peer relationships. Cultures may differ in the extent to which the development of specific friendships or group integration is encouraged (e.g., Sharabany, 2006). Sharabany and Wiseman (1993), for example, reported that children in Kibbutz communities focused on group involvement and had limited dyadic friendships. According to Sharabany (2006), dyadic friendships with high levels of affective involvement are not encouraged in at least some collectivistic societies because of the availability of other sources of emotional support, reduced privacy inherent in collectivistic lifestyles, and the potential threat of exclusive dyadic friendships to the cohesiveness of the larger group. Among the qualitative features of peer relationships, the functions that friendships and peer groups serve in children and adolescents' daily activities may be most likely to reflect cultural expectations such as those regarding individual independence and group commitment (Chen & French, 2008; Tietjen, 1989).

Friendship Functions: Enhancement of Self-Worth versus Instrumental Aid

The existing studies conducted with children in school context indicate that in general, the majority of children and adolescents, ranging from 70% to more than 90%, have reciprocal friends (children nominate each other as a friend) in most societies (e.g., Attili, Vermigli, & Schneider, 1997; French, Jansen, Riansari, & Setiono, 2003; Liu & Chen, 2003; Young & Ferguson, 1981). Major functions such as security-protection, companionship, intimate disclosure, instrumental assistance, and enhancement of self-worth emerge in friendships of youth in many cultures (French et al., 2006). Therefore, friendship may be a social resource for fulfilling some common needs of children and adolescents.

Nevertheless, cross-cultural research has revealed differences in friendship functions that are identified and appreciated by children in different societies. In Western cultures, support of friends is considered an important mechanism for children to develop positive views of self-worth (Sullivan 1953). This function is less salient in many non-Western cultures, where the development of the self is not considered an important developmental task. It has been found that whereas one of the major reasons for friendship among North American children is that friends make children feel good about themselves, Chinese (e.g., Chen, Kaspar, Zhang, Wang, & Zheng, 2004b; Cho, Sandel, Miller, & Wang, 2005) and Indonesian (French, Pidada, & Victor, 2005) children and children with an Arab and Caribbean background (Dayan, Doyle, & Markiewicz, 2001) often do not report the enhancement of self-worth as an important function of friendship.

Relative to self-validation, instrumental aid appears to be more important for friendships of children in many group-oriented cultures (Smart, 1999; Tietjen, 1989). Based on qualitative interviews, Way (2006) found that sharing of money and protecting friends from harm were salient aspects of the friendships of low-income Black and Hispanic adolescents in the United States. Instrumental assistance has also been found to be a highly salient feature of friendships in Asian nations such as China (Chen et al. 2004b), Indonesia (French et al. 2005), South Korea (French et al., 2006), and the Philippines (Hollnsteiner, 1979) and in Latino societies such as Cuba (Gonzalez, Moreno, & Schneider, 2004) and Costa Rica (DeRosier & Kupersmidt, 1991). In these societies, instrumental assistance may occur in various forms. For example, a theme that has often emerged from the interviews with Chinese adolescents in China, Taiwan, and the United States is the high appreciation of mutual assistance of friends in learning and school achievement (Chen et al., 2004b; Way, 2006).

The quality of children's friendships may also depend on specific social, cultural, and historical conditions (Chen & French, 2008). In Korea and some other Asian nations, for example, Confucianism has traditionally been considered the primary ideology that guides interpersonal interactions. According to French and his colleagues (French et al., 2005, 2006), the salience of loyalty and exclusivity in friendships in these nations may largely result from the Confucian value on trust and obligation between friends (French et al., 2006). Emotional expressivity in social interaction is typically encouraged in Latino societies to convey warmth and affection (Argyle, Henderson, Bond, Iizuka, & Contarello, 1986). The cultural values of emotional expressivity may be related to relatively intimate social relationships in Latino youth. Thus, future research on friendship should consider broad social and cultural factors.

Individual Autonomy versus Responsibility in the Peer Group

Most school-age children in the world are affiliated with a peer group (e.g., Chen, Chang, & He, 2003; D'Hondt & Vandewiele, 1980; Kiesner, Poulin, & Nicotra, 2003; Salmivalli, Huttunen, & Lagerspetz, 1997). Peer groups are often composed of same-sex members, with more mixed-sex groups appearing in late adolescence. Boys appear to be more likely to belong to groups and more susceptible to peer pressure than girls, and boys' groups tend to be larger than girls' groups in many countries (e.g., Benenson, Apostoleris, & Parnass, 1997; Dekovic, Engels, Shirai, De Kort, & Anker, 2002; D'Hondt & Vandewiele, 1980; Salmivalli et al., 1997; Sim & Koh, 2003).

In North America, involvement in peer groups increases from childhood to early adolescence, which is believed to be derived from the desire of youth to obtain support for personal autonomy from the family (Rubin et al., 2006). Once children enter the peer group, they are expected to learn independence and self-direction while maintaining positive relationships with others and eventually to acquire a sense of self-identity (Brown, 1990; Mead, 1934). Intensive interaction within the small clique is the major form of peer activity in childhood but tends to decline from middle childhood to adolescence, when children start to be affiliated with multiple groups and larger crowds (e.g., Brown 1990). During adolescence, a variety of peer groups can be identified, including those labeled as jocks, brains, populars, partiers, druggies, nerds, loners, and burnouts (e.g., Brown, 1990), indicating that peer groups are formed mainly based on adolescents' particular interests. As adolescents increasingly seek independence and attempt to avoid group restrictions, there is a general loosening of group ties, and adolescents' sense of belongingness declines steadily with age (see Rubin et al., 2006).

The tension between the pursuit of independence and personal identity and the commitment to group undertaking may be less evident in group-oriented cultures than self-oriented cultures. In group-oriented cultures, which emphasize commitment to social relationships, children and adolescents are encouraged to maintain strong social affiliation, identify with the group, and assume responsibility for the group (Sharabany, 2006). Accordingly, there is great pressure on group members to conform to group norms and make contributions to collective wellbeing (Azmitia & Cooper, 2004; Sharabany, 2006).

D'Hondt and Vandewiele (1980) have noticed that peer groups in Senegalese youth are organized on social and moral principles such as solidarity, unity, and struggle against social injustices. Similarly, children and adolescents in China often describe group activities in terms of how they are in accord with adults' social requirements and standards, such as maintaining interpersonal cooperation and school achievement (Chen, Chang, Liu, & He, 2008; Sun, 1995). Particular attention is paid to whether group activities are guided by the "right" social goals and whether these activities are beneficial to children's performance on socially valued tasks. In a series of studies conducted with Chinese children, Chen and colleagues (e.g., Chen, Chang, He, & Liu, 2005b) found that group prosocial–antisocial contexts were particularly important for individual development. Peer group prosocial–antisocial norms moderated the effects of parenting practices; whereas prosocial groups strengthened or facili-tated parental socialization effort to help children develop social and school competencies, antisocial groups undermined the contributions of supportive parenting to adaptive development (Chen et al., 2005b). Taken together, research findings indicate that cultural norms and values—especially those concerning socialization goals—are likely to affect the functions of children's friendships and the organization of peer groups, which in turn may affect the patterns and processes of social and cognitive development.

Culture and Peer Acceptance and Rejection

In the peer relationship literature (e.g., Rubin et al., 2006a), peer acceptance or likeability is often viewed as an index of personal social competence. This perspective does not fully recognize the social nature of peer acceptance and its culturally based regulatory function in human development. How a child is accepted by peers in larger contexts such as the classroom represents the over-all collective attitude toward the child on the basis of the social judgment of his/her behaviors and other attributes. Hartup (1983) has argued that peer acceptance is accounted for mainly by positively valued characteristics in the society, whereas peer rejection is predicted mainly by socially undesirable characteristics. At the same time, as an intrinsic social need (Sullivan, 1953)—particularly from middle childhood to early adolescence—peer acceptance serves as a motivational force for children to maintain or modify their behav-iors according to social expectations.

Behavioral Characteristics and Peer Acceptance and Rejection

Among various behavioral correlates and antecedents of peer acceptance and rejection, researchers are particularly interested in prosocial–cooperative behavior, aggression, and shyness–sensitivity (e.g., Masten et al., 1995; Rubin, Chen, McDougall, Bowker, & McKinnon, 1995). Prosocial–cooperative behavior appears to be associated robustly with peer acceptance in different cultures (e.g., Casiglia, Lo Coco, & Zappulla, 1998; Chen, Li, Li, Li, & Liu, 2000; Eisenberg, Pidada, & Liew, 2001). Children who display prosocial–cooperative behavior perform competently in social situations and thus are liked by peers. It has been argued that prosocial–cooperative behavior may have a more extensive impact on children's social and psychological adjustment, including peer relationships in Chinese and perhaps other group-oriented societies than in North American societies (Chen et al., 2000; Stevenson, 1991). There is little empirical evidence supporting this argument.

Children's aggressive behavior is generally associated with peer rejection and other adjustment problems because it may threaten the well-being of others. However, different consequences of aggressive behavior have been found across cultures. In cultures such as the Yanomamo Indians where aggressive and violent behaviors are considered socially acceptable or even desirable, aggressive children—particularly boys—may be regarded as "stars" and "heroes" by their peers (Chagnon, 1983). In some central and southern Italian communities, because of social and historical circumstances, aggressive and rebellious behaviors may be perceived by children as reflecting social assertiveness and competence (Casiglia et al., 1998; Schneider & Fonzi, 1996). Similarly, aggressive children may receive social approval and support from peers in some adolescent subcultures in North America (e.g., Rodkin, Farmer, Pearl, & van Acker, 2000). Apparently, aggressive children and adolescents in these communities and subcultures experience fewer social problems, such as peer rejection, than their counterparts in cultures that strongly disapprove aggression.

Aggressive behavior toward peers is strictly prohibited in many societies, and formal and informal practices are often applied to endorse this prohibition. For example, children engage in regular public evaluations in Chinese schools where they are required to evaluate themselves in terms of whether their behaviors reach the school standards. Peers and teachers provide feedback on the child's self-evaluations. The social interactive process makes aggressive children highly vulnerable to peer rejection as well as the development of negative self-perceptions and self-feelings (Chen et al., 2004a) because it is difficult in this circumstance for aggressive children to form inflated or biased views of their competence, like their counterparts in North America (Asher, Parkhurst, Hymel, & Williams, 1990).

Cross-cultural differences have been found more consistently in the relations between shyness--sensitivity and peer acceptance. Shy children are likely to be rejected by peers in North America (e.g., Cillessen, van Ijzendoorn, van Lieshout, & Hartup, 1992; Coplan, Prakash, O'Neil, & Armer, 2004; Gazelle & Ladd, 2003). Although research findings are not highly consistent with each other, the existing evidence indicate that shy children seem to experience fewer problems in peer acceptance in societies where assertiveness and autonomy are not valued or encouraged. Eisenberg et al. (2001) found, for example, that shyness in Indonesian children was negatively associated with peer nominations of dislike. Chen and colleagues (e.g., Chen, Rubin, & Li, 1995) conducted several studies in Chinese and Canadian children in the early 1990s and found that unlike their North American counterparts, shy Chinese children were accepted by peers and were more likely than others to obtain leadership status. Positive social relationships that shy children establish are, in turn, conducive to the development of positive attitudes toward self and others and the motivation to achieve success in other areas.

The Impact of Social Change on Relations Between Behavioral Characteristics and Peer Acceptance and Rejection

Chen, Cen, Li, and He (2005a) have recently explored how the massive social transformation in China affects relations between behavioral characteristics, particularly shyness–sensitivity, and peer acceptance and rejection. China has changed dramatically since the early 1980s, particularly in the past 15 years, toward a market-oriented society. There is evidence suggesting that traditional childrearing beliefs, attitudes, and practices (e.g., power assertion, lack of affective communication) have been changing among urban Chinese parents, especially those with a relatively high education. These parents increasingly realize that independence, expression of personal opinions, and self-confidence are required for adaptation to the new environment and that it is important to help children develop these qualities (Chen & Chen, 2010; Yu, 2002). Schools in China have also changed their education goals and practices to promote the development of assertive social skills. Relative to some other aspects of socio-emotional functioning, shyness may be particularly susceptible to the influence of the macro-level changes (Chen et al., 2006b). Shy, anxious, and wary behavior that impedes exploration and self-expression in stressful situations may no longer be regarded as adaptive in the new environment. Consequently, shy-inhibited children may be at a disadvantage in obtaining social approval and experience adjustment difficulties (Hart et al., 2000; Xu, Farver, Chang, Zhang, & Yu, 2007).

Using a cohort design in a study with elementary school children in urban China, Chen et al. (2005a) found that the relation between shyness and peer acceptance changed from positive in 1990 to negative in 2002. The results indicated that by the early part of the 21st century, as the country became more deeply immersed in a market economy, shy children, unlike their counterparts in the early 1990s, were perceived as incompetent and rejected by peers. Thus, the macro-level social, economic, and cultural changes in China have led to the decline in peer acceptance of shy children. An interesting finding of Chen et al.'s study (2005a) was that shyness was positively associated with both peer acceptance and rejection in 1998. Further analysis using the sociometric classification method revealed that whereas their counterparts were popular in 1990 and rejected in 2002, shy children were controversial in 1998. These results indicate ambivalent attitudes of peers toward shy children, which, to some extent, may reflect the cultural conflict between the new values of assertiveness and traditional Chinese values of self-control. Another interesting finding was that peer rejection was more sensitive than other aspects of adjustment such as academic achievement and depression to the change in social and cultural norms. The influence of contextual factors on school performance and psychopathological feelings may occur through complicated and prolonged interpersonal and intrapersonal processes. The finding supports the argument that peer attitudes and relationships serve as a major mediator of contextual influence on individual development (Chen et al., 2009).

Culture, Peer Relationships, and Individual Functioning:
A Contextual–Developmental Perspective

Developmental theorists have traditionally been interested in the role of socialization practices of adults in the society, especially parents and educators, in
transmitting cultural values to the young generation (e.g., LeVine et al., 1994;
Super & Harkness, 1986). Cultural influence on individual development is often
conceptualized as a vertical process from adults to children, although the latter
may be active participants in socialization (Edwards, Guzman, Brown, & Kumru,
2006; Goodnow, 2011; Rogoff, 2003). The socio-cultural theory (Vygotsky,
1978), for example, focuses on children's internalization of external symbolic
systems such as language and symbols, along with their cultural meanings, from
the interpersonal level to the intrapersonal level. According to this theory, an
important mechanism of internalization is collaborative, or guided, learning, in
which adults or experienced members of the society act as skilled tutors and
representatives of the culture and assist children in understanding and solving
problems. The assistance and guidance of more knowledgable members in children's activities are believed to be critical to the development of thought and
behavior (e.g., Goodnow, 1997; Rogoff, 2003; Vygotsky, 1978).

The socio-cultural theory and other vertical socialization perspectives indicate the importance of culture and culturally directed socialization practices
for human development. However, the processes of cultural influence on development, particularly in socio-emotional areas, are more complicated than
internalization of cultural systems or learning from senior members of the society. A major question, for example, is what motivates children to learn, accept,
and follow cultural expectations during socio-emotional development. Unlike
symbolic systems or tools for solving cognitive tasks, many of the cultural
norms and values endorsed in the society, such as those that serve to regulate
individual behaviors (e.g., self-control in resource-limited situations, helping
others when they need it), may not have inherent benefit *per se* and thus may
not be voluntarily appreciated by children. To maintain behaviors according to
certain cultural standards may even require personal sacrifice. Moreover,
although the instruction, guidance, and support of parents, teachers, and other
adults help children understand rules and learn appropriate behaviors, adult
influence becomes more indirect and inadequate as children develop greater
autonomy with age and as children engage in more social activities outside the
home and classroom. It is necessary to look into more context-relevant social
processes that are involved in cultural influence on development.

Based on the literature (e.g., Harris, 1995; Hinde, 1987) and the recent
cross-cultural research on peer relationships, Chen and colleagues (Chen &
French, 2008; Chen, Wang, & DeSouza, 2006b) have proposed a contextual–
developmental perspective on the links between cultural values and social
functioning and the role of peer interactions and relationships in shaping the
links. According to this perspective, social interactions and relationships serve
as an important context that mediates cultural influence on individual socio-
emotional and cognitive development. As discussed earlier, different cultures

may place different values on specific individual characteristics. For example, social initiative (the tendency to initiate and maintain social participation, as often indicated by reaction to challenging situations) is relatively more emphasized in Western self-oriented societies, whereas self-control/regulation (the ability to modulate behavioral and emotional reactivity in social interactions) is more valued in group-oriented societies (*see also* Rothbaum & Wang, 2011). Cultural values with regard to these two dimensions may be reflected in social behaviors such as aggression–disruption (high social initiative and low self-control), shyness (low social initiative and adequate control to constrain behaviors and emotions toward self), and aspects of social competence such as sociability and prosocial behavior (active social participation with effective control). Peer interactions and relationships may mediate cultural influence on development in multiple ways. Culture determines, in part, the extent to which children are allowed and encouraged to engage in peer activities, which in turn affect individual behaviors (Gaskins, 2000; Larson & Verman, 1999). Culture also guides socialization agents to organize social settings in which children interact and learn from each other (Super & Harkness, 1986; Whiting & Edwards, 1988). In addition, culture may explicitly or implicitly stipulate the developmental goals that children are encouraged to achieve through peer activities (French, Lee, & Pidada, 2006; Sharabany, 2006).

The contextual–developmental perspective (Chen, Chung, & Hsiao, 2009) particularly emphasizes the role of the social evaluation and response processes in building and facilitating links between culture and development. Specifically, during interactions, peers evaluate individual characteristics in manners that are consistent with the norms and values endorsed in the peer world. Moreover, peers may respond to these characteristics accordingly and express particular attitudes (e.g., acceptance, rejection) toward children who display the characteristics. Social evaluations and responses, in turn, may regulate children's behaviors and, ultimately, their developmental patterns. The need for intimate affect and mutual support within friendship, belongingness to the group, and peer acceptance in the larger setting (Sullivan, 1953) is the main source of motivational force that directs children to participate in peer interactions, to attend to social evaluations, and eventually to maintain or modify their behaviors according to culturally prescribed socialization goals. The general cultural belief system in the society may provide a basis for the social interaction processes through *(1)* specifying the expectations of individual behaviors in social settings; *(2)* promoting specific types of peer relationships such as close friendship versus the peer group in which social interactions occur; and *(3)* shaping the nature and organization of peer relationships, such as the functions of friendship, norms for peer group activities, and standards for overall peer acceptance and rejection.

By focusing on peer interaction processes, the contextual–developmental perspective inevitably pays attention to the active role of children in socialization. Children may actively engage in interactions and establish relationships through expressing their reactions (e.g., compliance, resistance) to social influence and through participating in constructing norms for social evaluations and other group activities (Corsaro & Nelson, 2003). Thus, the social processes are bidirectional and transactional in nature. At the cultural level, however, children in different societies may differ in their sensitivity and reaction to peer evaluation (e.g., Hwang, 1985). Cultures may also vary in the extent to which they allow and encourage children to maintain, adopt, and transform existing norms and values in the society and to develop new norms and values. Consequently, the dynamic processes of social interaction may occur in culturally distinct manners.

The production of new peer norms may be particularly evident in social interactions of immigrant children or children from immigrant families (e.g., Azmitia & Cooper, 2004; Chen & Tse, 2008; Way, 2006). The different, or even conflictual, cultural experiences of immigrant children in the home, the school, and other settings are likely to result in confusion, frustration, and distress (Berry, Phinney, Sam, & Vedder, 2006). However, mixed cultural backgrounds are also a resource for children to develop sophisticated peer cultures that incorporate diverse, and perhaps complementary, values and behavioral norms, such as responsibility, achievement, and independence (Conzen, Gerber, Morawska, Pozzetta, & Vecoli, 1992; Fuligi, 1998). The integrated cultural values play a unique role in shaping friendship functions, group organization styles, and eventually peer interaction processes (Way, 2006). For example, maintaining a balance between pursuing own ends and establishing group harmony (e.g., Maccoby, 1998) may be an important standard for social evaluations and responses in peer interactions. Thus, relationships with peers of different backgrounds provide opportunities for children to learn various social skills that allow them to function flexibly and effectively in different settings. Moreover, peer relationships that children form based on integrated and diverse values may be particularly beneficial for them to cope with stress in multiple areas during their adjustment to the challenging environment. In many contemporary societies that consist of families with diverse backgrounds, peer relationships serve as a buffering factor that protects children from developing social and psychological problems.

Conclusions and Future Directions

Cultural research has indicated the role of cultural norms and values in shaping the processes of peer interactions, the structural and functional features of friendships and groups, and behavioral antecedents and concomitants of peer acceptance and rejection. Through organizing these aspects of peer relationships, culture constructs distinct social contexts for children and adolescents to develop their socio-emotional characteristics and cognitive abilities according to socialization goals.

In the study of culture and peer relationships, researchers have relied mostly on cross-cultural comparisons. This type of research is important in revealing cultural variations in peer experiences. However, it provides limited information about how culture guides children to engage in peer interactions and establish peer relationships. Cross-cultural researchers are often interested in comparing children in Western self-oriented and non-Western or group-oriented societies. It is important to note that cultural exchanges and interactions may lead to the merging, co-existence, and integration of diverse value systems (Tamis-LeMonda et al., 2008). During globalization, for example, individual-istic ideologies and values such as assertiveness and autonomy have been introduced into many non-Western societies and exerted influence on social attitudes and behaviors of children and adults in these societies. Western values are likely to be integrated with the cultural traditions. It will be interesting to investigate how children engage in peer activities and develop their peer rela-tionships in culturally integrated and sophisticated settings.

Developmental researchers have long been interested in the processes in which culture is involved in human development. The contextual–developmental perspective I have proposed highlights the role of peer interactions as a social context in mediating the links between cultural values and individual socio-emotional and cognitive functioning (Chen et al., 2009). This perspective has guided our research effort over the past decade. However, the model is largely speculative; supporting evidence is needed for the general framework as well as specific components (e.g., similar and different effects of dyadic and group contexts on peer interactions). There is little research that examines directly how peer interactions and relationships mediate the linkage between culture and development, which may largely result from methodological difficulties. In a study of loneliness in Brazilian, Canadian, Chinese, and Italian children, Chen et al. (2004a) investigated how different cultural values of social behaviors were reflected in psycho-emotional distress through the mediation of friendship and peer acceptance/rejection. This study provided useful information about how culture, peer relationships, and psychological adjustment are associated with each other. However, investigating the cultural processes of human develop-ment is a complicated and long-term task. It may be necessary to use a multi-level (e.g., individuals nested within relationships in different communities and societies), multidisciplinary (e.g., sociological, anthropological, psycho-logical), and multimethod (e.g., quantitative, ethnographic, historical) approach to achieve a comprehensive and in-depth understanding of the issues.

According to the contextual–developmental perspective, cultural influence on social relationships and individual behaviors is a dynamic process in which children play an increasingly active role during development. The active role of children may be reflected in different aspects of peer interactions, including the choices of playmates, settings, and activities, and the reactions to peer influence (Edwards et al., 2006). From middle childhood, peer relationships provide a major social milieu in which children negotiate with each other to adopt existing cultural standards and create their own cultural norms for peer activities and mutual evaluations (Chen et al., 2009; Corsaro & Nelson, 2003). Despite the arguments about the dynamic and bidirectional nature of socializa-tion, however, the active role of children has received little attention in cross-cultural research. Therefore, it is crucial to engage in continuous exploration of the issues in the field of culture, peer relationships, and human development.

References

Argyle, M., Henderson, M., Bond, M., Iizuka, Y., & Contarello, A. (1986). Cross-cultural variations in relationship rules. *International Journal of Psychology, 21*, 287–315.

Ariel, S., & Sever, I. (1980). Play in the desert and play in the town: On play activities of Bedouin Arab children. In H. B. Schwartzman (Ed.), *Play and culture* (pp. 164–175). West Point, NY: Leisure Press.

Asendorpf, J. B. (1991). Development of inhibited children's coping with unfamiliarity. *Child Development, 62*, 1460–1474.

Asher, S., Parkhurst, J. T., Hymel, S., & Williams, G. A. (1990). Peer rejection and loneliness in childhood. In S. R. Asher & J. D. Coie (Eds.), *Peer rejection in childhood* (pp. 253–273). New York: Cambridge University Press.

Attili, G., Vermigli, P., & Schneider, B. H. (1997). Peer acceptance and friendship patterns among Italian schoolchildren within a cross-cultural perspective. *International Journal of Behavioral Development, 21*, 277–288.

Azmitia, M., & Cooper, C. R. (2004). Good or Bad? Peer influences on Latino and European American adolescents' pathways through school. *Journal of Education for Students Placed at Risk, 6*, 45–71.

Benenson, J. F., Apostoleris, N. H., & Parnass, J. (1997). Age and sex differences in dyadic and group interaction. *Developmental Psychology, 33*, 538–543.

Berry, J. W., Phinney, J. S., Sam, D. L., & Vedder, P. (2006). *Immigrant youth in cultural transition: Acculturation, identity, and adaptation across national contexts*. Mahwah, NJ: Erlbaum.

Berndt, T. J. (2002). Friendship quality and social development. *Current Directions in Psychological Science, 11*, 7–10.

Brown, B. B. (1990). Peer groups and peer cultures. In S. S. Feldman & G. R. Elliott (Eds.), *At the threshold: The developing adolescent* (pp. 171–196). Cambridge, MA: Harvard University Press.

Brown, B. B., & Klute, C. (2003). Friendships, cliques, and crowds. In G. R. Adams & M. D. Berzonsky (Eds.), *Blackwell handbook of adolescence* (pp. 330–348). Malden, MA: USishers.

Cairns, R. B., & Cairns, B. D. (1994). *Lifelines and risks: Pathways of youth in our time*. New York: Cambridge University Press.

Casiglia, A. C., Lo Coco, A., & Zappulla, C. (1998). Aspects of social reputation and peer relationships in Italian children: A cross-cultural perspective. *Developmental Psychology, 34*, 723–730.

Chagnon, N. A. (1983). *Yanomamo: The fierce people*. New York: Holt, Rinehart and Winston.

Chen, X., Cen, G., Li, D., & He, Y. (2005a). Social functioning and adjustment in Chinese children: The imprint of historical time. *Child Development, 76*, 182–195.

Chen, X., Chang, L., & He, Y. (2003). The peer group as a context: Mediating and moderating effects on the relations between academic achievement and social functioning in Chinese children. *Child Development, 74*, 710–727.

Chen, X., Chang, L., He, Y., & Liu, H. (2005b). The peer group as a context: Moderating effects on relations between maternal parenting and social and school adjustment in Chinese children. *Child Development, 76*, 417–434.

Chen, X., Chang, L., Liu, H., & He, Y. (2008). Effects of the peer group on the development of social functioning and academic achievement: A longitudinal study in Chinese children. *Child Development, 79*, 235–251.

Chen, X., & Chen, H. (2010). Children's social functioning and adjustment in the changing Chinese society. In R. K. Silbereisen & X. Chen (Eds.), *Social change and human development: Concepts and results* (pp. 209–226). London, UK: Sage.

Chen, X., Chung, J., & Hsiao, C. (2009). Peer interactions, relationships and groups from a cross-cultural perspective. In K. H. Rubin, W. Bukowski, & B. Laursen (Eds.), *Handbook of Peer Interactions, Relationships, and Groups* (pp. 432–451). New York: Guilford.

Chen, X., DeSouza, A., Chen, H., & Wang, L. (2006a). Reticent behavior and experiences in peer interactions in Canadian and Chinese children. *Developmental Psychology, 42,* 656–665.

Chen, X. & French, D. (2008). Children's social competence in cultural context. *Annual Review of Psychology, 59,* 591–616.

Chen, X., He, Y., De Oliveira, A. M., Lo Coco, A., Zappulla, C., Kaspar, V. et al. (2004a). Loneliness and social adaptation in Brazilian, Canadian, Chinese and Italian children. *Journal of Child Psychology and Psychiatry, 45,* 1373–1384.

Chen, X., Kaspar, V., Zhang, Y., Wang. L., & Zheng, S. (2004b). Peer relationships among Chinese and North American boys: A cross-cultural perspective. In N. Way and J. Chu (Eds.), *Adolescent boys in context* (pp. 197–218). New York: New York University Press.

Chen, X., Li, D., Li, Z., Li, B., & Liu, M. (2000). Sociable and prosocial dimensions of social competence in Chinese children: Common and unique contributions to social, academic and psychological adjustment. *Developmental Psychology, 36,* 302–314.

Chen, X., Rubin, K. H., & Li, Z. (1995). Social functioning and adjustment in Chinese children: A longitudinal study. *Developmental Psychology, 31,* 531–539.

Chen, X. & Tse, H. C. (2008). Social functioning and adjustment in Canadian-born children with Chinese and European backgrounds. *Developmental Psychology, 44,* 1184–1189.

Chen, X., Wang, L., & DeSouza, A. (2006b). Temperament and socio-emotional functioning in Chinese and North American children. In X. Chen, D. French, & B. Schneider (Eds.), *Peer relationships in cultural context* (pp. 123–147). New York: Cambridge University Press.

Cillessen, A. H., van Ijzendoorn, H. W., van Lieshout, C. F., & Hartup, W. W. (1992). Heterogeneity among peer-rejected boys: Subtypes and stabilities. *Child Development, 63,* 893–905.

Cho, G. E., Sandel, T. L., Miller, P. J., & Wang, S. (2005). What do grandmothers think about self-esteem? American and Taiwanese folk theories revisited. *Social Development, 14,* 701–721.

Coie, J. D., Dodge, K. A., & Coppotelli, H. (1982). Dimensions and types of social status: A five-year longitudinal study. *Developmental Psychology, 18,* 557–570.

Coie, J. D., Terry, R., Lenox, K., Lochman, J., & Hyman, C. (1995). Childhood peer rejection and aggression as predictors of stable patterns of adolescent disorder. *Development and Psychopathology, 7,* 697–714.

Conzen, K. N., Gerber, D. A., Morawska, E., Pozzetta, G. E., & Vecoli, R. J. (1992). The invention of ethnicity: A perspective from the U.S.A. *Journal of American Ethnic History, 11,* 3–41.

Coplan, R. J. & Armer, M. (2007). A "multitude" of solitude: A closer look at social withdrawal and nonsocial play in early childhood. *Child Development Perspectives, 1,* 26–32.

Coplan, R. J., Prakash, K., O'Neil, K., & Armer, M. (2004). Do you 'want' to play? Distinguishing between conflicted-shyness and social disinterest in early childhood. *Developmental Psychology, 40,* 244–258.

Corsaro, W. A., & Nelson, E. (2003). Children's collective activities and peer culture in early literacy in American and Italian preschools. *Sociology of Education, 76,* 209–227.

Dayan, J., Doyle, A. B., & Markiewicz, D. (2001). Social support networks and self-esteem of idiocentric and allocentric children and adolescents. *Journal of Social and Personal Relations, 18*, 767–784.

Dekovic, M., Engels, R. C. M. E., Shirai, T., De Kort, G., & Anker, A. L. (2002). The role of peer relations in adolescent development in two cultures: The Netherlands and Japan. *Journal of Cross-Cultural Psychology, 33*, 577–595.

DeRosier, M. E., & Kupersmidt, J. B. (1991). Costa Rican children's perceptions of their social networks. *Developmental Psychology, 27*, 656–662.

DeRosier, M., Kupersmidt, J., & Patterson, C. (1994). Children's academic and behavioral adjustment as a function of the chronicity and proximity of peer rejection. *Child Development, 65*, 1799–1813.

D'Hondt, W., & Vandewiele, M. (1980). Adolescents' groups in Senegal. *Psychological Reports, 47*, 795–802.

Dishion, T. J., Nelson, S. E., & Bullock, B. M. (2004). Premature adolescent autonomy: Parent disengagement and deviant processes in the amplification of problem behavior. *Journal of Adolescence, 27*, 515–530.

Dodge, K. A., Greenberg, M. T., Malone, P. S., & Conduct Problems Prevention Research Group (2008). Testing an idealized dynamic cascade model of the development of serious violence in adolescence. *Child Development, 79*, 1907–1927.

Dodge, K. A., Petit, G. S., McClaskey, C. L., & Brown, M. (1986). Social competence in children. *Monographs of the Society for Research in Child Development, 51* (2, Serial No. 213).

Edwards, C. P. (2000). Children's play in cross-cultural perspective: A new look at the Six Culture Study. *Cross-Cultural Research, 34*, 318–338.

Edwards, C. P., Guzman, M. R. T., Brown, J., & Kumru, A. (2006). Children's social behaviors and peer interactions in diverse cultures. In X. Chen, D. French, & B. Schneider (Eds.), *Peer relationships in cultural context* (pp. 23–51). New York: Cambridge University Press.

Eisenberg, N., Pidada, S., & Liew, J. (2001). The relations of regulation and negative emotionality to Indonesian children's social functioning. *Child Development, 72*, 1747–1763.

Espelage, D. L., Holt, M. K., & Henkel, R. R. (2003). Examination of peer-group contextual effects on aggression during early adolescence. *Child Development, 74*, 205–220.

Farver, J. M., Kim, Y. K., & Lee, Y. (1995). Cultural differences in Korean- and Anglo-American preschoolers' social interaction and play behaviors. *Child Development, 66*, 1088–1099.

Farver, J. M., & Shin, Y. L. (1997). Social pretend play in Korea- and Anglo-American preschoolers. *Child Development, 68*, 544–556.

French, D. C., Jansen, E. A., Riansari, M., & Setiono, K. (2003). Friendships of Indonesian children: Adjustment of children who differ in friendship presence and similarity between mutual friends. *Social Development, 12*, 605–621.

French, D. C., Lee, O., & Pidada, S. (2006). Friendships of Indonesian, South Korean and United States youth: Exclusivity, intimacy, enhancement of worth, and conflict. In X. Chen, D. French, & B. Schneider (Eds.), *Peer relationships in cultural context* (pp. 379–402). New York: Cambridge University Press.

French, D. C., Pidada, S., & Victor, A. (2005). Friendships of Indonesian and United States youth. *International Journal of Behavioral Development, 29*, 304–313.

Fuligni, A. J. (1998). The adjustment of children from immigrant families. *Current Directions in Psychological Science, 7*, 99–103.

Gaskins, S. (2000). Children's daily activities in a Mayan village: A culturally grounded description. *Cross-Cultural Research, 34*, 375–389.

Gazelle, H., & Ladd, G. W. (2003). Anxious solitude and peer exclusion: A diathesis-stress model of internalizing trajectories in childhood. *Child Development, 74*, 257–278.

Gonzalez, Y., Moreno, D. S., & Schneider, B. H. (2004). Friendship expectations of early adolescents in Cuba and Canada. *Journal of Cross-Cultural Psychology, 35*, 436–445.

Goodnow, J. J. (1997). Parenting and the transmission and internalization of values: From social-cultural perspectives to within-family analyses. In J. E. Grusec & L. Kuczynski (Eds.), *Handbook of parnting and the transmission of values* (pp. 333–361). New York: Wiley.

Goodnow, J. J. (2011). Merging cultural and psychological accounts of family contexts. In L. A. Jensen (Ed.), *Bridging cultural and developmental psychology: New syntheses in theory, research and policy* (pp. 73–91). New York: Oxford University Press.

Gosso, Y., Lima, M. D., Morais, S. E., & Otta, E. (2007). Pretend play of Brazilian children: A window into different cutlural worlds. *Journal of Cross-Cultural Psychology, 38*, 539–558.

Harris, J. R. (1995). Where is the child's environment? A group socialization theory of development. *Psychological Review, 102*, 458–489.

Hart, C. H., Yang, C., Nelson, L. J., Robinson, C. C., Olson, J. A., Nelson, D. A. et al. (2000). Peer acceptance in early childhood and subtypes of socially withdrawn behaviour in China, Russia and the United States. *International Journal of Behavioral Development, 24*, 73–81.

Hartup, W. W. (1983). Peer relations. In P. H. Mussen (Ed.), *Handbook of child psychology: Vol. 4. Socialization, personality, and social development* (4th ed., pp. 103–196). New York: Wiley.

Hartup, W. W. (1992). Social relationships and their developmental significance. *American Psychologist, 44*, 120–126.

Hartup, W. W., & Stevens, N. (1999). Friendship and adaptation across the life span. *Current Directions in Psychological Science, 8*, 76–79.

Hinde, R. A. (1987). *Individuals, relationships and culture.* Cambridge: Cambridge University Press.

Hollnsteiner, M. R. (1979). Reciprocity as a Filipino in value. In M. R. Hollnsteiner (Ed.), *Culture and the Filipino* (pp. 38–43). Quezon City, Phillippines: Atteneo de Manila University.

Hwang, K. K. (1985). Face and favour: The Chinese power game. *American Journal of Sociology, 92*, 944–974.

Kiesner, J., Poulin, F., & Nicotra, E. (2003). Peer relations across contexts: Individual-network homophily and network inclusion in and after school. *Child Development, 74*, 1328–1343.

Kinderman, T. A., McCollom, T. L., & Gibson, E., Jr. (1995). Peer networks and students' classroom engagement during childhood and adolescence. In K. Wentzel & J. Juvonen (Eds.), *Social motivation: Understanding children's school adjustment.* New York: Cambridge University Press.

Ladd, G. W. (1990). Having friends, keeping friends, making friends, and being liked by peers in the classroom: Predictors of children's early school adjustment? *Child Development, 61*, 312–331.

Ladd, G. W., Kochenderfer, B. J., & Coleman, C. C. (1996). Friendship quality as a predictor of young children's each school adjustment. *Child Development, 68*, 1181–1367.

Ladd, G. W., & Troop-Gordon, W. (2003). The role of chronic peer difficulties in the development of children's psychological adjustment problems. *Child Development, 74*, 1344–1367.

Larson, R. W., & Verma, S. (1999). How children and adolescents spend time across the world: Work, play, and developmental opportunities. *Psychological Bulletin, 125*, 701–736.

LeVine, R. A., Dixon, S., LeVine, S., Richman, A., Leiderman, P. H., Keefer, C. H., & Brazelton, R. B. (1994). *Child care and culture: Lessons from Africa*. New York: Cambridge University Press.

Liang, S. (1987). *The outline of Chinese culture*. Shanghai Teachers' University Press, Shanghai, China: Xue Lin.

Little, T. D., Brendgen, M., Wanner, B., & Krappmann, L. (1999). Children's reciprocal perceptions of friendship quality in the sociocultural contexts of East and West Berlin. *International Journal of Behavioral Development, 23*, 63–89.

Liu, M., & Chen, X. (2003). Friendship networks and social, school and psychological adjustment in Chinese junior high school students. *Psychology in the Schools, 40*, 5–17.

Maccoby, E. E. (1998). *The two sexes: Growing up apart, coming together*. Cambridge, MA: Harvard University Press.

Masten, A. S., Coatsworth, J. D., Neemann, J., Gest, S. D., Tellegen, A., & Garmezy, N. (1995). The structure and coherence of competence from childhood through adolescence. *Child Development, 66*, 1635–1659.

Mead, G. H. (1934). *Mind, self, and society*. Chicago: University of Chicago Press.

Moreno, J. L. (1934). *Who shall survive? A new approach to the problem of human interrelations*. Washington, DC: Nervous and Mental Disease.

Nsamenang, A. B. (2011). The culturalization of developmental trajectories: A perspective on African childhoods and adolescences. In L. A. Jensen (Ed.), *Bridging cultural and developmental psychology: New syntheses in theory, research and policy* (pp. 235–254). New York: Oxford University Press.

Parmar, P., Harkness, S., & Super, C. M. (2004). Asian and Euro-American parents' ethnotheories of play and learning: Effects on preschool children's home routine and school behaviour. *International Journal of Behavioral Development, 28*, 97–104.

Piaget, J. (1932). *The moral judgment of the child*. Glencoe, IL: Free Press.

Rodkin, P. C., Farmer, T. W., Pearl, R., & van Acker, R. (2000). Heterogeneity of popular boys: Antisocial and prosocial configurations. *Developmental Psychology, 36*, 14–24.

Rogoff, B., Mistry, J., Goncu, A., &Mosier, C. (1993). Guided participation in cultural activity by toddlers and caregivers. *Monographs of the Society for Research in Child Development, 236*, 58(8).

Rothbaum, F., & Wang, Y. Z. (2011). Cultural and developmental pathways to acceptance of self and acceptance of the world. In L. A. Jensen (Ed.), *Bridging cultural and developmental psychology: New synthesis in theory, research and policy* (pp. 187–211). New York: Oxford University Press.

Rubin, K. H., Bukowski, W., & Parker, J. G. (2006). Peer interactions, relationships, and groups. In N. Eisenberg (Ed.), *Handbook of child psychology: Vol 3. Social, emotional, and personality development* (pp. 571–645). New York: Wiley.

Rubin, K. H., Chen, X., McDougall, P., Bowker, A., & McKinnon, J. (1995). The Waterloo longitudinal project: Predicting internalizing and externalizing problems in adolescence. *Development and Psychopathology, 7*, 751–764.

Rubin, K. H., Coplan, R., & Bowker, J. (2009). Social withdrawal in childhood. *Annual Review of Psychology, 60*, 141–171.

Salmivalli, C., Huttunen, A., & Lagerspetz, K. (1997). Peer networks and bullying in schools. *Scandinavian Journal of Psychology, 38*, 305–312.

Sharabany, R. (2006). The cultural context of children and adolescents: Peer relationships and intimate friendships among Arab and Jewish children in Israel. In X. Chen, D. French, & B. Schneider (Eds.), *Peer relationships in cultural context* (pp. 452–478). New York: Cambridge University Press.

Sharabany, R., & Wiseman, H. (1993). Close relationships in adolescence: The case of the Kibbutz. *Journal of Youth and Adolescence, 22*, 671–695.

Schneider, B., H., & Fonzi, A. (1996). La stabilita dell'amicizia: Unostudio cross-culturale Italia-Canada [Friendship stability: A cross-cultural study in Italy-Canada]. *Eta Evolutiva, 3*, 73–79.

Sim, T. N., & Koh, S. F. (2003). Domain conceptualization of adolescent susceptibility to peer pressure. *Journal of Research on Adolescence, 13*, 58–80.

Smetana, J. (2002). Culture, autonomy, and personal jurisdiction. In R. Kail & H. Reese (Eds.), *Advances in child development and behavior* (Vol. 29, pp. 52–87). New York: Academic Press.

Smart, A. (1999). Expressions of interest: Friendship and *guanxi* in Chinese societies. In S. Bell & S. Coleman (Eds.), *The anthropology of friendship* (pp. 119–136). Oxford, UK: Berg.

Stevenson, H. W. (1991). The development of prosocial behavior in large-scale collective societies: China and Japan. In R. A. Hinde & J. Groebel (Eds.), *Cooperation and prosocial behaviour* (pp. 89–105). Cambridge, UK: Cambridge University Press.

Stevenson, H. W., Lee, S., Chen, C., Stigler, J. W., Hsu, C., & Kitamura, S. (1990). Contexts of achievement. *Monographs of the Society for Research in Child Development, 55*, (Serial n. 221).

Sullivan, H. S. (1953). *The interpersonal theory of psychiatry.* New York: Norton.

Sun, S. L. (1995). *The development of social networks among Chinese children in Taiwan.* Unpublished doctoral dissertation. University of North Carolina at Chapel Hill.

Super, C. M., & Harkness, S. (1986). The developmental niche: A conceptualization at the interface of child and culture. *International Journal of Behavioral Development, 9*, 545–569.

Tamis-LeMonda, C. S., Way, N., Hughes, D., Yoshikawa, H., Kalman, R. K., & Niwa, E. (2008). Parents' goals for children: The dynamic co-existence of collectivism and individualism in cultures and individuals. *Social Development, 17*, 183–209.

Tieszen, H. R. (1979). Children's social behavior in a Korean preschool. *Journal of Korean Home Economics Association, 17*, 71–84.

Tietjen, A. (1989). The ecology of children's social support networks. In D. Belle (Ed.), *Children's social networks and social support* (pp. 37–69). New York: Wiley.

Triandis, H. C. (1995). *Individualism and collectivism.* Boulder, CO: Westview Press.

Vygotsky, L. S. (1978). M. Cole, V. John-Steiner, S. Scribner & E. Souberman (Eds.), *Mind in society: The development of higher psychological processes.* Cambridge, MA: Harvard University Press.

Way, N. (2006). The cultural practice of close friendships among urban adolescents in the United States. In X. Chen, D. French, & B. Schneider (Eds.), *Peer relationships in cultural context* (pp. 403–425). New York: Cambridge University Press.

Wentzel, K. R. (2003). Sociometric status and adjustment in middle school: A longitudinal study. *Journal of Adolescent Research, 15*, 274–301.

Whiting, B. B., & Edwards, C. P. (1988). *Children of different worlds.* Cambridge: Harvard University Press.

Xu, Y., Farver, J., M., Chang, L., Zhang, Z., & Yu, L. (2007). Moving away or fitting in? Understanding shyness in Chinese children. *Merrill-Palmer Quarterly, 53*, 527–556.

Young, H. B., & Ferguson, L. R. (1981). *Puberty to manhood in Italy and America.* New York: Academic Press.

Yu, R. (2002). On the reform of elementary school education in China. *Educational Exploration, 129*, 56–57.

CHAPTER 6

Civil Societies as Cultural and Developmental Contexts for Civic Identity Formation

CONSTANCE FLANAGAN,
M. LORETO MARTÍNEZ, & PATRICIO CUMSILLE

Attention to Civil Societies as developmental contexts has been rare in developmental and cultural psychology as well as in political science. In this chapter, we draw from these three disciplines and argue that bridging paradigms are necessary to understand civil societies as developmental contexts where the civic and political identities of younger generations are formed. By *Civil Society*, we refer to that sector that is neither the market nor the government but that, in its practices, stabilizes and challenges those sectors. This third sector (Civil Society) includes families, schools, and faith-based and community-based organizations. We refer to these as mediating institutions because they are spaces where the political and economic principles of a society are interpreted—reinforced, challenged, and renegotiated (*see also* Goodnow, 2011). Political stability and political change occur in concert with the activities and relationships in those settings. Our thesis calls for a broader conceptualization of the political domain beyond its narrow framing as the business of government.

With respect to bridging developmental and cultural psychology, we suggest the following premise: Societies are economic and political systems that remain stable because they also are thinking systems—that is, the citizens in them share a set of ideas, values, and beliefs that explain (even naturalize) the political and economic arrangements of their social order.[1] Beliefs that are shared by a group have been called social representations (Moscovici, 1988), collective representations (Durkheim, 1912, 1995), and widespread beliefs (Fraser & Gaskell, 1990). Whatever we call them, the point is that our shared ideas and beliefs serve to regulate, maintain, and legitimate the principles on which our political or economic system is based (Miller, 1984). Besides reducing uncertainty and allowing individuals to act, shared beliefs serve relational functions—cementing relationships, developing group identities, and fulfilling needs for belonging and security (Shweder, 1996). Tenets of our shared beliefs also are reinforced in everyday interactions, communications, and in the practices of society's institutions, including, perhaps especially, formative ones.

Routine practices have been a focus of cultural psychology, but it is noteworthy that in the literature on Civil Society, references also are made to habits, mores, and civic cultures. These are discussed as mechanisms whereby the principles of the political system become internalized in the thoughts, feelings, and attitudes of citizens (Almond & Verba, 1963; de Tocqueville, 1848, 1965). For example, during the military rule in Chile, student councils were banned as a way of preventing any kind of youth voice in social organization, ideas, or activities that might challenge the regime. Instead, the government mandated a weekly practice in all of the nation's schools in which the national anthem and other national symbols of "unity" and "allegiance" were reinforced. When popular elections reinstated democratic rule in 1990, this practice was discontinued as values of freedom and human rights became central for citizenship.

Our point is twofold. First, through the repeated enactment of words, symbols, and activities, the political and economic system is stabilized. Second, despite these "stabilizing" practices in the institutions of Civil Society, political change happens and practices in mediating institutions play a part in this change as well. Through routine practices, affective or emotional feelings for the polity develop. As others have noted, children's understanding of political systems, societal institutions, or groups is often emotionally "hot," their affective regard often preceding factual knowledge and providing a frame for interpreting those "facts" (*see* edited volume by Barrett & Buchanan-Barrow, 2005). In their discussions of how "diffuse support" for the system develops in children, theorists in the early political socialization tradition made an important distinction between trust in the system and trust in particular incumbents in power: "*Every society introduces its members to the political system very early in the life cycle. To the extent that the maturing members absorb and become attached to the overarching goals of the system and its basic norms and come to approve of its structure of authority as legitimate, we can say that they are learning to contribute support to the regime*" (Easton & Dennis, 1967, p. 25, Italics added).

Further, we contend that children's experiences and, consequently, their interpretation of the policies and principles of their social order, vary according to the groups (gender, social class, caste, ethnicity) to which the children and their families belong. Here we draw from the notion of "selfways" in cultural psychology—that is, relationships and interactions in everyday contexts that form the contours of our lives and, through accumulated enactments, are the bases of our identities (Markus, Mullally, & Kitayama 1997). Because our focus is Civil Society, we have coined the term *groupways* to emphasize that children's lay theories about the political and economic system are refracted through lenses of the social class, caste, racial/ethnic, religious, and gender groups to which they belong. Thus, their political theories are likely to vary according to the way the tenets of their particular political and economic system play out for people "like them" (Flanagan & Campbell, 2003) and the "groupways" in which those tenets are enacted.

Several examples illustrate what we mean by "groupways." First, on the whole, contemporary Chilean youth are cynical about politicians, feeling that most do not represent the interests of youth. However, this sentiment is qualitatively different, as expressed by the most disadvantaged young people who feel that they and their group are marginalized not only by politicians but from society and its institutions. This feeling of social exclusion motivates some to want to destroy the social order (Martínez & Cumsille, 2009). Second, our concept of groupways is illustrated in research in Catalonia and the Basque Country, which shows consistent relationships between the language families speak at home and the personal importance that children as young as six years of age ascribe to particular national identities (Barrett, 2007).

Third, the concept of "groupways" also points to structural inequities in opportunities for civic identity formation. Activities such as student council or volunteer work can be thought of as mediational means or cultural tools (Vygotsky, 1978; Wertsch, 1995). Yet, according to work in the United States, such cultural tools for civic identity formation are unevenly distributed based on the social class and racial groups to which the youth belong (Kahne & Middaugh, 2009). Drawing from Erikson, the point is that youth from different social class or ethnic backgrounds will imagine and enact possible political selves based on "*ideological alternatives vitally related to the existing range of alternatives for identity formation*" (Erikson, 1968, p. 190, italics added). These alternatives also may vary according to the economic status and political latitude that an ethnic group enjoys in their local community. For example, Sanchez-Jankowski (1992) found that the range of political alternatives that Chicano parents in the United States framed for their children depended on the family's class position and the Chicano group's position in the larger community. In the ethnically stratified economy of San Antonio, lower-class parents worried that they would lose jobs and middle-class parents that opportunities for advancement would be blocked if teens engaged in political action. In the more dynamic Los Angeles economy, some lower -class parents discouraged activism, but others, frustrated by economic immobility, encouraged their children to make whatever political choices made the most sense to them.

Our concept of groupways also is illustrated in Barber's (2008) comparisons of the meaning associated with youths' political activism and identity formation in Bosnia and Palestine. Although the ethnic identity of each group figured centrally in the violence and oppression they experienced, the historical and intergenerational contexts were radically different. The experiences of the Palestinian youth were framed within the oral histories of their people passed down from parents and grandparents. This helped to clarify their identity and give meaning to their actions to advance the struggle of their people. In contrast, the Bosnian youth learned about their identities as Muslims through sudden attacks from Serbian people who had been their neighbors and friends. These youth lacked an intergenerational narrative that could bolster feelings of solidarity and motivate political action on behalf of their people. Instead, they experienced a collective identity as victims.

Finally, we discuss the construction of a sense of collective identity and of intergenerational and peer relations in the formation of this identity as a foundation for political stability and political change (*see also* Chen, 2011). Here we argue that through (both intergenerational and peer) relationships and activities in the institutions of Civil Society, youth construct a collective identity that is essential to sustaining Civil Society. That collective identity may correspond to or contest the political order. Thus, as younger generations come of age, collectively their actions contribute to political stability and political change.

Citizens and Nation-States: Prerogatives and Obligations

Citizens in every nation are bound to their polity by some compact or bargain with the state in which the citizens agree to live by laws in exchange for the state insuring citizens' security and welfare. On the one hand, notions of duty and obligation and, on the other, prerogatives, entitlements, protections, or rights describe a common structure that binds citizens with their nation. Although the structure of a social compact is universal, the specific tenets vary for different polities—that is, the degree to which the government, the market, or individuals are responsible for managing risk; the degree to which resources are distributed based on principles of equity, equality, or need; or the degree to which cultural diversity is celebrated or outlawed in public institutions, and so forth.

Cultures differ in how they define the obligations of citizens. For example, responsibility may be construed by some as a choice or, by others, a duty. The duties of citizens may be enforced by laws, by habits, by normative pressures, or by a combination of these. In some nations, citizens are bound by law to vote or to serve in the armed forces. State policies such as the age of compulsory schooling or definitions of child abuse and neglect are just some examples of the ways in which states act to protect children's welfare and prescribe what parents can/should do.[1]

The construal of prerogatives, entitlements, and rights is likely to differ as well. Within a social citizenship framework in which citizens are entitled to the provision of state services to meet basic needs, health care is conceived as a basic right. But rights also can be understood as matters of self-determination—that is, a citizen's right to voice his/her views, beliefs, and identities and the spaces for such expressions. The scarf affairs in France and Turkey (in which Muslim women wore head scarves in public buildings) point to the boundaries between private and public expressions of religious identities. In both cases, individual expressions of cultural/religious identities were considered a challenge to the secular state and the institutional neutrality intended to emphasize a shared (republican) identity in the public square and the reservation of religious expression to private spaces.

Concepts of prerogatives, obligations, and the very meaning of citizenship are regularly being recast. For example, China's state project of "growing the economy" encourages citizens to be entrepreneurial, to consume, and to nurture the unique talents of children in contemporary one-child families. This framing of citizens' duties and prerogatives contradicts those at the height of the socialist era when a citizen's identity was melded to the collective and references to individualism, privacy, and separation of one's fate from that of others were discouraged (Anagnost, 2008). Younger generations often play a special role in redefining the meaning of citizenship because they view the political arrangements of their society with a fresh lens. In this regard, the current generation of late adolescents and young adults in Chile is a good political barometer for the nation's future because they grew up in a post-Pinochet era. Research with these youth suggests that they are challenging formal definitions of citizenship that they perceive as ignoring the people and advocating for values of social inclusion, human dignity, and equality (Martínez, Silva, & Hernández, under review). Their perceptions that the people don't count in political decision making is, in fact, an incisive reading of the state of affairs insofar as government policies are based largely on decisions of political party elites rather than on citizen's referenda (Silva & Silva, under review). Political change occurs, in part, when citizens challenge normative beliefs and their actions motivate a public discussion on the rights and duties of citizens. The "Penguin Revolution" is a case in point. In 2006, Chilean secondary students organized to protest the unequal, multitiered (public and private) system of education and the low quality of the public schools. Students from across the educational tiers and representing different social strata were organized in a common cause. With the aid of cultural tools such as cell phones and the Internet, young people led the way and raised public consciousness about the inequalities of a highly segregated educational system (Domedel & Pena y Lillo, 2008). Not only did they motivate a public discussion, the student movement was supported by vast sectors of Chilean society and inspired teachers, health workers, and other unions to support their demands.

Notwithstanding these examples of political contestation, young people typically construct their political theories based on the political arrangements to which they are accustomed. An example is provided in analyses of data from the International Association for the Evaluation of Educational Achievement (IEA). When asked to choose from a list the important qualities that define a strong democracy, adolescents in the United States chose protecting human rights but were less likely than peers in other nations to support a proactive role for government in controlling the economy or distributing income (Baldi et al., 2001). That view is consistent with the minimal role that the government plays in providing social welfare or oversight of the market in the United States when compared to many countries. In a similar vein, adolescents from countries with a recent history of socialism and with low gross national product (Bulgaria and Russia) were more likely than their peers from free market systems to feel that the government should be responsible for economic matters (Torney-Purta, Schwille, & Amadeo, 1999). Finally, within a national context of gender inequality (i.e., low representation of women in government, legislature, and power positions), Chilean adolescents scored lower than the international IEA sample in their support of political rights for women (Ministerio de Educación, 2003). Further illustrating the significance of groupways in civic identity formation, Chilean males were more likely to endorse men's over women's rights in the labor market and in electoral politics, including their rights to be elected to Congress, despite the fact that the president of Chile at the time, was a woman.

The various articles in the United Nations Convention on the Rights of the Child allude to the responsibilities of governments (and their surrogates) to and for children and youth. Children's rights include those to nurturance, care, and protection from harm as well as to self-determination. As cultural psychology would predict, the meaning that children apply to rights reflects, in part, the individualistic versus collectivistic value orientation of their society (Berry, Poortinga, Segall & Dasen, 2006). So, for example, Cherney and Shing's (2008) three-nation comparison of 12-year-olds showed that Swiss children were the strongest advocates of self-determination rights, whereas Chinese-Malaysian and U.S. children advocated for more nurturance rights. However, if we want to understand how groupways operate within societies and contribute to variation in social meanings, a more nuanced conceptualization of societies beyond the individualist–collectivist polarization is needed (Green, Deschamps, & Páez, 2005; Oyserman, Coon, & Kemmelmeier, 2002). So Cherney and Shing also reported that youths' interpretations of rights varied according to the religious traditions of their families: Within the Chinese-Malaysian sample, Buddhists advocated more for self-determination than did their Christian peers.

The Convention on the Rights of the Child uses the term *rights*. To convey a similar concept, the political theorist Michael Walzer uses the term *prerogatives* to refer broadly to the entitlements or privileges associated with civic membership. His definition of a citizen is one who is "*a member of a political community, entitled to whatever prerogatives, and encumbered with whatever responsibilities are attached to membership*" (Walzer, 1989, p. 211, italics not in original). But the meaning associated with rights or prerogatives is culturally distinct. Rights may suggest an image of rights-bearing individuals who stand up for what they believe in opposition to others' beliefs. But scholars have pointed out that rights also are exercised in societies with a more interdependent understanding of the self. In these contexts, individuals are not speaking up for their own self-interest but rather for the common good (Rosemont, 2004; Wong, 2004). Indeed, Wong (2004) contends that some Confucian texts hold that officials have a duty to assert their right to speak up in the interests of the common good. By exercising this right, people resolve disagreements about what constitutes the public good and thereby enable the peaceful transformation of their community.

From our point of view, the cultural distinction is not whether members of a polity have rights but how the reciprocity between rights and responsibilities is construed within cultures with a more interdependent versus independent conception of the self. In cultures that emphasize the autonomy and separation of individuals from one another, where an individual's right to free expression is celebrated, the presumption is that an individual exercises free speech by expressing his/her opinions and interests. Such action is a mark of self-determination and it is assumed that s/he chooses rationally—that is, in his or her own self-interest. There is no duty to speak up. A citizen is free to be quiet if s/he chooses and s/he has no obligation to raise his/her voice for the common good. However, the rights-bearing citizen does have a responsibility—to constrain any exercise of individual rights that infringes on the rights of fellow citizens.

Ultimately, people's conceptions of prerogatives and obligations or rights and responsibilities are rooted in their social relations (Vygotsky, 1978, 1981). Those meanings are enacted within mediating institutions with families at the core. Here, work by Cigdem Kagitcibasi (2007) is highly relevant because she has related concepts of individualism and collectivism at the societal level with those of separate and relational selves at the individual and family level. According to Kagitcibasi, societies vary on the degree to which they promote personal agency/autonomy AND interpersonal distance, and these two dimensions underlie conceptions of self and other as well as interactional patterns within families. We believe these intersecting dimensions have implications for how civic identities are enacted in different cultures. According to this view, the simultaneous promotion of agency and interdependence, as opposed to agency and independence, would promote autonomous citizens who expressed their autonomy in caring and socially responsible relationships. In contrast, the expression of autonomy and independence would be more reflective of the rational choice model of individual decision making (*see also* Phinney & Baldelomar, 2011).

Incorporating Younger Generations into the Polity: Political Roles of Mediating Institutions

Mediating institutions (families, schools, community-based organizations, youth wings of political parties) play an important role in maintaining political stability. The state oversees and often regulates the formative institutions of society in one form or another (teacher certification, funding of youth services). Thus, mediating institutions are a context where the state's authority is distributed—enacted and interpreted. In their policies and practices, mediating institutions configure the behavioral and imaginative options children can consider and inform their normative beliefs.

Community-based organizations (CBOs; Scouts, 4-H, Young Pioneers) are good examples of the role that mediating institutions play in the political incorporation of younger generations. Besides encouraging constructive pro-social norms, youth organizations also stabilize political systems either overtly, by emphasizing specific ideological commitments, or more subtly, by communicating an affinity with national values. The practices of these organizations emphasize those principles that the organization considers central to the development of citizenship and character. In general, youth organizations serve a socially integrative function, developing a sense of belonging and positive affect in the next generation for the group and the larger community. CBOs provide structure for free time, a prosocial peer reference group, and adult mentors who typically are volunteering their own time to a community organization. Whether one is a member of the Scouts, the Young Pioneers, or 4-H, there are common practices of CBOs such as camping, team-building, wearing uniforms, marching in parades, earning badges, pledging allegiance to the organization and the nation, singing the national anthem, and raising the organization's and the nation's flag, often side by side.

The mores and practices of these organizations coupled with the infrastructure of such groups makes them ideal for rallying large numbers of young people toward patriotic and political ends. Typically a national organization has a common model for the structure and content of their youth groups at the local level as well as a communication strategy and a hierarchy of chapters, officers, and decision makers for the organization. Thus, members of youth organizations can be rallied to patriotic ends when the nation needs them. For example, in the 1950s, during the height of the Cold War, the Young Pioneers and Comsomol organizations in Central and Eastern Europe played an overt political role, encouraging the patriotic proclivities of young Soviet citizens. In contrast, during the 1960s and 1970s, Young Pioneers were known primarily for camping and environmental projects. Similarly, during the two world wars, 4-H Club work was partially abandoned so that the energy of the members could be devoted to raising food for the war effort. Victory gardens became a way that 4-H members could do their part for the nation (Van Horn, Flanagan, & Thomson, 1998). In summary, the routine practices of CBOs are quite similar, even in very different polities. However, as Vygotsky argued, those actions are governed by the meanings we impose on them with language. Thus, language, or "talk" as Peggy Miller (1996) describes it, constitutes the meaning a culture ascribes to a practice. We contend that it is in the language that accompanies practices and the way we talk about them—and not just the practices themselves—that the principles of our political and economic order are enacted and interpreted.

What do we mean by distinguishing a practice from the talk and the meaning associated with that practice? We offer an example from a study of youth in six nations (Australia, Bulgaria, Czech Republic, Hungary, Sweden, and the United States), which differed in the state's provision of social welfare in the mid 1990s when these data were collected. The teens were asked for their views about household chores and allowances. Across countries, teens felt that children should do household chores. However, the rationale for this practice varied according to the dominant principles of economic organization in those societies—youth from nations with a strong social welfare contract felt that doing chores taught children responsibility for the group. In contrast, in the United States and Australia, individual responsibility was the dominant reason. In these two nations, pocket money was more closely linked to specific chores, suggesting that youth had adopted dominant notions of wage work. In fact, 10% of the American youth actually endorsed a piece work principle—that is, contending that children should be paid an allowance according to each job or task they did at home (Bowes, Flanagan, & Taylor, 1998).

Although we have focused on CBOs to exemplify the role of mediating institutions, schools, religious organizations, work, and media also serve this role. Barrett (2007) summarizes three common sets of practices that schools in any society use to impact children's identification with the dominant culture of their nation: through explicit (and typically positive) instruction about the nation; through the ethnocentric biases of curricula that reflect choices about which cultural narratives should dominate; and through the adoption into daily practices elements of the nation's civil culture. We have discussed how CBOs can be rallied for political ends. Similarly, Barrett notes how school systems have been used strategically to unite diverse populations joined together in the formation of new states—for example, in the post-colonial world or in the formation of the Soviet Union after World War II.

The choice of which mediating institutions to study might differ in different cultural contexts. As Larson and Verma (1999) show, for adolescents in non-industrial populations, labor and unstructured leisure (both done with or near family members) claim major portions of time, whereas in the post-industrial societies of East Asia, adolescents' time is taken up largely by school work.

Values and Politics

When the political scientist David Easton (1953) described politics as the "authoritative allocation of values," he was referring to the competition for and distribution of resources in a society and to disagreements about how to resolve those differences. Values, in this sense, meant things of value (goods, services, wealth). But the values circulating in society at particular periods—whether those of the political elite or simply those with currency at particular times—also inform decisions about the allocation of resources. In a similar vein, Verba and Orren (1985, p. 2) held that "values are instrumental in shaping the public policies that give practical effect to political belief." In short, the ways in which different societies allocate resources and hardships, the bases on which they distribute services (universal entitlements, need, etc.) and pay for those services (user fees, income, property, or value added taxes), and changes in those policies over time reflect the dominant values and beliefs circulating in particular societies at particular times. That said, there is variation in the political values held by people within any system and people; even young people view policies through the lens of their own beliefs and values. For example, surveys of youth in Bulgaria, Hungary, and the Czech Republic, when these nations were in the throes of change from command to market economies, showed that youths' concerns about the economic changes were logically consistent with their political ideologies. Those who held socialist values—that is, those who endorsed the social welfare role of the state—were concerned that economic disparities were growing in their society. In contrast, their peers who held more liberal values contended that it was natural for a society to have both rich and poor and that anyone could make a good living if they worked hard and applied themselves (Macek, Flanagan, Gallay, Kostron, Botcheva, & Csapo, 1998).

Hegemonic World Views and Values

We have already discussed the phenomenon of widely shared beliefs as a basis for political stability. Next we argue that the dominant or mainstream views in most political systems are hegemonic, and it is difficult for alternative views to gain currency. This does not imply that all youth will conform to the dominant views, only that it is difficult for alternative perspectives to gain a foothold. Although different world views co-exist in any society, some gain hegemony and emerge as the received or "objective" truth. And, even if there is breadth in the range of information available to us, it is likely that we filter that information to reinforce our own perspectives. If there is a human motivation to believe that the world is just (Lerner, 1982), we are likely to selectively choose pieces of information and arguments to rationalize why our particular social order and its institutions are just. For example, comparisons of adolescents in security (Bulgaria, Czech Republic, Hungary, Sweden) versus opportunity societies (Australia, United States) revealed that, consistent with the principles of their economic order, youth in the former (security) endorsed the government's role in providing safety nets for citizens, whereas those in the latter (opportunity) were more likely to endorse individual meritocracy and to say that relying on government aid undermined personal initiative. However, in the three countries whose economies were changing from command to market structures in the decade of the 1990s, youths' views of a just world also reflected their family's social status and the implications of a changing economic structure for members of their group, for people "like them." The contrasting views were apparent in youths' views about the role that schools should play in their society. Whereas students attending vocational schools, whose parents typically had not gone on to higher education, were more likely to say that schools should help students find jobs (as had been the practice during the communist era), those in the higher track schools (whose parents tended to be in professional positions) were more likely to endorse the role of schools in aiding individual student autonomy, feeling that practices such as disagreeing with teachers helped students to become better independent thinkers (Flanagan & Campbell, 2003).

Insofar as repeated interactions in the settings where we spend time reinforce rather than challenge our political views, we gain confidence that ours are the right (perhaps the only) views. And we gain courage in expressing them, as one study of German youth after reunification suggests. Boehnke and colleagues found that xenophobic attitudes were higher in the Eastern than in the Western part of Germany but that such attitudes were especially high among students in the lowest school track (Boehnke, Hagan, & Hefler, 1998). One likely interpretation is that anti-foreigner sentiments were reinforced by fellow students in a homogeneous context and that in contrast to the active efforts in west German schools to combat xenophobia, no similar curricula had been in place in the GDR.

To contest the status quo, people need an alternative vision of the way things could be. Perhaps it is not surprising then that leaders of movements for social change typically have been exposed to alternative world views that inform their revolutionary visions. For example, in interviews with South African Black leaders in local government and Civil Society organizations, those who had contested apartheid discussed how the opportunities they had to leave their villages and attend college (albeit in the inferior system that apartheid allowed them) meant that they met students from other remote villages, could access media and news from the outside, and could compare the apartheid society that they lived in with a better world that they could imagine (Ngomane & Flanagan, 2003). Today, technologies such as the Internet overcome geographical and political boundaries and enable exposure to a wide range of political perspectives. The fact that such exposure can threaten political stability is a reason that authoritarian regimes control the flow of information and news. However, the decentralized, international, and user-driven nature of the Internet limits the success of these efforts.

Political Change and Generational Replacement

During periods of stability, we rarely reflect on the terms of the social compact that binds citizens with the state because our assumptions about how the system works and what behaviors are rewarded are generally reinforced. However, during times of change, our assumptions and behaviors may be out of sync with a changing reality. Research on the implications of German reunification for youth in the former GDR is illustrative. Despite the shared German language and culture, the political systems—the social contracts, if you will—of the two Germanies prior to reunification had very different implications for youth coming of age during this political transition. As in the other nations of the former Soviet bloc, centralized planning by the state and the links set up between schools and industries meant a relatively smooth and predictable transition from school to work. There was clarity but little variability in life paths. In contrast, the free market policies of a united Germany made it more incumbent on individuals to chart their futures and to identify paths to realize them. Individual psychological resources proved important for youths' capacities to negotiate the change. Specifically, feelings of personal efficacy prior to unification predicted young people's adaptation to the new system (Pinquart, Silbereisen, & Juang, 2004).

The role of older generations in political socialization is diminished in times of rapid social change. The world views and practices that worked in the old system are likely to be less valid in the new. Thus, in the countries of East Central Europe, behaviors that were functional in a socialist system when parents were young are poor guides for their children, as they negotiate the rules of a capitalist system. The rules of the system and the concepts one needs to function differ. For example, in a study comparing the economic concepts of Russian parents with their 11- to 14-year-old children, Fenko (2000, cited in Webley, 2005) found that the parents who had grown up in Russia's centrally planned economy had a poorer understanding of profit and its relevance for business when compared to their children who had come of age as Russia's market economy was forming. At the same time it must be said that parents also accommodate their practices to fit changing economic and political realities. Contemporary China is a case in point. The state's goal of "growing the economy" includes growing a middle class of parents who are encouraged to identify, nurture, and extract their child's latent potential. China's success in the global market has resulted in a middle class that invests, financially and psychologically, in early identification and intense nurturing of the skills and talents of their children (Anagnost, 2008). Notably, social class differences in lifestyles and parenting practices are flourishing and inequality is growing, despite the egalitarian ideology of communism and the "collective" values of Chinese culture.

Younger Generations' Roles in Political Change

Shared belief systems are powerful influences in a culture. Nonetheless, young people do not carbon copy a set of beliefs handed down to them by an older generation. Belief systems are resources from which individuals draw, but ultimately individuals construct their own views (Lightfoot & Valsiner, 1992). As Erikson (1968) noted, youth take an active role in re-interpreting, in the context of the historical era when they come of age, various tenets of the dominant ideologies of their societies: "youth can offer its loyalties and energies both to the conservation of that which continues to feel true and to the correction of that which has lost its regenerative significance" (p. 134).

Collectively, as younger generations assume their place as adult citizens, they are a force for political change. To explain why, generational replacement theorists have contrasted the period of youth with that of older adults (Delli Carpini, 2005). Drawing from Mannheim, generational theorists contend that young people should be more likely than their elders to contribute to political change because they have not yet settled into social roles or assumed adult responsibilities. Consequently, they have more freedom to explore different political perspectives. Typically youth are less committed than older adults to roles that constrain the futures they envision (Arnett, 2004). They also are more intellectually and psychologically flexible and more socially mobile. Thus, compared to their elders, it is easier for them to accommodate as well as contribute to social change. Because they are at the brink of adulthood, it also is more incumbent on them to consider what they are going to do in life. So it is not surprising that youth, more than their elders, are disproportionately represented in movements for social change. That said, politics is about power, and young people, as a group, typically hold little of it. Social institutions are designed by adults, and once established, they tend to self perpetuate (Rappaport, 1981). We have already discussed the Penguin Revolution in Chile as a social movement led by youth that rallied other sectors of society. In the end, however, the Penguin Revolution was co-opted by political parties, and the student leaders were integrated into government appointed committees to study school reforms. Ultimately, the legislation that resulted was a watered-down version of the original vision and fell short of enacting the changes promoted by the student movement.

The political issues that are salient when a generation comes of age shape the conditions of life as well as the conversations and debates in society at large. Opportunities for political action and, consequently, political identity formation vary at different historical moments and during periods of turmoil versus stability. If the period of one's youth intersects with a historical time of social discontinuity, it will likely increase within generation identification. According to Stewart and McDermott (2004), different forms of political engagement (e.g., conventional vs. protest politics) and the amount of political continuity or change they portend are shaped by different generations' relative tendency to identify horizontally (with peers) or vertically with their parents' generation. The political activities of several recent generations of Black South Africans provide a good case study. During the apartheid era in South Africa, the names of generations of Black youth reflected the political roles they played in the struggle against apartheid: Black Consciousness and Young Lions. In contrast, in the post-democracy generation, those who self-identified as political activists were more likely than their peers who did not to be active in local indigenous, religious, and community-based grassroots groups (Ngomane, 2004). The significance of indigenous roots also played out in the 2009 presidential election of Jacob Zuma, who celebrated his Zulu heritage and lifestyle during the campaign.

Parents' roles tend to be undertheorized in social movement literature. Yet intergenerational relationships figure in youths' decisions to be politically active. For example, in the struggle against apartheid, older generations of Black leaders said that their parents' struggles with grinding poverty were a major motivation for their activism (Ngomane & Flanagan, 2003). But when parents who were activists in their younger days advise their own children, they do so both as parents concerned about their children and in the political moment when their children are coming of age. So, for example, Chilean youth report that their parents, even those who were active against the military dictatorship in the 1980s, discourage their political activism in the new millennium. Young people were highly active in bringing down the military dictatorship in Chile, but contemporary Chilean youth tend to be disaffected from conventional politics (Martínez & Cumsille, 2010).

Civic Identity Is a Collective Identity

Citizenship is a collective identity. To develop that identity, younger citizens need opportunities to bond with others, to work collaboratively toward common ends, to appreciate how their interests are shared with others, and to understand that civic goals are achieved through collective action. According to social psychology, when individuals identify with a group, they are more willing to forego personal gain to enhance the collective good (Brewer & Gardner, 1996). Participation in civic/political activity (whether voting, donating to charity or doing community work, paying taxes, or doing national or military service) involves some personal sacrifice of time, money, resources, and self-gratifications in the interests of a larger common good. Thus, one of the purposes of formative institutions is to develop in younger generations a sense of connectedness to the group and the motivations and habits of pitching in for the benefit of the whole. According to longitudinal work, middle- and high-school students' feelings of solidarity with fellow students and of pride in membership in their school boosts the youths' social trust or faith in humanity, a belief that is highly related to pitching in for the common good (Flanagan & Stout, in press).

It may be more seamless to achieve this ethic of social responsibility in cultures where a relational self is modal, where interdependence rather than independence is the norm, and where the distinction between oneself and others is not so ardently emphasized in childrearing as it is in contexts where an independent construal of the self is customary (Kagitcibasi, 2007; Markus & Kitayama, 1991). Cultural practices may build into different stages of the life-course ways of forging interdependence, including gradually extending the community of "others" for whom one is responsible (Durham, 2008). In contrast, in cultures that emphasize an independent self, more pro-active and conscious efforts to connect personal rewards with actions to benefit the common good may be required. For example, motivational psychologists contend that sustaining the commitments of American volunteers to community or human service projects depends on the extent to which the activities and goals of the volunteer project match the motivational goals of the volunteer (Snyder, 2009). But motivation and civic commitment may be mutually reinforcing over time as youth engage—for example, in service projects with perceived benefits both to themselves and to others (Martínez, Silva, & Hernández, under review). Longitudinal research with youth activists in the United States suggests that a developmental transformation from self-centered to collectivist goals occurs for those youth who stick with the activist projects (Kirshner, 2009; Pearce & Larson, 2006).

Clearly there are cultural differences in the traditions and practices that achieve a sense of collective identity. But we would argue for the universal importance of achieving a collective identity in younger generations if Civil Society institutions are to be sustained. Further, we would argue that peers and adult authorities each have special roles in this process. An excellent example of the roles of youth and of adults in incorporating younger generations into the body politic is provided by Durham (2008) based on her field work in Botswana. In community gatherings, everyone is expected to listen to fellow members of the community, and the eldest members, who speak last, are expected to integrate the many voices of the community into a sense of "We": "They listen to the speeches of all the others, and then, when the time is right, they speak, referring to others' points, considering all the angles, and relating these to 'our customs' before forming and presenting their own understanding" (Durham, 2008, p. 171). Durham explains that in a culture where a person's life is organized around increasing interdependencies, youth is a period of building up a wide range of relationships, through peer groups (formal ones such as the Herero Youth Association and nonformal gatherings such as practicing traditional songs together) and adult–youth relationships (performing labor for a wide range of households). By participating in these "groupways," Botswanan youth build relationships and become integral members of their community.

A sense of the collective "WE" is not a static category, as research on immigrants attests. In the very process of immigrating, groups are faced with issues of group belonging and loyalty. As they bridge their sending and receiving cultures, immigrants find new ways to define the collective "WE" and to get engaged in the civic fray (Jensen, 2008, in press; Jensen, Arnett, & McKenzie, in press; Jensen & Flanagan, 2008). In the United States, Latino organizing for the Development, Relief and Education for Alien Minors (DREAM) Act and against exclusionary referenda in California united documented and undocumented immigrants in a common cause and identity (Bedolla, 2000; Seif, in press). Even group stereotypes can be a means through which youth develop a collective, sometimes political consciousness. For example, Arab-American adolescents, who were cognizant of media images of their ethnic group as an "enemy" of America well before 9/11, were less likely than their co-ethnic peers (who were not as sensitive to this image) to believe that the government in the United States was responsive to all people and were more likely to interpret personal experiences of prejudice as acts of intolerance against their group (Wray-Lake, Syvertsen, & Flanagan, 2008). Collective identities can develop within same-age (peer) relationships or in cross-age intergenerational relationships. Next we discuss the mechanisms whereby each plays a role in civic identity formation.

Peer Relations

Aristotle accorded a political role to friendship when he said that friends "hold states together." Because of their relatively equal status, peers may play a special role in a democratic social order. When youth are working collaboratively on a group project, what are the activities in which they engage? They negotiate what they will do and how as well as who will lead, represent, or coordinate. They argue over group goals and how best to achieve them. They hold one another accountable and criticize one another for failing to carry a fair share of the group's responsibility. The wrangling and work that peers do in common, assuming young people feel rewarded socially by it, also shape the civic dispositions of participants (to trust others and to pitch in). By working on group projects with peers, youth also develop a sense of collective efficacy. To be disposed to collective (civic) action, people need to feel that they can accomplish group goals by collaborating with others.

Peer relations should play a bigger role in civic identify formation in societies with greater age segregation. In contrast, in societies where younger and older generations spend more time together, the older generation might have a stronger influence on the political socialization of the younger with the potential for more intergenerational continuity in political beliefs and values (*see* Schlegel, 2011). That said, we should not assume that the direction of political influence is always from the older to the younger generation. Regular contact between younger and older generations opens the door for young people to introduce new ideas into the values, beliefs, and behaviors of the older generation. Of course, this presumes that the younger generation has first been exposed to new ideas in extra-familial contexts. But research has shown that even children who are too young to vote can influence their parents via engaging in political discussions and even affecting their parents' voting behaviors (McDevitt & Chaffee, 2000; Simon & Merrill, 1998).

Youths' Relationships With Adult Authorities in Mediating Institutions

If peers play a role in developing a sense of "WE," the political significance of nonfamilial adults may be more in the negotiation of authority, rights, and decision making. The state or government is both abstract and distal from youths' experiences. But there are adults with whom youth interact everyday who, in one way or another, embody the authority of the state (i.e., public school teachers and administrators, police). A young person's sense of membership in the polity and his or her beliefs that his or her views matter in that polity are shaped in part by experiences with adult authorities in local community institutions. Messages of inclusion and membership (who belongs, to whom do authorities attend in a serious way) are communicated in children's proximate interactions with those who wield power over their lives and suggest to the young person the status s/he and his or her group enjoy in the broader society.

The significance of proximate authorities in the development of a sense of political efficacy is underscored in Bandura's (1997, p. 491) discussion of collective efficacy:

> ". . . children's beliefs about their capabilities to influence governmental functioning may also be partially generalized from their experiences in trying to influence adults in educational and in other institutional settings with which they must deal."

His thesis is illustrated in one study of U.S. adolescents from different ethnic backgrounds, which found that students' perceptions that their teachers create a civil climate for learning (treat all students fairly, regardless of their background) were positively and significantly related to youths' beliefs in the principles of equal opportunity in America (that regardless of their background, individuals have an equal chance to succeed in America). This correlation between students' perceptions that teachers enact fair practices and that America is a fair society was especially strong for ethnic minorities (Flanagan, Cumsille, Gill, & Gallay, 2007).

At the same time, even when people have little faith in their government, relationships of trust and confidence built up through interactions with others at the grass roots level may stabilize polities. For example, Torney-Purta, Barber, and Richardson (2004) contend that in unstable or corrupt political regimes, face-to-face interactions with authorities at school may be a more solid basis for young people's development of trust in authorities than is trust in the authority of government. Thus, it may not be necessary to have demo-cratic government at the state level in order to have democratic institutions and relationships at the local community level. In summary, we are arguing for universal ends—that is, achieving feelings of membership and group identifi-cation—but for diversity of practices and of mediating institutions that achieve these ends in particular polities, at particular times, and for particular groups.

Community-Based Organizations as "Free Spaces"

We have already made the case that mediating institutions stabilize polities and develop allegiance for the system in younger generations. But if the principles of a social order are not merely reproduced but reconstructed and reinterpreted over time, then mediating institutions also contribute to political change.

Historically, in many different countries, non-government organizations, the institutions of Civil Society, have provided free spaces where citizens can debate and contest the status quo, imagine other political possibilities, and sometimes change the political system. Faith-based organizations have repeat-edly served such a role—promoting change on the left and the right of the political spectrum. For example, in the United States, religious leaders and organizations were instrumental in the abolitionist and Civil Rights Move-ments. In Poland, the Catholic Church joined Solidarity and the trade union movement in challenging the communist state. Notably, in the decade of the 1990s, the Catholic Church in Poland lost membership as its role in political change was outdated. Environmental organizations in Eastern Europe prior to 1989 are another good example. Although small, these groups contested the state's failure to protect the public welfare by failing to regulate and clean up industrial pollution in the air and rivers. In so doing, these groups raised for the average citizen questions about the terms of the social compact and whether the state was living up to its side of the bargain.

Each of these is an example of the role that non-government (Civil Society) organizations play in holding government accountable to provide for the welfare of the people and in providing free spaces where citizens can meet and act in concert. As the state responds, the roles of these non-governmental organizations (NGOs) and the young people who are members and leaders of these groups accommodate. For example, Un Techo para Chile is a not–for-profit youth-led organization that develops housing and social habilitation programs (microfinance, education) for the very poor in Chile. The vision and direct action of this NGO have engaged the interest and the time of young people, and consequently, the organization has grown exponentially both in membership and in international recognition. The success of this initiative has transcended political and national boundaries, as the program has been adopted in other Latin American countries that have followed the philosophy behind the initiative. Currently, the program is being implemented in 14 countries, organized in a network across Latin America (http://www.untechoparamipais.org/). Like many direct volunteer efforts, Un Techo Para Mi País provides young people with an opportunity to collaborate in a group project and to see the immediate benefits of their work for people who need housing. The sense of collective political efficacy can be greater in such work in contrast to volunteering for electoral politics where the impact of one's efforts are distal with less evidence of direct control. Nonetheless, savvy politicians are aware both of the political appeal of groups such as Un Techo para Chile and of the political and organizational skills that their leaders develop, as was evident in the appointments in 2009 of two of Un Techo para Chile's leaders to the presidential campaigns of competing candidates.

Similar Practices: Different Meanings for Sub-Groups of Youth

Community institutions mediate the relationship between individuals and the state. Those institutions can empower some youth while marginalizing or even oppressing others. For example, all youth may not get the message from teachers, police, or government that "they belong"—that "their views count." Thus, relationships and experiences in mediating institutions can be bases for developing feelings of cynicism or disaffection from the polity. For example, adolescents in the United States hold the police in lower esteem than do adults, but Black adolescents hold the police in lower esteem than do Latino, Native American, and White adolescents, in that order (Ceci, Markle, & Chae, 2005). Similarly, in a recent study of American youth, Gimpel and Pearson-Merkowitz (2009) found that compared to White youth, Latino and Black youth reported significantly lower feelings of political efficacy—that is, their capacities to affect the government. Some of this cynicism was anchored in their perceptions that the government neglected basic services such as street maintenance, trash collection, and snow removal in their communities. In short, these youth were developing a political consciousness that the government had not fulfilled the terms of the social contract in their communities.

A second way that the practices of mediating institutions may fail in political incorporation is in the case of a mismatch between a group's actions and experiences in a local institution and how that group is treated by the state;

in other words, the groups to which one bonds and with which one identifies may not identify with the polity or be treated like they count as members of the polity. Countless examples of ethnic minority groups come to mind, but the best may be that of ethnic Turks in Germany. Despite the fact that they have, for generations, lived, attended school, worked, and spoken the German language, they have been prohibited by law from becoming German citizens. Their everyday routines reflect more German than Turkish mores, but their collective identity as "WE" Turks in Germany does not map onto membership in the larger nation-state. So, even if the practices of mediating institutions reinforce a sense of affection and belonging to the local group and provide opportunities to have a voice, those experiences may not transfer to the polity. In an early essay, Easton (1975) made this distinction with respect to the object to which diffuse support was directed:

> "Diffuse support for the political authorities or regime will typically express itself in the form of trust or confidence in them. But for the political community the same kind of diffuse attitudes may appear as a sense of we-feeling, common consciousness or group identification" (p. 447).

Finally, Wertsch (1998) has shown that children respond in various ways to dominant historical narratives about their nation. Some embrace and identify with those narratives. Others actively resist, and still others learn the dominant narratives as "official history" but also learn unofficial accounts from their families and adopt these alternative narratives.

A Final Caveat

In the context of globalization, neither Civil Societies nor nation states are as self-contained as they once were. Supranational entities (the European Union, the World Trade Organization, the G-8, the World Bank) have resulted in a demise in the power of individual nations, especially in the developing world (Kassimir & Flanagan, in press). The fact that terms like *global citizen* and *stateless citizen* are now part of our lexicon alludes to the implications of these new realities for the meaning of citizenship. New inequalities associated with globalization also are captured in the dual meaning of "stateless citizens." The first connotation is a citizen who needs no state—the professional, fluent in many languages, able to find work in any nation, and protected by the state of his/her birth. The second is the migrant worker from the developing world who leaves the nation of his or her birth in search of work. Because both s/he and his or her sending nation are poor and lack power and because s/he has no civic status (often in fact an illegal or undocumented status) in the receiving nation, s/he is neither protected nor given rights in any state. These realities and new mediational means, such as the Internet, that transcend geographical borders and level the political playing field may transform the very meaning of politics and citizenship (Flanagan, 2008). In the end, the meaning of citizenship, whether global or confined to a state or ethnic group, has to be based on experiences of being part of a community or communities in which one can appreciate the links between one's own identity and future with that of others.

Conclusion

In their commentary on the extant body of work on children's understanding of society, Hatano and Takahashi (2005) wonder whether knowledge in this domain is privileged—that is, knowledge that human beings need to survive. They hypothesize that although the forms of organization in modern societies are relatively recent phenomena in human evolution, there are universal necessities of societal organization, including such things as resource distribution, division of labor, exchange, social status, which may be basic to the life of the human species. As in other domains, they consider this core part privileged, necessary for survival, and learned relatively early in life.

In this chapter we have argued that a social compact, a bargain of obligations and prerogatives that binds states and citizens, is such a universal necessity but that the specific tenets of this compact will vary. Further, we have suggested that there are common motivations underlying human development in the civic/political domain, including a sense of membership, solidarity, collective identity and of affective ties that fulfill the human need to belong.

Nations differ in their interpretations of the social compact and in their normative beliefs about what constitutes fair policy. Variability in children's societal cognition reflects such cross-national differences because policies affect the organization of everyday life and inform widespread normative beliefs. But differences in children's societal cognition also indicate ways that the terms of a society's social compact vary for different subgroups and the "groupways" in which those tenets are enacted.

To say that societal cognition is politically charged is to admit that politics concerns power, values, and policy decisions that affect groups and their members. Knowledge and understanding of this domain evolves from such experiences, and thus societal cognition is hot cognition, not emotionally, nor even morally neutral knowledge. Emotions impact our motivation to learn and our interpretation of 'the facts' in this domain.

Compared to their experience in and cognition about the natural world, children's understanding of Civil Society, institutions, government, and the economy is indirect and mediated. Mediating institutions where children spend time (families, schools, mass media, work, CBOs), their routine practices, and the interpretations of those practices through talk are universal means whereby younger generations are inculcated into the dominant narratives of their society and its institutions. Political and economic stability is generally maintained across generations because the practices of these institutions tend to reinforce dominant narratives and beliefs and children generally come to see the system they know as the one that is right and just. However, mediating institutions also are contexts where individuals, groups, and especially younger generations may question, contest, and reinterpret those narratives.

Acknowledgments

We thank Lene Arnett Jensen for very constructive editorial advice. We gratefully acknowledge the support provided by a Fulbright fellowship and the Escuela de Psicología at the Pontificia Universidad Católica de Chile awarded to Constance Flanagan, to the FONDECYT grant # 1085231 awarded to M. Loreto Martínez, and by a Resident Fellowship from the Spencer Foundation awarded to Constance Flanagan.

Note

1. State policies also reflect assumptions about developmental needs, competencies, and social roles, the length of childhood dependence, the duties of the state to provide for the needs of children and their preparation for adulthood, the culpability of children for their actions, etc. Consider the debates over the articles in the United Nations Convention on the Rights of the Child—on children's rights to protection and self determination and what they suggested about normative assumptions about developmental capacities.

References

Almond, G. A., & Verba, S. (1963). *The civic culture: Political attitudes and democracy in five nations.* Princeton, NJ: Princeton University Press.

Anagnost, A. (2008). Imagining global futures in China: The child as a sign of value. In J. Cole and D. Durham (eds.), *Figuring the Future: Globalization and the temporalities of children and youth* (pp. 49–72). Santa Fe, NM: School for Advanced Research Press.

Arnett, J. (2004). *Emerging Adulthood: The winding road from the late teens through the twenties.* New York: Oxford University Press.

Baldi, S., Perie, M., Skidmore, D., Greenberg, E., & Hahn, C. (2001). *What democracy means to ninth-graders: U.S. Results from the International IEA Civic Education Study.* Washington, DC: National Center for Educational Statistics, U.S. Department of Education.

Bandura, A. (1997). *Self-efficacy: The exercise of control.* New York: W.H. Freeman and Co.

Barber, B. K. (2008). Contrasting portraits of war: Youths' varied experiences with political violence in Bosnia and Palestine. *International Journal of Behavioral Development, 32*(4), 298–309.

Barrett, M. (2007). *Children's knowledge, beliefs, and feelings about nations and national groups.* East Sussex, UK: Psychology Press.

Barrett, M., & Buchanan-Barrow, E. (eds.). (2005). *Children's understanding of society.* East Sussex, UK: Psychology Press.

Bedolla, L. G. (2000). They and we: Identity, gender and politics among Latino youth in Los Angeles. *Social Science Quarterly, 81*, 106–122.

Berry, J. W., Poortinga, Y. H., Segall, M. H. & Dasen, P. R. (2006). Cross-*cultural psychology: Research and applications (2nd edition).* New York: Cambridge University Press.

Boehnke, K., Hagan, J., & Hefler, G. (1998). On the development of Xenophobia in Germany: The adolescent years. *Journal of Social Issues, 54*(3), 585–602.

Bowes, J. M., Flanagan, C., & Taylor, A. J. (2001). Adolescents' ideas about individual and social responsibility in relation to children's household work: Some international comparisons. *International Journal of Behavioral Development, 25*, 60–68.

Brewer, M. B., & Gardner, W. (1996). Who is this "We"? Levels of collective identity and self representations. *Journal of Personality and Social Psychology, 71*, 83–93.

Ceci, S. J., Markle, F. A, & Chae, Y. J. (2005). Children's understanding of the law and legal processes. In Barrett, M. & Buchanan-Barrow, E. (eds.), *Children's understanding of society* (pp. 105–134). East Sussex, UK: Psychology Press.

Chen, X. (2011). Culture, peer relationships, and human development. In L. A. Jensen (Ed.), *Bridging cultural and developmental psychology: New syntheses in theory, research and policy* (pp. 92–112). New York: Oxford University Press.

Cherney, I. D., & Shing, U. L. (2008). Children's nurturance and self-determinaiton rights: A cross-cultural perspective. *Journal of Social Issues, 64*(4), 835–856.

Delli Carpini, M. (2005). Generational Replacement. In L. Sherrod, C. A. Flanagan, R. Kassimir, & A. B. Syvertsen, (eds.), *Youth activism: An international encyclopedia* (pp. 282–284). Westport, CT: Greenwood Publishing.

Domedel, A. & Pena y Lillo, M. (2008). *El Mayo De Los Pinguinos.* Santiago, Chile: Editorial Universidad de Chile.

Durham, D. (2008). Apathy and agency: The romance of agency and youth in Botswana. In J. Cole & D. Durham, (eds.), *Figuring the future: Globalization and the temporalities of children and youth* (pp. 151–178). Santa Fe, NM: School for Advanced Research Press.

Durkheim, E. (1912/1995). *The elementary forms of the religious life.* Translated by Karen E. Fields. New York: The Free Press.

Easton, D. (1953). *The political system: An inquiry into the state of political science.* New York: Knopf.

Easton, D. (1975). A Re-Assessment of the concept of political support. *British Journal of Political Science, 5*(4), 435–457.

Erikson, E. H. (1968). *Identity: Youth and Crisis.* New York: W.W. Norton & Company.

Fenko, A. (2000). *Economic socialization in post-Soviet Russia.* Paper presented at the 27th International Congress of Psychology, Stockhom, July. Cited in Webley, 2004.

Flanagan, C. A. (2008). Private anxieties and public hopes: The perils and promise of youth in the context of globalization. In J. Cole & D. Durham, (Eds.), *Figuring the future: Globalization and the temporalities of children and youth* (pp. 125–150). Santa Fe, NM: School for Advanced Research Press.

Flanagan, C. A., & Campbell, B. (2003), with L. Botcheva, J. Bowes, B. Csapo, P. Macek, & E. Sheblanova. Social class and adolescents' beliefs about justice in different social orders. *Journal of Social Issues, 59*(4), 711–732.

Flanagan, C., Cumsille, P., Gill, S., & Gallay, L. (2007). School and community climates and civic commitments: Processes for ethnic minority and majority students. *Journal of Educational Psychology, 99*(2), 421–431.

Flanagan, C. A., & Stout, M. (in press). Developmental patterns of social trust between early and late adolescence: Age and school climate effects. *Journal of Research on Adolescence.*

Fraser, C. & Gaskell, G. (eds.), (1990). *The social psychological study of widespread beliefs.* New York, NY: Clarendon Press/Oxford University Press.

Gimpel, J., G., & Pearson-Merkowitz, S. (2009). Policies for civic engagement beyond the school yard. In J. Youniss & P. Levine, (eds.), *Engaging young people in civic life* (pp. 81–101). Nashville, TN: Vanderbilt University Press.

Goodnow, J. J. (2011). Merging cultural and psychological accounts of family contexts. In L. A. Jensen (Ed.), *Bridging cultural and developmental psychology: New syntheses in theory, research and policy* (pp. 73–91). New York: Oxford University Press.

Green, E., Deschamps, J. C. & Páez, D. (2005). Variations of individualism and collectivism within and between 20 countries: A typological analysis. *Journal of Cross-Cultural Psychology, 36*, 403–422.

Hatano, G., & Takahashi, K. (2005). The development of societal cognition: A commentary. In M. Barrett & E. Buchanan-Barrow, (eds.), *Children's understanding of society* (pp. 287–303). East Sussex, UK: Psychology Press.

Hobsbawm, E. (1983). Introduction: Inventing traditions. In E. Hobsbawm & T. Ranger (Eds.), *The invention of tradition* (pp. 1–14). Cambridge, UK: Cambridge University Press.

Jensen, L. A. (2008). Immigrants' cultural identities as sources of civic engagement. *Applied Developmental Science, 12*, 74–83.

Jensen, L. A. (in press). Immigrant youth in the United States: Coming of age among diverse civic cultures. In L. Sherrod, J. Torney-Purta, & C. Flanagan (eds.), *Handbook of Research on Civic Engagement in Youth*. Hoboken, N.J.: Wiley.

Jensen, L. A., Arnett, J. J., & McKenzie, J. (in press). Globalization and cultural identity developments in adolescence and emerging adulthood. In Schwartz, S. J., Luyckx, K., & Vignoles, V. L. (Eds.), *Handbook of Identity Theory and Research*. New York: Springer Publishing Company.

Jensen, L. A., & Flanagan, C. A. (Eds.). (2008). Immigrant civic engagement: New translations. *Applied Developmental Science, 12*, 55–56.

Kagitcibasi, C. (2005). Autonomy and relatedness in family context: Implications for self and family. *Journal of Cross-Cultural Psychology, 36*, 403–422.

Kagitcibasi, C. (2007). *Family, self, and human development across cultures (2nd edition)*. Mahwah, NJ: Lawrence Erlbaum.

Kahne, J. E., & Middaugh, E. (2009). "Democracy for Some: The Civic Opportunity Gap in High School." In J. Youniss & P. Levine, (eds.), *Policies for Youth Civic Engagement* (pp. 29–58). Vanderbilt University Press.

Kassimir, R., & Flanagan, C. (in press). Youth civic engagement in the developing world: Opportunities and challenges. In Sherrod, L., Torney-Purta, & Flanagan, C. (eds.), *Handbook of Research on Youth Civic Engagement*. Hoboken, N.J.: Wiley.

Kirshner, B. (2009). Power in numbers: Youth organizing as a context for exploring civic identity. *Journal of Research on Adolescence, 19*(3), 414–440.

Larson, R. W., & Verma, S. (1999). How children and adolescents spend time across the world: Work, play, and developmental opportunities. *Psychological Bulletin, 125*(6), 701–736.

Lerner, M. (1982). *The belief in a just world: A fundamental delusion*. New York: Plenum Press.

Lightfoot, C., & Valsiner, J. (1992). Parental belief systems under the influence: Social guidance of the construction of personal cultures. In I. Sigel, A. McGillicuddy-DeLisi, J. Goodnow (eds.), *Parental belief systems: The psychological consequences for children* (pp. 393–414). Hillsdale, NJ: Erlbaum.

Macek, P., Flanagan, C., Gallay, L., Kostron, L., Botcheva, L., & Csapo, B. (1998). Post-communist societies in times of transition: Perceptions of change among adolescents in Central and Eastern Europe. *Journal of Social Issues, 54*(3), 547–560.

Markus, H. R. & Kitayama, S. (1991). Culture and the self: Implications for cognition, emotion, and motivation. *Psychological Review, 9,* 224–253.

Markus, H. R., Mullally, P.,& Kitayama, S. (1997). Selfways: Diversity in modes of cultural participation. In U. Neisser & D. Jopling (eds.), *The conceptual self in context: Culture, experience, self-understanding* (pp. 13–61). Cambridge: Cambridge University Press.

Martínez, M. L. & Cumsille, P. (2009). Desarrollo cívico en jóvenes chilenos. Informe de resultados Proyecto FONDECYT 1085231.

Martínez, M. L. & Cumsille, P. (2010). Gender differences in civic involvement and political attitudes in Chilean adolescents. Jahrbuch Jugendforschung.

Martínez, M. L., Silva, C. & Hernández, A. C. (under review). ¿En qué ciudadanía creen los jóvenes? Psykhe.

McDevitt, M., & Chaffee, C. (2000). Closing gaps in political communication and knowledge. *Communication Research, 27,* 259–292.

Miller, J. G. (1984). Culture and the development of everyday social explanation. *Journal of Personality and Social Psychology, 46*(5), 961–978.

Miller, P. J. (1996). Instantiating culture through discourse practices: Some personal reflections on socialization and how to study it. In R. Jessor, A. Colby, & R. Shweder (eds.), *Ethnography and human development: Context and meaning in social inquiry* (pp. 183–204). Chicago: University of Chicago Press.

Ministerio de Educación (2003). Educación cívica y el ejercicio de la ciudadanía. Unidad de Curriculum y Evaluación.

Moscovici, S. (1988). Notes toward a description of Social Representations. *European Journal of Social Psychology, 18,* 211–250.

Ngomane, T. (2005). *Civic Participation: The emergence of political leadership in South Africa.* Unpublished doctoral dissertation. The Pennsylvania State University.

Ngomane, T., & Flanagan, C. (2003). The road to democracy in South Africa. *Peace Review, 15,* 267–271.

Oyserman, D., Coon, H. M. & Kemmelmeier, M. (2002). Rethinking individualism and collectivism: Evaluation of theoretical assumeptions and meta-analysis. *Psychological Bulletin, 128,* 3–72.

Pearce, N. J., & Larson, R. W. (2006). How teens become engaged in youth development programs: The process of motivational change in a civic activism organization. *Applied Developmental Science, 10,* 121–131.

Phinney, J. S., & Baldelomar, O. A. (2011). Identity development in multiple cultural contexts. In L. A. Jensen (Ed.), *Bridging cultural and developmental psychology: New syntheses in theory, research and policy* (pp. 161–186). New York: Oxford University Press.

Pinquart, M, Silbereisen, R. K., & Juang, L. P. (2004). Changes in psychological distress among East German adolescents facing German unification: The role of commitment to the old system and self-efficacy beliefs. *Youth and Society, 36*(1), 77–101.

Rappaport, J. (1981). In praise of paradox: A social policy of empowerment over prevention. *American Journal of Community Psychology, 9,* 1–21.

Rosemont, H. (2004). Whose Democracy? Which Rights? A Confucian Critique of Modern Western Liberalism. In S. Kwong-Loi & D. B. Wong (eds.), *Confucian Ethics: A comparative study of self, autonomy, and community* (pp. 49–71). Cambridge, UK: Cambridge University Press.

Sanchez-Jankowski, M. (1992). Ethnic identity and political consciousness in different social orders. *New Directions for Child Development, 56,* 79–93, San Francisco: Jossey-Bass.

Schlegel, A. (2011). Adolescent ties to adult communities: the intersection of culture and development. In L. A. Jensen (Ed.), *Bridging cultural and developmental psychology: New syntheses in theory, research and policy* (pp. 138–158). New York: Oxford University Press.

Seif, H. (in press). The Civic Life of Latina/o Immigrant Youth: Challenging Boundaries and Creating Safe Spaces. In L. Sherrod, J. Torney-Purta, & C. Flanagan (eds.), *Handbook of Research on Civic Engagement in Youth*, Hoboken, NJ: Wiley.

Shweder, R. (1996). True ethnography: The lore, the law, and the lure. In R. Jessor, A. Colby, & R. Shweder (eds.), *Ethnography and human development: Context and meaning in social inquiry* (pp. 15–52). Chicago: University of Chicago Press.

Silva, E., & Silva, C. (under review). La Economía Política de las Motivaciones de Jóvenes Líderes para la Participación Social.

Simon, J., & Merrill, B. D. (1998). Political socialization in the classroom revisited: The Kids Voting Program. *Social Science Journal, 35*, 29–42.

Snyder, M. (2009). In the footsteps of Kurt Lewin: Practical theorizing, action research, and the psychology of social action. *Journal of Social Issues, 65*(1), 225–245.

Stewart, A. J., & McDermott, C. (2004). Civic engagement, political identity, and generation in developmental context. *Research in Human Development, 1*(3), 189–203.

De Tocqueville, A. (1848/1965). *Democracy in America.* J. P. Mayer (Ed.). G. Lawrence trans. Garden City, New York: Doubleday. (Original work published 1848).

Torney-Purta, J., Barber, C. H., & Richardson, W. K. (2004). Trust in government-related institutions and political engagement among adolescents in six countries. *Acta Politica, 39,* 380–406.

Torney-Purta, J., Schwille, J., & Amadeo, J. (Eds). (1999). *Civic education across countries: Twenty-four national case studies from the IEA Civic Education Project.* Amsterdam: IEA.

Van Horn, B., Flanagan, C., & Thomson, J. (1999). Changes and challenges in 4-H: Part 2. *Journal of Extension, 37*(1), 1–5. http://www.joe.org/joe/1999february/index.php

Verba, S. & Orren, G. (1985). *Equality in America: The view from the top.* Cambridge, MA: Harvard University Press.

Vygotsky, L. S. (1978). *Mind in society: The development of higher psychological processes.* Cambridge, MA: Harvard University Press.

Vygotsky, L. S. (1981). The genesis of higher mental functions. In J. V. Wertsch (Ed.), *The concept of activity in Soviet psychology* (pp. 144–188). Armonk, NY: Sharpe.

Walzer, M. (1989). *Citizenship.* New York, New York: Cambridge University Press.

Webley, P. (2005). Children's understanding of economics. In M. Barrett & E. Buchanan-Barrow (eds.), *Children's understanding of society* (pp. 43–68). East Sussex, UK: Psychology Press.

Wertsch, J. V. (1995). The need for action in sociocultural research. In J. V. Wertsch, P. Del Rio, & A. Alvarez (eds.). *Sociocultural studies of mind.* Cambridge, UK: Cambridge University Press.

Wertsch, J. V. (1998). *Mind as action.* New York: Oxford University Press.

Wong, D. B. (2004). Rights and community in Confucianism. In S. Kwong-Loi & D. B. Wong (eds.), *Confucian Ethics: A comparative study of self, autonomy, and community* (pp. 31–48). Cambridge, UK: Cambridge University Press.

Wray-Lake, L., Syvertsen, A. B., & Flanagan, C. (2008). Contested citizenship and social exclusion: Adolescent Arab-American Immigrants' views of the "Social Contract." *Applied Developmental Science, 12,* 84–92.

CHAPTER 7

Adolescent Ties to Adult Communities

The Intersection of Culture and Development

ALICE SCHLEGEL

This chapter addresses one intersection between culture and human development, specifically adolescent development. It focuses on the context and extent of adolescents' integration into the settings and activities of adults across cultures and the attitudinal and behavioral consequences of integration or segregation. Adolescents are involved with adults in many ways: as family members, receivers of abstract or practical knowledge, neighbors, and sometimes friends. Different cultures bring together adolescents and adults in different ways, for different purposes, and to differing degrees. We ask not only how relationships with adults affect adolescents but also how involvement with adolescents affects the lives of adults.

A cultural perspective on human development takes us away from a focus solely on the individual—and even on the individual *within* a particular setting—to the interaction between the individual and the cultural environment. The unit of analysis is not the individual alone but, rather, what ways and to what degrees the individual is formed by and responds to the cultural context. The goal is to understand how features that make up a cultural context build on the universal mental and behavioral characteristics of our species to influence the ways in which adolescents act in the world around them.

This perspective gives rise to three questions. First, how does a cultural approach add to the understanding of adolescent development? Second, how does a developmental perspective, specifically regarding adolescents, add to an understanding of culture? And finally, what is the bridge between culture and adolescent development?

I will address the first two questions later, in the Discussion section of this chapter, after we have examined concrete examples of the relation between cultural conditions and adolescent responses. As to the third, cultural features are linked to development from childhood to adulthood through the set of socialization practices and processes that transmit the knowledge of appropriate behavior and the beliefs, attitudes, and emotions that accompany that behavior. Cultural transmission occurs directly, as adults (and, sometimes, older children) instruct children and organize the settings within which they learn, work, and play. It occurs indirectly as children watch and imitate, informally learning what are and are not appropriate behaviors, emotions, and attitudes. We study adolescent socialization by observing the ways adolescents are treated, and how they behave, within the constraints and opportunities provided to them by the culture of their community. The culture of the community includes the way people communicate through action, speech, gesture, and ritual acts; but it also includes built structures and objects that people use for shelter, as tools, for esthetic pleasure, or to communicate ideas, attitudes, and emotions (*see* Valsiner, 2011).

Adolescent socialization has two distinct aspects. The conscious goal is to prepare adolescents for their future adulthood, but a concurrent purpose is to teach and reinforce culturally appropriate behavior as adolescents. Socialization is both future- and present-oriented, a process of preparing individuals for future ways of thinking and acting while simultaneously reinforcing the attitudes and behaviors appropriate to their present point in the life cycle. In adolescence, these orientations may be in conflict, one probably universal example being preparation for some degree of adult autonomy, even in collectivist cultures, which can be at odds with the dependence and subordination expected of people who are not yet adults (but *see* Lebra, 1990).

Cultural anthropology has a long history of research into the ways that children are socialized in different cultures. Ethnographies over the last 50 years or so often include a chapter on the life of children from birth to puberty. Child-rearing has been a major focus in the subfield of cultural anthropology known as psychological anthropology. But until recently, adolescence as a developmental stage has been neglected in these works; it is as if culture were fully learned, and social adulthood achieved, by the arrival of reproductive capacity. Even after Mead's (1928) influential study of adolescent girls in Samoa, there was only sporadic interest in topics dealing with adolescence outside of courtship customs (where the courting pair are adolescents) and puberty ceremonies. These ceremonies were commonly believed to advance young people from childhood to adulthood, although the Samoan study and others (such as those by Elwin [1947] and Wilson [1951]) clearly showed that a socially marked stage of life between childhood and adulthood existed in the pre-industrial and nonliterate societies they examined.

One exception to this, an example of cultural influences on adolescent personality, comes from my own field research in the 1960s on the Hopi Reservation in northern Arizona. I found it odd that in this sexually egalitarian society, where women were dominant in the home and participated fully in public life, there was a general fear that a girl might commit suicide should she be rejected by the boy she had set her heart on marrying. Since young husbands came to live in the homes of their wives, nubile girls, a few years after menarche, made the proposal of marriage, which might or might not be accepted. The period between the proposal and its acceptance or rejection was universally recognized as a time of considerable anxiety for the girl, as no self-respecting boy would agree to give up his bachelor freedom in an instant. But given that every normal woman did marry, why such intense fear of rejection?

The answer was based on my study of Hopi home life and the cultural themes I elicited through the use of the Thematic Apperception Test (Schlegel, 1973). I related this anxiety about male acceptance to the importance of fathers, both symbolically and actually, in a young girl's life, in face of the reality of frequently broken marriages and the withdrawal of the father from his daughter's daily existence. (His sons, however, would see him often in the all-male activities of the village.) Cultural practices both promoted fathers' emotional involvement and made it problematic for girls.

Anxiety over male rejection in courtship, I concluded, was a displacement of an earlier anxiety over perceived rejection by the most emotionally salient masculine figure, the father. Recognition of this anxiety was expressed as a cultural theme of suicide due to rejection, although no one could report a specific known case. Thus, rejection anxiety seemed to be a cultural product rather than a realistic fear or one arising universally during development. In contrast to the anxious Hopi adolescents, the saucy girls of the Trobriand Islands of Melanesia seemed to have little anxiety about rejection, as the boys were the ones who had to win *their* favors (Malinowski, 1932).

Two research projects, both initiated in the 1970s, marked a revival of general interest in adolescence on the part of anthropologists. One, the Adolescence Project under the direction of John and Beatrice Whiting, resulted in a series of monographs on adolescent life in four communities with very different cultures (Condon, 1987; Burbank, 1988; Davis & Davis, 1989; Hollos & Leis, 1989). At about the same time, Herbert Barry (a psychologist) and I (an anthropologist) began our cross-cultural study: The Adolescent Socialization Project. The major resulting publication (Schlegel & Barry, 1991), and the data set on which it was based (Barry & Schlegel, 1990), provide much of the information for this chapter.

Adolescent–Adult Relations

Psychological research on adolescence is replete with studies of adolescents' relations to parents, peers, friends, and romantic interests and of their behavior within settings such as the family, the school, and the workplace. Yet, when I did an informal survey of some current textbooks of adolescent psychology, I was struck by what was omitted: discussions of adolescent participation in community life. There might be mention of programs, designed by adults, to encourage this, such as opportunities to volunteer in service organizations or to take part in activities that teach civic responsibilities (Flanagan, Martínez, & Cumsille, 2011). Mentorship programs, by which an adolescent and a volunteer mentor are matched, also received attention. However, there was little mention of sustained informal social exchanges between adolescents and adults outside the family, of the inclusion of adolescents in adult-centered settings, or of community services organized by adolescents themselves. This is probably because such exchanges, inclusion, and services are not common in the United States, and their absence is not likely to be noticed by researchers whose observations have been confined to American adolescents.

When American adolescents do have sustained contacts with adults, these adults are most frequently those with designated authority over them: parents, teachers, coaches, youth-group leaders, and, if they are employed, employers and supervisors. The jobs that teenagers hold rarely integrate them into a group of adult colleagues (Greenberger & Steinberg, 1986; Staff et al., 2009). Outside the home, American adolescents typically spend most of their time in peer-centered settings, in which they outnumber adults, such as schools, sports teams, formal youth groups, and leisure-time peer groups. Those who grow up in long-established towns or long-settled urban neighborhoods know their adult neighbors and often have more access to adult kin other than parents, but the cultural norm in America has become one of age segregation, particularly adolescent segregation. Adults generally believe that this is what adolescents themselves prefer.

This is in marked contrast to the traditional pre-industrial cultures that were the field of study for most anthropologists (as well as most historians of social life). In such cultures, adolescents spend much of their days as workers at home or as apprentices in a business, profession, or trade, learning the skills they will need in the future. They most often do this alongside the adults, family members or others, who are training them for adult work as they benefit from their labor. This is true both for unschooled societies and those traditional societies in which adolescents spend part of their day in school. Along with the work, and possibly the schooling, that prepares them for adult productivity, adolescent peer groups may have civic responsibilities, working for the public good in coordination with adult community members. Adolescence, in such cultures, is a time of both economic and social apprenticeship, under the guidance and supervision of their elders. This is true at all social levels, for the elite as well as for adolescents of lower social position.

The contemporary American way of dealing with this developmental period by segregating adolescents from adult community life deviates from this time-honored pattern. In this chapter, I shall use the findings of the cross-cultural study of adolescent socialization in traditional cultures (Schlegel & Barry, 1991), which suggest that there are important developmental consequences of the cultural features of age integration or age segregation, to adolescents themselves and to the communities in which they live. Moving on to contemporary societies other than the United States, I shall examine whether such segregation is inevitable in modern societies that prepare young people for life in an industrial economy.

The Study of Adolescent Socialization
Across Cultures

A cross-cultural study, which collects data amenable to statistical analysis from a fairly large sample, imposes certain constraints. This approach takes each culture, operationally defined as a set of beliefs and practices pinpointed by time and place, as a unit in the sample and looks at patterns that appear with some regularity across cultures, although they are widely separated in space and face different environmental conditions. The data come from a number of sources and were initially recorded for widely different purposes by anthropologists and other ethnographers. This limits the amount and kind of data that can be used. In field research, anthropologists attempt to reach an empathic understanding of another way of life, but that is not the purpose of large-scale cross-cultural research. In that kind of study, the researcher attempts to find patterns of behavior or expressive culture and to uncover the reasons, either practical or motivational, for them.

In our research on adolescent socialization (Schlegel & Barry, 1991), we relied on existing ethnographic descriptions, by anthropologists and others, for data on adolescents in 186 traditional societies. The data set consisted of variables coded from the ethnographers' observations of behavior and their reports on cultural beliefs and values. The fact that the analyses resulted in statistically significant findings, and these findings reinforced one another without being redundant, gave us confidence that they were not simply coincidental or artifacts of the method.

Although we fully realized the limitations of our data, we nevertheless designed questions related to the adolescent self (Schlegel & Barry, 1991: Chapter 9). Herbert Barry was the primary figure in the design of these questions. Our framework was a set of character traits inculcated through child and adolescent socialization practices. Measures of compliance included sexual restraint, obedience, responsibility, conformity, and trust. Measures of assertion included sexual expression, self-reliance, competitiveness, aggressiveness, and achievement. For each of these traits, we were able to get information from enough societies to perform statistical tests (from 45 to 149 societies, depending on the trait). Girls and boys were coded separately, allowing for the possibility that socialization for character traits differs between the sexes. (In fact, one of the findings was that this is generally not true: a culture that strongly socializes one sex for a trait will do the same with the other.)

As is true for any set of ethnographic data, whether comparative or from a single culture, it is the analysis that leads to understanding: trying to answer the "why" of the findings. Here, one goes beyond descriptions and correlations to try to explain not just behavior (e. g., the X were responding to condition Y), but also the motivation for it. Because we cannot enter the minds of the subjects, we can only infer motivation—ultimately, by trying out the possibilities and, through a process of elimination, arriving at the most probable. In this case, several test results pointed in a single direction, which was that there were differences between those adolescents who were more integrated into adult groups and those who were less integrated.

We found that age segregation was related to features of antisocial behavior and to socialization for competitiveness and aggressiveness. We also found that girls display much less antisocial, competitive, and aggressive behavior than boys: without overlooking sex differences in the brain, are there cultural reasons for this? The challenge was to try to understand these findings.

Antisocial Behavior

The results of four statistical tests support one another and indicate that close and sustained contact with multiple adults benefits adolescents. Two are direct measures; they show that the amount of contact is correlated with a measure of antisocial behavior. Given that we were restricted to using ethnographic information—that is, cultural information—about antisocial behavior rather than being able to assess it directly, we measured cultural beliefs about this behavior. We asked whether it was expected that a fair number of adolescents would behave badly. This expectation exists in modern American culture, although most parents hope that their children will not be among that number. It is captured in such expressions as "boys will be boys." Parents and others often excuse behaviors that victimizes others, regarding them as mere pranks, especially if it is difficult or impossible for the victims to retaliate. Our assumption was that if antisocial behavior was common in adolescence, it would be recognized and tolerated, deplored, or both, depending on circumstance. The two most common forms of antisocial behavior among boys in the sample were violence (mainly fighting) and theft.

Tolerance of antisocial behavior should not be confused with tolerated and even encouraged aggression as a form of punishment of those who violate community norms. Communities as widely separated and with cultures as different as Congo Pygmy settlements, 18th- to 19th-century English, French, and German villages, and 20th-century American Chinatowns allowed teenage boys to punish neighbors or strangers who threatened community well-being (Schlegel & Barry, 1991). In such cases, adolescents, who are inferiors in the age hierarchy, are permitted and encouraged to act in ways that would cause lasting social damage if performed by adults against adults of equal social status. Adolescents, generally considered to be less responsible for their actions than adults, can be excused for what adults cannot do without losing their dignity or causing lasting enmity.

Cultures differ according to the number of waking hours adolescents spend alone or with other people such as family members, adults of the same sex or both sexes, and peers. Cultures also differ in whether at least some proportion of adolescents are believed and expected to misbehave. We tested the hours of contact against presence or absence of an expectation of antisocial behavior. Because the adults outside the family with whom adolescents in our sample had the most contact were men for boys and women for girls, we asked only about same-sex adults. As it turned out, in too few cultures were girls expected to misbehave for us to be able to test. I shall discuss the implications of this at a later point.

The first test showed that in cultures where the contact between boys and adult men was above the mean, antisocial behavior was not likely to be expected ($p = 0.024$). As this finding could be influenced by boys' close supervision by family members, we tested for contact with adult men outside the family. The results were similar ($p = 0.014$). This indicates that integration into the company of men is likely to diminish boys' antisocial behavior to the point where it is not recognized as an expected feature of adolescence. In the majority of societies, adolescent boys work, or are otherwise in close and sustained contact, with groups of adult men in which the adults outnumber the boys. This contact of boys with adults outside the family usually occurs when men and boys are engaged in goal-oriented activities that require team effort, like productive work or a community project. Adolescent boys do not generally mingle with men during leisure hours.

Boys' Competitiveness and Aggressiveness

The third and fourth statistical tests also lend support to the proposition that close and sustained contact with a number of adults benefits adolescents, but they use different measures. The independent variable is household form, and the dependent variables are competitiveness and aggressiveness as traits inculcated in adolescents by socialization processes. The rationale for these tests was the hypothesis that these traits would decline as more adults surrounded the adolescent, for the child could not compete with nor aggress against a number of adults without failure in the first instance and undesirable consequences in the second. From large to small number of primary adults in the average household, the three most widespread household forms in the world are extended-family, stem-family, and nuclear-family households. Primary adults are those persons anchored to the household who have responsibility for its welfare and claims on its benefits. We did not anticipate our findings, which was that it is the mid-sized stem-family household, rather than the large extended-family household, that is related to a lesser likelihood of competitiveness ($p = 0.087$, trend) and aggressiveness ($p = 0.031$, significant).

The Affects of Household Form

The nuclear-family household, a common form worldwide and the norm for modern and modernizing societies, consists of two primary adults, although other adults such as widowed elders or household helpers may also reside in the home, often on a temporary basis. The extended-family household, infrequently found in most of traditional Eurasia but common throughout Africa and native North and South America in earlier times, comprises at least two married couples of the same generation, usually brothers and their wives, along with their children. The parents of these brothers also live in the household during their lifetimes. Thus, the household in which the children grow up contains at least six primary adults or more if additional married siblings live in the household or if any of the men have more than one wife (*see also* Nsamenang, 2011).

In the stem-family household, which was the most common form in large parts of pre-industrial Europe and Asia, the older couple resides with the married son or, less often, the daughter, who will inherit the house along with any associated rights over tangible or intangible property. In this form, unmarried siblings (usually younger brothers and sisters of the heir) may also live there as the "bachelor uncles" and "maiden aunts" of their nephews and nieces, at least until they marry or move away for other purposes. (It was these young men and women without prospects of inheritance who peopled the monasteries, convents, and armies and comprised the servant classes and pool of landless laborers in pre-industrial Europe and Asia.) Many of the non-heirs never marry. Those sons who do manage to marry, unless they marry an heiress and enter an established household, form a nuclear family—the first generation of a future stem family. If this new family remains in the community, then it often becomes the poor relations and client family of the heir's house.

The rather surprising result that it is the stem family, rather than the extended family, that dampens competitiveness and aggressiveness required a rethinking of the issue of contact between adolescents and adults. It was not the number of primary adults, *per se*, in the household but the ratio of adults to children that made the difference. Let us assume four living children, adolescents or younger, per married couple. In the nuclear-family household, the adult to child ratio is 1:2. In the extended-family household with three couples, two brothers and their wives (with eight children) plus the senior couple, the ratio is 1:1 1/3. If any of the men had additional wives producing children, the ratio of adults to children would be even lower, approaching or exceeding that of the nuclear family. In the stem-family household, the ratio is 1:1 or higher. This implies that the higher the ratio of primary adults to children in the household, the likelier the children are to be involved with them, for the attention of each adult is less dispersed the smaller the group of children.

Heirs and non-heirs had different socialization needs. As civilizations of Asia and Europe throughout history expanded their territories, and later as nations of early modern Europe established their colonies, opportunities for entrepreneurship and for employment in newly established enterprises arose. This opened opportunities for boys whose future did not include inheritance, so long as they were willing and able to take the risks of moving out and competing for resources. Socialization practices had to accommodate to this economic and social reality. First-born sons, the usual heirs, likely were more socialized for obedience and conformity, whereas greater leeway was provided to later-born sons, regardless of whether parents were aware of this.

In pre-industrial Europe, for example, school and home discipline trained for compliance, but competitive sports and, in some parts, tolerance of boys' pranks rewarded competitiveness and aggressiveness. The dual nature of boys' socialization, for compliance and assertion, is reflected in the fact that the association of competitiveness with the stem-family household is only a trend rather than a significant probability. Boys could be put on the path of compliance or assertiveness, and the one they followed was likely to be determined as much by future prospects as by individual tendencies. Girls, on the other hand, were much more socialized for compliance, for their futures as wives, maiden aunts, or (in both Europe and Asia) nuns generally offered little scope for aggressive or competitive action, although as individuals they might be more aggressive or competitive than the approved cultural norm.

Sex Differences in Contact With Adults

So few societies in the sample expected adolescent girls to misbehave that we were unable to test for antisocial behavior in girls. Following the line of reasoning that an expectation of some delinquency is associated with low contact with same-sex adults, we can explain girls' general compliance with the norms by the high level of integration of girls into groups of women. Boys work alongside men and are involved with them in special-purpose activities, but their leisure time is usually spent apart from men. The boys' peer group is frequently off on its own, out of sight. Even when they are in the same general social space, boys are usually on the periphery of the men's group. Girls generally work alongside women, and they are frequently incorporated into groups of women during leisure hours as well. This was the case for all cultures in the sample, even those that permitted premarital sexual freedom, so it cannot be explained by close supervision to protect virginity, which in any case was valued in only a minority of cultures in the sample (Schlegel, 1991).

Girls often meet with their peers in these all-female gatherings. In ethnographic photographs and descriptions, one often finds two or more adolescent girls standing or sitting together surrounded by women, relatives and neighbors. The degree of contact and involvement with adults of the same sex was greater for girls than for boys in all the cultures in the sample, and they were more compliant. There may be additional reasons for the greater compliance of girls than of boys, and one might ask why girls are not extruded from women's groups as boys are from men's groups or why girls do not seek the company of peers away from adults as much as boys do. Whatever the underlying cause or causes for this sex difference, girls spend more time in adult-centered settings than boys, and it is likely that the compliance of girls is directly related to this feature of social organization.

Socialization Within Significant Social Groups

As infants, children are initially acted on by their culture. As their bodies and minds mature, they learn to act within it. Part of children's socialization—particularly in adolescence when their physiques and brains are approaching final adult form—is learning how to act on their culture, that is, to use it to their advantage and to try to change it when desirable and possible. Children learn to

follow the rules. To be successful adults, adolescents must learn the rules for changing the rules and breaking the rules (Flanagan, Martínez, & Cumsille, 2011).

Infants bring to this process the capacities and temperaments molded by
genetic inheritance and prenatal conditions. As children grow, each experience
is filtered through a screen of previous experiences and understandings. With
the maturing forebrain (Steinberg et al., 2006), children and adolescents gain
the ability to weigh the needs or wants of the present against considerations
of the future. As children respond to their significant social groups (the social
environments that contribute most to their socialization), they learn their culture and become able to anticipate the responses of others to their behavior.
This is not to suggest that only significant social groups contribute to cultural
learning but rather that cultural learning, is more sustained and intensive within
these groups than within the general social environment of the neighborhood
or community.

The earliest significant social group is the family. Even when children are
surrounded by many people, their closest bonds are to their caretakers. At
around age 7, the peer group becomes a second significant social group (Rogoff,
2003). Adolescents in most cultures are brought into a third group that consists
of some or all of the adults of the community, usually of the same sex as the
adolescent (Schlegel & Barry, 1991).

In each case, the significant group provides important social and emotional
resources and, sometimes, material ones as well. Family resources are obvious
and need no further comment. The peer group provides allies and cooperative
partners, as well as competitors against whom to test one's strengths. The
importance of the peer group continues, and in fact increases, in adolescence
(Brown & Larson, 2009; Chen, 2011). In traditional societies and within
sectors of modern societies, today's adolescent peers will be tomorrow's adult
peers, the source of allies and partners in political, social, and economic
exchange networks.

To adolescents in most cultures, some or all of the adults of their community
become a major social group because they set and remove barriers and provide
resources. Adults decide who will be acceptable as a son- or daughter-in-law,
who is a reliable worker, who has the potential for leadership, and whom to
mentor. Adolescents who consistently misbehave may be socially supported by
their families, but they will be unable to gain resources from the larger community of adults, while these resources might be granted to a worthy adolescent without family support. For example, even in as rank-conscious a culture
as the traditional Hopi Indians, a poor boy of a low-ranking clan can be brought
as a son-in-law into the matrilocal household of a high-ranking girl—a kind of
Cinderella in reverse. This will only happen if the boy has impressed the girl's
male and female kin, the ones with veto power over her choice of husband,
who see him as a hard worker and a loyal and dutiful son-in-law.

Significant social groups are culturally defined and may well differ from
one culture or sector of a national or regional culture to another. In some cultures, the families of adolescents encompass a circle of kin who all play a role
in socializing each other's children, while in others the only important kin are

parents, siblings, and possibly grandparents or an uncle or aunt. Adolescents, more than younger children, can choose their significant peers if their social environment is large enough to offer a choice. In small communities or neighborhoods this is not possible, and there is only one group of same-sex adolescents at any one time. The community refers to those adults, outside of family members as defined above, with whom the adolescent is in frequent contact. For many American adolescents, these are mainly authority figures and sometimes the parent of a friend, but in traditional societies and some modern ones, adolescents interact freely and often with adult neighbors and fellow workers.

Responses to Significant Social Groups

One way of looking at adolescence within a culture is to consider how these three significant social groups claim the attention of adolescents, assuming that adolescents must adapt to all three: family, peers, and the community of adults. Is there consistency in what each of these groups expects of the adolescent, or is the young person torn between orienting toward one or two at the expense of the other or others? What are the consequences of orienting more toward family, or toward peers, or toward the larger community?

Only in rare cases (such as the early Israeli kibbutzim where children and adolescents lived apart from their parents) were adolescents expected to be oriented more to the community, and secondarily to peers, than to the family. In most cultures, the family still has primary importance, although the degree of attachment to peers, measured by time spent with peers and obligations to them, varies considerably.

There is no indication in the anthropological literature that a strong involvement with peers necessarily conflicts with strong attachment to the family. Two pre-industrial cultures are examples of extreme cases of peer involvement without such conflict. These are the Muria Gond, a tribal people of the central Indian state of Madhya Pradesh, as they were in the 1970s and earlier, and the Nyakyusa of southwestern Tanzania as they were in the 1930s.

The Muria are known for their dormitories (*ghotul*) for adolescents of both sexes (Elwin, 1947; Gell, 1992), a feature also found in some other cultures. Young people spent most of the day at home working with their families, but in the evenings they congregated in the village dormitory for singing, games, and sleeping, with or without a partner of the opposite sex. Although coercive sex was not approved, some sexual activity was expected. Young people should change partners to avoid becoming too closely attached to any one person, a strategy that was not always successful. These adolescents showed little conflict with their family members. (That conflict, between sons and parents especially, arose later for other reasons [Gell, 1992]). The community gave the ghotul the responsibility of doing certain chores of community maintenance, which they did in apparent good spirits. Parents expected and encouraged their children to join the ghotul.

The Nyakyusa were even more peer-oriented (Wilson, 1951). It was common throughout Africa for adolescent boys and youths to sleep in men's clubhouses or other separate quarters until they married, but the Nyakyusa carried this further. There, boys established a permanent village next to that of their parents. A group of boys ages 10 or 11 established the new village, where they slept in huts they built themselves. They continued to eat at home and work in their fathers' fields until they married and brought their wives into the new village. A village began with about a dozen boys, and by the time the original inhabitants were between ages 16 and 18, the village was closed and a new village started by the younger boys. Thus, the cooperating male group comprised boys, and later married men, with an age-span of about 6 to 8 years. Young men did not marry until about age 25, at which time they were given their own fields to farm. Thus, fathers and their several sons worked together until the father was ready to retire from heavy work. Men remained close to their mothers, who would come to live with them when they were widowed. Girls remained at home until marriage. There is no evidence of parent–child conflict during adolescence.

These examples show that there is no inherent dissonance between attachment to the family and attachment to peers. In fact, some separation of adolescents, especially boys, from their families is so common as to be considered one variant of normal adolescent development. It is quite likely that many cultures use an orientation to peers, by promoting peer relations, to deflect any intergenerational conflict that might arise as adolescents make the necessary transition toward establishing themselves as adults. The easiest way to deal with rambunctious teenage boys may be just to get them out of the way.

Tensions between fathers and sons are more likely when the household includes the much younger secondary wives—closer in age to the son than to the father—of polygynous men, as was fairly common in African cultures, including the Nyakyusa. Potential for intergenerational conflict, which exists for other reasons, might also give rise to the practice of separating adolescents from their families to some degree. But in the cases just discussed, as in most other cases of traditional societies that promoted strong peer affiliations, young people continued to work with or otherwise associate closely with family members.

Peer attachment also need not militate against involvement with the community—that is, adults other than family members. The Muria adolescents had specific duties to their village, under the direction of village elders. The Nyakyusa were seemingly unique in Africa in that adolescents and youths were responsible to and for each other but not to their natal community. Throughout that continent, males and, in some cultures, females were divided into age sets, beginning in childhood. Each set, consisting of age peers, had certain responsibilities to the community at large, overseen by the village or town elders (Nsamenang, 2011; Wilson, 1951).

The energy of youth has been put to use in many cultures by incorporating peer groups within adult-centered social structures. Adolescent group participation in these goal-directed community activities was found in the villages and towns of 19th-century Japan, Hungary, and Malaysia, to name a few. Wherever older adolescent boys were warriors-in-training, the boys' peer group cooperated closely with the adult men in learning the skills of warfare.

Adolescent–Adult Relationships in Modern Societies

We have seen that adolescents are involved with adults in at least the majority of pre-industrial cultures. But do schooling, labor laws that restrict subadult employment, and general social conditions prevent this kind of involvement in modern industrial societies? I will respond with my observations of adolescents in two modern societies. I conducted field research in Germany (Frankfurt & Nürnberg in 1994–1997 and in a village on the Rhine in 1999) and in Siena, Italy, in the summers of 2000, 2001, and 2003.

The German research of 1994 to 1997 focused on blue-collar adolescent apprentices in several occupations: chemical production, electronics, shoe-making and repair, and cabinetry. Apprentices entered their 3-year programs at about age 16, alternating between time spent in the workplace and in the state-run vocational schools that combined academic studies with studies geared toward their vocations. In the factory-run training programs of the chemical and electronics businesses, they were in an in-house school-like setting for the first year under the tutelage of trainers, skilled workers selected for that position. For the following 2 years, they spent increasing time on the factory floor (the chemical plant) or out on the job (electronics). Here they worked alongside adult workers, learning not only the job but also the behavior and the attitudes appropriate to their work. Even though the chemical plant was dark and reeked of chemicals, and electronic work was exacting and demanding, every apprentice preferred that aspect of their training. They insisted on being called "workers," not "students," and they were proud of being considered colleagues by the older, more experienced workers.

The apprentices in the job shops worked directly under journeymen rather than the *Meistern*, the master craftsmen, who owned the shops. Journeymen tend to be younger, in their twenties and early thirties, although some remain in the category throughout their working lives. The adolescents my researchers and I spoke to liked and admired their journeyman supervisors and tried to win their approval through good work and good behavior. Apprenticeship lore is full of tales of woe, exploitation and even bad treatment, but both the laws and general attitude toward young people in Germany seem to have relegated that to a less enlightened past. My sample was too small to make any general statement, but union officials I spoke to, who were not likely to cover up misuse of future members, did not complain about mistreatment of apprentices. On the contrary, everyone agreed that this is a useful part of socialization for those adolescents, about two-thirds of the adolescent population, who will not go on to university (cf. Hamilton & Hamilton, 2009).

In addition to the many apprenticeship programs for both blue- and white-collar occupations, Germany has another institution, the *Verein*, or club, which brings adolescents and adults together in informal relationships. There is a Verein for almost any interest: volunteer firefighting, hunting, gardening, choral singing, sports, chess, history, and so forth. To be a Verein, a club is legally registered with the municipality and can claim certain benefits, like some monetary support. This is because it is widely believed in Germany that the Vereine promote civic responsibility and cooperation and are a positive force in community life. In my field work in the Rhineland village, I observed adolescent involvement in Vereine, particularly the local voluntary firefighters' association, a Verien that appeals strongly to men and boys.

Adolescents usually join Vereine at about age 15 or 16, although some Vereine, like sports clubs, welcome families. In their club activities, the adolescents and adults act together to meet common goals. After the meetings, members usually relax in the clubhouse or a local eating and drinking establishment over snacks and beer, wine, and soft drinks. The legal age of public consumption of beer and wine in Germany is 16, so young members (those not preferring soft drinks) can join their elders in moderate consumption of alcohol. This, along with mealtime consumption of small amounts of alcohol at home, is accepted as a way of teaching young people how to drink responsibly. In this setting, there is free conversation among all present, although adolescents do not generally talk as much as adults.

One of the apprentices in the apprenticeship study, a rather clumsy boy not much admired by his more adroit fellows, told us that he spent most of his free time in a chess club, where he played with adults and was respected for his ability. Another boy, also one of the less competent, lived for his bicycle club. In both cases, their low status in the peer group seemed to be more than compensated by their involvement with the adults, as well as any other adolescents, in their clubs. It is quite usual in Germany for most adolescents to spend good parts of their working and leisure time with adults. Some of these adults may be family members, other kin, or neighbors, but many will be adults whom the young people would otherwise not have a chance to meet if it were not through their apprenticeship or Verein membership.

The research in Siena was devoted to the activities of adolescents in the *contrade*, the 17 districts of the city. Each contrada has its clubhouse, its symbols of identity, and its traditions. The contrade own property, which they rent out to support contrada activities. Members pay dues according to ability, and they are expected to put in time working for the good of the contrada. In return, they receive social support, useful information, and often favors from other members, as well as a social center.

Adolescents are important in contrada activities and are recognized as such. Boys have the more active roles: they supervise and train younger boys in contrada responsibilities, and they act as bartenders in the clubhouse. (Bars in Italy do serve alcoholic drinks, mainly wine, but the main beverage is coffee as most alcohol is consumed at mealtime.) Girls work with the women as they prepare food for contrada dinners or sew contrada flags and costumes for the parades that are a colorful part of Sienese life. Adolescents of both sexes help set up, serve, and clean up at contrada dinners.

All of these activities are done alongside adults. Although some adolescents are more involved in contrada life than others, the large majority seem to value their contrada activities and intend to continue participating in them. In several cases reported to me, contrada leaders helped troubled young people get out and stay out of difficulty; in fact, it is not unusual for police to report an adolescent caught in illicit behavior to the president of his or her contrada. The object is to exert social control, rather than to punish under the law, and to keep the young person out of trouble in the future.

Siena is unusual, perhaps unique, in having adapted its medieval civic structure to modern life. The involvement of adolescents with adults in this city cannot be generalized to Italy or even Tuscany. However, it does serve as a modern example of one kind of institution that brings the generations together in close working relations, as do the Vereine and apprenticeship programs of Germany.

How Adults Matter in the Lives of Adolescents

Adults provide the resources adolescents need, at present and in the near future. One of these resources in traditional societies is help in getting a spouse. To gain a spouse, young people have to be worthy in the eyes of potential in-laws, and they cannot alienate their own kin, who may also be involved in their marriage decisions. As the example of the Hopi boy given earlier attests, even a person without family resources can be an appealing son-in-law if he has the right personal qualifications.

Other resources may be jobs, or apprenticeships, or help in getting into a school or other institution. People have long memories, and reputations established in adolescence tend to stick; so other things being equal, adolescents in settled communities see it to their advantage to impress elders who control resources. This is likely to be less important where adolescents will move away later and leave their reputations behind, as is often the case in geographically and socially mobile modern societies. They may not be as dependent on local elders for help in getting a job, or for any other future needs, as those who stay in the community.

One oft-heard complaint in modernizing cultures is that young people have lost respect for their elders. In fact, young people often do not need those particular elders to put them on the road to successful adulthood, and so they are unwilling to endure the subordination that traditional customs of respect require (Arnett, 2011). Other adults, such as potential employers, may be more important in their calculus. It is often people other than parents or close kin who provide school fees, apprenticeships, casual employment, or other resources of a contractual nature, in modern or modernizing societies as well as in some traditional ones. Some adolescents' social networks may not provide them with any adults who can help them. In that case, the cost of subordination is not recompensed by any gain in benefits.

There is more to the relations between adolescents and community adults, however, than just a calculus of material and social costs and benefits. Social life is not just about gain and loss and the exchange of information and ideas.

One of the most important services that adults can provide to adolescents is to help them regulate their emotions, as individuals and in social interchange. Reward, as praise or just social acceptance, is of little value unless it comes from people the individual respects, and punishment, such as scoldings or social rejection, will have little impact beyond the immediate if the punishers are of no importance to the individual. Role models are taken most seriously when there is an emotional attachment to the admired figure. Adults who would have lasting influence on adolescents and teach them the ways of adulthood are most effective if they cultivate a strong personal bond. Institutionalized mentorship programs, where the adolescents do not freely choose the mentors to follow, are not always successful in this regard (Rhodes & Lowe, 2009).

Integration with adults allows adolescents to form friendships with adults in a natural setting, where the adult and the adolescent come together by choice and common interest. Adult friends can be very helpful to adolescents as mentors and guides. Their companionship can provide respite when relations with the family or the peer group go sour. The choirs or chess clubs or sports teams that include adolescents along with adults offer alternative social relations to the sometimes stressful relations with peers, especially to adolescents who feel their peers do not accept them. We saw this with the apprentices who seemed not to be bothered by their low status with work peers, because their emotional affiliation was with the members of their Vereine, most of them older than the boys.

In short, it is in the community of adults that adolescents can observe, and gradually begin to practice, adult behavior. They learn what is and is not acceptable to adults, something their peers cannot teach them. If they find a special friend there, they enlarge their sphere of learning and emotional support. Segregation from adult company denies them these sources of learning, and it puts barriers to the formation of friendships that give comfort and wisdom, unencumbered by peer competition and insecurity and free from the tensions of parental authority. The larger community of adults can have special importance to adolescents from families that do not provide adequate socialization or emotional support—providing, of course, that the community itself is not dysfunctional.

Discussion: Cultural Approaches to Adolescent Socialization

The view taken here is that culture's locus is the minds of individuals in a communicative system, and it is transmitted and developed primarily through their social communication (cf. Habermas 1987, pp. 136 ff.). The major means of social communication are actions to be observed and speech to be understood, both to be interpreted by the individual, although material objects and structures can also convey messages. Individuals grow up surrounded by witnessed actions, heard speech, observed objects. Some of these are salient and some are simply cultural noise, trivial or transient phenomena. A task of the developing mind is to make sense of all of this.

Cultural transmission becomes socialization when the neophyte—be it child, immigrant, or visiting anthropologist—begins to reduce chaos to comprehension. The first step in socialization is probably imitation, whether conscious or under the stimulus of mirror neurons. Mirror neurons may also provide the mechanism of "emotional contagion" by which we "catch" the emotions of those around us. This serves as the basis for the culturally variable patterns of emotional responses that individuals attach to objects, specific words, gestures, and acts. Through cognitive processes, individuals learn the behavioral rules and explicit meanings of symbols that characterize their culture.

The theme of this chapter has been socialization as the bridge between culture and human development. We return to the earlier questions of how a cultural approach adds to the understanding of adolescent development and how a developmental perspective adds to the understanding of culture.

Culture and Adolescent Development

The body of this chapter is devoted to the first of these questions. We have seen two ways in which knowledge of culture can aid our understanding of human development. One way is through detailed studies of individual cultures. A benefit of studying other cultures is that it expands our vision of the possible by expanding our knowledge of what actually exists. At the very least, it shakes any belief that what we know from American culture is necessarily universal (cf. Arnett, 2008).

The Hopi case shows that female fear of male rejection has both situational and psychogenic causes: the present situation revives earlier childhood anxieties, even in the face of all evidence that all women marry. The Muria Gond and the Nyakyusa illustrate the absence of an inherent conflict between attachment to peers and attachment to the family. In fact, these cases suggest that adults devise cultural practices to encourage attachment to peers, getting the adolescents out of the house when there may be tensions at home over authority and subordination or for other reasons. Do Americans isolate adolescents from adult-based settings as a means of avoiding intergenerational conflict? Or is age segregation an unplanned consequence of other factors in our society? This question lends itself to research from a number of different disciplinary perspectives.

The German and Italian cases demonstrate that modern social arrangements do not necessarily put an end to adolescent–adult integration; on the contrary, these cultures include practices that encourage such integration. Are there sectors of American society that also practice age integration? If so, how do they do it?

Comparative research across cultures is another way that cultural knowledge contributes to an understanding of human development. Ideally, comparative research reveals patterns of association, and it is through the analysis of these patterns that we can come to understandings of behavior within individual cultures, such as our own.

Take the results of the cross-cultural study on age integration and segregation. One research question this leads to is whether there are any differences
between two groups within a sample of American adolescents, those with and
those without extensive contacts with adults, close relationships with adults
outside the home, or both. These groups could be compared on several dimensions of personality and behavior or physical or mental health. Inherent in this
kind of study, however, is the problem of self-selection, which would have to
be met through careful research design.

Adolescent Development and Culture

The characteristics of human development also affect culture. Unlike social
animals, in which one or both sexes are extruded from whatever the home base
is at puberty, humans keep their reproductive and sexually interested, but
unmated, offspring at home. The intensified sexuality of adolescence presents
a challenge to all societies, and cultural practices are invented or borrowed to
manage adolescent sexuality (Schlegel, 1995).

While the avoidance of close inbreeding is found in almost all animal species, cultures turn this natural propensity into a cultural feature, with incest
taboos and kin-related marriage restrictions that often go far beyond the biological boundaries of close inbreeding. These elaborations are interwoven with
other cultural features related to kinship and marriage. Concern over childbirth
outside of marriage is very widespread across cultures, for almost everywhere,
regardless of the kinship system, children have strong relationships with
fathers' families and depend on them for various kinds of resources. Thus, even
where adolescents have sexual freedom, there are cultural practices to prevent
pregnancy or otherwise deal with it (Schlegel, 1991).

Healthy adolescents are strong and energetic, but they are still subordinate
to parents and elders. This makes them an ideal labor pool for family production and community service in many cultures. Healthy adolescents are also
generally physically attractive, "the flower of the village" as the Trobriand
Islanders call them (Malinowski, 1932). They provide public entertainment as
they show off their skill and beauty, to other adolescents and the community,
through dancing and sports performances. Much research into contemporary
adolescence deals with the ways adolescents respond to or within the structures
created by adults, such as families, schools, and the workplace. It may be time
to think about ways that adolescents already contribute to the community and
how these can be expanded to make our young people feel, and be, useful
members of society.

Conclusion

Can we change our culture to accommodate the integration of adolescents as
contributing members of adult-based structures and institutions? This last
question has implications for social policy. Given social inertia, it is unlikely

that any major changes would come quickly. There have been attempts to introduce apprenticeship programs at the high school level, such as one modeled after the German program (Schlegel, 1996), but such programs have never become widespread.

One attainable measure would be to give social and financial support to organizations that integrate adolescents with adults in pro-social activities. If civic leaders were convinced that this is good public policy, then this support would be easy to justify. Some organizations that do this, such as community orchestras, already exist. These should be encouraged. But this will not happen on a large scale until adult–adolescent integration is seen as socially useful.

References

Arnett, J. J. (2008). The neglected 95%: Why American psychology needs to become less American. *American Psychologist 63*: 602–614.

Arnett, J. J. (2011). Emerging adulthood(s): The cultural psychology of a new life stage. In L. A. Jensen (Ed.), *Bridging cultural and developmental psychology: New syntheses in theory, research and policy* (pp. 255–275). New York: Oxford University Press.

Barry, H. III & Schlegel, A. (1990). *HRAF research series in quantitative cross-cultural data, vol. IV: Adolescence.* New Haven, CT: Human Relations Area Files.

Brown, B. B. & Larson, J. (2009). Peer relations in adolescence. In R. M. Lerner and L. Steinberg (Eds.), *Handbook of adolescent psychology*, 3rd ed., Vol. 2 (pp. 74–103). Hoboken, NJ: John Wiley & Sons.

Burbank, V. K. (1988). *Aboriginal adolescence: Maidenhood in an Australian community.* New Brunswick, NJ: Rutgers University Press.

Chen, X. (2011). Culture, peer relationships, and human development. In L. A. Jensen (Ed.), *Bridging cultural and developmental psychology: New syntheses in theory, research and policy* (pp. 92–112). New York: Oxford University Press.

Condon, R. G. (1987). *Inuit youth: Growth and change in the Canadian Arctic.* New Brunswick, NJ: Rutgers University Press.

Davis, S. S. & Davis, D. A. (1989). *Adolescence in a Moroccan town: Making social sense.* New Brunswick, NJ: Rutgers University Press.

Elwin, V. (1947). *The Muria and their ghotul.* London: Oxford University Press.

Flanagan, C., Martínez, M. L., & Cumsille P. (2011). Civil societies as cultural and developmental contexts for civic identity formation. In L. A. Jensen (Ed.), *Bridging developmental approaches to psychology: New syntheses in theory, research and policy* (pp. 113–137). New York: Oxford University Press.

Gell, S. M. S. (1992). *The ghotul in Muria society.* London: Oxford University Press.

Greenberger, E. & Steinberger, L. (1986). *When teenagers work: The psychological and social costs of teenage employment.* New York: Basic Books.

Habermas, J. (1987). *The theory of communicative action, vol. Two: Lifeworld and system: A critique of functionalist reason.* Boston, MA: Beacon Press.

Hamilton, S. F. & Hamilton, M. A. (2009). The transition to adulthood: Challenges of poverty and structural lag. In R. M. Lerner & L. Steinberg (Eds.), *Handbook of adolescent psychology*, 3rd ed., vol. 2 (pp. 492–526). Hoboken, NJ: John Wiley & Sons.

Hollos, M. & Leis, P. E. (1989). *Becoming Nigerian in Ijo society.* New Brunswick, NJ: Rutgers University Press.

Lebra, T. S., (1990). Skipped and postponed adolescence of aristocratic women in Japan: Resurrecting the culture/nature issue. In A. Schlegel (Ed.), *Ethos: Special Issue on Adolescence 23*: 79–102.

Malinowski, B. (1932). *The sexual life of savages in northwestern Melanesia*. London: Routledge and Kegan Paul.

Mead, M. (1928). *Coming of age in Samoa*. Ann Arbor, MI: Morrow.

Nsamenang, A. B. (2011). The culturalization of developmental trajectories: A perspective on african childhoods and adolescences. In L. A. Jensen (Ed.), *Bridging cultural and developmental psychology: New syntheses in theory, research and policy* (pp. 235–254). New York: Oxford University Press.

Rhodes, J. E. & Lowe, S. R. (2009). Mentoring in adolescence. In R. M. Lerner & L. Steinberg (Eds.), *Handbook of adolescent psychology*, 3rd ed., Vol. 2 (pp. 152–190). Hoboken, NJ:Wiley.

Rogoff, B. (2003). *The cultural nature of human development*. Oxford, UK: Oxford University Press.

Schlegel, A. (1973). The adolescent socialization of the Hopi girl. *Ethnology 12*: 449–462.

Schlegel, A. (1991). Status, property, and the value on virginity. *American Ethnologist 18*: 719–734.

Schlegel, A. (1995). The cultural management of adolescent sexuality. In P. Abramson and S. Pinkerton (Eds.), *Sexual nature, sexual culture* (pp. 177–194). Chicago, IL: University of Chicago Press.

Schlegel, A. (1996). *The Fox Valley youth apprenticeship program*. Unpublished report to the Menasha Corporation Foundation and the Fox Cities Chamber of Commerce and Industry.

Schlegel, A. & Barry, H. III. (1991). *Adolescence: An anthropological inquiry*. New York: Free Press.

Staff, J., Messersmith, E. E., & Schulenberg, J. E. (2009). Adolescents and the world of work. In R. M. Lerner & L. Steinberg (Eds.). *Handbook of adolescent psychology*, 3rd. ed., vol. 2 (pp. 270–313). Hoboken, NJ:Wiley.

Steinberg, L., Dahl, R., Keating, D., Kupfer, D. J., Masten, A. S., & Pine, D. (2006). Psychopathology in adolescence: Integrating affective neuroscience with the study of context. In D. Cicchetti & D. Cohen (Eds.), *Developmental psychopathology, vol. 2: Developmental neuroscience.* (pp. 710–741). Hoboken, NJ: John Wiley & Sons.

Valsiner, J. (2011). The development of individual purposes: Creating actuality through novelty. In L. A. Jensen (Ed.), *Bridging cultural and developmental psychology: New syntheses in theory, research and policy* (pp. 212–232). New York: Oxford University Press.

Wilson, M. (1951). *Good company: A study of Nyakyusa age villages*. Oxford, UK: Oxford University Press.

PART III

DEVELOPMENTAL SELVES
AND CULTURE

CHAPTER 8

Identity Development in Multiple Cultural Contexts

JEAN S. PHINNEY & OSCAR A. BALDELOMAR

Identity formation takes place at the crux of development and culture. According to Erikson (1968), the process of achieving an identity is located "in the core of the individual and yet also in the core of his [sic] communal culture" (p. 22). One's developing sense of self is inevitably entwined in, and reflective of, one's cultural context. Shweder and colleagues (Shweder et al., 2006) state that "The self can be conceptualized as a primary locus of culture-psyche interaction. . . It is where the individual, a biological entity, becomes a meaningful entity—a person as a participant in social worlds" (p. 749). An identity is formed as a result of the actions and decisions of an individual in response to both developmental needs (e.g., to resolve questions of purpose and goals in life and achieve a coherent sense of self) and the actual and perceived opportunities and affordances in the cultural community in which he or she lives. The study of identity formation addresses the interplay of developmental pressures and cultural factors. Research on the topic can lead to a better understanding of the ways by which development and culture are linked and interactive.

In this chapter, we explore the process of identity formation in diverse cultural contexts. We first review work that demonstrates the interdependence of identity development and the cultural context in which it takes place. We then discuss ways of conceptualizing culture as a factor in identity development. We review the widely used identity status model of identity formation as proposed by Marcia (1966) and describe a modified model of this process that recognizes and allows for alternative cultural settings. We discuss the contemporary reality that identity formation most often occurs in multiple cultural contexts.

We then examine the process with reference to specific domains of identity formation—namely, occupational, ethnic, national, religious, and gender identities. We conclude with some thoughts about the implications of our view of identity development and culture as interdependent.

Identity Development in Cultural Context

The field of developmental psychology has long acknowledged the role of context in development. Current developmental theories, deriving largely from the seminal work of Bronfenbrenner (1979), acknowledge the role of the environment, broadly defined, in developmental processes. The ecological context of human development is conceptualized by Bronfenbrenner in terms of "a nested arrangement of concentric structures, each contained within the next" (p. 22): the microsystem, mesosystem, exosystem, and macrosystem. Bronfenbrenner emphasizes the relations between and among these systems in the process of development but implies that they are conceptually separate. The macrosystem, described as the "overarching patterns of ideology and organization of the social institutions common to a particular culture or subculture" (p. 8), thus refers to what is more commonly called the cultural context.

Bronfenbrenner can be given credit for raising the awareness of developmental scholars to the cultural context, but his model places little emphasis on the interactions among contexts (*see* Goodnow, 2011). More recently, theorists have attempted to explain the ways in which individual and environmental factors mutually influence each other throughout development and across contexts. Developmental systems theory (Lerner, 1999) stresses the complex interactive relations that exist among multiple levels of the environment, from the proximal family and school levels to the institutional and cultural systems that make up the wider world of the developing child. With the work of Lerner and others (e.g., Overton, 1998; Tharakad, Mistry, & Dutta, 2010), the important role of the context has become increasingly recognized in developmental psychology.

In the past, however, the study of identity formation has showed less concern with the context in comparison to many other areas of development. The neglect of context is surprising, given the fact that the writings of Erikson (1963, 1968), who introduced the concept of identity to psychology, pointed out that identity development occurs in a reciprocal relationship between the individual and the cultural context. Recently, the conception held by some identity researchers of a self-contained individual developing an identity apart from contextual constraints and resources has been broadly criticized (Bosma & Kunnen, 2001; Cote & Levine, 2002). Baumeister and Muraven (1996) suggest that identity is best thought of as an adaptation to a social, cultural, and historical context. Hammack (2008) elaborates a model of identity in cultural context that emphasizes the construction of identity through social interaction and social practice. In a recent theoretical examination of identity formation, Schachter (2005) notes that "different contexts constrain, enhance, interact with, and even constitute basic developmental processes and, complementarily, that individuals create, choose, maintain, change, and constitute their contexts of development" (p. 376).

When context has been examined in relation to identity formation, the proximal environment of family and community has most often been the focus (e.g. Beyers & Goossens, 2008). Although culture pervades every aspect of individual lives, this pervasive reciprocal interaction is rarely acknowledged. The reciprocal relation between individual and context means that culture permeates the process of identity formation not just at a macro-level but at every level of analysis. Culture is not at the periphery of identity formation but at its center (Jensen, 2003, 2008; Jensen, Arnett, & McKenzie, in press). This point is important when considering the different levels at which identity has been studied, including personal identity, social identity, and cultural identity. Although these ways of partitioning one's identity are useful for understanding different aspects of the construct, in our view all identity, whether personal or social, is saturated by the cultural context. No identity is culture-free.

The reciprocity of identity and cultural context is evident in a number of characteristics of identity formation. First, identity develops as the person engages in social relations (Fiske, 1991) that are culturally patterned or scripted. The essence of identity development is balancing the self in reference to the other (Kroger, 2004)—that is, the nature of identity is relational; one's identity serves to distinguish oneself from others and to link oneself with others. In this way identity development is "a process of recognizing and being recognized by 'those who count'" (Kroger, 2004, p. 11). The relational nature of identity is particularly evident in work from cultures that emphasize the interdependent self. For example, in a study of contextual factors associated with identity transitions in Japan, Sugimura (2007) examined how adolescent females make use of and incorporate others' opinions, expectations, needs, and worldviews into their own identity explorations and decision-making processes.

Second, identity formation is situated within a cultural context, and the range and type of identity options available to individuals vary across cultural contexts. For example, occupation can range from a single option with little variations in nomadic tribes and farming communities to the wide range of careers available in more technological societies (Arnett, 2010). These occupational options are adaptive to the individual's environment. In this way, individuals choose and develop their identities in relation to the contingencies of their cultural contexts. Thus, the value and meaning of an identity option can only be assessed within its cultural context.

Third, individuals are not culturally neutral in forming their identities; identity pursuits are never impartial or value-free. Young members of a society find the available identity options meaningful to them because their communities raise and condition them to perceive these options as significant. Developing individuals are influenced by cultural notions of personhood associated with their identity options and the particular processes of identity formation endorsed by their cultural community. This connection between cultural ideals of personhood and identity is supported by the cultural group's ethnotheory of development, the group's indigenous and informal theory on how development should occur. For example, central to the development of the Zinacantan Maya women of Mexico is their identity as weavers on a backstrap loom (Greenfield, 2004). Weaving is considered a stage of development for girls, starting as young as age 5, when they have "enough 'soul' or 'spirit' . . . [an element] necessary because weaving is so hard: frustrating, taxing, time-consuming, and intellectually demanding" (Greenfield, 2004, p. 52). They become skillful weavers by mid-adolescence, thus enhancing their marriageability.

Fourth, normative identity development follows cultural goals. Cultural communities have goals about the development of their younger members, and these goals are guided by their cultural ideals and values (Greenfield, 1994; Jensen, 2010; Rogoff, 2003). What a community considers a "mature" or "desirable" identity for their youth varies according to cultural norms. To attain culturally sanctioned goals, the older generations prepare age-appropriate tasks to guide the development of their children and adolescents (Greenfield, 1994; Schlegel, 2010), and children develop as cultural beings through participation in these activities. These young members' identity development is strongly influenced by their cultural communities' expectations. In the interplay of the individual and the cultural context, adults have a greater impact than children on the cultural processes leading to identity development; children and adolescents have less opportunity to affect the cultural process and exert their own agency. However, as we discuss later, across cultures and ages, individuals may act in ways contrary to the prevailing cultural norms and follow alternative routes to identity.

Conceptualizing the Cultural Context

Recognition of the interplay of development and culture in identity formation leads to the question of how to conceptualize culture in terms of its role in development. Markus and Hamedani (2007) point out two distinct approaches to this question, depending on whether culture is conceptualized as "social influence" or as "process." In the social influence approach, cultures are thought of as distinct categories characterized by particular values, attitudes, and practices that affect the individual. Cultures in this sense can best be understood through comparative studies, where culture is considered as a grouping variable represented by individuals from different identifiable cultural groups, such as Japanese and American. Empirical differences in values, attitudes, and behaviors among individuals from these groups are studied and interpreted as showing the influence of the differing cultural contexts. With regard to identity, researchers working in this tradition examine how differences between cultural groups lead to variation in the way identities develop and in the characteristics of the resulting identities.

In contrast, conceptualizing culture as a process leads identity scholars to a focus on "how one becomes and exists as a cultural being, emphasizing that the cultural and the psychological, the environmental and the individual, cannot be separated. . . The sociocultural and psychological exist in mutual interdependence with one another" (Markus & Hamedani, 2007, p. 27). This approach is in accord with current thinking about development and culture; however, developing research paradigms within this approach is difficult, a fact that may explain in part the limited amount of research in the area. Qualitative methods, such as interviews and narratives (e.g., Hammack, 2008; Schachter, 2005; Sugimura, 2007) are seen as necessary for gaining understanding of the complex processes involved.

In psychology, the most influential theoretical tool to study cultural differences in development has been the distinction between individualism and collectivism (I/C), or independence and interdependence (Hofstede, 1980; Markus & Kitayama, 1991; Triandis, 1988). This distinction refers to the ways in which individuals relate to each other and experience social reality. Collectivistic cultures emphasize the interdependence of the individuals and their groups (e.g., family, church, ethnic group, tribe, etc.); individualistic cultures emphasize the independence of individuals and their groups. Based on the I/C distinction, Markus and Kitayama proposed two types of cultural self-constructs: An individualistic culture constructs the self as independent from others, autonomous, unique, and valuing personal achievement; a collectivistic culture constructs the self as interdependent, connected with others, valuing subordination of individual goals to the needs of the group.

Although the I/C distinction has been useful in studying cultural differences, psychologists do not agree on how best to apply it in studying psychological phenomena. Many theoretical positions have been proposed about the I/C distinction, ranging between two extremes, from a strict dichotomy, where cultures are either individualistic or collectivistic (e.g., Markus & Kitayama, 1991; Triandis, 1995) to a denial that cultures can be characterized in such a way (e.g., Nucci & Turiel, 2000). In general, critics of the I/C distinction claim that cultures are heterogeneous and multidimensional rather than homogeneous and unidimensional (Raeff, 2006). Some critics emphasize agency over cultural patterns, arguing that the I/C distinction does not account for heterogeneity in people's judgments about different kinds of social situations (Turiel, 1985).

In this chapter, we propose that the I/C distinction and its related constructs are relevant to the study of identity development because of its implications regarding the relational nature of identity. Individualism and collectivism imply different cultural ways of balancing the self and others in the process of identity formation (Baldelomar, under review). However, we acknowledge that although cultures exhibit recognizable patterns, cultures are not monolithic; they are not solely individualistic nor solely collectivistic. We also acknowledge that individual agency plays an important role in identity development in all cultures. These important points will be evident later in our discussion.

Developmental psychologists have used the I/C distinction to examine how cultures differ in their goals for children's development as independent or interdependent beings and the developmental practices associated with these goals. Greenfield and colleagues (1994; Greenfield, Keller, Fuligni, & Maynard, 2003) have proposed two idealized, cultural pathways of development: an independent pathway that promotes choice, individualization, and self-expression and an interdependent pathway that promotes conformity, tradition, and replication (e.g., Greenfield, 1994; Greenfield et al., 2003). These two idealized pathways are universal and "applicable to all developmental domains" (Greenfield et al., 2003, p. 464); thus, the process of identity development could be explained in terms of these pathways. In the following sections, we elaborate on how the I/C distinction can inform our understanding of the interplay between culture and identity formation.

The Identity Status Model of Identity Formation

In developmental psychology, one of the most influential models of identity formation is Marcia's (1966) identity status model. Identity statuses mark specific outcomes or positions along the identity formation process. For Marcia, the process of identity formation is composed of two basic processes: exploration and commitment. *Exploration* is the process of searching for an adequate identity choice among the available options; this search is supposed to lead to an identity commitment. *Commitment* is the making of a decision to adopt a particular identity option. By combining high and low levels of exploration and commitment, Marcia identified four basic identity statuses: achievement (high exploration, high commitment), moratorium (high exploration, low commitment), foreclosure (low exploration, high commitment), and diffusion (low exploration, low commitment). As individuals develop their identity, they move through these different statuses (e.g., from moratorium to achievement, etc.). However, in Marcia's model, only change leading to an identity-achieved status is considered progressive (e.g., from diffusion to moratorium, etc.). Thus, identity achievement is the most preferred and ideal status, followed by moratorium as the forerunner of identity achievement; foreclosure and diffusion come last, in that order.

The identity status model was developed in a North American setting and reflects the view that an individualistic process of identity formation is normative. Although the status model identifies two types of identity commitments, achievement and foreclosure, the model indicates that an achieved identity is the preferred or more mature status. Whereas foreclosed commitments reflect the identities of others (e.g., parents, authority figures, or reference groups), achieved commitments are based on individual choice and autonomous preference. Moreover, the process of exploration is defined exclusively as an individualized process of choice, rendering foreclosure as bypassing the identity formation process (e.g., Kroger, 2004). In contrast, in cultural contexts where tradition is highly valued, a foreclosed identity may be considered a normative achievement. As Schlegel (1995, 2010) has noted, in traditional cultures adolescents spend a lot of time with adults, often engaged in joint family and work tasks. Girls, in particular, are seldom seen without the presence of adults. This type of context is conducive to an identity formation process that places less emphasis on independence and autonomy and more on interdependence. It is thus apparent that the identity status model is not readily applicable to cultural contexts where interdependence is valued over independence as normative (Baldelomar, under review).

The Cross-Cultural Identity Status Model

To understand cultural variation in the identity formation process, Baldelomar (under review) has proposed the *cross-cultural identity status model*. This model extends the original status model by explaining identity development in cultural contexts where interdependence is valued over independence. Based on Markus and Kitayama's (1991) concept of independent/interdependent self-construals, the model identifies two types of identity achievements as cultural goals for identity development: an *independent* identity achievement and an *interdependent* identity achievement. These achievements are defined in relational terms, by the role others play in the process of identity formation. The goal for an independent identity achievement is to highlight the differences between self and others by forming an individualized identity commitment. The goal for an interdependent identity achievement is to adopt or internalize the identity commitments of the cultural community.

As shown by the solid lines in Figure 8–1, each type of identity achievement is associated with a culturally different identity formation process. Applying Greenfield and colleagues' cultural pathways of development (1994; Greenfield et al., 2003), an independent pathway (lower branch of Fig. 8–1) promotes choice, individualization, and self expression; an interdependent pathway (upper branch of Fig. 8–1) promotes conformity, tradition, and replication. Each pathway of development leads to a different kind of identity achievement. An independent identity achievement reflects self-preferences, autonomy, and individualized values. An interdependent identity achievement reflects generational continuity. Thus, these two types of identity achievements constitute culturally different goals for identity development. As is explained later, the solid lines in Figure 8–1 represent culturally normative processes, whereas the dashed lines represent the counter-cultural options for reaching an identity commitment that some individuals may take in opposition to each cultural pathway of identity formation.

The process of identity development depends on the range of identity options structured and presented by the cultural community. In cultures with an independent identity achievement as the desired outcome, many identity options are available to facilitate individualism and self-expression. In cultures with an interdependent identity achievement as the desired outcome, there is a narrower range of identity options, options that in some cases may be very similar to each other. As Arnett (1995) has pointed out, children are socialized narrowly or broadly, depending on the range of individual variation allowed in

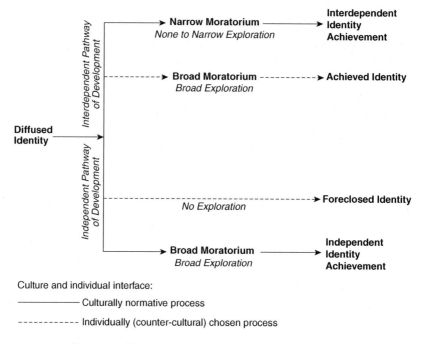

FIGURE 8.1 Sequence of identity statuses by cultural pathways of development

each culture. Baldelomar (under review) proposes that the type of socialization employed during childhood prepares adolescents for different types of identity exploration, narrow and broad, each corresponding to the different ranges of identity options and cultural expectations in identity outcomes. As shown in Figure 8–1, narrow exploration is employed in the interdependent pathway, where there are few options, and broad exploration is employed in the independent pathway, which offers many choices. Baldelomar argues that Marcia's (1966) original identity statuses describes exclusively an independent pathway of development, in which exploration is conceived only as broad.

Narrow and broad explorations are not only related to different ranges of identity options, but they also refer to different ways of thinking and evaluating these options. Baldelomar (under review) hypothesizes that broad exploration involves critical thinking, to facilitate comparing and contrasting the many different identity options. In contrast, narrow exploration involves the relative absence of critical thinking, to facilitate the internalization of an available identity from authority figures. Thus, because the identity status of moratorium is both an indication of exploration and the precursor of an identity achievement, narrow moratorium leads to an interdependent identity achievement (upper, solid line of Fig. 8–1), and broad moratorium leads to an independent identity achievement (lower, solid line of Fig. 8–1).

Identity formation takes place in different *domains*—that is, areas that individuals or cultures consider important to identity, such as occupation, religion, ethnicity, and gender. Identity domains can differ in the extent to which they are ascribed to one by others or freely chosen. There is variation across cultures as to whether a domain is ascribed or chosen, with traditional cultures typically ascribing identity in more areas than modern developed societies. For ascribed domains, exploration is mostly narrow, aimed at gaining deeper understanding of the given identity. Some ascribed identities may be so heavily scripted that they may not offer the possibility of exploring from a narrow range before committing to them. Conversely, when there are many options to choose from, individuals can explore broadly.

The categories of narrow versus broad and ascribed versus chosen are relative categories—that is, they are considered a matter of degree and defined in relation to each other. For example, an important tradition of many East Asian cultures is that of arranged marriages, in which parents choose the mates for their children. This type of marriage leaves no choice to the children and thus is a heavily ascribed process. This tradition has survived even in highly technological communities in the modified form of semi-arranged marriages (Sandhu & Mani, 1993); it has been modified as a result of increasing individualism through globalization. Parents influence the mate-selection process but do not make a choice without the consent of their children. For adolescents, a semi-arranged marriage offers more choice, as they date the potential mates whom their parents present to them or seek their parent's approval before dating a potential mate whom they have met. Nevertheless, relative to the mate-selection process common in the West, a semi-arranged marriage is still a narrow process of exploration, although not as narrow as it used to be.

Given that identity domains can vary in the range of identity options, in their ascribed or chosen nature, and in the type of exploration required to achieve a normative identity, the cross-cultural identity status model conceives the interdependent and independent cultural pathways of development as being domain-specific. This conceptualization fits well with the view that cultural groups are not monolithically independent or interdependent in all areas of life. Moreover, research using Marcia's identity statuses has shown that individuals can have different identity statuses across different domains (Goossens, 2001). Thus, the independent–interdependent distinction should not be applied to a cultural group as a whole, but rather to individual identity domains. Therefore, identity domains are the focus of cross-cultural comparisons to study variations of the identity formation process. Researchers can study *between-culture variability* in identity formation by comparing whether cultural groups employ an interdependent, independent, or no developmental pathway in a particular identity domain.

The cross-cultural identity status model also accounts for *within-culture variability* in identity development by considering individual differences. The model assumes that not all individuals will follow the prescribed developmental pathways to develop an identity commitment, and some could even pursue proscribed identity options. Individuals may deviate from the culturally supported pathways of identity development in three possible ways, with these deviations occurring on a domain-specific basis.

First, individuals may choose to develop a type of identity commitment different from the one that is culturally desired. Although some individuals may concur with their cultural group that it is desirable to develop an identity commitment in a particular domain, they may choose to do so through a process that is not culturally supported, thus creating within-culture variability in identity formation. The dashed lines in Figure 8–1 represent counter-cultural ways of reaching an identity commitment. In relation to an independent pathway of development, the counter-cultural option is a foreclosed identity commitment; in relation to an interdependent identity pathway, the counter-cultural option is an individualistic, achieved identity.

The second possibility of within-culture variability occurs when individuals do not develop an identity in a particular domain despite the availability of a cultural pathway. They do not participate in the process of identity development and remain in a diffused identity status despite their cultural community's expectations. The third possibility occurs when individuals develop identity commitments despite the cultural indifference or lack of expectation for forming an identity in a particular domain. These within-culture variations in the process of identity formation highlight the fact that the process is highly interactive—that is, individual characteristics or preferences interact with the options available within a given cultural community.

To illustrate the process of identity development across diverse cultural contexts, we examine four key identity domains: occupation, religion, ethnicity/nationality, and gender. For each domain, we discuss independent and interdependent identity pathways and then consider the case of multicultural settings, where multiple pathways are available and development requires negotiating among them. Although our initial discussion focuses on separate domains, identity domains do not exist independently of each other but, rather, interact in complex ways in identity formation (Cole, 2009). We conclude our examination of identity formation with some examples of these interactions.

Occupational Identity Formation

Achieving an occupational identity is the core developmental task in Marcia's (1966) paradigm, and an occupational identity is rated as the most important identity across diverse ethnic groups in the United States (Phinney & Alipura, 1990). Marcia's theory originated in a North American context and is based on the assumption that a wide range of occupational options is available. American society is characterized by the ideal that one can be whatever one wants to be, and most young people are given the opportunity to explore broadly. The independent pathway is the dominant, perhaps "default," developmental pathway for occupational identity formation, involving broad exploration of multiple options followed by a commitment. Nevertheless, even in this context, some individuals may follow a counter-cultural pathway and become foreclosed on the first job available or remain drifters.

In contrast, in traditional collectivistic cultures, children are generally expected to follow their parents into similar occupations and often to take over their parents' trade. This pathway may involve narrow exploration, as adolescents get involved in apprenticeships, leading to an interdependent achieved identity when the trade or occupation is learned with sufficient expertise. Nevertheless, some young people may defy cultural expectations and reject the ascribed identity. They may achieve an independent identity, perhaps by going outside the immediate community, moving from occupation-specific villages such as farm or fishing villages, into more urbanized contexts, looking for a wider range of occupational options.

Increasingly, societies worldwide are heterogeneous, consisting of diverse cultural groups and communities (Bhatia, 2007; Hermans & Kempen, 1998). Individuals living in such culturally diverse societies are exposed to a wide range of occupational choices not only from their own cultural community but also from other cultures via the media and internet. For adolescents who belong to collectivistic societies or ethnic groups in multicultural societies, the occupational expectations of their parents or group may be highly traditional, whereas the youth themselves see many alternatives. Immigrant adolescents, in particular, are likely to experience competing pressures from their ethnic culture and from the larger society regarding appropriate occupational goals. Immigrant parents often have strong desires for their children to enter professions that promise clear economic benefits, such as business or medicine. In contrast, peers and school personnel expose them to a range of alternative career options, stressing the need for individuals to pursue their own personal dreams. Often for these youth, an occupational identity cannot be freely chosen but must be negotiated among varying constraints related to the cultural communities in which they live. Few if any models have been developed to make sense of the complexity of occupational identity formation in multicultural contexts. However, a body of research exploring the actual experiences of individuals who form identities in the context of differing expectations from two or more cultures is beginning to appear.

A study of U.S. American youth (ages 14–22 years) from four different cultural backgrounds (European, Mexican, Armenian, and Korean) used vignettes to explore the way young people negotiate the conflicting pressures of the two cultural frameworks in the occupational domain (Phinney, Kim-Jo, Osorio, & Vilhjalmsdottir, 2005). A vignette portrayed a situation in which the adolescent wanted to pursue a course of study and career different from the one strongly urged by the parents. The young people read the vignette and then wrote open-ended responses regarding what they would do in the situation and their reason for doing it. The results showed clear differences among the ethnic groups. Young people from the immigrant groups, compared to the European Americans, showed greater interdependence in this situation, being more likely to consider their parents' feelings and wishes and to seek a way to meet both their own needs and those of their parents. An Armenian adolescent, reflecting both independent and interdependent cultural values, said she would study what her parents wanted, but she would also take courses in her own area of interest. As a reason for her actions, she stated, "That way [I will] be satisfied, and [I'll] satisfy [my] parents as well" (unpublished data). In their actions, the immigrant youth found ways to show respect to their parents, as expected within their ethnic culture, while also making their independent choices, as expected in American culture. The young people's responses to this vignette illustrate the interplay of agency and cultural influence that underlies identity formation in culturally mixed settings. Thus, in multicultural settings, young people may use a mixture of independent and interdependent pathways in the process of identity formation.

Religious Identity

Like occupation, religion is seen in most North American and European societies as a domain in which one's identity can be freely chosen. A recent poll showed that 44% of American adults have either switched the religious affiliation in which they were raised, moved from being unaffiliated with any religion to being affiliated with a particular faith, or dropped any connection to a specific religious tradition altogether (Pew Forum on Religion & Public Life, 2008). Most youth in Europe and America follow an independent identity pathway, exploring broadly their religiosity and then making a commitment to a religious identity.

However, in other countries or cultures, religion may be an ascribed identity to which one is assigned based on one's background. Young people are strongly socialized to internalize the religion of their community. In some cases, being a member of a religious group requires one to be born into the group, because conversion is prohibited or rarely admitted, as it is the custom of the Druze, the Yezidis, and the Mandaeans of the Middle East (Buckley, 2002; Maisel, 2008, August; Obeid, 2006). Individuals growing up in these communities are expected to explore narrowly and to develop an interdependent religious identity achievement, which is vital for the continuation of these communities.

In multicultural settings, young people are exposed to contrasting socialization from their own family and cultural community and from other cultures or societies with very different religious values and traditions. Adolescent Muslim immigrants in Western Europe and the United States present an interesting case because the formation of a Muslim identity requires continual decisions between Muslim and non-Muslim behaviors. Muslim girls in the Netherlands wrestle with decisions about whether to wear a headscarf and have a boyfriend (Ketner, Buitelaar, & Bosma, 2004). Some young women decide not to wear a scarf, despite strong cultural pressures. Others choose to wear the scarf, suggesting conformity to traditional cultural norms. However, because there is room for choice, the decision does not represent foreclosure. Rather, it may be considered an interdependent achieved identity, as defined earlier—that is, they choose to adopt traditional religious behaviors but only after giving it serious thought.

Ethnic and National Identities

The ethnic and national identities that individuals form are based on member-ship in a particular group or society. These group identities may involve a strong sense of affiliation with other members of the group and with the group as a whole. In some cases, ethnic and national identities may overlap or be indistinguishable, as in nations such as Japan with homogeneous populations and a distinctive culture. Even in more ethnically diverse nations, members of a majority group may not distinguish an ethnic identity from a national identity. For a dominant ethnic group in their cultural homeland, such as Han Chinese in China, ethnicity may be confounded with national identity. Most members of the White majority in the United States have only a vague concept of their ethnicity as European American as distinct from their national identity as American.

However, it is useful to make a distinction between ethnic and national iden-tities because of their different implications for developmental pathways, depending on the particular group and the context. Ethnic identity refers to a sense of peoplehood based on one's ancestry and is associated with one's cul-tural values and traditions. It is an ascribed identity, into which one is born, although ethnic groups themselves are fluid and dynamic, changing with his-torical and social events. In contrast, national identity refers to a sense of mem-bership in a sovereign political entity. It can generally be acquired by becoming a resident or citizen of the nation, although some countries are resistant to new members. We first examine ethnic identity formation and then consider the development of national identity in terms of cultural context.

Ethnic Identity

When ethnic groups exist in relative isolation, with limited contact with other groups, there is likely to be little choice as to how to live in the community as group member. Young people are assumed to follow an interdependent path-way, either asserting their group membership without much thought and remain-ing foreclosed or engaging in narrow exploration as they learn the customs and traditions of their group and achieve interdependent ethnic identities.

This situation, however, is increasingly rare, as more ethnic groups co-exist with other groups or as part of a larger society. This relationship may be one of relative dominance, weakness, or equality, with implications for the develop-mental process. When an ethnic group dominates in a setting, such as Han Chinese in China, European Americans in the United States, or Mestizos in Costa Rica, ethnicity is likely to have little salience. European Americans tend to rate their ethnic identity as unimportant to them (Grossman & Chamaraman, 2009; Phinney & Alipuria, 1990; Waters, 2000). Most are diffuse; they have given little thought to the issue of ethnicity and are unsure about its meaning. Exceptions to this generalization are members of the dominant majority who are in very diverse contexts or in settings where they are the minority; in such cases, they may feel motivated to explore their own ethnicity. In addition, individuals from European backgrounds in the United States, such as Irish or German, unlike those from, say, Asia or Africa, have a choice as to whether maintain ties with their ethnic origin (Waters, 1990); for personal reasons, they may choose to explore in depth and decide whether or not they wish to commit to a specific ethnic identity.

The more usual situation worldwide is for ethnic groups to exist as non-dominant minorities within larger political entities. In such cases, ethnic identity is a highly salient identity that typically elicits considerable explora-tion. Ethnic identity has perhaps been most widely studied in immigrants—particularly in the United States (Phinney, 1990)—but increasing diversity and the greater numbers of migrants moving across borders has led to an increase in concern with ethnic identity worldwide (Berry, Phinney, Sam, & Vedder, 2006). Among the many minority groups in which ethnicity is salient are indig-enous groups such as Aboriginal Australians and the Sami of the Scandinavian countries, lower status groups such as Koreans in Japan, Blacks in the United States, and lower caste groups in India.

As a developmental process, ethnic identity formation for indigenous, minority, and immigrant adolescents involves exploration of the meaning and implications of their ethnicity (Phinney & Ong, 2007b). Because ethnicity is generally ascribed, these adolescents do not have the option of exploring other ethnicities (unless it is possible for them to "pass" as a member of another group), so their exploration might be mostly narrow. However, because they live in multicultural contexts, there may be different ways to internalize and express one's ethnicity, in terms of values, language usage, and cultural prac-tices. Survey measures of ethnic identity show minority youth generally scor-ing very high on exploration, as well as on their commitment to their group. A well-developed ethnic identity involves an awareness and understanding of one's cultural heritage and a secure sense of oneself as a member of a particular cultural group.

Despite a considerable body of research on ethnic identity formation (Phinney & Ong, 2007a), there is still little understanding of the actual unfold-ing of the process by which an ethnic identity is constructed in interaction with the cultural context. Several recent studies have explored aspects of this process and provide insight into the interplay of development and culture. Some of the earliest research on group identity (Clark & Clark, 1947), carried out with young Black children, suggested the social influence of a pervasive culture that denigrates Blacks. In this research, young Black children showed a consistent choice of White dolls over Black dolls as being nicer, prettier, and preferred playmates. More recent work has indicated that the immediate context also serves as a social influence on the adolescents from diverse ethnic groups (Way, Santos, Niwa, & Kim-Gervey, 2008). Way and col-leagues interviewed adolescents in New York schools in which virtually all the students were from ethnic minority groups (Puerto Rican, Dominican, Black, and Chinese-American), but the social status of the groups in the schools varied widely, with the Puerto Ricans having the highest status and the Chinese-Americans the lowest. Although the expressed ethnic identities of the adolescents showed the influence of their group's status, the students did not passively accept the status hierarchy. Many adolescents, particularly those from lower status groups, showed a variety of ways of resisting and accommodating to the status differences. The resulting ethnic identities were not simply a reflection of the existing social hierarchies; rather, they were the product of the way adolescents responded to and interacted with the school context. Thus, the way ethnic identities are developed is dependent on the interaction between identity formation process and the cultural context in which it takes place.

National Identity

National identity has been studied far less than ethnic identity, and existing research has been carried out mainly in Western European and North American— that is, in predominantly individualistic—contexts. However, results from a study that examined national identity among more than 4000 children and youth from 10 different countries in both Western and Eastern Europe found that "different groups of children living in different national and state contexts exhibit different patterns of [national] identity development" (Barrett, 2007, p. 252). Although this study did not consider developmental changes in the sense discussed in this chapter, the findings do suggest wide variability both within and across countries. For example, Armenian and Georgian children attending the same schools in Tblisi differed widely in the extent to which they considered themselves Georgian (Barrett, 2007). We can speculate that the differing cultures of diverse countries contribute to differing pathways by which young people form a national identity.

In multicultural settings, the context is highly complex, involving two or more cultures and the interactions among them. In such settings, minority youth are faced with the task of simultaneously developing an ethnic and a national identity. An extensive literature on acculturation has explored the extent to which immigrants adopt a national identity in their country of settlement and retain their ethnic identity (Phinney, Berry, Liebkind, & Vedder, 2006). Based on data from 13 culturally European or North American countries, Phinney and colleagues (2006) described four different acculturation profiles, based on whether immigrants developed and maintained both identities (integrated or bicultural), only one identity (ethnic or national), or neither identity (diffuse or marginalized). These profiles reflect, in part, the individual preferences and choices of immigrant youth, but they are also influenced by the context. The bicultural profile is significantly more common in societies that have a history of immigration and a large proportion of immigrants, such as the United States and Canada (Phinney et al., 2006).

The profiles, like the identities themselves, develop in the interaction of the individual and the context. This interactive process is evident in a study of 46 Mexican-American adolescents (Phinney & Devich-Navarro, 1997) in culturally diverse American high schools. The students were interviewed about their sense of being Mexican and American and the meaning and implications of their group membership. They also completed a survey of the strength of their ethnic and American identities and of their attitudes toward other ethnic groups. The results showed that the adolescents differed widely in their perceptions of being American. In response to whether they saw themselves as more ethnic or more American, one group of students, termed *blended biculturals*, reported that they were "both," or "like half and half. . . To me it is the same thing." In discussing the meaning of American identity, these adolescents expressed the attitudes that America is "a very diverse culture," "people have come from all different places," and "as an American . . . you are part of everything in American society." In contrast, a second group of students, termed *alternating biculturals*, felt that they were bicultural, but they reported situational differences in how they saw themselves—more ethnic in some settings, more American in others. Their perceptions of America reflected this distinction. The concept of being American was more abstract, related to the idea of freedom or a better life but with little sense of inclusion. These differing perceptions of being American were related to differences in outcomes. The blended biculturals had more positive attitudes than the alternating biculturals toward members of ethnic groups other than their own. The study illustrates the interaction of person and context in identity formation; it was not the context alone but the differing perceptions of the context that lead to different identity outcomes.

A challenge that young people from minority cultures face in forming a national identity is resolving differences between the culture of the larger society and that of their ethnic culture. There is a substantial literature describing differences in values, attitudes, and practices between American culture and that of many immigrants in the United States (Fuligni, Tseng, & Lam, 1999; Phinney, Ong, & Madden, 2000). Young people in immigrant families often are expected to defer to parents and to show respect to a greater extent than is expected in American culture. These differences must be negotiated by ethnic minority group youth as they develop an identity. The study cited earlier (Phinney et al., 2005), in which immigrant youth responded to situations of cultural conflicts with their parents, provides numerous examples of the way in which immigrant young people balance the competing cultural expectations. Typical vignettes involved potential conflicts, such as wanting to go to a friend's party rather than attend a family dinner or dating someone from another ethnic group contrary to parental wishes. The results showed the adolescents' attempts to meet both cultural expectations and exercise their own autonomy. The results also revealed the way these change with age. Younger adolescents in some cases disagreed with their parents, but they were more likely than older ones to defer to their parents, and they gave reasons reflecting interdependence: "I would do what is best for my family," or "I love and respect my parents; I would honor their reasons." Older adolescents were more likely to follow their own wishes, but their autonomy was tempered by consideration and respect for parents: "I respect my parents but at the same time I'm an adult, and I make my own decisions," or "I'd go to the party, but I'd apologize the next day to the whole family." It is through the negotiation of these cultural differences in specific situations that an individual forms ethnic and national identities.

Multicultural settings involve more than the social influences of the two cultures on the child. They also involve disparities in power and dominance among the various groups represented in the setting. The broader cultural context encompasses the reality that the values and practices of one group have higher status or preference than the other, and that members of one group have privileges and advantages lacking in the other group. Immigrant youth face not only cultural differences but also the lower status of their own group and the experience of discrimination. Within this broader cultural context, ethnic and national identity formation for some youth is a process of attempting to develop a coherent identity within a context that is not welcoming to them. In the study of bicultural youth described earlier (Phinney & Devich-Navarro, 1997), some of the adolescents denied that there were or could be Americans. They made comments such as "I'm not part of two cultures," "Everything is so White," and "No one in my family is White." Others acknowledged the problem but focused on a larger perspective. An adolescent who described herself as bicultural stated that American culture was "a very diverse culture. . . I do not think there is any true blood American; people have come from all different places." The way in which the young person views a society becomes part of the process of forming a national identity. The formation of both ethnic and national identities is an interactive process involving both the intergroup situation of the society and the perceptions and attitudes of the individual regarding that situation. We can speculate that the differing cultures of diverse countries influence the pathways by which young people form a national identity.

Gender Identity

Gender is a universally ascribed identity, perhaps because it is one of the most salient and visible markers of human differences. The gender label assigned at birth largely determines the way children are socialized and what their identity options will be. Cultures prescribe, with varying degrees of flexibility, the appropriate roles that males and females can or should enact (Williams & Best, 1990). Children learn their gender identities as they participate in the gendered roles of their cultural communities and follow the patterns of the adult interactions. Because gender identity is highly ascribed in most settings, exploration is likely to be relatively narrow, particularly in traditional communities and in remote rural areas. In contrast, in complex urban settings, many more gender options are available, and exploration and negotiation of many alternatives can take place. However, there has been relatively little research on the development of gender identity (Kroger, 2007) and even less on gender identity across cultures. Research has focused on gender and cultural differences, rather than on developmental processes. For example, Kashima and colleagues (1995) found that in both Western cultures (United States and Australia) and Eastern cultures (Japan and Korea), women scored higher than men on relatedness.

The topic of gender identity formation across cultures is a complex topic that we cannot explore in depth here. Because of the prominence of the gender identity domain in all cultures, it interacts with and influences other identity domains. We explore this topic in the following section.

Interaction of Identity Domains

As noted earlier, identity domains interact in complex ways in identity formation. Recent research on intersectionality has explored the ways in which identities such as ethnicity, gender, and social class interact (Cole, 2009). For example, Azmitia, Syed, and Radmacher (2008) describe how gender and ethnicity jointly influence the career decisions of an Asian and a Latina college student. Domains also differ in prominence as well as depth across cultural contexts. A domain with a great personal or social significance may be prioritized over other identity domains, influencing what are perceived as acceptable identity options and restricting the range and type of exploration in these areas.

At the cultural group level, gender identity tends to be a dominant domain to which other identity domains are subordinated. Cultural groups often have conceptions of what is appropriate for women to pursue in occupation and how they should develop their religious identity. But subordination of other domains to a single identity domain can also be voluntary, based on individual preference. Even in a secular society, a religious identity may play a dominant role for some individuals. Using the guiding principles drawn from their religious commitments, they limit the range of exploration and the identity possibilities for other identity domains. For example, individuals may restrict the pool of potential occupations to options that have direct connection to their religious group such as priesthood or missionary work. They might also limit their gender roles according to the teachings of their religious community.

The interaction of religious and occupational identity is illustrated in the case of identity formation when a person with a traditional religious identity commitment is confronted with modern scientific values. An in-depth case study by Schachter (2005) describes a young man, Gil, who grew up in a homogeneous religious neighborhood in Israel and considered himself a modern Orthodox Jew. When his interest in science led him to study physics, he wrestled with the contradictions between the two "cultures"—a religious worldview and a scientific one. In this case, the two identity domains present such different values and beliefs that no simple resolution is possible. He was unwilling to give up either and eventually arrived at a position that allowed him to "get on with his life by making tentative commitments to an indefinite and changing world" (pp. 387–388). Conflicts such as these are likely to be increasingly common in complex modern societies, giving rise to mixed independent and interdependent identity pathways.

Socio-economic status varies widely both within and across cultural groups and interacts with the process of identity formation. In the developing world, more affluent families may adopt Western, individualistic patterns of child-rearing, socialization, and consumption (e.g., children having their own rooms and their own gadgets, like cell phones). These patterns are likely to support a pathway to an independent identity achievement. Adolescents from non-affluent families would be more likely to follow narrower, more traditional identity options because of their economic constraints. Saraswathi (1999) notes that in India, adolescents from lower socio-economic groups are expected to have a smooth continuity between childhood and adulthood. Girls learn to be homemakers through early assignment of childcare and chores. For boys, economic pressures may prevent them from advanced schooling and force them to enter the work force. In contrast, boys from middle socio-economic groups may be encouraged to continue their education. Wealthier adolescents, with access to cash and perhaps their own car, have more independence.

Cultural Change and Identity Development

Any discussion of cultural differences risks the danger of portraying cultures as static entities that remain constant over time. However, cultures are continually changing and evolving on their own as well as being influenced by changes worldwide. Four types of changes, in particular, have important implications for identity formation: technological advances, immigration, globalization, and historical events of great social significance.

Technological advances can affect ascribed identities such as gender. Traditionally, the gender roles have been defined along the lines of biology and reproduction, with childbirth being the task of women. Until the arrival of modern birth control methods, most women expected to be pregnant or nursing during most of their adult life. In addition, because of the baby bottle, infant feeding is not limited to women anymore. Adopting changes such as these implies a change in the range of identity alternatives for gender identity.

Immigration is a major source of cultural change. In their new environments, immigrants face a different range of identity choices, a range that sometimes is wider than that offered by their original community. For example, Shenzhen, formerly a fishing town across the border from Hong Kong, is now a booming industrial town in China, where the rural poor—especially young females—go looking for new opportunities. Most of them listen to "At Night You're Not Lonely," the top-rated radio show in Shenzhen (population 12 million), which was designed to reach the immigrant population. The host of the show, Hu Xiao Mei, explains her main message: "I tell the women in my audience to respect themselves, think independently and take control of their lives . . . because the world we face and the fast changing environment are beyond anyone's imagination. Everyone needs time to grow up. All people, me included, have to gradually grow up" (On The Media, 2008, June 20b). Thus, these immigrant women are encouraged to adapt to their new context by exploring broadly and pursuing an independent identity achievement.

The effects of globalization are ubiquitous through increased economic trade and media coverage. In China, for example, pirated DVDs and American TV shows available on the Internet have changed the identity expectations of young people in many urban centers. It is common for them to download shows such as "Prison Break," "24," "Desperate Housewives," and "Sex in the City" (On The Media, 2008, June 20a). A woman in her early twenties, from Shanghai, commented: "I think this is maybe the reason why we often watch American TV shows, such as 'Ugly Betty' [or] 'Friends,' because we have maybe [a] generation gap with [people] 10 years older than us, maybe our big sisters, big brothers. They don't like to watch that because their life and the life in TV are not similar. They [the TV programs] are more similar of us" (On The Media, 2008, June 20a).

Some large-scale, historical events carry such social significance that they can change the usual process of identity formation by opening or restricting the array of identity options (Crockett & Silbereisen, 2000). When former European socialist countries adopted a market economy, the range of occupational possibilities was significantly widened. But this event also changed the type social skills needed for success under the new system, skills such as willingness to take risks and impression management (Crockett & Silbereisen, 2000). The process of occupational identity formation had to be adapted to the new social order that demanded an independent identity achievement.

Even the identity options of ascribed domains such as ethnic identity can be changed by historical events. The election of Barack Obama has broken old stereotypes that used to define who was a Black American. For example, studious Black adolescents are often tarred by their same race peers as "acting White" for liking school. Obama's election has the potential to change such perception (McWhorter, 2008). In addition, because identity options are to some extent based on role models, the image of a Black president can provide a powerful model to youth of color. However, some types of social change may restrict the array of identity options. The recent resurgence of the Taliban in certain areas of Afghanistan has meant the closing of schools for girls and the enforcement of traditional religious restrictions on women (Nelson, 2007, April 5), thus constraining their exploration of gender roles and occupation.

Implications for Research and Policy

The complexity of the interactive processes of identity development and cultural processes present a daunting challenge for researchers and policymakers. Our view of identity development as interactively entwined with the cultural context means that any efforts to understand the process must consider multiple factors. From the developmental perspective, the individual can be seen as an agent with developmental needs to form a coherent sense of self across various domains important to his or her life. Thus, one starting point for research is to focus on the individuals being studied. How are they working on identity issues? What domains are important to them? What kinds of exploration are they engaging in? What kinds of decisions have they made or avoided? However, to address these questions, it is essential to define the cultural context in which they have developed and the kinds of exposure they have to other cultural communities and to cultural change.

The model we have presented specifies the different possibilities of interaction between culture and individual agency that give rise to differences between and within cultures. These possibilities are defined by two factors: *(1)* the kinds of developmental goals and pathways of identity formation that cultural communities have (or lack) in particular identity domains and *(2)* the extent to which individuals follow the cultural processes available in their communities. Numerous hypotheses can be developed from the combination of these factors. For example, within traditional cultures and among ethnic groups from these cultures, more individuals will show interdependent identity achievement. Traditional cultural communities in the midst of rapid social change toward individualism will have a mixture of independent and interdependent identity achievements in those domains affected by the change.

Those instances in which individuals follow their cultural community's orientation highlight within-culture consistencies that can be used to study differences between cultures. Conversely, instances in which individuals part ways from their communities represent within-culture variability. Thus, the cross-cultural status model describes both cultural consistencies and variations in the process of identity formation; it allows generalizations as well as group-specific variations. The more culture-specific features of identity development are found in the identity options themselves and the meanings associated with these options.

Longitudinal studies are needed to examine identity formation processes in situations of exposure to multiple cultures or of rapid cultural change. Such research has the potential to illuminate the many ways in which individuals and their cultural contexts make each other up.

Policymakers need to be aware of the complex interactive processes that influence identity and avoid simplistic solutions to promoting positive identity formation. Particularly in some traditional and minority communities, extensive identity exploration may not be expected or valued. Thus, appropriate identity pathways may be quite different from those common in dominant groups and in highly developed countries.

Conclusions

Theoretical descriptions of identity development are converging on the view that an individual's identity formation process is inseparable from the immediate and larger cultural contexts in which the individual lives. Culture can be understood as part of identity formation in two ways. First, culture can be considered as a coherent set of values, attitudes, and practices that is an *influence* on identity development at all levels, from daily contacts within the family to the prevailing societal norms about how best to practice one's religion or find an occupation. Cultural influence can be studied by means of comparisons between differing contexts. Second, culture is a *process* that is evident in identity formation in the way "youth negotiate their multiple identities or manage their domain-specific identities" (Bosma & Kunnen, 2008, p. 287). Culture as process is best studied through analysis of day-to-day interactions in which individuals deal with identity challenges in specific settings. These two approaches are complementary rather than opposing, and each contributes to our understanding of development in cultural context.

Although a comprehensive contextual theory of identity development does not yet exist (Schachter & Ventura, 2008), a step toward it is the cross-cultural identity status model (Baldelomar, under review). This model suggests that individuals follow different pathways of identity formation, depending on their own needs and goals and on the opportunities and constraints offered by their cultural context. Because this model is applicable to all contexts, separate theories for each culture are not needed. The model considers different cultural orientations (independent or interdependent) and identity statuses (e.g., foreclosed or achieved) in different domains. Cultural comparisons might show that in a given domain, most individuals are achieved in one culture and foreclosed in another. However, the process of identity formation, based on variation in the extent and type of exploration and the degree of commitment, is similar across cultures. To understand identity formation within a particular context, it is essential to examine the options, or lack of options, in that context, as well as the values and attitudes that underlie the choices that do exist.

In summary, identity development and culture do not constitute separate topics with differing implications for psychology. Rather, they are inextricably linked, resulting in complex processes that we are just beginning to understand. Identity researchers can contribute to this exciting field of inquiry by focusing on the ways in which development and culture interact in the process of identity formation.

Note

The preparation of this chapter was supported in part by grants to Oscar Baldelomar from the Ford Foundation and from the Foundation for Psychocultural Research-UCLA Center for Culture, Brain, and Development.

References

Arnett, J. J. (1995). Broad and narrow socialization: The family in the context of a cultural theory. *Journal of Marriage and the Family, 57*(3), 617–628.

Arnett, J. J. (2010). Emerging adulthood: The cultural psychology of a new life stage. In L. A. Jensen (Ed.), *Bridging cultural and developmental psychology: New Syntheses in Theory, Research and Policy.* New York: Oxford University Press.

Azmitia, M., Syed, M., & Radmacher, K. (2008). On the intersection of personal and social identities: Introduction and evidence from a longitudinal study of emerging adults.

In M. Azmitia, M. Syed & K. Radmacher (Eds.), *The intersections of personal and social identities* (Vol. Number 120, pp. 1–16). San Francisco: Jossey-Bass.

Baldelomar, O. A. (under review). Identity development and culture: A theoretical integration of the identity status model and the interdependent-independent self.

Barrett, M. (2007). *Children's knowledge, beliefs, and feelings about nations and national groups.* New York: Psychology Press.

Baumeister, R., & Muraven, M. (1996). Identity as adaptation to social, cultural, and historical context. *Journal of Adolescence, 19,* 405–416.

Berry, J., Phinney, J., Sam, D., & Vedder, P. (2006). *Immigrant youth in cultural transition: Acculturation, identity, and adaptation across national contexts.* Mahwah, NJ: Erlbaum.

Beyers, W., & Goossens, L. (2008). Dynamics of perceived parenting and identity formation in late adolescence. *Journal of Adolescence, 31*(2), 165–184.

Bhatia, S. (2007). Rethinking culture and identity in psychology: Towards a transnational cultural psychology. *Journal of Theoretical and Philosophical Psychology, 27/28*(2/1), 301–321.

Bosma, H., & Kunnen, S. (2001). Determinants and mechanisms in ego identity development: A review and synthesis. *Developmental Review, 21,* 39–66.

Bosma, H., & Kunnen, S. (2008). Identity-in-context is not yet identity development-in-context. *Journal of Adolescence, 31*(2), 281–289.

Bronfenbrenner, U. (1979). *The ecology of human development: Experiments by nature and design.* Cambridge: Harvard University Press.

Buckley, J. J. (2002). *The Mandaeans: Ancient texts and modern people.* New York: Oxford University Press.

Clark, K., & Clark, M. (1947). Racial identification and preference in Negro preschool children. In T. Newcomb & E. Hartley (Eds.), *Readings in social psychology.* New York: Holt.

Cole, E. (2009). Intersectionality and research in psychology. *American Psychologist, 64,* 170–180.

Cote, J., & Levine, C. (2002). *Identity formation, agency, and culture.* Mahwah, NJ: Erlbaum.

Crockett, L. J., & Silbereisen, R. K. (2000). Social change and adolescent development: Issues and challenges. In L. J. Crockett & R. K. Silbereisen (Eds.), *Negotiating adolescence in times of social change* (pp. 1–13). New York: Cambridge University Press.

Erikson, E. H. (1963). *Childhood and society.* New York: Norton.

Erikson, E. H. (1968). *Identity: Youth and crisis.* New York: Norton.

Fiske, A. P. (1991). *Structures of social life: The four elementary forms of human relations: Communal sharing, authority ranking, equality matching, market pricing.* New York: The Free Press.

Fuligni, A., Tseng, V., & Lam, M. (1999). Attitudes toward family obligations among American adolescents with Asian, Latin American, and European backgrounds. *Child Development, 70,* 1030–1044.

Goodnow, J. J. (2011). Merging cultural and psychological accounts of family contexts. In L. A. Jensen (Ed.), *Bridging cultural and developmental psychology: New Syntheses in Theory, Research and Policy* (pp. 73–91). New York: Oxford University Press.

Goossens, L. (2001). Global versus domain-specific statuses in identity research: A comparison of two self-report measures. *Journal of Adolescence, 24*(681–699).

Greenfield, P. M. (1994). Independence and interdependence as developmental scripts: Implications for theory, research, and practice. In P. M. Greenfield & R. R. Cocking (Eds.), *Cross-cultural roots of minority child development* (pp. 1–37). Hillsdale, NJ: Lawrence Erlbaum Associates.

Greenfield, P. M. (2004). *Weaving generations together: Evolving creativity in the Zinacantec Maya.* Santa Fe, NM: SAR Press.

Greenfield, P. M., Keller, H., Fuligni, A., & Maynard, A. (2003). Cultural pathways through universal development. *Annual Review of Psychology*(54), 461–490.

Grossman, J., & Chamaraman, L. (2009). Race, context, and privilege: White adolescents' explanation of racial-ethnic centrality. *Journal of Youth and Adolescence*(38), 139–152.

Hammack, P. (2008). Narrative and the cultural psychology of identity. *Personality and Social Psychology Review, 12,* 222–247.

Hermans, H., & Kempen, H. (1998). Moving cultures: The perilous problem of cultural dichotomies in a globalizing society. *Identity: An International Journal of Theory and Research, 4,* 145–169.

Hofstede, G. (1980). *Culture's consequences: Comparing values, behaviors, institutions, and organizations across nations.* Thousand Oaks, CA: Sage.

Jensen, L. A. (2010). The cultural-developmental theory of moral psychology: A new synthesis. In L. A. Jensen (Ed.), *Bridging cultural and developmental psychology: New Syntheses in Theory, Research and Policy.* New York: Oxford University Press.

Jensen, L. A. (2008). Immigrants' cultural identities as sources of civic engagement. *Applied Developmental Science, 12,* 74–83.

Jensen, L. A. (2003). Coming of age in a multicultural world: Globalization and adolescent cultural identity formation. *Applied Developmental Science, 7,* 188–195.

Jensen, L. A., Arnett, J. J., & McKenzie, J. (in press). Globalization and cultural identity developments in adolescence and emerging adulthood. In Schwartz, S. J., Luyckx, K., & Vignoles, V. L. (Eds.), *Handbook of Identity Theory and Research.* New York, NY: Springer Publishing Company.

Kashima, Y., Yamaguchi, W., Kim, U., Choi, S., Gelfand, M., & Yuki, M. (1995). Culture, gender, and self: A perspective from individualism-collectivism research. *Journal of Personality and Social Psychology, 69,* 925–937.

Ketner, S., Buitelaar, M., & Bosma, H. (2004). Identity strategies among adolescent girls of Moroccan descent in the Netherlands. *Identity: An International Journal of Theory and Research, 4,* 145–169.

Kroger, J. (2004). *Identity in adolescence: The balance between self and other.* New York: Routledge.

Kroger, J. (2007). *Identity development: Adolescence through adulthood* (2nd. ed.). Newbury Park, CA: Sage.

Lerner, R. (1999). Theories of human development: Contemporary perspectives. In R. Lerner (Ed.), *Handbook of Child Psychology, Fifth edition* (Vol. Volume 1: Theoretical models of human development, pp. 1–23). New York: Wiley.

Maisel, S. (2008, August). Social change amidst terror and discrimination: Yezidis in the new Iraq [Electronic Version]. *The Middle East Institute Policy Brief,* 1–9. Retrieved May 16, 2009 from http://www.mideasti.org/policy-brief/social-change-amidst-terror-and-discrimination-yezidis-new-iraq.

Marcia, J. E. (1966). Development and validation of ego identity status. *Journal of Personality and Social Psychology, 3,* 551–558.

Markus, H. R., & Hamedani, M. G. (2007). Sociocultural psychology: The dynamic interdependence among self systems and social systems. In S. Kitayama & D. Cohen (Eds.), *Handbook of cultural psychology.* New York: The Guilford Press.

Markus, H. R., & Kitayama, S. (1991). Culture and the self: Implications for cognition, emotion, and motivation. *Psychological Review, 98*(224–253).

McWhorter, J. (2008). What Obama means for Black America: A new reality—without a revolution. *Forbes.*

Nelson, S. S. (2007, April 5). Taliban wages war on Afghan girls' schools. *NPR World.*

Nucci, L. P., & Turiel, E. (2000). The moral and the personal: Sources of social conflicts. In L. P. Nucci, G. B. Saxe & E. Turiel (Eds.), *Culture, thought, and development.* Mahwah, NJ: Earlbaum.

Obeid, A. (2006). *The Druze and their faith in Tawhid.* Syracuse, NY: Syracuse University Press.

On The Media. (2008, June 20a). Brand China.

On The Media. (2008, June 20b). Journalism with Chinese characteristics.

Overton, W. (1998). Developmental psychology: Philosophy, concepts, and methods. In W. Damon (Ed.), *Handbook of child psychology: Vol 1. Theoretical modelsl of human development* (5th ed., pp. 107–187). New York: Wiley.

Pew Forum on Religion & Public Life. (2008). U.S. Religious Landscape Survey. Religious affiliation: Diverse and dynamic [Electronic Version]. Retrieved April, 29 2009 from http://religions.pewforum.org/pdf/report-religious-landscape-study-full.pdf.

Phinney, J. (1990). Ethnic identity in adolescents and adults: Review of research. *Psychological Bulletin, 108*(3), 499–514.

Phinney, J., & Alipuria, L. (1990). Ethnic identity in college students from four ethnic groups. *Journal of Adolescence, 13*, 171–184.

Phinney, J., Berry, J., Liebkind, K., & Vedder, P. (2006). The acculturation experience: Attitudes, identities, and behaviors of immigrant youth. In J. Berry, J. Phinney, D. Sam & P. Vedder (Eds.), *Immigrant youth in cultural transition: Acculturation, identity, and adaptation across national contexts* (pp. 71–116). Mahwah, NJ: Erlbaum.

Phinney, J., & Devich-Navarro, M. (1997). Variations in bicultural identification among African American and Mexican American adolescents. *Journal of Research on Adolescence, 7*, 3–32.

Phinney, J., Kim-Jo, T., Osorio, S., & Vilhjalmsdottir, P. (2005). Autonomy and relatedness in adolescent-parent disagreements: Ethnic and developmental factors. *Journal of Adolescent Research, 20*, 8–39.

Phinney, J., & Ong, A. (2007a). Conceptualization and measurement of ethnic identity: Current status and future directions. *Journal of Counseling Psychology, 54*, 271–281.

Phinney, J., & Ong, A. (2007b). Ethnic identity development in immigrant families. In J. Lansford, K. Deater-Deckard & M. Bornstein (Eds.), *Immigrant families in contemporary society* (pp. 51–68). New York: Guildford Press.

Phinney, J., Ong, A., & Madden, T. (2000). Cultural values and intergenerational value discrepancies in immigrant and non-immigrant families. *Child Development, 71*(2), 528–539.

Raeff, C. (2006). Multiple and inseparable: Conceptualizing the development of independence and interdependence. *Human Development, 49*, 96–121.

Rogoff, B. (2003). *The cultural nature of human development.* New York: Oxford.

Sandhu, K. S., & Mani, A. (Eds.). (1993). *Indian communities of Southeast Asia.* Singapore: Institute of Southeast Asian Studies.

Saraswathi, T. S. (1999). Adult-child continuity in India: Is adolescence a myth or an emerging reality? In T. S. Saraswathi (Ed.), *Culture, socialization, and human development: Theory, research, and applications in India* (pp. 213–232). New Delhi: Sage.

Schachter, E. (2005). Context and identity formation: A theoretical analysis and a case study. *Journal of Adolescecent Research, 20*(3), 375–396.

Schachter, E., & Ventura, J. (2008). Identity agents: Parents as active and reflective participants in their children's identity formation. *Journal of Research on Adolescence, 18*(3), 449–476.

Schlegel, A. (1995). A cross-cultural approach to adolescence. *Ethos, 23*(1), 15–32.

Schlegel, A. (2010). Cultural approaches to adolescent development: The significance of age integration or segration. In L. A. Jensen (Ed.), *Bridging cultural and developmental psychology: New Syntheses in Theory, Research and Policy.* New York: Oxford University Press.

Shweder, R., Goodnow, J., Hatano, G., Levine, R., Markus, H., & Miller, P. (2006). The cultural psychology of development: One mind, many mentalities. In R. Lerner (Ed.), *Handbook of child psychology* (6th ed., Vol. 1, pp. 716–792). Hoboken, NJ: Wiley.

Sugimura, K. (2007). Transitions in the process of identity formation among Japanese female adolescents: A relational viewpoint. In R. Josselson, A. Lieblich & D. McAdams (Eds.), *The meaning of others: Narrative studies of relationships* (pp. 117–142). Washington, DC: American Psychological Association.

Tharakad, S., Mistry, J., & Dutta, R. (2010). Hindu lifespan conceptions. In L. A. Jensen (Ed.), *Bridging cultural and developmental psychology: New Syntheses in Theory, Research and Policy.* New York: Oxford University Press.

Triandis, H. C. (1988). Collectivism and individualism: A reconceptualization of a basic concept in cross-cultural psychology. In C. Bagley & G. Verma (Eds.), *Personality, cognition, and values: Cross-cultural perspectives of childhood and adolescence* (pp. 60–95). London: MacMillan.

Triandis, H. C. (1995). *Individualism and collectivism.* Boulder, CO: Westview Press.

Turiel, E. (1985). *The development of social knowledge: Morality and convention.* Cambridge, UK: Cambridge University Press.

Waters, M. (1990). *Ethnic options: Choosing identities in America.* Berkeley, CA: University of California Press.

Waters, M. (2000). Multiple ethnicities and identity in the United States. In P. Spickard & W. J. Burroughs (Eds.), *We are a people: Narrative and multiplicity in constructing ethnic identity* (pp. 23–40). Philadelphia: Temple University Press.

Way, N., Santos, C., Niwa, E., & Kim-Gervey, C. (2008). To be or not to be: Exploration of ethnic identity development in context. In M. Azmitia, M. Syed & K. Radmacher (Eds.), *The intersections of personal and social identities.* San Francisco: Jossey-Bass.

Williams, J., & Best, D. (1990). *Sex and psyche: Gender and self viewed cross-culturally.* Thousand Oaks, CA: Sage.

CHAPTER 9

Cultural and Developmental Pathways to Acceptance of Self and Acceptance of the World

FRED ROTHBAUM & YAN Z. WANG

This chapter examines cultural differences in parental acceptance of children and how such differences foster differences in children's acceptance of themselves and their world. Acceptance refers to beliefs, feelings, values, and actions that convey acknowledgment and approval. Parental acceptance is a key dynamic in theories of socialization (Ainsworth, Blehar, Waters, & Wall, 1978; Baldwin, Kallhorn, Breese, & Huffman, 1949; Baumrind, 1971) and in theories of child and adult mental health (Hayes, Strosahl, & Wilson, 1999; Rogers, 1961). Although these theories are often assumed to apply universally, they are authored by European Americans, are based on European American values and assumptions, and are supported by evidence predominantly from European American samples. Even investigators focused on cultural differences in acceptance have been heavily influenced by European American theories (e.g., Rohner, 2004).

We agree with these investigators that acceptance is of universal importance, but we claim that there are important cultural differences in acceptance that have often been ignored. One dimension of cultural difference involves the target of acceptance. In some cultures, caregivers are relatively more accepting of their children's individual selves, whereas in other cultures, caregivers are relatively more accepting of the world in which their children are embedded. Another dimension involves the nature of acceptance. In some cultures, acceptance tends to be evaluative and positive (approving), whereas in others acceptance tends to be non-evaluative. Acceptance is non-evaluative when it is acknowledging and neutral as opposed to approving (i.e., positive). We believe that caregivers in European American and East Asian communities differ with regard to both of these dimensions. Because children's acceptance is based on parental acceptance, children also differ in their acceptance of themselves versus their world and in their positive versus non-evaluative acceptance.

In this chapter, "European American" communities refer to North American and Northern and Western European communities. Most of the communities studied were in the United States. "East Asian" communities refer to Confucian- and Buddhist-influenced communities in China, Japan, and South Korea. The research from which we draw focuses on *predominantly middle class, majority group individuals from urban areas*, so our claims apply primarily to those individuals.

In moving away from a one-size-fits-all view of acceptance, we advocate efforts to identify general cultural differences as opposed to highly specific and particular differences. That is why we group together cultures with similar philosophical traditions (e.g., a shared Judaic–Christian vs. a Buddhist–Confucian belief system). Identifying general distinctions leads to a middle ground between a universalist approach common in developmental psychology and a theory-for-every-culture approach that can result from an extreme focus on cultural uniqueness (*see also* Tharakad, Mistry, & Dutta, 2011). Finding that middle ground lies at the heart of this volume.

While focusing on general differences between communities in their ways of accepting children, we are mindful of important differences within communities. Within-culture variation pertaining to ethnicity, region, religious affiliation, rural versus urban, and social class (Kitayama, Ishii, Imada, Takemura, & Ramaswamy, 2006; Snibbe & Markus, 2005) often rivals variation between communities. There are also historical changes, some of which are related to globalization. For example, in the past 30 years there has been a dramatic increase in the number of European Americans—scholars first and, because of their influence, parents and educators—who have adopted East Asian practices involving acceptance, including educators and clinicians working with parents (Kabat-Zinn, 2005).

Clearly, the task of bridging cultural and developmental accounts of acceptance requires more than a comparison of developmental processes in two groups of communities. At a minimum, it requires an appreciation of cultural crossovers as well as cultural differences. Crossover occurs at the individual level as well as the subgroup (e.g., SES and urban–rural) level; it occurs because the same developmental processes occur in all peoples, although the emphasis on those processes varies in different cultures. Our ultimate goal is to provide nuanced and varied portraits of the universal cultural phenomenon of acceptance.

In the first part of this chapter we examine cultural differences in two processes fundamental to acceptance: people's views of the malleability of the self versus world (i.e., to what extent are self's characteristics changeable by the self vs. to what extent is the world changeable by self?) and in people's proneness to be evaluative versus non-evaluative (i.e., do people more often convey approval of others or non-evaluative acknowledgment of them?). The research we review examines cultural differences, but it largely ignores developmental issues; in fact, the vast majority of studies have been conducted with a single age group (young adult college students). Although our ultimate goal is to bridge the cultural and developmental research, we begin by reviewing research largely concerned with adults.

In the second part of this chapter, we demonstrate how differences in adult patterns relate to differences in caregiving practices with children. We review evidence that European American as compared to East Asian caregivers are relatively more accepting of their children's individual selves and that they communicate their acceptance by emphasizing children's positive qualities. By contrast, East Asian caregivers are relatively more accepting of the world in which their children are embedded, and they communicate their acceptance through relatively non-evaluative feedback about the circumstances surrounding their children.

Cultural Differences in Views About, and Acceptance of, Self and World

Although caregivers worldwide are aware that children and aspects of the world have both fixed and malleable qualities, caregivers in different cultures give unequal weights to both. Fixed (also called "entity") qualities refer to dispositions adhering to a relatively invariant set of laws that are difficult or impossible for individuals to influence, such as genetically determined characteristics or fate. Fixed qualities are often seen as causal of outcomes. Note that fixed qualities may be changable—albeit not by self. Malleable (also called "incremental") qualities refer to features that are amenable to control, such as a muscle that is strengthened by exercise and the meaning one makes of events (Dweck, 1999). Below, we review evidence that East Asians as compared to European Americans are more likely to view the world (e.g., social norms, and people's roles as designated by norms) as fixed, in the sense that the self cannot change it, and that European Americans are more likely to view the self (e.g., abilities and traits) as fixed.

Our notion of self corresponds to Markus & Kitayama's (1991) notion of the independent self. Our notion of world is closely tied to those authors' notion of the interdependent self. However, the notion of world as used in this chapter goes beyond the issue of self-identity and interpersonal relationships. By "children's world," we mean the people, norms, customs, and settings that surround children, as well as children's relationships with all of these aspects of their world.

Malleable Versus Fixed Views of the Self

Studies directly comparing U.S. and East Asian views about individuals' ability to change themselves *generally indicate more fixed views of persons in the*

United States than East Asia. For example, Dweck, Chiu, and Hong (1995b, p. 331) report data demonstrating that "the proportion of malleable theorists is appreciably greater in the Hong Kong sample [as compared to several of the American samples]." These authors cite the work of Stevenson et al. (1990), who found that among educators, there was "a far greater belief in malleable intelligence and in the importance of effort . . . in East Asian cultures, compared to the relatively greater emphasis in European American cultures on fixed intelligence and the role of ability (vs. effort) in influencing achievement" (p. 330).

Similarly, Heine et al. (2001) found that participants in the United States were more likely than those in East Asia to view abilities as fixed as opposed to as malleable. Instructing Americans that ability is malleable (and, thus, effort matters) led to increased persistence, but the same instruction provided no new information to Japanese and it did not lead to an increase in their persistence. By contrast, presenting participants with information that abilities are fixed led to opposite effects. Norenzayan, Choi, and Nisbett (2002) found that participants in the United States were more likely than those in East Asia to endorse fixed views of personality—that is, to claim that people are unable to change their own personality. It appears that the cultural differences pertain to diverse realms of self.

There are many studies that provide *indirect* evidence that European Americans have more fixed views of self than East Asians. The frequent finding that a fixed view of self is associated with attributions to self's dispositions (reviewed in Dweck, Chiu, & Hong, 1995a, and Dweck, 1999), combined with the well-replicated finding that European Americans as compared to East Asians are more likely to attribute outcomes to self's dispositions (e.g., Choi & Nisbett, 1998; Miyamoto & Kitayama, 2002; Morris & Peng, 1994; *see also* Lehman et al., 2004) lend support to our conclusion that European Americans have relatively more fixed views of the self.

Malleable Versus Fixed Views of the World

In addition to indicating that European Americans are relatively more likely to consider self as stable and as causing outcomes (i.e., as fixed entities), the above studies indicate that East Asians are more likely to attribute events to situations—that is, to view the self as able to change as a result of situational factors (e.g., Norenzayan, Choi, & Peng, 2007). This finding is consistent with the notion that East Asians have a more malleable view of self and a more fixed view of the world. East Asians anticipate more variability in an actor's behavior and more often attribute this variability to situational constraints such as role obligations and social pressure, implying a malleable self and a world that causes outcomes (Fiske, Kitayama, Markus, & Nisbett, 1998).

We use the term *fixed world* to refer to self's inability to change the world; the world is fixed to the extent that there is not potential for the self to influence it. Concluding that people cannot change the world is not the same as concluding that the world is not changeable. Influenced by "Naïve Dialecticism,"

East Asians do tend to see the world as constantly changing (Ji, Peng, & Nisbett. 2000). However, evidence reviewed below indicates that East Asians view the world as fixed in the sense that it is not potentially changeable by the self. These two points do not contradict each other. In fact, it is possible that frequent changes in the world, which follow from relatively invariant laws that are difficult or impossible for self to influence, make the world even more unpredictable and unchangeable by the self.

There is direct evidence of cultural differences in malleable versus fixed beliefs about the world. More than two-thirds of Hong Kong students reported fixed views of the world (Chiu & Hong, 1999, studies 1 and 2; e.g., "Our world has its basic and ingrained dispositions, and you really can't do much to change it,") as compared to approximately one half of U.S. students (Dweck et al., 1995b). Similarly, Chiu et al. (1997, p.936) found "an overwhelming belief in a fixed world" in Hong Kong, but roughly equivalent amounts of fixed world and malleable world beliefs in the United States. Because malleable and fixed views were operationalized as mutually exclusive, a belief in a fixed world implies a belief that the world is not malleable.

Morling, Kitayama, and Miyamoto's (2002) findings also suggest that malleable views of the world are more common among Americans than East Asians. Compared to Japanese students, American students were able to recall more, and more recent, episodes in their daily lives in which they were able to influence or change the "surrounding people, events or objects according to your own wishes" (p. 313). Moreover, the situations described by Americans evoked stronger feelings of self efficacy (i.e., a feeling that they were able to do something because of their power, competence, or effort) than those described by the Japanese. Even the Japanese saw the American-generated influence situations (i.e., those recalled by the Americans) as higher on efficacy than the Japanese-generated influence situations.[1]

As mentioned earlier, compared to European Americans, East Asians are more likely to explain outcomes in terms of the power of the social situation (Choi, Nisbett, & Norenzayan, 1999). East Asians are also more likely to attribute outcomes to norms, roles, obligations, and social pressure (Choi et al., 1999; Fiske et al., 1998; Hallahan, Lee, & Herzog, 1997). Because things seen as fixed tend to be seen as causal (Dweck et al., 1995a), these findings are consistent with the claim that East Asians have more fixed views of the world.

Fixed views of the world help explain East Asians' greater compliance with, and accommodation to, other people and external forces. Among East Asians there is an "emphasis on occupying one's proper place and engaging in appropriate action . . . and adherence to norms and traditions" (Cheung et al., 2001, p. 425). Relatedly, East Asians are more likely than Americans to attribute causality to collective-level agents—organizations and groups (Menon, Morris, Chiu, & Hong, 1999). In the sphere of occupational performance, "Asians . . . expect individuals to display . . . fit with the relatively fixed external environment" (Chen, 2007).

The findings above add to and are consistent with the review by Weisz, Rothbaum, and Blackburn's (1984) of cultural differences in primary and secondary control, including findings involving locus of control. According to those authors, Japanese are more likely to view outside forces as causal of events and Americans are more likely to view the individual as causal. In particular, Japanese are more likely than Americans to view chance and fate as determining outcomes and to view individuals as exerting little influence when acting alone. As noted above, views of causality are closely associated with fixed views.

Because European Americans have a more malleable view of the world, the primary–secondary control model predicts that European Americans are more likely than East Asians to view the self as able to change aspects of the world. Morling et al. (2002) found that American, as compared to Japanese, participants could more easily recall situations in which they influenced or changed the surrounding people, events, or objects according to their own wishes (i.e., a malleable view of the world). By contrast, Japanese participants could more easily recall situations that involved self-adjustment (i.e., a malleable view of self) than Americans (*see* Morling & Evered, 2006 for other cultural evidence).

People Accept Things They See as Fixed: On Self and World Acceptance

We claim that people are more invested in accepting aspects of the self or world that are seen as fixed and uncontrollable than things seen as malleable and able to be controlled. There are several interrelated dynamics involved here. First, things seen as fixed are assumed to have greater causal power than are things that are seen as malleable (Dweck et al., 1995a). People understandably are more invested in accepting things that have influence over them and their world than things that lack such influence. Second, fixed things are more likely to be seen as a locus of worth or value. Things possess worth in part because they can be counted on; it is often unwise to invest in, depend on, and value things that can be changed. Third, there is little motivation to accept things that self can change. Accepting malleable things is likely to undermine determination to change them. For these reasons, people are typically unwilling to accept, and are more likely to negatively evaluate, things that they view as malleable and improvable (Duval & Silvia, 2002).

Although we distinguish between acceptance of self and world, we realize that the two forms of acceptance often go hand-in-hand. Caregivers who foster children's acceptance of their world are also likely to foster children's self-acceptance. Secure attachment entails both forms of acceptance (Bartholomew & Shaver, 1998). However, when the status quo is challenged and pressure for change mounts, such as when what self wants is different from what the world allows, the cultural dynamics described above lead to imperfect reciprocity of self and world acceptance. These dynamics have implications for childrearing, as explained below.

Because European American caregivers tend to view the world as malleable and as capable of improvement, they are less likely to encourage their children to accept the world as it is—they do not want children to be too tolerant or positive about something the children may decide to change. The same logic applies to East Asians; because they tend to view the self as malleable and improvable, they are less likely to encourage their children to accept themselves. As a work in progress, the self benefits more from a focus on its limitations and inadequacies than from self-acceptance (Heine, 2001).

In all cultures people seek self-acceptance (Heine, 2005a, 2005b; 2007; Sedikides Gaertner & Vevea, 2005), but their pathway to, as well as their emphasis on, self-acceptance differs. In particular, cultures differ in the extent to which self-acceptance depends on the world's—especially others'—acceptance of self. Concern with the world's acceptance, referred to as *face* concerns, is the focus of East Asians more than of European Americans (Cohen, Hoshino-Browne, & Leung, 2007). A focus on the world's acceptance of self is predicated on acceptance of others' perspective and on the norms that shape that perspective. By contrast, European Americans often dismiss the importance of others' acceptance of self, particularly when a focus on others' acceptance is seen as undermining self-direction and autonomy (Heine, 2005a, 2007; Heine & Hamamura, 2007; Suh & Diener, 2001).

Cultural Differences in Non-Evaluative Versus Positive Acceptance

Our second claim is that compared to European Americans, East Asians are more prone to *non-evaluative*, as opposed to positive, acceptance of themselves and their world. This applies to caregivers' acceptance of their children and, as a result, to children's acceptance of self and the surrounding world. Caregivers who provide non-evaluative acceptance are open to and acknowledge their children and their circumstances, often affectionately, but they refrain from positive evaluations. Their focus is on maintaining equanimity and avoiding evaluations, especially negative ones.

We base these claims on cultural differences in goal orientations. European Americans are more invested in promotion goals and pursuing ideals or positive gains, and East Asians are more invested in prevention goals and avoiding aversive outcomes or losses. For example, European Americans are more likely to seek out and uncritically accept praise and other positive feedback, whereas East Asians are more likely to focus on negative information about, and mistakes made by, the self (Lee, Acker, & Gardner, 2000). Heine (2007) draws a similar conclusion: East Asians have "an orientation toward avoiding negative outcomes" rather than seeking positive ones. An orientation to avoid negative outcomes is consistent with a tendency to seek non-evaluative forms of acceptance. In both cases, people strive to prevent negative feedback rather than to increase positive feedback.

Research on culture, emotion, and well-being provides further evidence of these differences. European Americans pay more attention to positive emotions, as well as to other positive aspects of life, than do East Asians and Asian Americans (Diener, Scollon, Oishi, Dzokoto, & Suh, 2000; Oishi, 2002;

Oishi & Diener, 2003; Schimmack, Radhakrishnan, Oishi, Dzokoto, & Ahadi, 2002). Suh, Diener, Oishi, and Triandis (1998) show that the frequency of positive emotion is less strongly associated with life satisfaction for people in collectivist cultures such as Korea and Japan. In China there is a general attitude that intense emotions are dangerous, irrelevant, or cause illness and that the moderation or suppression of emotions is highly valued (Butler, Lee, & Gross, 2007; Klineberg, 1938; Potter, 1988; Wu,1982)

In a cross-national comparison, Eid and Diener (2001) found that people in China have the lowest frequency and intensity scores of both positive and negative affect. Recent findings indicate that compared to European Americans, East Asians are higher on suppression of both positive and negative emotion; moreover, for East Asians, suppression is associated with more adaptive functioning (Matsumoto et al., 2008). The greater preference for muted expressions of emotion in East Asia may result from the value placed on harmony, group cohesion, facilitation of status and power differentials, social order, maintenance of the status quo, and propriety. Because intense emotions, both positive and negative, work against the preservation of these values, intense emotions are avoided (Markus & Kitayama, 1994; Matsumoto et al., 2008; Triandis, 2005).

Similar findings are obtained when the focus is on attitudes about oneself and one's life. On average, European Americans hold more positive attitudes toward their lives and themselves (Chang & Asakawa, 2003; Heine & Lehman, 1995) and enjoy a higher level of global life satisfaction and self-esteem than Asian Americans, Japanese, or Koreans (Diener, Diener, & Diener, 1995; Oishi & Sullivan, 2005). A link between positive emotions and positive attitudes contributing to those emotions among European Americans has long been assumed; for example, measures of self-esteem frequently employed in studies in the United States (Rosenberg, 1979) combine items assessing positive emotions about the self and positive attitudes toward the self.

Two qualifications of these cultural differences are needed. First, people worldwide express both positive and non-evaluative acceptance; the differences we highlight are matters of degree rather than kind. For example, people everywhere engage in some degree and some form of positive acceptance (i.e., positive self-regard) (Heine et al., 1999). Second, the *positive* acceptance of European Americans is but one manifestation of their *evaluative* orientation. The findings reviewed above indicate that compared to East Asians, European Americans are more likely to express negative emotions and attitudes as well as positive ones (Cole & Dennis, 1998). Negative emotions and evaluations are part-and-parcel of the process of identifying what is positively accepted and what constitutes happiness (e.g., the caregiver's happiness about the child and the child's happiness about him/herself). Positive acceptance allows for greater highs but also risks greater lows, as compared to non-evaluative acceptance, which fosters a state of calmness.

There is precedent for distinguishing between types of acceptance. Dictionary definitions as well as operational definitions employed by parent–child researchers emphasize two relatively distinct notions: *(1)* approval, favorably receiving, and positive regard, all of which are evaluative and positive, and

(2) openness, non-judgment, compassion, and seeing things as they are/being objective, which are non-evaluative. We claim that European American lay-persons and researchers tend to emphasize positive acceptance of children and their children's abilities. Positive acceptance is neither open nor objective. It is contingent on searching for and finding favorable qualities.

The desire for positive acceptance leads to cognitive distortions. Seeking positive evaluation leads to biases (Heine, 2005b) and positive illusions (Taylor & Brown, 1988). By contrast, a focus on non-evaluative acceptance leads to greater awareness of things as they are. Non-evaluative notions of acceptance, which have been relied on heavily in recent psychotherapy research in the United States (Hayes et al., 1999; Segal et al., 2002), are borrowed from Eastern (primarily Buddhist) notions of mindful awareness and common humanity.

Integrating the Two Claims : Targets and Natures of Acceptance

Here we integrate the two claims regarding acceptance and apply them to parents' caregiving of children. We propose the following two hypotheses. First, compared to European American caregivers, East Asian caregivers are more invested in accepting their child's world (including role obligations and norms), which they see as relatively fixed, and their acceptance of the child's world is likely to be relatively non-evaluative. As a result, East Asian children are more likely to accept their world non-evaluatively. Second, European American caregivers are more invested than East Asian caregivers in accepting their children's internal qualities, which they see as relatively fixed, and their acceptance of these qualities is likely to be evaluative and positive. As a result, European American children are more likely to positively accept themselves.

These claims regarding acceptance relate to larger cultural distinctions. European Americans' focus on positive acceptance of self relates to their emphasis on an independent self (Markus & Kitayama, 1991) and on individual uniqueness (Hsu, 1983; Triandis, 1995). As a result of their self-conceptions, European Americans are invested in viewing themselves as possessing self-worth—that is, competence, sociability, and likability. European American parents are more likely than East-Asian parents to seek and find evaluative features, such as intelligence, talent, beauty, a smile, or a sense of humor, that explain why their children are worthy and valuable. By contrast, East Asians' orientation to acceptance of the world and to non-evaluative acceptance relates to their focus on an interdependent self (Markus & Kitayama, 1991). Their orientation to acceptance also relates to their collectivism (Triandis, 1995), their situation-centeredness (Hsu, 1983), and their tendency to change the self to fit the world (Weisz et al., 1984). These foci explain why East Asians are more invested in, and tend to base acceptance on, their common humanity and common circumstances rather than on self's positive qualities.

To date, research on cultural differences in acceptance of self and world has focused on adults. Research on malleable versus fixed views, and on positive versus non-evaluative orientations, has also focused on adults. The research on adult acceptance has been almost completely segregated from the developmental research on parents' acceptance of children. Our goal is to bridge this gap.

Childrearing

This section reviews evidence regarding socialization practices that shape children's acceptance of self and world. The evidence shows that: *(1)* European American caregivers are generally more invested in fostering children's positive acceptance of fixed aspects of the self, as evident in the focus on children's esteem, efficacy, competence, agency, and *(2)* East Asian parents are generally more invested in fostering children's non-evaluative acceptance of fixed aspects of the world, as evident in their focus on children's relationships, the collective, norms, roles, duties, and fate. We review evidence regarding five aspects of socialization: fostering of values, closeness, sensitive caregiving, praise and criticism, and exercise of control.

Fostering of Values: Harmony and Accommodation Versus Autonomy and Self-Assertion

There are important differences in the values socialized in European American and East Asian communities (Dennis, Cole, Zahn-Waxler, & Mizuta, 2002; Rothbaum et al., 2000b; Stevenson & Stigler, 1992). In now-classic studies of parents' folk theories about childrearing and the moral tales parents share with their children, Miller and colleagues found striking differences in parents' focus on valuation of the self (Miller, Wang, Sandel, & Cho, 2002; Miller, Wiley, Fung, & Liang, 1997). Open-ended interviews with European American, as compared to Taiwanese, mothers indicated a greater focus on supporting and enhancing children's self-esteem—for example, by highlighting their willfullness, their clever ways of getting what they want, and putting the best face on transgressions (Miller, Sandel, Liang, & Fung, 2001). Self-esteem is seen as fostering persistence in overcoming external obstacles, consistent with a view of the external world (or at least of the obstacles it poses) as malleable.

For their part, Taiwanese mothers were more concerned that their children behave in ways expected and desired by the culture. Their stories highlighted children's transgressions and were often intended to extract confessions. Taiwanese parents believe they have an important role in training children to improve themselves, which hinges on an assumption that the self is malleable. Their underlying message is that self-improvement is needed to accommodate external, fixed realities. For these parents, self-esteem is seen as problematic in that it can interfere with children's willingness to accommodate to external demands. Taiwanese mothers believe self-esteem can cause children to become frustrated in the face of failure and interfere with children's receptivity to correction from others.

Differences in values stem in part from East Asians' insistence on filial piety, a concept for which there is no exact European American equivalent. East Asian children are expected to accept their parents unconditionally, regardless of the treatment they have received. A recent and popular form of Japanese-inspired therapy, Morita, builds on this principle by encouraging clients to focus on the *assumption* of the mothers' goodness (i.e., goodness that is based on giving birth to the child); from this perspective even abusive parents should be accepted (Ozawa-de Silva, 2007). Themes of piety, evident in stories that are still popular in Japan (DeVos, 1998), epitomize East Asians' unconditional acceptance of the outside world—particularly adult authority.

Closeness: Constant Proximal Contact Versus Distal Contact With Separations

Whereas it is common for European American parents to be apart from their children, most of the world's population, including East Asians, spends much more time together—especially in infancy and especially at night (Harkness & Super, 1995; Latz, Wolf, & Lozoff, 1999; *see also* Tharakad, Mistry, & Dutta, 2011). Extensive body contact with caregivers has been observed in East Asia, including co-sleeping and co-bathing and prolonged holding and carrying of young children (Rothbaum et al., 2000a, b; *see* Shweder, Jensen, & Goldstein, 1995, regarding similar findings in India). Closeness and proximity is also demonstrated by including young children in, as compared to segregating them from, most of adults' daily life experiences (Rothbaum et al., 2000b).

The East Asian communication pattern also maximizes closeness. Choi reports that Korean mothers and young children are "attuned to one another in a fused state" and "mothers merged themselves with their children" in contrast to Canadian mothers who "withdraw themselves . . . so that the children's reality can remain autonomous" (1992, p. 38). Clancy's (1986) description of Japanese–U.S. differences closely parallels Choi's description of Korean–Canadian differences (*see also* Rothbaum et al., 2000b).

Compared to European American children, East Asian children are more often given the message that their dependency needs will be accepted. This is seen, for example, in the emphasis on amae (indulgence of dependency needs) in Japan (Rothbaum & Kakinuma, 2004; Rothbaum, Kakinuma, Nagoaka, & Azuma, 2007). Early indulgence is associated with low externalizing (aggressive, antisocial) behavior, and it promotes relationship harmony (Rogoff, 2003; Schlegel, & Barry, 1991). However, these gains in relatedness are offset by losses in autonomy—restriction of infants' movement and promotion of passivity (Edwards, 1995; Saarni, Mumme, & Campos, 1998). There is evidence of an inverse association between parental warmth and child autonomy in China (Chen et al., 1998).

The greater closeness and proximity practiced in East Asian communities foster in infants and young children a view of themselves as continuously influenced by benevolent outside forces. External agents who almost constantly meet children's needs are likely to be accepted and viewed as fixed and causal.

European American children, whose separation from caregivers means that their care is largely dependent on their own initiative, are more likely to view themselves as active, exploring, mastery-oriented causal agents of environmental change (Rothbaum et al., 2000c).

European American parents are more likely to view extreme closeness as enmeshment. They tend to provide care that is responsive to infants' signals and self-assertion, which promotes children's view of themselves as positive causal agents. European American parents put more emphasis on distal forms of contact, such as face-to-face and eye-to-eye interaction. Keller et al. (2004) found that these forms of distal contact are more common in individualistic than collectivistic communities.

Although European American mothers are less physically close to their children than are mothers in other cultures, including East Asian cultures, they are more likely to serve as playmates for their children and to enjoy distal contact with them (e.g., via infant seats, walkers, and play pens) and brief, demonstrative expressions of warmth/contact (e.g., hugging, kissing and praise). European American mothers are also high on "object stimulation"—they frequently direct the child's attention to the environment to manipulate it (LeVine et al., 1994; Rogoff, 2003; Rothbaum et al., 2000b; Uzgiris & Raeff, 1995; Whiting & Edwards, 1988). Compared to Japanese children, U.S. children have repeatedly been found to engage in more exploration of the environment, which requires distance from caregivers and fosters children's causal agency vís-a-vís the outside world (Rothbaum et al., 2000c).

This pattern of behavior—that is, modest amounts of physical proximity and contact combined with high levels of distal, brief, and demonstrative contact as well as directing children's attention outward–meshes well with European American theorists' notion of optimal caregiving. For example, Ryan and Deci (2000) play down the importance of high-level closeness and contact: "proximal relational supports may not be necessary for intrinsic motivation." Indeed they note that "many intrinsically motivated behaviors are happily performed in isolation" (p. 71). An emphasis on distal, brief, and demonstrative contact reflects a belief that early relatedness that includes opportunities for separation paves the way for later exploration of the physical world and of relationships with new partners. Too-close ties with others can thwart this progression.

Research in European American communities indicates that the attachment and exploration systems are closely linked. Although seemingly universal, this link is cultivated to different degrees in different communities. To strengthen the link, young children need experiences with separations and reunions and with venturing forth on their own into the environment and returning to the caregiver (secure base). When these opportunities are relatively rare, as they are in East Asian communities, children are not likely to manifest high levels of exploration or autonomy. In fact, separations (i.e., leaving the child with strangers or alone) and reunions are not common for infants in many other societies, which is why the Strange Situation is often overly stressful for them (Miyake, Chen, & Campos, 1985; Rothbaum, Kakinuma, Nagaoka, & Azuma, 2007).

Children in these societies are almost always in the presence of caregivers they know well—siblings, extended family members, or surrogate mothers.

The attachment–autonomy link, which is well-documented in research with European American samples, is supported by European American caregivers' positive evaluation of the individual child. For the child to possess the internal strength and resources to function freely and independently, s/he must have self-confidence and self-esteem as well as a secure attachment relationship. Parents' positive evaluations foster children's self-esteem, autonomy, and security (Bartholomew & Shaver, 1998; Cassidy & Shaver, 2008).

Pressures on European American children to obtain autonomy from parents continue into adolescence (Schlegel, 2011). Adolescents' and their parents' expectations regarding the timing of autonomy are earlier in European American than non-European American countries (Kwak, 2003; Smetana, 2002). There is more pressure for teens to separate from parents in the United States than in China (Dubas & Gerris, 2002) or Japan (Rothbaum et al., 2000b). Also contributing to European American teens' quest for autonomy are their loosely knit in-groups and the ease of exploring outside relationships. In European American communities, there is a close link between acceptance of dependency needs and autonomy (Feeney, 2007). We suggest that acceptance of dependency needs is effective in fostering autonomy among European American youth because satisfaction of those needs is determined by their self-assertion; youth have responsibility for determining when, where, how, and how much meeting of dependency is appropriate. The youth best able to navigate these responsibilities are those that have confidence in themselves—those who have positive views of, and are able to rely on, themselves.

In summary, in East Asian communities, relatedness entails more constant and close physical contact from the earliest period, and correspondingly less self-agency vís-avís the external world. This kind of constancy, closeness, and early indulgence builds tight and guaranteed relationships and makes the recipient of indulgence obligated to others. Thus, children in East Asian communities develop a relatedness that involves acceptance of external forces, as evidenced by enduring commitment, loyalty, and duty; their relatedness involves relatively less acceptance of inner needs and self-direction, as evidenced by autonomy. East Asian children are expected to accept their parents and their world unconditionally. In contrast, in European American communities, the child is accepted as a positive causal agent, and the child accepts the caregiver conditionally, dependent on the caregiver's responsiveness to his/her own agency.

Sensitive Caregiving: Anticipation Versus Responsiveness

Because of the constant and close proximity between caregivers and infants in East Asia, caregivers are highly attuned to the child's needs (Choi, 1992; Rothbaum & Kakinuma, 2004). This enables caregivers to be proactive, to anticipate and minister to the child's needs even before the child sends overt signals (Rothbaum, Nagaoka, & Ponte, 2006; Trommsdorff & Friedlmeier, 2010).

When children's needs are seamlessly anticipated, they view caregivers *as powerful agents* who are able to read their minds, and they are motivated to *accommodate themselves* to these omnipotent others (Rothbaum & Trommsdorff, 2006; Rothbaum et al., 2000b; Rothbaum et al., 2006).

By contrast, the European American child's distal contact makes his/her expressiveness—particularly overt verbal expressiveness—imperative. According to Keller et al. (2004, p. 12), distal contact "informs infants of their uniqueness and self-efficacy." Caregivers' responsiveness to the infant's self assertion reinforces the infant's sense of *personal agency* and of the *external world's malleability* in response to its will. European American caregivers believe that too much anticipation of the child's needs undermines the child's expression of its own will. There is less investment in children's learning to change themselves (self-malleability) and more investment in exploring and having an effect on the surrounding world (self-determination, self-efficacy). Constant separations and reunions—especially separations associated with the child's exploration of the environment—foster the child's sense of choice, acting on preferences and ultimately, mastery of the world (Rothbaum et al., 2000b; 2000c).

The indulgence common in many East Asian cultures—especially Japan—involves unconditional acceptance of children's expressions of distress and helplessness. By contrast, the emphasis in European American communities is on responsiveness to positive signals, particularly signals indicating the child's autonomy-seeking and related needs for self-esteem, self-expression, and self-assertion (Dennis, Cole, Zahn-Waxler, & Mizuta, 2002; Morelli & Rothbaum, 2007; Trommsdorff & Friedlmeier, 2010). Bridges (2003, p. 170) claims that "attachment and autonomy may be linked in part because the same sort of contingent consistently responsive and affectively positive caregiving that is linked with secure attachment is also linked with the facilitation of mastery motivation." These claims capture well European American experiences and European American forms of responsiveness—that is, modest warmth, distal contact (closeness without restraint), absence of indulgence, and an emphasis on responsiveness to autonomy seeking.

Praise and Criticism: Fostering Self-Improvement Versus Self-Regard

U.S. parents' praise is often "person-oriented" rather than directed at specific behaviors (Kamins & Dweck, 1999; Huntsinger, Jose, Rudden, Luo, & Krieg, 2001; Markus & Kitayama, 1994), thereby reinforcing the child's sense of himself as stable (fixed) and as an agent of change. Parents who inform children that they are good, smart, or talented convey the message that their children are fixed rather than a malleable. As compared to praise in East Asia, there is more praise in the United States for initiative and behavior chosen by the child, as well as praise for acting on the world as opposed to in concert with the world or in response to external demands (Wang, Wiley, & Chiu, 2008). Interviews about socialization goals indicate that almost all U.S. parents, but no Chinese parents, strive to build, cultivate, and protect their children's self-esteem because they view it as leading to increased learning about the world and attempts to master it (Miller et al., 2002).

East Asian parents are less likely to encourage the child's self-esteem and self-enhancement and more likely to encourage self-effacement, self-criticism, and self-improvement (Henderlong & Lepper, 2002; Miller, Wiley, Fung, & Liang, 1997). East Asians' view of the self as malleable makes positive self-evaluation less important; relatively more importance is placed on effort, self-improvement, and viewing the self through the eyes of others (Cohen, Hoshino-Browne, & Leung, 2007; Heine, 2005a; Muramoto, 2003). East Asian parents often highlight the perils of praise, including increases in children's frustration, stubbornness, and *unwillingness to be corrected* (Miller et al., 2002).

When East Asian parents administer praise, it is often in response to the child's doing what he is told to do, and parents administer praise in anticipation of the child's engaging in "correct" action (Wang et al., 2008). The tendency to link praise with adherence to expectations is reflected in the Chinese word for praise ("guai"), which refers to obeying, listening, understanding, and following norms (Wang et al., 2008). Praise in East Asia is more often directed at a malleable self that seeks to adhere to absolute standards and socially sanctioned roles and norms. Praise among European Americans, by contrast, is more often directed at a fixed self that initiates personally preferred options.

There are corresponding differences in criticism. European American caregivers avoid criticism when it is seen as damaging the child's self-esteem (Miller et al., 2002; Wang et al., 2008). Asian parents, by contrast, emphasize the importance of focusing on children's transgressions and "assiduously correcting their mistakes" (Miller et al., 2002, p.235). Because East Asian caregivers do not see the child as a fixed entity, they do not view criticism as conveying that the child is bad in a stable sense. Their criticism is relatively benign in that they assume that children are motivated to learn correct behavior and that failure to do so simply reflects their immaturity rather than stable characteristics (Lewis, 1995).

Exercise of Control

The type of caregiving found to be optimal in the West is authoritative—the child benefits most when parents set clear expectations and are firm, while providing warmth and remaining open to the child's perspective and preferences (i.e., promoting self-agency). Authoritarian parenting leads to poor child functioning because it undermines the child's view of the self as positive and as able to influence the world (Baumrind, 1971; Chao, 1996). These findings pertain best to European Americans. Chao and Tseng (2002) cite more than 20 studies of greater parental control and exercise of authority in East Asia and less encouragement of autonomy. The concept of guan, or training, captures well the East Asian notion of optimal caregiving (Chao, 1996). *Guan* refers to fostering the child's willingness to *improve the self* (a malleable self-view) and to adhere to norms and authority (a fixed view of the world). There is no comparable term in European American countries, where socialization of children's self-improvement is less socially valued. Guan relates to various aspects of well-being (e.g., perceived health and life satisfaction) in East Asia but not the United States (Stewart et al., 2002).

Shaming and empathy training are common forms of psychological control in East Asia (Chao & Tseng, 2002; Wu et al., 2002; Clancy, 1986; Fung, 1999). Because the social hierarchy and norms are fixed and non-negotiable, shaming and empathy training are seen as appropriate ways of ensuring that the child will attune himself to others' expectations. By contrast, U.S. parents believe that "practices such as shaming children, disciplining too harshly or making invidious comparisons, should be avoided because they damage self esteem" (Miller et al., 2002, p. 231; *see also* Barber, 2002). Too much empathy is seen as potentially pathological in the West because children must assert their own views, even in the face of opposing views of more powerful others (Rothbaum et al., 2000b). Children's voice is more attended to (Rothbaum, Morelli, Pott, & Liu-Constant, 2000) and their efforts to negotiate with, and thereby *influence others*, are reinforced (Kuczynski & Hildebrandt, 1997; Weisner, 1984). By contrast, East Asian parents believe they know best what their children need, and they are more likely to let their own voice overshadow their child's voice (Rothbaum et al., 2000a).

Policy Implications and Conclusions

In summary, we claim that East Asians', as compared to European Americans', greater non-evaluative acceptance of the world and lesser positive evaluation of the self relates to differences in the values they foster in their children and in their childrearing practices and beliefs involving closeness, sensitivity, praise/criticism, and control.

Specifically, East Asians' non-evaluative acceptance of the world stems in large part from their caregivers': emphasis on harmony with and accommodation to benevolent outside forces; proximity and near-constant contact with infants; ability to anticipate whether and how children's needs should be met; praise and criticism intended to foster children's self-improvement and acceptance of externally determined standards; and assumptions that socialization agents, norms, and roles are appropriate and should be acknowledged as the agents of control. We maintain that these types of care are especially likely to be provided by adults who accept the world in non-evaluative ways.

By contrast, European American adults' positive acceptance of the self stems in large part from their caregivers': emphasis on autonomy and self-assertion; distal closeness with infants; responsive care that encourages children to positively regard themselves and to assert their wills; praise intended to foster children's positive self-regard; and assumptions that children are basically good and should be acknowledged as agents of control. We maintain that these types of care are especially likely to be provided by adults who positively accept themselves.

Earlier we commented that different types of acceptance, representing the four possibilities formed by crossing self versus world acceptance with positive versus non-evaluative acceptance, occur in all cultures. The differences in degree of occurrence and emphasis arise in large part because they confer distinct advantages in particular settings. The most obvious advantages of positive acceptance of self is that it makes people feel good about themselves—it leads to positive emotion and self-esteem. In communities where happiness and self-esteem are highly valued, that type of acceptance will also be highly valued. The most obvious advantages of non-evaluative acceptance of the world is that it is unconditional and transcendent—the child is assured that acceptance is constant and pervasive—it does not only, nor mainly, apply to the self. In communities where harmony and unity are valued, so, too, will that type of acceptance be valued.

One policy implication of our claims is that socialization agents should be made aware of both types of acceptance and of the contexts in which each is optimal. Just as children benefit most when their independent and interdependent selves are fostered in different settings, they are also most likely to benefit when the type of acceptance they receive is well-matched to the demands of the situation. For example, within the political sphere, acceptance of self as fixed and as able to improve a malleable world encourages youth to challenge the existing order and to initiate reforms (*see also* Flanagan, Martínez, & Cumsille, 2011). By contrast, acceptance of world as fixed and as able to improve a malleable self encourages youth to make sacrifices and concessions needed of individual members when the larger group is struggling to cope with external threats. Because acceptance can foster willful self-expression as well as yielding to social hierarchy and to outside constraints, socialization agents should be mindful of the situations in which to foster each type of acceptance.

In this chapter, we borrowed from the largely segregated literature on cultural differences in adults' acceptance and socialization influences on children. Next, research is needed regarding how adults' beliefs affect childrearing and get recreated through childrearing. Investigators should test how caregiving practices related to self versus world acceptance influence children from different cultures. We expect that children will benefit most from practices reflecting the type of acceptance typical of their culture (cf. Iyengar & Lepper, 1999). We also expect that self and world acceptance will have consistent effects across cultures—that is, self-acceptance will foster more exploratory, autonomous behavior, and world acceptance will foster more accommodative, harmonious behavior. Demonstrating these differences across and within cultures will provide direct evidence of the kind of bridging of development and culture with which this chapter is most concerned.

Is it possible to provide children both positive and unconditional acceptance? European American parents seemingly believe they can. To do so, they commit themselves to finding favorable characteristics. For example, parents who recognize their children are low in intelligence will emphasize abilities on which their child is likely to score high—athleticism, artistic talent, or sociability. This explains the appeal of concepts like multiple intelligences (Gardner, 1999) and unconventional forms of intelligence (Sternberg, 1999). These concepts are well-tailored for parents determined to positively accept their children by finding the ability, or abilities, on which their children perform best.

The search for both positive and unconditional acceptance explains the appeal of Rogers' notion of unconditional positive regard. We contend that in the long run, positive acceptance of the child is necessarily conditional: It is based on an evaluation that the child has met specified criteria and thus carries with it the possibility of negative evaluations and rejection. Yet the notion of unconditional positive regard highlights the possibility of cultural cross-over.

Cross-over is also evident when East Asians seek positive self-acceptance ("self-esteem;" Sedikides et al., 2005). East Asians' more indirect forms of self-esteem enhancement involve "relationship esteem," "face," securing the esteem of others, self-improvement, and fulfilling valued roles as opposed to possessing valued traits (Heine, 2005a). In other words, the indirect self-esteem of East Asians involves acknowledgment of and receptivity to aspects of self's world, including the people in it, relationship harmony, worldviews, collectivist norms, and fate (Sedikides et al., 2005, p. 539). This indirect self-esteem should not be equated with traditional forms of self-esteem, especially positive evaluation of the independent self. However, it highlights the fact that no culture corners the market on fundamental human needs (*see also* Jensen, 2011).

The larger point is that people in all cultures probably have a mix of different types of acceptance, despite the inherent contradictions between them. People cannot simultaneously prioritize acceptance of the child's independent self and the child's world, and they cannot simultaneously provide positive and non-evaluative acceptance. Still, all people seek and achieve a balance between these competing types of acceptance.

Each form of acceptance has its advantage—each fosters qualities that provide more benefits in some settings than in others. To alter forms of acceptance, then, it is probably necessary to change the settings and circumstances for which children are being prepared. In many cases, changes in acceptance and in settings occur in tandem. For example, shifts from authoritarian toward more democratic and child-centered practices in China, which are likely to lead to increased positive acceptance of the self, are accompanying the Westernization, urbanization, and one-child policy in that country (Chang, Schwartz, Dodge, & McBride-Chang, 2003; *see also* Chen, 2011). Seeking to change either our childrearing practices leading to acceptance or the environment surrounding our children without changing both is likely to meet with heavy resistance. Forms of acceptance work best when they are consistent with the settings in which they occur.

People's need for acceptance and the types of benefits acceptance provides are largely universal. Yet the contextual and psychological factors that make each form of acceptance more or less optimal vary greatly from culture to culture.

Note

1. The finding that certain situations reflect self-efficacy across culture indicates that people from different cultures (in this case Japanese and Americans) tend to have similar interpretations of events. Although cultural values influence people's perception

and memory of situations (e.g., whether they attend to self-changing-world vs. world-changing-self situations), people also appear to share common understandings about those situations. An analogy can be made to language development, which entails wide variation from one community to another but also shared vocalizations and linguistic structures.

References

Ainsworth, M. D. S., Blehar, M. C., Waters, E., & Wall, S. (1978). *Patterns of attachment: A psychological study of the strange situation.* Hillsdale, NJ: Erlbaum.

Baldwin, A. L., Kalhorn, J., & Breese, F. H. (1949). The appraisal of parent behavior. *Psychological Monographs, 63*, No. 299.

Barber, B. (Ed.). (2002). *Intrusive parenting: How psychological control affects children and adolescents.* New York: American Psychological Association.

Bartholomew, K., & Shaver, P. R. (1998). Methods of assessing adult attachment: Do they converge? In J. A. Simpson & W. S. Rholes (Eds.), *Attachment theory and close relationships* (pp. 25–45). New York: Guilford Press.

Baumrind, D. (1971). Harmonious parents and their preschool children. *Developmental Psychology, 4*, 99–102.

Bridges, L. J. (2003). Autonomy as an element of developmental well-being. In M. Bornstein, L. Davidson, C. Keyes, & K. Moore (Eds.), *Well being: Positive development across the life course* (pp. 167–175). Mahwah, NJ: Erlbaum.

Butler, E. A., Lee, T. L., & Gross, J. J. (2007). Emotion regulation and culture: Are the social consequences of emotion suppression culture-specific? *Emotion, 7*, 30–48.

Cassidy, J. & Shaver, P. R. (Eds.) (2008). *Handbook of attachment: Theory, research and clinical applications.* New York: Guilford.

Chang, E. C., & Asakawa, K. (2003). Cultural variations on optimistic and pessimistic bias for self versus a sibling: Is there evidence for self-enhancement in the West and for self-criticism in the East when the referent group is specified? *Journal of Personality and Social Psychology, 84*, 569–581.

Chang, L., Schwartz, D., Dodge, K. A., & McBride-Chang, C. (2003). Harsh parenting in relation to child emotion regulation and aggression. *Journal of Family Psychology, 17*, 598–606.

Chao, R., & Tseng, V. (2002). Parenting of Asians. In M. H. Bornstein (Ed.), *Handbook of parenting: Vol. 4. Social conditions and applied parenting* (2nd Ed., pp. 59–93). Mahwah, NJ: Erlbaum.

Chao, R. K. (1996). Chinese and European American mothers' beliefs about the role of parenting in children's school success. *Journal of Cross-Cultural Psychology, 27*, 403–423.

Chen, J. (2007). *Society, culture, and performance forecast: The role of occupational mobility and the belief in the fixed world.* Unpublished doctoral dissertation, University of Illinois.

Chen, X. (2011). Culture, peer relationships, and human development. In L. A. Jensen (Ed.), *Bridging cultural and developmental psychology: New syntheses in theory, research and policy* (pp. 92–112). New York: Oxford University Press.

Chen, X., Hastings, P., Rubin, K. H., Chen, H., Cen G., & Stewart, S. L. (1998). Child-rearing attitudes and behavioral inhibition in Chinese and Canadian toddlers: A cross-cultural study. *Developmental Psychology, 34*, 677–686.

Cheung, F. M., Leung, K., Zhang, J. X., Sun, H. F., Gan, Y. Q., Song, W. Z., & Xie, D. (2001). Indigenous Chinese personality constructs: Is the five-factor model complete? *Journal of Cross-Cultural Psychology, 32*, 407–433.

Chiu, C., Dweck, C. S., Tong, Y., & Fu, H. (1997). Implicit theories and conceptions of morality. *Journal of Personality and Social Psychology, 73*, 923–940.

Chiu, C., & Hong, Y. (1999). Social identification in a political transition: The role of implicit beliefs. *International Journal of Intercultural Relations, 23*, 297–318.

Chiu, C. Y., Hong, Y., & Dweck, C. (1997). Lay dispositionism and implicit theories of personality. *Journal of Personality and Social Psychology, 73*, 19–30.

Choi, I., & Nisbett, R. E. (1998). Situational salience and cultural differences in the correspondence bias and actor-observer bias. *Personality and Social Psychology Bulletin, 24*, 949–960.

Choi, I., Nisbett, R. E., & Norenzayan, A. (1999). Causal attribution across cultures: Variation and universality. *Psychological Bulletin, 125*, 47–63.

Choi, S. H. (1992). Communicative socialization processes: Korea and Canada. In S. Iwawaki, Y. Kashima, & K. Leung (Eds.), *Innovations in cross-cultural psychology* (pp. 103–121). Lisse, The Netherlands: Swets & Zeitlinger.

Clancy, P. M. (1986). The acquisition of communicative style in Japanese. In B. B. Schieffelin & E. Ochs (Eds.), *Language socialization across cultures* (pp. 213–250). New York: Cambridge University Press.

Cohen, D., Hoshino-Browne, E., & Leung, A. K.-Y. (2007). Culture and the structure of personal experience: Insider and outsider phenomenologies of the self and social world. In M. P. Zanna (Ed.), *Advances in Experimental Social Psychology, 39*, 1–67. San Diego, CA: Elsevier Academic Press.

Cole, P. M., & Dennis, T. A. (1998). Variations on a theme: Culture and the meaning of socialization practices and child competence. *Psychological Inquiry, 9*, 276–278.

Dennis, T. A., Cole, P. M., Zahn-Waxler, C., & Mizuta, I. (2002). Self in context: Autonomy and relatedness in Japanese and U.S. mother-preschooler dyads. *Child Development, 73*, 1803–1817.

DeVos, G. A. (1998). Confucian family socialization: The religion, morality and aesthetics of propriety. In W. H. Slote, & G. A. DeVos (Eds.), *Confucianism and the family*. New York: State University of New York Press.

Diener, E., Diener, M., & Diener, C. (1995). Factors predicting the subjective well-being of nations. *Journal of Personality and Social Psychology, 69*, 851–864.

Diener, E., Scollon, C. K. N., Oishi, S., Dzokoto, V., & Suh, E. M. (2000). Positivity and the construction of life satisfaction judgments: Global happiness is not the sum of its parts. *Journal of Happiness Studies, 1*, 159–176.

Dubas, J. S., & Gerris, J. R. (2002). Longitudinal changes in the time parents spend in activities with their adolescent children as a function of age, pubertal status, and gender. *Journal of Family Psychology, 16*, 415–426.

Duval, T. S., & Silvia, P. J. (2002). Self-awareness, probability of improvement, and the self-serving bias. *Journal of Personality and Social Psychology, 82*, 49–61.

Dweck, C. S. (1999). *Self-Theories: Their role in motivation, personality and development*. Philadelphia, PA: Taylor and Francis/Psychology Press.

Dweck, C. S., Chiu, C. Y., & Hong, Y. (1995a). Implicit theories and their role in judgments and reactions: A world from two perspectives. *Psychological Inquiry, 6*, 267–285.

Dweck, C. S., Chiu, C. Y., & Hong Y. (1995b). Implicit theories: Elaboration and extension of the model. *Psychological Inquiry, 6*, 322–333.

Edwards, C. P. (1995). Parenting toddlers. In M. H. Bornstein (Ed.), *Handbook of Parenting: Vol. 1. Children and parenting* (pp. 41–63). Mahwah, NJ: Erlbaum.

Eid, M., & Diener, E. (2001). Norms for experiencing emotions in different cultures: inter- and intranational differences. *Journal of Personality and Social Psychology, 81*, 869–885.

Feeney, B. C. (2007). The dependency paradox in close relationships: Accepting dependence promotes independence. *Journal of Personality and Social Psychology, 92*, 268–285.

Fiske, A. P., Kitayama, S., Markus, H. R., & Nisbett, R. E. (1998). The cultural matrix of social psychology. In D. T. Gilbert, S. T., Fiske, & G. Lindzey (Eds.), *Handbook of social psychology* (pp. 915–981). New York: McGraw-Hill.

Flanagan, C., Martínez, M. L., & Cumsille P. (2011). Civil societies as cultural and developmental contexts for civic identity formation. In L. A. Jensen (Ed.), *Bridging developmental approaches to psychology: New syntheses in theory, research and policy* (pp. 113–137). New York: Oxford University Press.

Fung, H. (1999). Becoming a moral child: The socialization of shame among young Chinese children. *Ethos, 27*, 180–209.

Gardner, H. (1999). *Intelligence reframed: Multiple intelligences for the 21st century.* New York: Basic Books.

Hallahan, M., Lee, F., & Herzog, T. (1997). It's not just whether you win or lose, it's also where you play the game: A naturalistic, cross-cultural examination of the positivity bias. *Journal of Cross-Cultural Psychology, 28*, 768–778.

Harkness, S., & Super, C. (1995). Culture and parenting. In M. H. Bornstein (Ed.), *Handbook of parenting: Vol. 2. Biology and ecology of parenting* (pp. 211–234). Mahwah, NJ: Erlbaum.

Hayes, S., Strosahl, K., & Wilson, K. (1999). *Acceptance and commitment therapy: An experiential approach to behavior change.* New York: Guilford Press.

Heine, S. J. (2005a). Constructing good selves in Japan and North America. In R. M. Sorrentino, D. Cohen, J. M. Olsen, & M. P. Zanna (Eds.), *Cultural and social behavior: The Ontario symposium* (pp. 95–116). Mahwah, NJ: Lawrence Erlbaum Associates Publishers.

Heine, S. J. (2005b). Where Is the Evidence for Pancultural Self-Enhancement? A Reply to Sedikides, Gaertner, and Toguchi (2003). *Journal of Personality and Social Psychology, 89*, 531–538.

Heine, S. J. (2007). Culture and motivation: What motivates people to act in the ways that they do? In S. Kitayama, & D. Cohen (Eds.), *Handbook of cultural psychology* (pp. 714–733). New York: Guilford Press.

Heine, S. J. & Hamamura, T. (2007). In search of East Asian self-enhancement. *Personality and Social Psychology Review, 11*, 1–24.

Heine, S. J., Lehman, D. R., Ide, E., Kitayama, S., Takata, T., & Matsumoto, H. (2001). Divergent consequences of success and failure in Japan and North America: An investigation of self-improving motivations and malleable selves. *Journal of Personality and Social Psychology, 81*, 599–615.

Heine, S. J., & Lehman, D. R. (1995). Cultural variation in unrealistic optimism: Does the West feel more invulnerable than the East? *Journal of Personality and Social Psychology, 68*, 595–607.

Heine, S. J., Lehman, D. R., Markus, H. R., & Kitayama, S. (1999). Is there a universal need for positive self-regard? *Psychological Review, 106*, 766–794.

Henderlong, J., & Lepper, M. R. (2002). The effects of praise on children's intrinsic motivation: A review and synthesis. *Psychological Bulletin, 128*, 774–795.

Hsu, F. L. K. (1983). *Rugged individualism reconsidered: Essays in psychological anthropology.* Knoxville, TN: University of Tennessee Press.

Huntsinger, C., Jose, P. E., Rudden, D., Luo, Z., & Krieg, D. B. (2001). Cultural differences in interactions around mathematics tasks in Chinese American and European

American families. In C. C. Park, A. L. Goodwin & S. J. Lee (Eds.), *Research on the education of Asian and Pacific Americans* (pp. 75–103). Greenwich, CT: Information Age Publishing.

Jensen, L. A. (2011). The cultural-developmental theory of moral psychology: A new synthesis. In L. A. Jensen (Ed.), *Bridging developmental approaches to psychology: New syntheses in theory, research, and policy* (pp. 3–25). New York: Oxford University Press.

Ji, L., Peng, K., & Nisbett, R. E. (2000). Culture, control, and perception of relationships in the environment. *Journal of Personality and Social Psychology, 78,* 943–955.

Kabat-Zinn J. (2005). *Coming to our senses: Healing ourselves and the world through mindfulness.* New York: Hyperion.

Kamins, M. L., & Dweck, C. S. (1999). Person versus process praise and criticism: Implications for contingent self-worth and coping. *Developmental Psychology, 35,* 835–847.

Keller, H., Lohaus, A., Kuensemueller, P., et al. (2004). The bio-culture of parenting: Evidence from five cultural communities. *Parenting: Science and Practice, 4,* 25–50.

Kitayama, S., Ishii, K., Imada, T., Takemura, K., & Ramaswamy, J. (2006). Voluntary settlement and the spirit of independence: Evidence from Japan's "northern frontier." *Journal of Personality and Social Psychology, 91,* 369–384.

Klineberg, O. (1938). Culture and emotional expression. *Journal of Abnormal and Social Psychology, 33,* 517–519.

Kuczynski, L., & Hildebrandt, N. (1997). Models of conformity and resistance in socialization theory. In J. E. Grusec & L. Kuczynski (Eds.), *Parenting and the internalization of values: A handbook of contemporary theory* (pp. 227–256). New York: Wiley.

Kwak, K. (2003). Adolescents and their parents: A review of intergenerational family relations for immigrant and non-immigrant families. *Human Development, 46,* 15–36.

Latz, S., Wolf, A. W., & Lozoff, B. (1999). Cosleeping in context: Sleep practices and problems in young children in Japan and the United States. *Archives of Pediatrics and Adolescent Medicine, 153,* 339–346.

Lee, A. Y., Aaker, J. L., & Gardner, W. L. (2000). The pleasures and pains of distinct self-construals: The role of interdependence in regulatory focus. *Journal of Personality and Social Psychology, 78,* 1122–1134.

Lehman, D. R., Chiu, C. Y., & Schaller, M. (2004). Psychology and culture. *Annual Review of Psychology, 55,* 689–714.

LeVine, R. A., Dixon, S., LeVine, S., et al. (1994). *Child care and culture: Lessons from Africa.* New York: Cambridge University Press.

Lewis, C. C. (1995). *Educating hearts and minds: Reflections on Japanese preschool and elementary education.* New York: Cambridge University Press.

Markus, H. R., & Kitayama, S. (1991). Culture and the self: Implications for cognition, emotion, and motivation. *Psychological Review, 98,* 224–253.

Markus, H. R., & Kitayama, S. (1994). The cultural construction of self and emotion: Implications for social behavior. In S. Kitayama, & H. R. Markus (Eds.), *Emotion and culture: Empirical studies of mutual influence* (pp. 89–130). Washington, DC: American Psychological Association.

Matsumoto, D., Yoo, S. H., & Nakagawa, S. (2008). Culture, emotion regulation, and adjustment. *Journal of Personality and Social Psychology, 94,* 925–937.

Menon, T., Morris, M. W., Chiu, C., & Hong, Y. (1999). Culture and the construal of agency: Attribution to individual versus group dispositions. *Journal of Personality and Social Psychology, 76,* 701–717.

Miller, P. J., Sandel, T. L., Liang, C. H., & Fung, H. (2001). Narrating transgressions in Longwood: The discourses, meanings, and paradoxes of an American socializing practice. *Ethos, 29*, 159–186.

Miller, P. J., Wang, S., Sandel T., & Cho G. E. (2002). Self-esteem as folk theory: A comparison of European American and Taiwanese mothers' beliefs. *Parenting: Science and Practice, 2*, 209–239.

Miller, P. J., Wiley, A. R., Fung, H., & Liang, C. H. (1997). Personal storytelling as a medium of socialization in Chinese and American families. *Child Development, 68*, 557–568.

Miyake, K., Chen, S., & Campos, J. (1985). Infant temperament, mother's mode of interaction, and attachment in Japan: An interim report. *Monographs of the Society for Research in Child Development, 50*(1–2, Serial No. 209): 276–297.

Miyamoto, Y., & Kitayama, S. (2002). Cultural variation in correspondence bias: The critical role of attitude diagnosticity of socially constrained behavior. *Journal of Personality and Social Psychology, 83*, 1239–1248.

Morelli, G. & Rothbaum, F. (2007). Situating the child in context: Attachment relationships and self-regulation in different cultures. In S. Kitayama & D. Cohen (Eds.), *Handbook of cultural psychology* (pp. 500–527). Guilford Press: New York.

Morling, B., & Evered, S. (2006). Secondary control reviewed and defined. *Psychological Bulletin, 132*, 269–296.

Morling, B., Kitayama, S., & Miyamoto, Y. (2002). Cultural practices emphasize influence in the United States and adjustment in Japan. *Personality and Social Psychology Bulletin, 28*, 311–323.

Morris, M. W., & Peng, K. (1994). Culture and cause: American and Chinese attributions for social and physical events. *Journal of Personality and Social Psychology, 67*, 949–971.

Muramoto, Y. (2003). An indirect self-enhancement in relationship among Japanese. *Journal of Cross-Cultural Psychology, 34*, 552–566.

Norenzayan, A., Choi, I., & Nisbett, R. E. (2002). Cultural similarities and differences in social inference: Evidence from behavioral predictions and lay theories of behaviors. *Personality and Social Psychology Bulletin, 28*, 109–120.

Norenzayan, A., Choi, I., & Peng, K. (2007). Cognition and perception. In S. Kitayama & D. Cohen (Eds.), *Handbook of cultural psychology* (pp. 569–594). New York: Guilford Publications.

Oishi, S. (2002). The experiencing and remembering of well-being: A cross-cultural analysis. *Personality and Social Psychology Bulletin, 28*, 1398–1406.

Oishi, S., & Diener, E. (2003). Culture and well-being: The cycle of action, evaluation and decision. *Personality and Social Psychology Bulletin, 29*, 939–949.

Oishi, S., & Sullivan, H. W. (2005). The mediating role of parental expectations in culture and well-being. *Journal of Personality, 73*, 1267–1294.

Ozawa-de Silva, C. (2007). Demystifying Japanese therapy: An analysis of Naikan and the Ajase complex through Buddhist thought. *Ethos, 35*, 411–446.

Potter, S. H. (1988). The cultural construction of emotion in rural Chinese social life. *Ethos, 16*, 181–208.

Rogers, C. R. (1961). *On becoming a person.* Oxford, UK: Houghton Mifflin.

Rogoff, B. (2003). *The cultural nature of human development.* New York: Oxford University Press.

Rohner, R. P. (2004). The parental "acceptance-rejection syndrome": Universal correlates of perceived rejection. *American Psychologist, 59*, 830–840.

Rosenberg, M. (1979). *Conceiving the self.* New York: Basic Books.

Rothbaum, F., & Kakinuma, M. (2004). Amae and attachment: Security in cultural context. *Human Development, 47*, 34–39.

Rothbaum, F., Kakinuma, M., Nagaoka, R., & Azuma, H. (2007). Attachment and amae: Parent-child closeness in the United States and Japan. *Journal of Cross-Cultural Psychology, 38,* 465–486.

Rothbaum, F., Morelli, G., Pott, G., & Liu-Constant, Y. (2000a). Immigrant-Chinese and Euro-American parents' physical closeness with young children: Themes of family relatedness. *Journal of Family Psychology, 14,* 334–348.

Rothbaum, F., Nagaoka, R., & Ponte, I. (2006). Caregiver sensitivity in cultural context: Japanese and U.S. teachers' beliefs about anticipating and responding to children's needs. *Journal of Research in Childhood Education, 21,* 23–40.

Rothbaum, F., Pott, M., Azuma, H., Miyake, K., & Weisz, J. (2000b). The development of close relationships in Japan and the United States: Path of symbiotic harmony and generative tension. *Child Development, 71,* 1121–1142.

Rothbaum, F., & Trommsdorff, G. (2007). Do roots and wings complement or oppose one another: The socialization of relatedness and autonomy in cultural context. In J. Grusec and P. Hastings (Eds.), *Handbook of socialization* (pp. 461–489). New York: Guilford Press.

Rothbaum, F., Weisz, J., Pott, M., Miyake, K., & Morelli, G. (2000c). Attachment and culture: Security in Japan and the U.S. *American Psychologist, 55,* 1093–1104.

Ryan, R. M., & Deci, E. L. (2000). Self-determination theory and the facilitation of intrinsic motivation, social development, and well-being. *American Psychologist, 55,* 68–78.

Saarni, C., Mumme, D. L., & Campos, J. (1998). Emotional development: Action, communication, and understanding. In N. Eisenberg (Ed.), W. Damon (Series Ed.), *Handbook of child psychology: Vol. 3. Social, emotional, and personality development* (5th ed., pp. 237–309). New York: Wiley.

Saraswathi, T. S., Mistry, J., & Dutta, R. (2011). Reconceptualizing lifespan development through a Hindu perspective. In L. A. Jensen (Ed.), *Bridging cultural and developmental psychology: New syntheses in theory, research and policy* (pp. 276–299). New York: Oxford University Press.

Schimmack, U., Radhakrishnan, P., Oishi, S., Dzokoto, V., & Ahadi, S. (2002). Culture, personality, and subjective well-being: Integrating process models of life satisfaction. *Journal of Personality and Social Psychology, 82,* 582–593.

Schlegel, A. (2011). Adolescent ties to adult communities: the intersection of culture and development. In L. A. Jensen (Ed.), *Bridging cultural and developmental psychology: New syntheses in theory, research and policy* (pp. 138–158). New York: Oxford University Press.

Schlegel, A., & Barry, H. (1991). *Adolescence: An anthropological inquiry.* New York: Free Press.

Sedikides, C., Gaertner, L., & Vevea, J. L. (2005). Pancultural self-enhancement reloaded: A meta-analytic reply to Heine (2005). *Journal of Personality and Social Psychology, 89,* 539–551.

Segal, Z. V., Williams, J. M. G., & Teasdale, J. D. (2002). *Mindfulness-based cognitive therapy for depression: A new approach to preventing relapse.* New York: Guilford.

Shweder, R. A., Jensen, L. A., & Goldstein, W. (1995). Who sleeps by whom revisited: A method for extracting the moral goods implicit in practice. In J. J. Goodnow, P. J. Miller & F. Kessel (Eds.) New Directions in Child Development. *Contextualizing Development: A Practice Perspective, 67,* 21–39.

Smetana, J. G. (2002). Culture, autonomy, and personal jurisdiction in adolescent-parent relationships. In H. W. Reese and R. Kail (Eds.), *Advances in child development and behavior,* Vol. 29 (pp. 51–87). New York: Academic Press.

Snibbe, A. C., & Markus, H. R. (2005). You can't always get what you want: Educational attainment, agency, and choice. *Journal of Personality and Social Psychology, 88*, 703–720.

Sternberg, R. J. (1999). The theory of successful intelligence. *Review of General Psychology, 3*, 292–316.

Stevenson, H. W., Lee, S., Chen, C., Stigler, J. W., Hsu, F. & Kitamura, S. (1990). Contexts of achievement: A study of American, Chinese, and Japanese children. *Monographs of the Society for Research in Child Development, 55*(1/2), 1–119.

Stevenson, H. W., & Stigler, J. W. (1992). *The learning gap: Why our schools are failing and what we can learn from Japanese and Chinese education.* New York, NY: Summit Books.

Stewart, S. M., Bond, M. H., Kennard, B. D., Ho, L. M., & Zaman, R. M. (2002). Does the Chinese construct of guan export to the West? *International Journal of Psychology, 37*, 74–82.

Suh, E. M., & Diener, E. (2001). The role of the self in life satisfaction judgment: Weighing emotions and social information differently. In E. Diener, S. Oishi, & R. E. Lucas (Eds.), *Annual Review of Psychology, 54*, 403–425.

Suh, E., Diener, E., Oishi, S., & Triandis, H. C. (1998). The shifting basis of life satisfaction judgments across cultures: Emotions versus norms. *Journal of Personality and Social Psychology, 74*, 482–493.

Triandis, H. C. (1995). *Individualism and collectivism.* Boulder, CO: Westview Press.

Triandis, H. C. (2005). Issues in individualism and collectivism research. In R. M. Sorrentino, D. Cohen, J. M. Olson, & M. P. Zanna (Eds.), *Culture and social behavior: The Ontario Symposium,* (Vol. 10, pp. 207–225). Mahwah, NJ: Erlbaum.

Trommsdorff, G., & Friedlmeier, W. (2010). Preschool girls' distress and mothers' sensitivity in Japan and Germany. *European Journal of Developmental Psychology, 7*, 350–370.

Uzgiris, I. C., & Raeff, C. (1995). Play in parent-child interactions. In M. H. Bornstein (Ed.), *Handbook of parenting: Vol. 4. Applied and practical parenting* (pp. 353–376). Hillsdale, NJ: LEA.

Wang, Y., Wiley, A. R., & Chiu, C.-Y. (2008). Independence-supportive praise versus interdependence promoting praise. *International Journal of Behavior Development, 32*, 13–20.

Weisner, T. S. (1984). A cross-cultural perspective: Ecocultural niches of middle childhood. In A. Collins (Ed.). *The elementary school years: Understanding development during middle childhood.* Washington, DC: National Academy Press.

Weisz, J. R., Rothbaum, F. M., & Blackburn, T. C. (1984). Standing out and standing in: The psychology of control in America and Japan. *American Psychologist, 39*, 955–969.

Whiting, B. B., & Edwards, C. P. (1988). *Children of different worlds: The formation of social behavior.* Cambridge, MA: Harvard University Press.

Wu, D. Y. H. (1982). Psychotherapy and emotion in traditional Chinese medicine. In A. J. Marsella & G. M. White (Eds.), *Cultural conceptions of mental health and therapy* (pp. 285–301). Dordrecht, The Netherlands: Reidel.

Wu, P., Robinson, C. C., & Yang, C. (2002). Similarities and differences in mothers' parenting of preschoolers in China and the Unites States. *International Journal of Behavioral Development, 26*, 481–491.

CHAPTER 10

The Development of Individual Purposes

Creating Actuality Through Novelty

JAAN VALSINER

Novelty has been a major conceptual puzzle for developmental science. As something that has not yet been encountered it defies our habits of classification of phenomena into established categories. Thus, it can go unnoticed—although we try to fit anything new into the already established systems of categories. Yet to make sense of development, it cannot go unnoticed, as it is the very core of any development. So it needs to gain conceptualization; yet that cannot happen in terms of the previously known (i.e., not novel) categories.

In our lives, the experience of novelty is pervasive. We can observe new formations in all biological, psychological, social, and cultural phenomena— change in relation to any previous state of affairs presents itself as novelty. As development is defined as constructive transformation of form in irreversible time through the process of the constant organism—environment interchange (Valsiner & Connolly, 2003)—novelty is both the result of the previous and the basis of upcoming: development.

Recognizing the central focus of novelty creates a very complex conceptual problem for the study of development: trying to make sense of what is *not yet* present (but is likely to emerge) on the basis of what we can observe. What is observable now may vanish as something new becomes observable. Development entails the unity of *evolution* and *involution*, as James Mark Baldwin (1930) understood over a century before us (*see* Fig. 10–1).

Any recognition of the unity of disappearance and emergence sets up a very difficult task for a scientist because the object of investigation is always fuzzy.

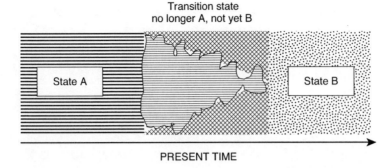

FIGURE 10.1 Development as unity of the disappearing (involution) and appearing (evolution) in time.

As one can see from Figure 10–1, there is no difficulty for an observer to distinguish between A ("that what was") and B ("that what now has emerged")—this fits the common sense uses of Aristotelian logic (focusing on the "Law of excluded middle"). However, development happens precisely outside of the realm covered by classical logic—in the fuzzy "zone" in which A *no longer* is clearly observable and B is *not yet* equally clearly observable.

However, *traces* of A and B are possibly visible in the transition state, which creates an empirical analysis problem for researchers who want to study development. By existing (non-developmental) habits of creating knowledge—by assigning categories—to the selected fuzzy phenomena, they can demonstrate high intercoder agreement in the case of A, as well as in the case of B, but not in the transition state (Valsiner, 1994). The non-developmental methodology of using intercoder agreement as a reliability indicator would lead the researchers to eliminate a focus on the transition state and study only the "reliable" As and Bs. It is obvious from Figure 10–1 that this amounts to elimination of the very phenomenon—development—that is declared to be the object of the study. The frequent critiques of child psychology not being developmental (Cairns, 1986; Cairns et al., 1996; Gottlieb, 1997; Valsiner, 2006) thus reveal a more fundamental problem of psychology's methodology in general that was very well-phrased by Ludwig Wittgenstein half a century ago:

> The confusion and barrenness of psychology is not to be explained by calling it a "young science". . . The existence of the experimental method makes us think we have the means of solving the problem which trouble us: though problem and method pass another by. (Wittgenstein, 1958, p. 232)

How can one overcome such confusion? All empirical research into development is of scientific value only if built on clear axiomatic premises from which particular theoretical perspectives are derived. Any strictly developmental perspective needs to accept the open-systemic nature of developmental phenomena, with two consequences: a focus on novelty and the inevitability of uniqueness of developmental phenomena. Yet that uniqueness has general order.

Development as Unfolding of Uniqueness

The emphasis on novelty construction in development is based on the basic assumption of the open-systemic nature of development. Open systems are wholes—consisting of parts and their relationships[1]—that are in an exchange relation with their environment. As Ludwig von Bertalanffy has clarified the concept:

> A system is closed if no material enters or leaves it; it is open if there is import and export and, therefore, change of the components. Living systems are open systems, maintaining themselves in exchange of materials with environment, and in continuous building up and breaking down of their components. (Bertalanffy, 1950, p. 23)

Thus, an open system is any distinct entity—a cell, a person, a forest, a family, an orchestra, a crowd, or a country—that takes in resources from its environment, processes them in some way, and produces something new that is taken outward into the environment. Such system depends on its environment—it exists only because of that relationship—as well as on interactions between its component parts or subsystems[2]. All biological, psychological, and social organisms exist and develop only because of their permanent exchange relationships with their environments.[3] Hence, models that explain processes of development are those that either imply their dynamic interchange or take it into account in direct ways. Developmental phenomena are self-organizing systems, rather than ontological objects—entities or "things."

Who develops is the particular open system in direct relation with its environment—not an abstracted "average system." Developmental psychology belongs to the general idiographic science—science that generalizes from particular, individual cases (systems) that have unique histories. This means that evidence about some phenomenon that is based on the study of inter-individual variability (usually termed "individual differences" in a sample) cannot be interpreted as if it reflects the intra-individual variation (over time) in any of the persons in the sample. Open-systemic phenomena are non-ergodic. Peter Molenaar (2004, 2007) has made it explicit:

> ... psychology as an idiographic science restores the balance by focusing on the neglected time-dependent variation within a single individual (*IAV*). It brings back into scientific psychology the dedicated study of the individual, prior to pooling across other individuals. Each person is initially conceived of as a possibly unique system of interacting dynamic processes, the unfolding of which gives rise to an individual life trajectory in a high-dimensional psychological space. Bringing thus back the person into scientific psychology, it can be proven that her return is definitive this time. Classical theorems in ergodic theory, a branch of mathematical statistics and probability theory, show that most

psychological processes will have to be considered to be nonergodic. (Molenaar, 2004, p. 202).

Non-ergodicity of psychological phenomena renders most of the work done in psychology over the past half-century moot. The practice of treating **inter**-individual variability (which we usually label "variance") as if it adequately reflected **intra**-individual (temporal) variability is not possible on axiomatic grounds. By rejection of the axiom of ergodicity in psychology, we invalidate the interpretations of group-based data that are applied to individuals. That psychology—like common sense thinking—has been forcing "crowd" (population)-based findings on individual cases is a result of social (and linguistic, Valsiner, 1986) convention.

Developing on the Margins of Irreversible Time

The human being is always on the border of oneself and of the "world around," attempting (by culture) to achieve the unachievable and going **beyond** the horizons (Smith, 1999). Yet in that process of purposive efforts, the very limits—horizons—are **extended** through culture. It is exactly in the capacity of culture to make movement from the real (here-and-now) to the constructed (imaginary there-and-then) possible (Boesch, 2005), enabling both the pleasures of aesthetic kind and horrors of wars and genocides. It also sets up the tasks of "building bridges"—such as the collective effort in the present volume (*see also* Goodnow, 2011).

Open systems are constructed on the boundary of the past and the future as the actual trajectory of their life-course of the organism becomes constructed out of a field of possibilities. Self-organization in biological systems. . .

. . . is a process in which a pattern at the global level of a system emerges solely from numerous interactions among the lower-level components of the system. Moreover, *the rules specifying interactions among the system's components are executed using only local information, without reference to the global pattern.* (Camazine et al, 2001, p. 8, added emphasis)

The focus of Camazine et al. on "local information" may fit the behavioral development of species lower on the evolutionary scale but requires the addition of *purposiveness* at the higher level of the evolutionary process. The latter is most clear in *Homo sapiens*, where development entails *culturally created purposiveness* through the use of semiotic mediators. When taking an open-systems approach, we look both inward and outward. We are interested in relationships and patterns of interaction between subsystems and their environments within the organization. We also look for relationships and reciprocal influences between the organization and the environment outside its formal boundary—an analog of a "membrane" (Valsiner, 2007). Such membranes can be structural (between a cell and its environment, between person and the environment) as well as temporal (between the past and the future).

The "Zone of Proximal Development" As Boundary
Between Past and Future

The concept of "zone of proximal development" (ZPD) has a curious history (*see* Valsiner & van der Veer, 1993; van der Veer & Valsiner, 1991). Its selective appropriation in psychology is a good example of developmental researchers' struggle with the phenomena of emergence.

From the "traditional" (non-developmental) psychology's standpoint, it is a strange concept to use. Aside from its non-translatability into an "operational concept" or a "measure," it poses a number of theoretical problems. First, it entails a reference to a *zone*, rather than to a *point*. Most of psychology's concepts are point-like signs, in relation to which various statistical concepts ("true score," "reliability," etc.) are applied in the act of "measurement." Second, it is a concept applicable only for an *individual case at the given time*, although psychology's understanding of "development" has been highly varied in contemporary psychological discourse, ranging from loosely formulated ideas about "age group differences" (or "age effects") to narrowly definable structural transformation of organisms in irreversible time and within context. It is only the latter look at development that can fit with the ZPD concept. Finally, to complicate the matters even further, contemporary psychologists have to wrestle with the qualifier of "proximal" (or "potential" or "nearest"), as it is the connecting link between the field theoretic "zone" and the concept of "development" in this complex term.

To understand the emergence of the use of ZPD in Vygotsky's discourse, it is important to bear in mind the consistent emphasis on developing psychological processes that form the holistic dynamic structure of the child's mental development. Vygotsky's effort to explain human ontogeny led him to bring together the developmental theory and traditions of pedology (child study). This duality of focus—on developmental theorizing and pedological (test-based "diagnostic") applications—was Vygotsky's field of argumentation. In the same manuscript where the basic idea of social rearing of not-yet-developed processes is expressed, we can trace the roots of thinking that later serve as illustrations for this concept (in "The Problem of Cultural Age," Vygotsky, 1931/1983). ZPD in later uses—especially in North America—has taken that example of social assistance conditions as if it is the core of the concept.

However, it is not that. The ZPD, in its "pure" form, is a concept strictly applicable to the development of a single organism within its environment, without any reference to social assistance. In one of his lectures devoted to play at Leningrad Pedagogical Institute in 1933, Vygotsky focused on play as the core of the teaching–learning process (*obuchenie*) in development. Explicitly, he argued that play creates the ZPD:

> *In play the child is always higher than his average age, higher than his usual everyday behavior;* he is in play as if a head above himself. The play contains, in a condensed way, as if in the focus of a magnifying glass, all tendencies of development; the child in play as if tries to accomplish a jump above the level of his ordinary behavior.

The relationship of play to development should be compared with that of teaching-learning to development. Changes of needs and consciousness of more general kind lie behind the play. Play is the resource of development and it creates the zone of nearest development. Action in the imaginary field, in imagined situation, construction of voluntary intention, the formation of the life-plan, will motives– this all emerges in play and . . . makes it the ninth wave of preschool age development. (Vygotsky, 1933, 1966, pp. 74–75, added emphasis)

Here is the paradox that stands in the way of empirical use of Vygotsky's ZPD concept: It refers to the hidden processes of the present that may become explicated in reality only as the present becomes the (nearest) past, whereas the (nearest) future becomes the present. However, any empirical research effort (including Vygotskian "teaching experiments" using the "method of double stimulation") can take place only within the present (given the constraint of irreversibility of time). It is for that reason that the ZPD concept could not be specified by Vygotsky in any more detail than a general emphasis on the need to pay attention to the processes of development that are constructing the new "present" that is currently "future"—on the basis of the functional organization of the child in the actual "present." ZPD was not to be a concept usable for empirical investigations—it was devised as a rhetoric device in Vygotsky's dialogue with his contemporary educational practices.

The ZPD was a strong argument against the use of intelligence tests and any other "measurement" techniques that depicted children's present levels of development but remained moot to their futures. It pointed to the need to study processes of development "online" but provided very little opportunity for how such studies could be done. A contemporary effort to work out the specifics of such development is reflected in the construction of the Trajectory Equifinality Model (TEM; Sato, 2009; Sato et al, 2007).

The Trajectory Equifinality Model

In its minimal form, the TEM is depicted in Figure 10–2. It is obvious that it requires the analysis of complex phenomena—as these unfold in time—into units that cross the time barrier of future and past, including memories of past dialogues between the then-actualized A versus then-potential (not eventually actualized) B trajectories. The two trajectories of the past bifurcation point— A and B—define the field of multiple possibilities out of which only one (A) became actualized. The relation {A<>B} as it is being reconstructed at the present becomes coordinated with the potential opposition {C<>D} (Fig. 10–2). The range specified by C and D defines the boundaries of what Sato calls "zone of finality," the range of possible immediate futures (ZPD in Vygotsky's terms).

The TEM is not merely a description of unfolded trajectories but a mechanism that generates future actualized trajectories on the basis of past contrasts of the actual and the potential directions. It is a "dialogue" between two fields: the (yet unknown) future as constrained by C and D, with the remembered (reconstructed) past marked by the range of A and B.

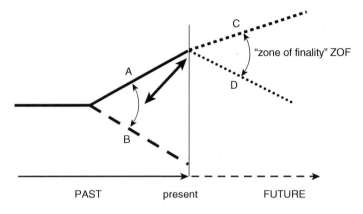

FIGURE 10.2 The locus of coverage by the TEM of the coordination of the past and the future.

While providing a new light on the processes of negotiation that happen within ZPD, the TEM also brings to our attention the need to enrich psychology's theoretical toolkit. First, note that three of the four components in the whole are non-real (in terms of the life of the person)—B (never occurred but was a possibility), C, and D (not yet tried out, just borders of possibilities). Only A is "real," in the sense of having happened in the development of the person. The claim by Lee Rudolph—that psychological concepts cannot be represented by real numbers (Rudolph, 2006a, 2006b, 2006c; Valsiner & Rudolph, 2008)—is substantiated by TEM. Second, the negotiation of {A<>B} and {C<>D} occurs in the boundary of past and future. In this sense, development happens as a "membrane" event (Valsiner, 2007a). As such, they work for producing novelty; however, whether the novelty produced stays or vanishes depends on its transition "upward" in the hierarchy of levels of organization of development.

Multilevel Nature of Developmental Processes

Developmental science investigates transformation of structures at different levels of generality—phylogeny, cultural history, ontogenesis, mesogenesis, and microgenesis. Each of these levels of processes are characterized by its own functional time unit—for example, a period of 1 million years in phylogeny may be a reasonable time frame to use, whereas for cultural history of a social representation of some king 500 years may suffice. Ontogeny is limited to the maximum length of the organism's lifetime, whereas microgenesis may be limited to developmental transformations that occur from duration of milli- or microseconds to those that merge with mesogenetic organizational level. The latter feeds into ontogenesis by creating relative stability of microgenetically established and mesogenetically practiced new forms.

Developmental psychology—among other developmental sciences—is the arena where differentiation and hierarchical order prevail (Ehrenfels, 1890, 1932, 1937). Undoubtedly it is an order of processes that is functional for relating with the dynamic environment and dynamic in its adjustment of its form. These properties of the developing systems render the traditional focus on "measurement" in psychology (Michell, 1999, 2004) misfitting with the nature of the phenomena. It is simply impossible to "measure" the "true state" of a phenomenon that is in the process of movement from one state to another, never passing through a previous (momentarily "true") state. The latter is also never "true" as an entity but a negotiated temporary central point of oppositely located manifolds of vectors (Fig. 10–3). In that figure, the seemingly determinable central point (CP) is a result of the set of vectors of mutually opposite kind (A and non-A to E and non-E). Although it is technically possible to fixate it in the flow of movement in time and assign it some number as an act of "its measurement," this construction of a sign fails to represent the complexity of the process that functions in the phenomena (Rosenbaum & Valsiner, in press).

The hierarchical systems view of developmental processes is elaborated in the theory of *probabilistic epigenesis* (Gottlieb, 1997, 2003). In addition to the fourfold separation of the levels of organization (genetic activity, neural activity, behavior, and environment), the phenomena of human psychology require further differentiation of levels beyond the behavioral one into the inclusion of higher mental functions into the scheme (*see* Fig. 10–4). The principle of *bounded indeterminacy* (Valsiner, 1987)—setting the constraints for defining subdomains of not yet determined futures—applies to all levels of Figure 10–4, both in terms of "upward" (genetic → neural → behavioral → mental → volitional) and "downward" (volitional → mental → behavioral → neural → genetic) chains of constraining the functioning of each next level by setting up

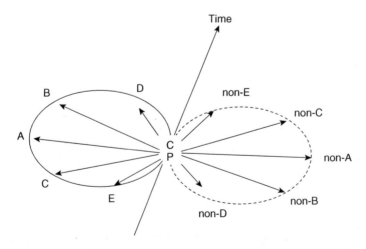

FIGURE 10.3 Any "measurable point" of psychological phenomena as a unique temporary result of a manifold of oppositions (based on Valsiner, 2006).

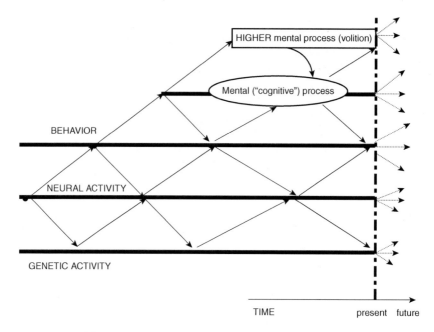

FIGURE 10.4 Hierarchical organization of human biological and psychological functions.

boundary conditions. Psychology operates within the realm of the upper part of the scheme—behavioral, mental, volitional levels—of the organization, without (obviously) denying the relevance of the lower levels, and with guidance of the lower levels from above (in terms of "medium downward causation" as specified by Emmeche, Køppe and Stjernfeldt, 2000, p. 25).

The hierarchical organization of the developmental process guarantees its redundant equifinality—a functionally similar mental outcome (way of thinking) can emerge both on the basis of generalization from the behavioral level as well as through the downward specification of the volitional to mental constraining. Redundancy—possibility to accomplish a particular outcome via more than one means—is a consequence of the open-systemic nature of all development. In a hierarchical system, a similar outcome (something as ordinary as drinking a glass of water) can occur on the basis of upward causative chain ("I am thirsty") as well as by a downward chain ("drinking water is good for my health").

At the level of human beings—self-reflexive and purposive—the emerged patterns become functional in a feed-forward loop of "downward causality" (Emmeche, Køppe, & Stjernfeldt, 2000). This is the qualitative specific of psychology, in biological systems, as indicated above; it need not be considered. That makes psychology's search for adequate conceptual systems belonging to a class of generality that is far from the "measurement" of assumed ontological properties "of" the given system (Michell, 2004; Valsiner & Rudolph, 2008). When viewed from the open-systemic basis, psychologists' favorite objects of measurement—"intelligence," "personality dimensions," "attitudes," and so forth—are ephemeral artifacts of no scientific value, similarly to the role "ether" played in physics. Subsequently, claims of "predicting" outcomes from one to another of these entities—usually in the case of application of regression analysis—are artifacts as well. Psychology has misplaced its precision of analysis by treating processes as if these are measurable entities.

It should be obvious from Figure 10–4 that the use of any linear model that presumes a singular pathway of development is theoretically inappropriate for developmental psychology. Instead, the multitrajectory models of the application of the dynamic systems (van Geert, 2003) fit the developmental phenomena. Developmental models may benefit from dynamic structural images (e.g., that of a web; Fischer & Bidell, 1998) rather than attempt to ascribe numbers to complex phenomena (Porter, 1995).

Even if numbers are assigned, the focus on what these numbers represent can be constructed in variable ways. The accumulation of evidence can be viewed from different standpoints—those of stability (concentration upon the averages or prototypes) or variability (here, inter-individual variability or "individual differences"). Psychology as a non-developmental discipline has assumed the former stance with a clearly inadequate basis:

> The uncritical use of the assumption of normal distribution—the bell-shaped curve—dominated psychology and social sciences. But in this assumption, something important was overlooked. Researchers tended to forget or never learned how the bell-shaped curve had been mathematically derived and defined. The normal distribution occurs when both the following conditions are satisfied: (1) The fluctuations are *random*; (2) they are *independent* of one another. But psychological and social events are neither random nor independent. Therefore it is *illogical* to assume a normal distribution. (Maruyama, 1999, p. 53)

By this singular look at the misfit of the axiomatic basis of the statistical method and the nature of psychological phenomena, Maruyama has elegantly cleaned the base for building new methodological perspectives by introducing into science the notion of *deviation-amplifying processes* (which are working in coordination with deviation-counteracting—that is, equilibrating processes; Maruyama, 1963). Open systems are not merely characterized by their variability, but they generate increasing variability. Together with such increasing intra-individual variability—widening of the range of novelty—constraints to keep that variability within managable bounds are set up as well. It is here—in the domain of increasing variability together with efforts to reduce it—where developmental and cultural psychology build the bridge over the traditions of "measurements"-oriented psychology. Because the issue of development is that of structural transposition—from one context to another, and from one form of a structure to an altered (developed–progressed or regressed) form— the question of units of analysis becomes central for translating theoretical schemes into empirical investigations.

Units of Analysis: Minimal Structural Wholes
in Steady State and in Transformation

Psychology's analysis units are necessarily complex ones—entailing the multi-
level structure of development and its duration in irreversible time. The developmental thinkers from the beginning of the 20th century attempted to make
sense of the whole–part relationships in different ways—through the notion of
abduction or retroduction (Charles S. Peirce—Pizarroso & Valsiner, 2009),
creative synthesis (Wilhelm Wundt), "vertical" transfer of experience from one
context to another via the notion of generalization, or, most importantly,
through dialectical synthesis (Lev Vygotsky). The latter is the form of development where culture, as semiotic mediation, acquires its crucial role (Rosa &
Valsiner, 2007). The whole to be studied is a living form—it is a structure, that
cannot be understood without considering the constant dynamically interacting
parts, essential to life, stemming from present as well as from the past. However, Vygotsky's kind of dialectical synthesis entails strict consideration of the
thesis (A), antithesis (non-A), their relation (contradiction), and overcoming of
the latter through creating novelty (synthesis).

This structural-dynamic look at the unit of analysis led Vygotsky to formulate the general idea of what a unit of analysis needs to be like in psychology:

> Psychology, as it desires to study complex wholes . . . needs to change the meth-
> ods of analysis into elements by the analytic method that reveals the parts of the
> unit [literally: breaks the whole into linked units—*metod . . . analiza, . . . razchle-*
> *niayushego na edinitsy*]. It has to find the further undividable, surviving features
> that are characteristic of the given whole as a unity—*units within which in mutu-*
> *ally opposing ways these features are represented* [Russian: *edinitsy, v kotorykh v*
> *protivopolozhnom vide predstavleny eti svoistva*].[4] (Vygotsky, 1999, p. 13)

Such generalization arises through the formal operations the researchers
perform on the phenomena to make sense of them. Its root metaphor has been
the contrast between water and its components (oxygen and hydrogen), which
are used in making the point of the primacy of the Gestalt over its constituents
widely in the late 19th- through early 20th-century developmental theorizing.
Quite obviously, the properties of water are not reducible to those of either
hydrogen or oxygen. Hence, the whole (water) is more than a mere "sum" of
its parts. Furthermore, it is universal: the chemical structure of water remains
the same independent of whatever biological system (e.g., human body, cellu-
lar structure of a plant) or geological formation (e.g., an ocean, or a coffee
cup!) in which it exists.

Developmental Units: "Minimally Structured Wholes," But Wholes That Are Transformable

Developmental focus is even more complex than the solution of the use of
dialectical units—an essentially Gestalt claim, with the addition of the notion
of dialogical opposition between the parts. The water analogy, which was good

for fortifying the Gestalt quality notion, is here misleading: The oxygen and hydrogen are in chemistry given as "harmoniously fitted" into the chemical structure of water, rather than in a "state of contradiction" or "friction" with one another. It is from these latter notions of friction, opposition, and contradiction that development is to be discerned—so water in and of itself does not "develop" (i.e., establish a new form of chemical structure, despite changing its substantive qualities under varied conditions—solid ice, liquid substance, and evaporating steam[5]).

It is easy to see how Vygotsky's dialectical units (into opposing parts of the whole) go beyond the water analogy. A developmental unit of analysis is one of a structure **{X<contradicting>Y}** together with a set of catalytic conditions **C {a,b,c}** that specify how a new structure **{X<contradicting>Z}** can emerge. Together with charting out the pathways to synthesis, inherent in that unit is the constraining of options—the structure of the unit rules out some possible courses for emergence. Vygotsky found that holistic unit in word meaning, as that meaning includes a variety of mutually opposite and contradicting versions of "personal sense" (*smysl*). Through the dynamic oppositions—contradictions—between subunits (of "personal sense") of the meaning (*znachenie*), the latter develops. Thus we have a hierarchical unit, where the transformation of the *znachenie* at the higher level of organization depends on the dialectical syntheses emerging in the contradictory relationships between varied *smysl*'s at the lower level. And conversely, the emerged new form of *znachenie* establishes constraints on the interplay of *smysl*'s at the lower level. The *loci* of developmental transformations are in **the relationsships between different levels of the hierarchical order**, not at any one level (*see* Fig. 10–4).

Despite this hyperdynamic nature of developing phenomena we are able to detect—and even reify—moments of relative stability within them. Hence, we encounter the conceptual paradox of development; to study it, we create abstract fixed conceptual schemes that attempt to capture the non-fixed (and unfixable) phenomena. On what conceptual background is such effort plausible? It is here that cultural psychology creates the bridge between the uniqueness of actual development and its communication across unique personal experiences. Although our experience is unique, we can understand one another's experience through cultural meaning systems.

Cultural Psychology As a "Bridge"

Cultural psychology has long history—going beyond that of independent psychology[6]—yet it has become notable in psychologists' discourses again in the last two decades (Valsiner, 2001a). Among other directions in cultural psychology, the focus on semiotic mediation is interesting. The central point of the semiotic direction in cultural psychology is simple: **human beings create signs and let these signs regulate their lives** (Boesch, 1991, 2008; Chaudhary, 2004; Lonner & Hayes, 2007; Shweder & Sullivan, 1990; Valsiner, 1999, 2001b,

2002, 2007). Individual purposes are culturally guided. From the immediate life meanings, persons create deeply subjective and abstracted—personal gods or shrines, which are at times personified in terms of deities (Oliveira & Valsiner, 1997; Valsiner, 1999), or images of idealized "social others"(e.g., Baoule "wooden spouses"—Ravenhill, 1996; Vogel, 1997). All of these cultural forms are semiotic resources and become symbolic resources (Zittoun, 2006; Zittoun et al, 2004) when put to human life practices. We act "on our own free will," not recognizing that the very concept of "free will" and its corollary ("I want THIS [and not THAT]!") are results of the internalization and externalization process in relation of the self with the social context.

Meaning-Making

In the generalized form, acts of personal–cultural meaning construction can be summarized by the following process description:

(a) **The PERSON constructs MEANING COMPLEX labelled X...**

$\downarrow$

(b) **... proceeds to OBJECTIFY it by FIXING ITS FORM... ,**
(e.g., internal—internalized social norm, or external—monument, picture of deity, figurines for luck, rituals)

$\downarrow$

(c) **... and starts to act *AS IF* the objectified, meaning complex X is an external agent that controls the PERSON**

$\downarrow$

(d) **... and proceeds to create the imperatives—the purposes—by which the meaning complex X *SHOULD be used* by oneself and others as a guideline (or norm)**

Most of the World's religious architecture, art, rituals, and reasons for all kinds of quarrels result from this simple projective–constrictive process. We construct the meanings that lead us to reconstructing the objective world, and the reconstructed world guides our further construction of meanings. Both the Notre Dame Cathedral and the McDonalds arches are architectural objective realities in this subjective chain of meaning construction. Most importantly, constructed meanings are projected outward "to the society" and turned into social imperatives by which individuals organize their lives by their own "free will" or by socio-moral-legal forms of social coercion.

Cultural psychology is a part of general psychology. Human feeling, thinking, and willingness are regulated by signs created by the very persons who succumb to their regulatory powers. It is here where culture enters into the human *psyche*—as an inherent constituent of the psychological functions, rather than some "influence" from "outside." Yet in the common sense presentation of the story the attribution to "influences from outside," even using the term *culture* as a meaning for specifying to "which outside" the causality is attributed is rampant. It acquires the role analogous to *society*, *social environment*, and so forth (in contrast to *nature*, *genes*, etc.) in upholding a socially established normative dichotomy of internal/external contrasts. In contrast to such common language (attributional) use of the word *culture*, the scientific use of it is distinguished by denial of making statements like "Culture *causes* X, Y, Z." Culture—in the sense of semiotic mediation, or activity settings (rituals, etc.)—is inherent in the functioning of the human *psyche*, not an external "impact" or "cause."

Universality of the Generalization and Specification Process

Two processes can be present in the regulatory hierarchies: **abstracting generalization** and **contextualizing specification**. Abstracting generalization creates new levels of semiotic regulators, removing the re-co-pre-presentational role increasingly further toward higher complexity of abstraction. For example, human values are generalizations of abstracted kind. Extremely general terms like *love*, *justice*, *freedom*, and so forth, are meaningful in their generalized (and hypergeneralized—that is, absolutized) abstractness. As such, these generalized signs can be brought to bear upon regulating very specific contexts (by a process I call **contextualizing specification**). They operate in very concrete settings—linking their abstracted properties with the specifics of a here-and-now setting.

Example: The Use of Fun

Nobody can exactly define the term *fun*, but its use is possible across an immense variety of concrete contexts. So, North American English speakers can "have fun" doing almost anything—from doing nothing to working hard on their self-created hobbies. When you are eating at a restaurant, the waiter may come and ask, "*Are you **having fun** with your steak?*" and you may be uncertain what is implied. You hear people boasting how some event was "*a lot of fun,*" and again it is uncertain what it means. People can set up "fun" as the criterion for improvement by making "*having **more** fun*" one's personal goal-orientation. The ill-defined meaning of fun even becomes part of labeling of commercial enterprises (*see* Fig. 10–5) in countries where the connotations of the English language are very remote.

The meaning of "fun" itself is in principle indeterminate in two ways. First, within a person's personal culture, it is an abstracted overgeneralization from a wide variety of personal life experiences of the past, linked with the language notion of "fun." The contrast here is with the opposite ("non-fun"), which helps to specify boundary of the two for specific referents (e.g., "X is fun, Y is not fun"). Second, and more importantly, for interpersonal communication, the notion of "fun" is completely indeterminate in its meaning—it is a field of such feeling (rather than a point). For the reason of its overgeneralized vagueness, it is easily usable for creating a state of illusory intersubjectivity. Whatever my

FIGURE 10.5 The display of *fun* as a shop name in Madrid Barajas Airport.

personal–cultural background for making any statement, it is not revealed in the statement itself, which remains a widely open sign-"blurb." This makes it usable as an indiscriminate meaning displayed in public (Fig. 10–5)—the mundane experience of shopping (that could be framed by other meanings, such as "boredom," "work for beauty," or "seduction"). In reality, the fashion shop owners expect their clients to enter to shop and choose between different fashion brands, and as anybody knows, such choices are very difficult to make. But the notion of fun is expected to color that mundane decision making between products. Promoter signs provide a meaningful orientation for future anticipated experiences. The actual experiences will be preflavored, which is done through *promoter signs*.

Human meaning-making is future-oriented in its temporal extension— inevitably so, because our lives proceed through irreversibility of time. This extension comes through setting up specific signs of various abstractness that begin to function as guiders of the range of possible constructions of the future. These signs—or parts of signs—operate as **promoter signs** (in analogy with the sequences in human genetic organization that promote the expression of other parts of the gene). The implementation of the three ethics (Jensen, 2011) in everyday life social practices is pre-oriented by such signs of generalized (and hypergeneralized; Valsiner, 2005, 2007b) kind. The desire to wear festive clothing on Sundays, which may seem a deeply personal wish, is prepared by the cultural–developmental template.

Every semiotic mediator can be functioning as a promoter sign—guiding the possible range of variability of meaning construction in the future. Figure 10–6

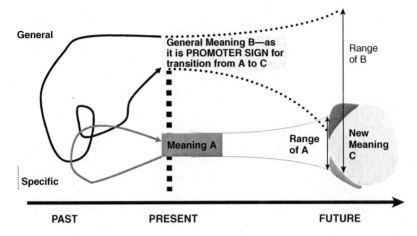

FIGURE 10.6 The promoter function of signs at different levels of generalized abstraction.

is an extended version of the notion of enablement by signs (Valsiner, 2003 p. 7.7; Fig. 3B). Each meaning (i.e., sign) that is in use during the infinitely small time "window" we conveniently call "the present" is a semiotic mediating device that extends from the past to the possible, anticipated (but not knowable) future. The promoter role of these signs is a feed-forward function: they set up the range of possible meaning boundaries for the unforeseeable— yet anticipated—future experiences with the world. **The person is constantly creating meaning ahead of the time** for occasions when it might be needed— orienting oneself toward one or another side of the anticipated experience and thus preparing oneself for it. Every new experience of the future proceeds through the prism of constructive meaning-making through a semiotic hierarchy of various kinds of signs (Valsiner, 2005), ranging from hypergeneralized fields (such as all-encompassing feelings or values, or promises of *fun* in doing ordinary everyday tasks) to verbally accessible mediators (that can be visible in self-narratives), and finally in the "snippet reactions" to everyday local triggers in a context.

Promoter signs organize contexts within which meaning-making occurs. In that function, they set the meaning orientation for most everyday life contexts, making the presence of culture so ordinary that it is invisible (*see* Goodnow, 2011; Jensen, 2011). The signs in the present do not determine how, in precise terms, the upcoming experience will be experienced. Instead, they are promoters of the **ranges** of possible future meaning making, rather than specific meanings. The range includes each and every point within the constraints that specify the boundary of the meaning field. Hence, each and every possible specific meaning is included in the range that is afforded by the promoter signs. As an example, consider the expectations of a young couple—and their kin groups—who are preparing for a major life-course ritual: a wedding. All preparations by all participants are guided by the hypergeneralized promoter sign (of field-like nature; Valsiner, 2005); most naturally, that sequence of events is a happy occasion for everybody[7]. Each particular action in preparation—finding financial resources for all the one-time-use paraphernalia of the ritual—would be flavored with the feeling of "*of course* it is *such a happy* event." The fatigue of the bride and groom in succumbing to all normative features of the preparations and of the ceremony itself—or even the fear of some parts of these normative events[8]—would not be allowed to dominate the occasion as a social event. Of course individuals involved in the event will create their own personal senses out of it—which may involve boredom of the long procedures, jealousies of the kind of wedding the bride and groom get, insufficiency of the amount of alcohol available, and many other interpretations of the event that still goes down as marked by "happy memories" for all participants. The photographs and films taken of the wedding will remain, even after the couple is not so happily divorced a few years later.

Different semiotic mediators operate in parallel and at different levels of abstractive generalization. The "high-time" nature of a wedding can be modulated by other semiotic mediators—creating a complex of an ambivalent kind that still may be socially presented along the lines of a dominant promoter sign. Concurrent meanings in the present are setting the stage for the negotiation of the boundaries of meanings in the future (*see* Fig. 10–6, the context of new meaning C out of the relation of ranges of A and B). The meaning of any experience is a complex of many simultaneously functioning affective oppositions (*see* Fig. 10–3 above)—it is a field of tensions from which new meanings emerge.

General Conclusion: Universality of Semiotic Mediation and the Nature of Context

The semiotic cultural look at meaning construction is an example of a universal abstract theory that is expected to fit the psychological processes of any person within any society (and any historical period). In the context of this volume, the semiotic perspective represents a solution to the problem of tension between "one-size-fits-all " and "one-for-every-society" perspectives in cultural psychology in the form of "one-GENERAL-theory-GENERATES-all"—all versions of inevitably unique particular psychological phenomena.

The present theoretical model specifies the ways in which the human being can face future challenges at the present, but which particular forms the sign construction takes, how deep (or shallow) its hierarchical structure, and how temporary or quasi-permanent it might be are issues not specified by this version of cultural–psychological theory. It is rooted in Vygotsky's focus on dialectical nature of human development and elaborated in life-course psychology by the TEM. The making of individual purposes is a process of anticipating the future relationships with the changing context. Novelty is the ever-present (transitory) link between what these future relations are and how they relate with the already known. Human development is being made on the borderline of the past and the future—creating the notion of the present as if it were a solid state of being, rather than an ephemeral state of eternal becoming. Culture—by way of processes of semiotic mediation—makes that possible.

Notes

1. The minimal system—here a **closed** system—is {a-R-b}, where a and b are parts of the system, and R = relationship. R can be either formal (e.g., correlational—most widely used in psychology) or functional, indicating the ways in which the parts relate with one another (e.g., terms like *feed into*, *dominate over*, *share,* etc., are examples of functional relations).

2. An open system is given by [{aRb}E c], where c is the environment and E exchange relation of the system {aRb} with that environment. The focus of investigation is on how the two relations—intrasystemic and of the system with the environment—are coordinated. **Forms of coordination** become the central concept in such analyses, rather than attribution of causality to one or another agentive entity (a,b,c) viewed without their systemic relations.

3. See, for example, Phinney and Baldelomar (2011), who point out that much of work on identity formation in psychology has been done without considering the context as immediate interlocutor of the self.

4. It is important to note that the intricate link with the dialectical dynamicity of the units—which is present in the Russian original—is lost in English translation, which briefly stated the main point: "Psychology, which aims at a study of complex holistic systems, must replace the method of analysis into elements with the method of analysis into units" (Vygotsky, 1986, p. 5). Yet it remains unclear in the English translation what kinds of units are to be constructed, whereas in the Russian original it is made evident.

5. Of course, the water example is a good rhetoric linking point of the Gestalt (parts<>whole) discourse in the history of psychology with that of contemporary cultural psychology: by semiotic transformation of meaning the same liquid becomes either "pure" or "contaminated," acquires magic properties ("holy") and becomes accepted as a commercial commodity ("bottled water" sold for profit of some, and "healthy living" of others; Wilk, 2006). The liquidity of meaning matches—or surpasses—that of the liquid!

6. The first professorship in psychology was that established in *Völkerpsychologie* at University of Bern in 1860, antedating Wilhelm Wundt's Leipzig laboratory by 19 years.

7. This can even be encoded in language—the German term for wedding, Hochzeit, translates literally as "high time."

8. Consider the history of "virginity testing" of the bride on the wedding night in many societies—public display of blood-marked bedclothes after the first night.

References

Baldwin, J. M. (1930). James Mark Baldwin. In C. Murchison (Ed.), *A history of psychology in autobiography.* Vol. 1 (pp. 1–30). New York: Russell & Russell.

Bertalanffy, L. von (1950). The theory of open systems in physics and biology. *Science, 111,* 23–29.

Boesch, E. E. (1991). *Symbolic action theory and cultural psychology*. New York: Springer.

Boesch, E. E. (2005). *Von Kunst bis Terror*. Göttingen: Vandenhoeck & Ruprecht.

Boesch, E. E. (2008). On subjective culture: In response to Carlos Cornejo. *Culture & Psychology, 14*(4), 499–512.

Cairns, R. B. (1986). Phenomena lost. In J. Valsiner (Ed.), *The role of the individual subject in scientific psychology*. New York: Plenum.

Cairns, R. B., Elder, G., and Costello, E. J. (Eds.) (1996). *Developmental science*. New York: Cambridge University Press.

Camazine, S, Deneubourg, J.-L., Franks, N. R., Sneyd, J., Theraulaz, G., and Bonaneau, E. (2001). *Self-organization in biological systems*. Princeton, NJ: Princeton University Press.

Chaudhary, N. (2004). *Listening to culture: Constructing reality from everyday talk*. New Delhi: Sage.

Ehrenfels, C. (1890/1988a). Über Gestaltqualitäten (1890/1922). In C. von Ehrenfels, *Philosophische Schriften*. Vol 3. *Psychologie Ethik Erkenntnistheorie* (pp. 128–167). München: Philosophia Verlag

Ehrenfels, C. (1932/1988b). On Gestalt qualities (1932). In B. Smith (Ed.), *Foundations of Gestalt theory* (pp. 121–123). München: Philosophia Verlag.

Ehrenfels, C. (1937/1988c). Über Gestaltqualitäten (1937). In C. von Ehrenfels, *Philosophische Schriften*. Vol 3. *Psychologie Ethik Erkenntnistheorie* (pp.168–170). München: Philosophia Verlag.

Emmeche, C., Køppe, S., and Stjernfeldt, F. (2000). Levels, emergence, and three versions of downward causation. In P. Andersen, C. Emmeche, N. Finnemann and P V. Christiansen (Eds.), *Downward causation: Minds, bodies and matter* (pp. 13–34). Aarhus: Aarhus University Press.

Fischer K. W., & Bidell, T. R. (1998). Dynamic development of psychological structures in action and thought. In W. Damon & R. Lerner (Eds.), *Handbook of child psychology*. 5th edition. Vol. 1. *Theoretical models of human development* (pp. 467–562). New York: Wiley.

Goodnow, J. (2011). Merging cultural and psychological accounts of family contexts. In L. A. Jensen (Ed.), *Bridging Cultural and Developmental Psychology: New Syntheses in Theory, Research and Policy* (pp. 73–91). New York: Oxford University Press.

Gottlieb, G. (1997). *Synthesizing nature/nurture*. Mahwah, N.J.: Erlbaum.

Gottlieb, G. (2003). Probabilistic epigenesis of development. In J. Valsiner & K. J, Connolly (Eds.), *Handbook of developmental psychology* (pp. 3–17). London: Sage.

Jensen, L. A. (2011). The cultural-developmental theory of moral psychology: A new synthesis. In L. A. Jensen (Ed.), *Bridging Cultural and Developmental Psychology: New Syntheses in Theory, Research and Policy* (pp. 3–25). New York: Oxford University Press.

Lonner, W. J., and Hayes, S. A. (2007). *Discovering cultural psychology: A profile and selected readings of Ernest E. Boesch*. Charlotte, NC: Information Age Publishing.

Maruyama, M. (1963). The second cybernetics: Deviation amplifying mutual causal processes. *American Scientist, 51*, 164–179.

Maruyama, M. (1999). Heterogram analysis: where the assumption of normal distribution is illogical. *Human Systems Management, 18*, 53–60.

Michell, J. (1999). *Measurement in psychology*. Cambridge: Cambridge University Press.

Michell, J. (2004). The place of qualitative research in psychology. *Qualitative Research in Psychology, 1*, 307–319. [www.QualReserchPsych.com]. last accessed 1-6-10

Molenaar, P. C. M. (2004). A manifesto on psychology as idiographic science: Bringing the person back into scientific psychology, this time forever. *Measurement: Interdisciplinary research and perspectives, 2*, 201–218.

Molenaar, P. C. M. (2007). Psychological methodology will change profoundly due to the necessity to focus on intra-individual variation. *IPBS: Integrative Psychological & Behavioral Science, 41*(1), 35–40.

Oliveira, Z. M. R., & Valsiner, J. (1997). Play and imagination: the psychological construction of novelty. In A. Fogel, M. C. D. P. Lyra, & J. Valsiner (Eds.), *Dynamics and indeterminism in developmental and social processes* (pp. 119–133). Mahwah, NJ: Lawrence Erlbaum Associates.

Phinney, J. S., and Baldelomar, O. A. (2011). Identity development in multiple cultural contexts. In L. Arnett Jensen (Ed.), *Bridging Cultural and Developmental Psychology: New Syntheses in Theory, Research and Policy* (pp. 161–186). New York: Oxford University Press.

Pizarroso, N., and Valsiner, J. (2009). Why developmental psychology is not developmental: Moving towards abductive methodology. Paper presented at SRCD, April, 3.

Porter, T. (1995). The political philosophy of quantification. In T. Porter, *Trust in numbers: The pursuit of objectivity in science and public life* (pp. 73–86) Princeton, NJ: Princeton University Press.

Ravenhill, P. L. (1996). *Dreams and reverie images of otherworld mates among the Baoule, West Africa.* Washington, DC: Smithsonian Institution Press.

Rosa, A., & Valsiner, J. (2007). Socio-cultural psychology on the move: semiotic methodology in the making. In J. Valsiner & A. Rosa (Eds.), *The Cambridge Handbook of Sociocultural Psychology* (pp. 692–707). New York: Cambridge University Press.

Rosenbaum, P. J., and Valsiner, J. (in press). The Un-Making of a Method: From Rating Scales to the Study of Psychological Processes. *Theory & Psychology.*

Rudolph, L. (2006a). The Fullness of Time. *Culture and Psychology, 12*(2), 157–186.

Rudolph, L. (2006b). Mathematics, Models and Metaphors. *Culture and Psychology, 12*(2), 245–265.

Rudolph, L. (2006c). Spaces of Ambivalence: Qualitative Mathematics in the Modeling of Complex Fluid Phenomena. *Estudios de Psicología, 27*(1), 67–83.

Sato, T. (Ed.). (2009). *TEM: Trajectory Equifinality Model.* Tokyo: Shinsei [in Japanese].

Sato, T., Yasuda, Y., Kido, A., Arakawa, A., Mizoguchi, H., & Valsiner, J. (2007). Sampling reconsidered: Idiographic science and the analyses of personal life trajectories. In J. Valsiner and A. Rosa (Eds.), *Cambridge Handbook of Socio-Cultural Psychology* (pp. 82–106). New York: Cambridge University Press.

Shweder, R. A., and Sullivan, M. A. (1990). The semiotic subject of cultural psychology. In L. Pervin, (Ed.), *Handbook of personality* (pp. 399–416). New York: Guilford Press.

Smith, B. (1999). Truth and the visual field. In J. Petitot, F. J. Varela, B. Pachoud and J.-M. Roy (Eds.), *Naturalizing phenomenology: Issues in contemporary phenomenology and cognitive science* (pp. 317–329). Stanford, CA: Stanford University Press.

Valsiner, J. (1986). Between groups and individuals: Psychologists' and laypersons' interpretations of correlational findings. In J. Valsiner (Ed.), *The individual subject and scientific psychology* (pp. 113–152). New York: Plenum.

Valsiner, J. (1987). *Culture and the development of children's action.* Chichester, UK: Wiley.

Valsiner, J. (1994). Bidirectional cultural transmission and constructive sociogenesis. In W. de Graaf & R. Maier (Eds.), *Sociogenesis reexamined* (pp. 47–70). New York: Springer.

Valsiner, J. (1999). I create you to control me: A glimpse into basic processes of semiotic mediation. *Human Development, 42,* 26–30.

Valsiner, J. (2001a). The first six years: Culture's adventures in psychology. *Culture & Psychology, 7*(1), 5–48.

Valsiner, J. (2001b). Process structure of semiotic mediation in human development. *Human Development, 44,* 84–97.

Valsiner, J. (2002). Irreversibility of time and ontopotentiality of signs. *Estudios de Psicologia, 23*(1), 49–59.

Valsiner, J. (2003). Beyond social representations: A theory of enablement. *Papers on Social representations, 12,* 7.1–7.16 [http://www.psr.jku.at/].

Valsiner, J. (2005) Soziale und emotionale Entwicklungsaufgaben im kulturellen Kontext. In J. Asendorf (Ed.), *Enzyklpädie der Psychologie*. Vol. 3. *Soziale, emotionale und Persönlichkeitsentwicklung*. Göttingen: Hogrefe.

Valsiner, J. (2006). Ambivalence under scrutiny: returning to the future. *Estudios de Psicologia, 27*(1), 117–130.

Valsiner, J. (2007). Looking across cultural gender boundaries. *IPBS: Integrative Psychological & Behavioral Science, 41*(3–4), 219–224.

Valsiner, J. (2007b). *Culture in minds and societies*. New Delhi: Sage.

Valsiner, J. (2009). A persistent imitator. In J. Valsiner (Ed.), *James Mark Baldwin's Genetic Theory of Reality*. New Brunswick, NJ: Transaction.

Valsiner, J., & Van der Veer, R. (1993). The encoding of distance: The concept of the zone of proximal development and its interpretations. In R. R. Cocking & K. A. Renninger (Eds.), *The development and meaning of psychological distance* (pp. 35–62). Hillsdale, NJ: Lawrence Erlbaum Associates.

Valsiner, J., & Connolly, K. J. (2003). The nature of development: The continuing dialogue of processes and outcomes. In J. Valsiner & K. J. Connolly (Eds.), *Handbook of developmental psychology* (pp. ix–xviii). London: Sage.

Valsiner, J., and Rudolph, L. (2008). Who shall survive? Psychology that replaces quantification with qualitative mathematics. Paper presented at the 29th International Congress of Psychology, Berlin, July, 21.

van Geert, P. (2003). Dynamic systems approaches and modeling of developmental processes. In J. Valsiner & K. J. Connolly (Eds.), *Handbook of developmental psychology* (pp. 640–672). London: Sage.

van der Veer, R. & Valsiner, J. (1991). *Understanding Vygotsky: A quest for synthesis*. Oxford: Basil Blackwell.

Vygotsky, L. S. (1931/1983). Istoria razvitia vyshhikh psikhicheskikh funktsii. In L. S. Vygotsky, *Sobranie sochinenii*. Vol. 3. *Problemy razvitia psikhiki* (pp. 6–328). Moscow: Pedagogika.

Vygotsky, L. S. (1933/1966). Igra i ee rol' v psikhicheskom razvitii rebenka. *Voprosy Psikhologii, 12*(No. 6): 62–76.

Vogel, S. M. (1997). *African art in Western eyes*. New Haven, CT: Yale University Press.

Vygotsky, L. (1986). *Thought and language*. 2nd ed. Cambridge, MA: MIT Press.

Vygotsky, L. S. (1999). *Myshlenie i rech*. 5th edition. Moscow: Labirint.

Wilk, R. (2006). Bottled water: the pure commodity in the age of branding. *Journal of Consumer Culture, 6*(3), 303–325.

Wittgenstein, L. (1958). *Philosophical investigations*. Oxford: Blackwell.

Zittoun, T. (2006). *Transitions*. Greenwich, CT: Information Age Publishers.

Zittoun, T., Duveen G., Gillespie, A., Ivinson, G., and Psaltis, C. (2003). The use of symbolic resources in developmental transitions. *Culture & Psychology, 9*(4), 415–448.

PART IV

DEVELOPMENTAL PHASES
AND CULTURE

CHAPTER 11

The Culturalization of Developmental Trajectories

A Perspective on African Childhoods and Adolescences

A. BAME NSAMENANG

We cannot afford to ignore the extant body of knowledge on child and youth development gained through more than a century of scientific research. But we must be keen on what the ethnocentrism of scientific psychology, a Euro-Western article of export whose theories and methods are not unalterable inductions from facts, portends for Africa. We must critique the current state of the science from concerned awareness that the "most creative theories are often imaginative visions imposed upon facts; the source of imagination is also strongly cultural" (Gould, 1981, p. 22). Science, like culture, influences what scientists see and how they see it and, more critically, what scientists report, ignore, or fail to notice, as when serendipitous research findings are not reported. We must also question and endeavor to "correct" a state of the field wherein Euro-Western developmental indicators are being "forced"—often inappropriately—on the rest of humanity.

Imagine that "at least 86 percent of all children and adolescents" live in the non-European, non-White Majority World (Gielen & Chumachenko, 2004, p. 84), but the norms to judge their appropriate development originate in the Euro-West. Such cultural imperialism is usurpatory in two ways. On one hand, Africa's rich cultural heritage is denigrated and considered anti-progressive, and on the other hand the right to produce scientific knowledge of global importance is denied to residents of Africa. If scientific knowledge about phases of life is dominated by one culture, and it does not matter which culture (Ardila, 1982), then it will always ignore or exclude crucial developmental phenomena and processes in other cultures, especially the African.

This chapter presents phases of an Africentric developmental trajectory and the social ecology of development and the principles and processes that frame child and adolescent development so that we might indeed learn something about part of the world's understudied majority in a global age when "all cultures can contribute scientific knowledge of universal value" (UNESCO, 1999, p. 1). We need to endeavor to know something about child and youth development in Africa before we can fine-tune the type of universalistic policies and programs we see applied today to its realities.

I undertook this task aware of the sparseness and unsystematic nature of published research on African childhoods and adolescences. I have pieced the chapter together with literature from different fields and diverse sources as well as drawn upon my own work and insider knowledge. I have framed the discourse within the purview of the culturally structured daily lives of Africa's timeless family traditions to highlight the importance of settings in supplying the markers of biobehavioral development. This contribution is not only for Africa but for the larger community of developmental researchers. I hope that my discursive style would not only instigate a fresh look at developmental science in Africa but would also yield new knowledge for apt social policies (*see* Goodnow, 2011) to address the unspoken wish of Africa's young generations to "please know us before you try to help us."

Africa is a single geographical entity but international interest groups and global structural systems fracture it into an Islamic North Africa associated with the Arab world and a low-status sub-Saharan Africa, a split that accentuates the plurality of African childhoods and adolescences. Clearly, African cultures are not homogeneous, but there are sufficient commonalities in its cultural tools and deep psychosocial structures to enable drawing common features of childhoods and adolescences from the African cultural universe. So, this chapter represents broad strokes of childhoods and adolescences in Africa's 53 countries that differ in size, vegetation, population, social and economic development, as well as cultural, linguistic, and ethnic composition. I must hasten to add that the African commonalities I infer here represent only the "common quality" (Maquet, 1972) perceivable as one traverses Africa's "bewildering diversity and extraordinary dynamism" (Olaniyan, 1982, p. 1).

In the chapter, I adopt a novel conceptualization that does not dichotomize cultural and developmental psychology and that acknowledges the developmental impact of cultural settings. The model does not perpetuate the theoretic error of separating the developing person from the environment (Nsamenang, 1992a). This conceptual outlook instead fuses biology and culture into developmental outcomes because the individual is "never concretely encountered independent of the situation through which he [or she] acts, nor is the environment ever encountered independent of the encountering individual" (Ittelson, 1973, p. 19).

The chapter has four sections. First, I provide an historical synopsis of developmentally focused research conducted in Africa. The second section sketches an Africentric developmental trajectory discerned from research with the Nso of Cameroon, with corroborative evidence from across the continent. I describe an African life-course that is cyclical from birth to the afterlife, and I give special attention to the life phases of childhood and adolescence. The third section focuses on the social ecology of development in African cultural worlds, highlighting how children and adolescents develop and are "useful" to family and themselves within dense familial settings and peer cultures. In the fourth section, I discuss general implications of the research for policy in the African context. This discussion is informed by the historical synopsis provided at the outset.

Historical Synopsis of Developmental Research in Africa

Considerable psychological research has been carried out in Africa, much of it itinerant cross-cultural research by expatriate researchers. Except for South Africa where systematic psychological research and developmental science is emerging, programmatic research is notable across Africa by its scarcity. In my view, the history of developmental research in Africa can be divided into four periods

First, elements of psychology arrived in Africa with the colonial services of governance, evangelism, education, health, security services, and so forth. Having rejected or reviled Africa's knowledge systems, lifestyles, and forms of intelligence, the European and American voyagers published the earliest racist literature purportedly representing the psychology of Africans. Captain Richard Burton, the 19th-century British explorer, for example, wrote of the failure of Africans to develop from primitive to civilized, whereas Sir Samuel Baker described the African mind to be as "stagnant as the morass which forms its puny world" (Davison, 1969, p. 24). Thus, Ellis (1978) clarifies how European voyagers, merchants, missionaries, and colonial agents of the pre- and post-colonial periods referred to the irrationality and gullibility of Africans.

Early anthropological research sought to understand stagnated development in the Dark Continent (Forde, 1963) or to "civilize" the purportedly savage African mind (Goody, 1977). A developmental topic that attracted early research curiosity was the precocity of physical development of the African child compared to that of the Western child. Wober (1975) reviewed this research and attributed the accelerated physical development of African children to excessive contact and physical handling. He also noted that African children began to lag behind the European American children, as the African children were weaned abruptly with the birth of the next sibling.

Today's developmental science was preceded by racist views and is evolving on scientific approaches dominated by Anglo-American perspectives. African data were presented as failing to conform to developmentally appropriate

European and American norms, rather than being reported as developmental data in their own right. Even today, Africa's developmental indices are explored and established in comparison to those of European Americans. Thus, reports of the substantive but disparate cross-cultural research done in Africa have tacitly rejected and still largely disdain patterns of African child and youth development but with surprise that Africans "refused" to accept and act on such patronizing reports.

The second research phase was marked by a gradual shift from interest in specific abilities and personality profiling in comparison with Western markers to a focus on the developmental impact of cultural settings. In the *Six Cultures Study of Childrearing,* B.B. Whiting (1963) moved the field of psychological anthropology toward a more systematic, measurement-oriented approach to human abilities and psychological characteristics. In the domain of social development, LeVine (1973) in his early work hinted that Gusii parents in Kenya were not overtly affectionate with their infants and toddlers. Ainsworth (1967), on the basis of a "strange situation" where Bagandan (Ugandan) infants reacted to a White woman whom they saw in their community for the first time, described lack of face-to-face interactions between Bagandan mothers and their infants. Similarly, Goldschmidt (1975) purported a pattern of "idle hands and absent eyes" in mothers' interactions with infants among the Sebei of Kenya and Uganda. On the other hand, the Kilbrides' (1975) studies among the Baganda corroborated findings by Super and Harkness (1974) that East African parents influenced the social behavior of their infants through smiling and talking to the infants. Two African psychologists, Ohuche and Otaala (1981), provided a macro-level description of the contexts of African children. Cognizant of the divergences in perspectives to cultural research, Super and Harkness (1986), with data from East Africa and New England in the United States, offered the developmental niche (a sociological–anthropological framework) and three-componential theoretical model with which to understand children and their psychosocial differentiation in their various cultural contexts. Munroe et al. (1981) published the first comprehensive handbook on cross-cultural human development, which integrated anthropological and psychological research, including insightful glimpses from data bases obtained from across Africa.

The third period was devoted to measuring abilities in African children, with keen interest in cognitive development. Cole et al. (1971) expanded and enriched the field by comparing performance on cognitive tests between Liberian and American respondents and concluded that performance outcomes on cognitive tasks was more dependent on situational factors than on underlying differences in cognitive abilities. The 1970s and 1980s were indeed a watershed period in cross-cultural research on measuring human abilities and development of cognitive and social competencies. Whiting and Whiting (1975) provided the roadmap for the role of culture on child development in the *Children of Six Cultures*, and Berry (1976) sketched the ecology of cognitive styles and demonstrated the impact of acculturation on cognitive development with respect to figure-ground perceptual abilities with a Central Africa subsample.

Munroe and Munroe (1975) published the first textbook on cross-cultural developmental research, with some data from childrearing research in East Africa. Mundy-Castle (1974) introduced the distinction between academic or technological intelligence and social intelligence. From their research on Piaget's theory, Dasen et al. (1978) revealed the "birth" of intelligence in the Baoule of Cote d'Ivoire. Erny (1787) offered an educational perspective on the developmental landscape of the African child. Serpell (1984) critiqued cognitive development research and psychological testing in Africa and disclosed that the studies were designed to determine how well African children performed the "tricks" of Western schooling rather than to understand the abilities of African children within the conditions under which they were actualized. The differences observed in test scores between African children and Western comparative samples were interpreted as "developmental deficits" and not perhaps the result of cultural and other differences.

In the fourth phase, indigenization efforts away from cross-cultural comparisons toward efforts to understand Africans in their own terms became increasingly discernible from the early 1990s. African and some Africanist scholars began to develop a psychology that makes sense in the African cultural circumstances and by which to gain understanding of the African mindset and intersubjectivity. Earlier, Serpell (1977) initiated research into African forms of intelligent behavior by charting the perceptions of intelligence in rural Zambia. Kathuria and Serpell (1999) later developed a language-reduced test, the *Panga Muntu Test* (Make-A-Person Test), suitable for use by children in rural Africa. The test presents children with wet clay and the children are asked to "make" a person with the clay. The children's figures are then quantitatively scored for accurate representation of human physical characteristics. Sternberg and colleagues (2001) studied the relationship between academic and practical intelligence by developing a Test for Tacit Knowledge for Natural Herbs with Luo children of a rural community in Kenya. The test sampled from common illnesses in the Luo community and standard herbal treatments for those illnesses in that community. Given the significance of schooling and the adoption of European languages for school instruction in much of Africa (Serpell, 1993); research has also focused on the interfaces of African mother tongues and the learning of European languages (e.g., Fai, 1996; Veii & Everatt, 2005).

Whereas Nsamenang (1992a, 2004) emphasized a contextualist approach and sketched an indigenous African developmental trajectory, Tape (1993) explored indigenous cognitive abilities in Ivorian adolescents. Serpell (1994, p. 18) judged Nsamenang's research as resonating with the developmental ideas and childrearing practices of parents across many African communities, and Dasen (1993, p. 156) recognized Tape's research as "a good beginning of the development of a truly African psychology." Ngaujah (2003, p. 9) underscored "the affective nature" of Nsamenang's theory of indigenous African education and wished Missionaries and others could draw from it "a healthy respect for the people of Africa."

Recently, LeVine (2004) specified some lessons from his African research: Sub-Saharan African mothers have "a practical understanding of infant care and development contrasting sharply with expert knowledge in the child development field" (p. 149). "Gusii mothers raised their infants and toddlers according to a different set of standards [. . .] the Gusii infant study, permits us to see that alternative patterns of care based on different moral and practical considerations can constitute normal development that had not been imagined in developmental theories" (LeVine, 2004, p 159–163). Arnett (2007) edited an *International Encyclopedia of Adolescence* that published chapters on 20 African countries.

Developmental science in Africa has moved beyond the early overtly racist approaches, as well as approaches that often emphasized the deficits in African children's abilities and their caregivers' childrearing approaches. By now, African research aims to understand African children and caregivers on their own terms. Also, African scholars are increasingly contributing to the scientific enterprise. Yet a significant gap remains in knowledge about the local eco-culture. In an effort to begin to fill this gap, I next outline how Africans conceptualize childbearing and childrearing.

The Social Ecology of African Childbearing and Childrearing

A holistic African theory of the universe is pronatalist and imputes a theocentric value on fertility and childbearing (Nsamenang et al, 2008). As Musoke (1975, p. 315) noted, African "elders formulate a pattern of behavior which they consider fulfills the wishes of their ancestors" to guarantee childbearing and childrearing. Accordingly, African cultures tacitly oblige men and women to become parents, hence the deeply ingrained desire for biological children "in the hearts of both men and women," as "they regard procreation as their first and most sacred duty" (Nsamenang, 1992a, p. 130).

African social thought and religious norms advocate parenthood as an ultimate path to personal fulfillment. The acceptable reproductive institution is marriage, which is best contracted between a mature man and woman (Nsamenang, 2002). Accordingly, "normative" African adulthood is best visualized as being "married with children" (Nsamenang, 1992a; Arnett, 2011). The culturally acceptable way to procreate and have socially integrated children in much of Africa is through a family constituted through marriage although the number of children gotten out of wedlock is steadily increasing in every community. In Kenya, as in most African countries, the family can be defined as all persons connected by blood, marriage, fostering or exchange of children between families, and shared cultural, economic, and psychosocial tools for adaptation (Bradley & Weisner, 1997). The African does not think of the family in its nuclear form but, rather, in its extended or joint form. The conjugal pair is the hub of the extended family, and they are connected to a dense kinship networks where all share in the care, socialization, and education of the young (Nsamenang, 2002). The African institution of marriage acknowledges the partnership between a man, as pater, and a woman, as mater, in ultimate reproductive fitness. Therefore, African men and women are expected to be *Better Together* (Riccio & Kristina, 1996) as reproductive and farming partners. In traditional Cameroon, for example, the family is the productive unit within which a farmer is not considered as an individual male or female but a marital couple and children in farming relationships. Farm work is organized to involve adults and children, such that a horizontal division of farming duties by sex is combined with a vertical distribution between adults and young people.

Furthermore, most African cultures separate childcare skills from the life period of parenthood and situate childcare training as a familial commitment for children and adolescents to learn (Nsamenang, 2008a) as part of a "shared management, caretaking and socially distributed support" of the family (Weisner, 1997, p. 23). In comparison, Euro-Western cultures concede childcare mainly to adults. During the pre-colonial era when African mothers left home to go to the farm or social events or the neighborhood, extended family members and older siblings—especially older female children—were readily available to care for infants and toddlers. In addition, indigenous Africa had its own systems of "public training" to transfer norms, knowledge, and skills to youth to ease their transition into adulthood, which I have identified later for some African ethnic polities under stages of social selfhood.

Wober (1975) referred to the positive attitudes and receptive social networks into which African children were born. Zimba (2002) recently confirmed this with a review of evidence for the southern Africa region that revealed an "indigenous network of support" reserved for newborns and their mothers. Similarly, in both West and East Africa, newborns are treasured and nurtured in a deep and comforting sense of tradition and community that receives and sustains newborns (Nsamenang 1992b). In the post colony, relative and sibling caregivers are no longer readily available although preteen and adolescent babysitters are still useful in more intricate childcare arrangements. "The Nigerian urban working mother," for example, "is able to play the dual roles of being a mother and an employee successfully due to the availability of childcare services such as homemaids, nannies, day care centres, nursery schools and kindergarten" (Ogbimi & Alao, 1998, p.48).

But today, too, the social ecology of most of Africa's children and adolescents is anything but comfortable. They face a terrible minefield of problems, including sexually transmitted diseases and AIDS, many preventable diseases, abject poverty, uncontrolled urbanization, family disruptions, and lack of social security from poor governance. Nevertheless, the majority of Africa's children and youth still successfully navigate their developmental adversities into outstanding achievements and productive adulthood. The African family that is still the best security net for children and Africa's peer cultures are important, and their developmental significance requires further study. For example, although the extended African family initiates children's cultural learning and introduces them into participative community life and life-long self -learning and responsibility, most youngsters spend waking lot of time in peer cultures that are useful and influential developmental spaces but that have not received the research and policy attention commensurate to their developmental impact.

An Africentric Developmental Trajectory

Ontogenesis refers to the development of an individual organism over its life span. An African theory of the universe posits social ontogenesis in three phases of selfhood—namely, social selfhood or the experiential self and two metaphysical phases of spiritual selfhood and ancestral selfhood. The notion of the life cycle is implicit in developmental science, but an African developmental theory explicitly espouses a circular path to being human (Nsamenang, 1992a, 2005c; Ramokgopa, 2001). Social ontogeny draws on African life journeys (Serpell, 1993) to acknowledge the cultural transformation of the child into a viable "cultural agent" of a particular community, systematically through periods of an unbroken circle of existence in the sense of the indestructibility of energy—the human life force. As children develop through these life stages, they gradually and are "deliberately" made to enter into and assume particular levels of personhood, personal identity, and "being" connected to the human community and the universe.

Traditional African families are aware that some genetic factors could subvert inclusive fitness. Hence, they take premarital precautions to exclude "shameful diseases" such as mental illness and convulsive seizures in prospective spouses. In addition, African cultural practices subject pregnant women and their spouses to behavioral taboos that guide sexual intercourse, specific food items, and emotional distress, among others, to optimize the health of the unborn child and mother (Zimba & Otaala, 1995).

The experiential self or social selfhood begins at birth and extends to biological death. Social selfhood refers to the living individual and various reasons across ethnic cultures; this phase more effectively begins from the ritual incorporation of the child into the human community through naming. Newborns are thought to have "special links with the spirit world." In the Nso community, "children are not thought to belong to this world until they have been incorporated into the community of the living through naming" rituals (Nsamenang, 1992a, p. 142). It is more difficult to accept the death of children and youth who are still at the early stages of social ontogeny; death is more easily accepted for old persons. Accordingly, the death of a child or adolescent is more painfully mourned by the Nso of Cameroon than that of an aged person. The first and last stages of social selfhood connect with the two non-existential components of personhood. The newborn takes on a social selfhood into an existing human community, whereas the dying person takes on an ancestral selfhood into the spirit world. Ancestral selfhood follows biological death and extends to the ritual initiation of the dead into spiritual selfhood. Some ancestors lived good and virtuous lives and therefore are fondly remembered as the *loving dead* (Nsamenang, 2005a). As "spiritual presences" (Ellis, 1978), ancestors are important in African cosmologies because they are believed to "monitor" the behaviors and role fulfillment of the living and therefore act as inhibitory influences on impropriety and other vices. It is not naive to hypothesize that these indigenous behavioral checks tend to more forcefully promote prosocial attitudes and hospitable values and interpersonal harmony than does any revealed religion or legal and constitutional code, at least among the Nso of Cameroon. One source of the mystery of death revolves around the uncertainty about which community of the dead one would transit into in the afterlife—that of the loving dead or that of the dreaded evil dead.

Stages of Social Selfhood

An African theory labels the living person a *social selfhood*, the primary subject matter of developmental science. The theory identifies seven stages of social selfhood that add to the two metaphysical phases to give a total of nine distinct phases of the human life cycle (*see* Nsamenang, 1992a, 2005a). The developmental stages within an African theory that encompass the conventional stages of childhood and adolescence include the neonatal period, social priming, social apprenticeship, social entrée, and social internment. The fully developed phases of life are adulthood and old age/death, including ancestral and spiritual selfhoods.

African child and adolescent development is ordained primarily by social and affective agendas. Nevertheless, African cultures implicitly acknowledge the role of biology but more actively invest on social and affective development. Accordingly, responsibility training and social competence are essential tasks that traverse all stages and begin from an early age. Within Africa's cultural worlds, responsibility is more valued than cognition, *per se*, in that a child or adolescent cannot be responsible without being cognitive. Africans cherish cognition not as an end in itself but as a means to social ends; it is subordinated to servicing human needs or enhancing children's social competencies. Some children and youth are cognitively alert and high academic achievers but not so responsible, which often worries their parents and relatives.

The stages of African social ontogeny are recognized, not on the criterion of chronological age but on predominantly biology-based social markers, such as the birth cry, smiling, falling off of the umbilical stump, teething, walking, generosity, social connectedness, marriage, and so forth. Stages are marked by distinctive developmental tasks, defined within the framework of the culture's integrative conception of children, family, and their welfare.

The first stage is the period of the newborn that is marked by celebration for the "gift" of life and the safety of his/her birth. This is accompanied by verbalizations about the kind of socialized adult the newborn should become. In some ethnic communities, such as the Nso of Cameroon, children are not named at birth but only after the umbilical stump falls off. Nso people believe that babies whose umbilical stumps have not detached belong more to the spirit than to the world of the living and could literally be "taken away" (i.e., die) at any moment. "Just as the ancestors are thought to have gone from the land of the living, though not far, the newborn are regarded as not fully and securely with the living and are thought to have special links with the spirit world" (Ellis, 1978, p. 42). In fact, the separation of the umbilical stump is a decisive developmental indicator among the Nso that marks the end of the period of the neonate. Accordingly, soon after the umbilical stump falls off, a naming ceremony, which is often symbolic today, confers a name on the child to integrate him or her into the community of the living. In general, Nso names situate a child in the family tree, but more remarkably, they carry autobiographical significance for the child's individuality.

The second ontogenetic period approximates the stage of infancy. It is prosocial in that the "quality" of such biological markers or reflexes as crying, sucking, babbling, grasping, smiling, sitting, and standing are indicators for normalcy. As precursors of social functioning, the absence of these biological pointers causes considerable concern, as when there is no birth cry or when a child does not babble.

The third stage is social apprenticeship (childhood) during which children are gradually and systematically inducted into the canonical ways of their family and culture. At various levels of social maturation, the child is expected, each according to sex and ability, to learn and to attempt to enact family or social roles. "The principal developmental task is [for the child] to recognize, cognize, and rehearse social roles" toward which s/he is being prepared (Nsamenang, 1992a, p. 146). The peer group plays a pivotal role in this task because older peers or sibs "engage in activities during interaction [in peer cultures] that are within the scope of actions that the younger child is capable of reproducing immediately or slightly after observation" (Zukow, 1989, p. 85).

The fourth stage, social entrée or puberty, is heralded by biological changes that become assessable in social functioning. Some societies practice initiation rituals, which mark the end of this stage, examples of which are the *poro* (for boys) and the *sande* (for girls) in Liberia (Gormuyor, 1992), the voodoo convents in Benin (*Hounkpè*, 2008), the *bogwera* (for boys) and the *bojale* (for girls) in Botswana (Shumba & Seeco, 2007), and the rites of passage in Cameroon (Tchombe, 2007) and Kenya (Harkness & Super, 1992). These developmental rituals transition children into the fifth stage, when a naive novice transitions into the status of a socialized neophyte. It is a period of internment for social induction and definitive socialization for graduated entry into the status and roles of adulthood, the most cherished ontogenetic stage.

African Developmental Principles and Processes During Childhood and Adolescence

An important way to understand childhood and adolescence as social constructs (Jenks, 1982) is to explore how such constructions mirror or instantiate cultural interpretations of the non-adult phases of life—that is, the extent to which cultures attribute incompetence and "completeness" or "incompleteness" to the nature of the child or teenager (Prout & James, 1990). The immaturity of children and adolescents is a biological fact, but the ways in which this immaturity is understood and made meaningful is a fact of culture (La Fontaine, 1986). African theories position children in their unfolding abilities and competencies, "not as a set of organisms to be molded into a pattern of behavior specified in advance as educational outcomes, but as newcomers to a community of practice, for whom the desirable outcome of a period of apprenticeship is that they would appropriate the system of meanings that informs the community's practices" (Serpell, 2008, p. 74). Children's personas and developmental experiences in families and communities shape and channel their innate biological characteristics into cultural paths (Shweder, 1995), thus the human neonate rapidly transforms into an "agent" of the socializing culture. In this way, many African children and adolescents are not conventionally "raised," but they "emerge" by themselves into adulthood as *participants in cultural communities*" (Rogoff, 2003, p. 3).

Foundational African developmental principles reflect botanical metaphors, such as *seed* and *plant* or *grain du monde* (universal seed) (Erny, 1968) and mix cropping (Nsamenang, 2004, 2008a). These metaphors connote a gradual unfolding of human potentials and qualities as well as the successive attainment of levels of personhood at various stations of development. The "unfolding" happens within the imperatives of an identifiable culture and its cultural tools and meaning systems. An inherent assumption with the garden metaphors that is a seminal principle of developmental science is self-generated or maturational learning and development, which improves with appropriate tending or cultivation in different sociocultural fields at various stages of development. An exemplar of such development is the story of Camara Laye's boyhood and emergence into adulthood in rural and urban Guinea and France, presented in *The African Child* (1977).

Developmental learning is learning that is vital to children's survival and development and that can be acquired during development in cultural circumstances without the usual institutions of the school. Education is a basic necessity because to survive, thrive, and relate to others and "nature," every human being must acquire vital knowledge of self, the environment, and the universe (Nsamenang, 2004). Developmental learning can be achieved with parents, other adults, and peers, even by self-directed children. Self-education and child-to-child learning are in dire need of exploration.

In African family traditions, children are trained from an early age to participate in self-care and family maintenance chores. Parental values prime and socialize the norms that foster children's self-emergence and participatory learning in the social and economic activities of the family and community. At each developmental milepost, the child faces a distinct task, conceived in terms of important transitions between patterns of social participation that focus on the culture's definition of children, family, and their welfare. Children are offered stage- and sex-appropriate opportunities to make sense of adult roles toward which they are primed. Education is designed in African family traditions to socialize responsible intelligence through children's active participation in acceptable and valued social and economic activities (Nsamenang, 2006). Depending on the children's perceived level of competence at any developmental stage, for example, they "assist" with such domestic chores as cleaning the house and compound, tending animals, and running errands to deliver important messages or bring articles as well as caretaking of younger sibs.

Africa's Pedagogies and Peer Cultures as Developmental Spaces

The centerpiece of African pedagogies is participative engagement and responsible maturation toward adulthood. Indigenous pedagogies permit toddlers and youngsters to learn in participatory processes in the home, community, religious service, peer cultures, and so forth through "work–play" activities, with little to no explicit didactic support (Pence & Nsamenang, 2008, p. 23). Tacit ethnotheories posit children's innate capacity to be agents of their own developmental learning in multi-age peer groups in which parental values and actions prime responsible intelligence by permitting older children to serve as peer mentors to younger charges (Nsamenang & Lamb, 1995). "Child work" is an essential African cultural mode of preparing the next generation, and it is understood by both the family and the young as necessary for the family and for the youngster's developmental learning (Nsamenang, 2008a). With Africa's traditions of "child work," children "do" tasks, even difficult ones, on their own.

In Cameroon, most of children's "work" is undertaken with peers and in child-to-child sociability and peer mentorship than with parents or other adults or teachers. This is more commonplace in rural settings and urban slums. Most mothers are only partially available to guide and supervise child babysitting and sibling caretaking. The peer culture also offers opportunities for children to play, work, and learn together, free from parental supervision and adult control. Accordingly, the freedom of the peer culture breeds creativity and challenges children to cultivate prosocial values and altruism, to defer to elders and more competent peers, to address and resolve conflicts, and to take perspective to notice needs and serve them (Nsamenang, 2002). Peer group relationships during adolescence can influence development in complex ways because they provide peer-controlled learning spaces, particularly as peers can be and are agents of their own socialization and education. For example, a multi-age peer setting can and does foster intergenerational transfer of knowledge and skills.

Adolescence ends with social internment, when an adolescent completes basic learning of the culture and its modus operandi. A normally developing person adjusts to the requirements of every milepost of development and begins to take on responsibility in the adult world. But the end of adolescence does not automatically confer adult status, as "adequate" adulthood is defined by marriage and parenthood. "By taking part in different tasks of social life, by observing his [or her] seniors, by listening to and later by joining [adult] discussions, the adolescent acquires a sense of solidarity and responsibility as he [or she] completes his [her] physical, intellectual and practical education" (Cameroon, 1981, p. 34) in the family, community, and activity settings of the peer culture at various stages of childhood and adolescence.

Individuation and Psychosocial Differentiation

Defining the self, or spelling out who one is, and relating to social others are essential developmental tasks for every "station of life." I perceive self-construal in two components: a personal perspective that implies an ongoing clarification of "who am I" as the one and only *individuum*, distinct from the non-self in general and the collective in particular, and a cultural view of what personhood in one's current developmental status is in own culture.

During development, the child increasingly defines and sharpens her or his self-concept; the child individuates and forms social relationships with others. By seeing human offspring in their *becoming* (Erny, 1968), implying the unfolding of biological potentialities and social competencies, Africans tacitly acknowledge that self-concept emerges and evolves with a maturing self-awareness that confers self-direction and deliberate search for or choice of the environments and experiences that increasingly hone self-identity and goal-directed behavior toward desired or imagined personal status, either of sovereign individuality or relational individuality. In actuality, autonomy develops better in relatedness (Kagitçibasi, 2009).

The African child or adolescent individuates or evolves a self-identity by being interconnected to others in dense social relationships across developmental phases. The metaphor for identity development is polycropping, not monoculture—that is, the emphasis on self-definition and identity formation is on the shared and social rather than the unique and individual aspects of personhood (Nsamenang, 2008b; *see also* Phinney & Baldelomar, 2011). African parents sensitize children from an early age to seek out others, to extract 'intelligences' and to define self, particularly in peer groups, by gaining "significance from and through their relationships with others" (Ellis, 1978, p. 63). Zimba (2002, p. 94) described one instance of self-definition with the Zulu of South Africa, as nurturing *umuntu umuntu ngabantu*, which literally translates into "a person is only a person with other people". This view downplays sovereign individuation, implying that the sense of self cannot be attained without reference to the 'community' of other humans. In a nutshell, "the process of developing a sense of self is a process of connecting individual personal identity to a changing social identity, depending on a child's ontogenetic group affiliations" (Pence & Nsamenang, 2008, p. 41). By fostering children's close identification with peer groups, traditional social values in many African cultures can be seen to partially align with Erikson's (1968) focus on social development. African developmental rites of naming, marriage, death, and so forth, typically extend and transition the identity of the individual through assimilating her or him into meaningful social roles and relationships (Pence & Nsamenang, 2008). The "life" of the peer group in some societies is life long.

The history of psychology in Africa reveals how Europe exported elements of that discipline in its "civilizing mission" of governance, evangelism, and services development into African colonies. The roots of scientific psychology in Africa are in anthropological research, which produced mainly racial images of African habits and practices. Psychology persists today with this extraverted outlook (Owusu-Bempah & Moffitt, 1995) in theories and methods that are Anglo-American; the focal research topics are more germane to Western realities and interests than to those of Africa's appalling condition. As such, psychology largely loses "sight of the soil out of which the existing [African] society has grown and the human values it has produced" (Kishani, 2001, p. 37). Wober (1975) perhaps read scientific psychology as an "export" commodity from European Enlightenment to predict that it would be different in the hands of Africans.

Africa has contributed significantly to developmental science, but the bulk of printed contributions has been made by non-Africans and obviously contains their cultural imprints. The accentuating effort by Africans to develop psychology that is meaningful and useful for Africa's multiple needs is consistent with Wober's (1975) prediction. It can be interpreted as a proactive post-colonial search for own-knowledge empowerment through outgrowing *received* psychology and into a generative process of "extracting" relevant knowledge and guiding principles from Africa's worldviews and timeless traditions, albeit in confrontation of global schisms and macro-level challenges. Callaghan's (1998, p. 32) wise counsel during crisis of social change is that "if we could continue to listen to, and learn from, the African worldview, seeing a holistic and integrated way of looking at the family and the universe, we might see things in a new way." In the next section, I raise the issue of the crucial link between research and policy in Africa.

Policy Research

The enshrinement in the U.N. *Convention on the Rights of the Child* (UNCRC), itself sometimes critiqued as an overly Euro-Western document (e.g., Reid, 2006), nevertheless supports the right to a cultural identity for every child and prescribes sensitivity to the original culture of the group into which a person was born (United Nations, 1989, Article 7.1). "In a globalized world, local culture must be the anchor of identity" (Nsamenang, 2008b, p. 13), because no people entirely dislodged from their cultural roots have ever made progress with collective development. Some major areas of social policy research include family law; equity in marriage, parenthood, and household duties; education of boys and girls; reproductive health for children and adolescents; and social services, particularly for children and adolescents with disabilities and in adversity. Shared parenting is a child's right, and researchers and policy planners need to do more to understand and take into account what states and communities should do to give every child that right, as well as ensure implementation of Article 18 of the Convention that promotes parenting as a partnership between fathers and mothers. An important issue is the extent to which various forces have modified "traditional" family structures and the roles of parents, children and state parties to precipitate a crisis of social change (Weisner et al., 1997). Given that the family is the main productive and caregiving unit, the main thrust of efforts to improve the circumstances of Africa's children and youth, should focus on the home, where the "everyday love, support and reassurance that children [and youth] receive from families and communities" exert, in principle, high-impact effects on their developmental outcomes (Richter et al., 2006, p. 9).

A rights-based approach, however, requires overcoming some challenges. First, researchers should understand the core provisions of the UNCRC and Commission on Women's Rights and what they signify for their research. Second, policy and services ought to deal effectively with the tensions and apprehensions caused by schisms from various sources, such as scientific positioning, women in the work force, equity debates, and human capital flight that literally take "men away from their families, increasing father absence". In South Africa, for example, the pattern of father presence in the lives of children has changed since the end of apartheid (Townsend, Madhavan, & Garey, 2005). Third, most African countries overly rely on foreign expertise to translate international instruments and policy guidelines into local situations. The "received" instruments and guidelines, like theories and methods, become virtual "prescriptions," as the policies and procedures that follow on from these were rarely suitably customized to Africa's realities.

African scholars are constrained to address the universalizing Anglo-American images of childhood and adolescence instead of speaking about Africa's children and youth in their home tufts. They do so using Euro-Western theories, logic systems, and epistemologies. For example, researchers have thus far sought to capture and compare the inner motives of Africans with individualism-draped instruments that, *a priori,* are insensitive to the relational mindsets and sociogenic life paths of African children and adolescents. In this regard, Pence and Nsamenang (2008) raised issue with practices of disseminating data-gathering tools that privilege Anglo-American indicators that pathologize African patterns of development. Fourth, relational individualism or collectivism does not erase a sense of a distinct and separate *individuum*. It is scientific myopia not to notice modes of cognition and expression of individuality in collectivistic societies. The crux of the matter about research and intervention for children's and adolescents' development pivots on whether the self is situated in connectedness to others or in the autonomy of purportedly self-serving ends.

Conclusion

Africa yearns for understanding of its appalling state and "acceptance" of its child and youth cultures as a precondition for policy and interventions. Interactive contextualism presses for research and policy that "represent the particular context that determines why the project is there, what it is doing and how it is doing it" (Smale, 1998). The need is to be aware that the universal human need to thrive and become an integrated member of own society is socialized and canalized in the world's diverse cultures into different endpoints of development (Nsamenang, 2009).

All this invites contextualist thinking and rights-based approaches as reflected in the UNCRC, which has become "a basic document for the professionals involved in the field of the social protection of children" (Nsamenang, 2008a, p. 212). Although international efforts are determining how best to actualize the participation of young citizens as provided for in the UNCRC, simultaneous international advocacy persists in condemning the centuries-old productive agency of Africa's children and youth, "which disables almost 70 percent of the continent's population, instead of working to enhance and learn from it" (Nsamenang, 2008a, p. 211).

An Africentric developmental research should not ignore the supportive role of the extended family and ubiquitous African peer cultures, with their child-to-child templates as significant developmental spaces. A research focus on Africa's circular developmental trajectory and on African cultures would extend and enrich the frontiers of the discipline. Furthermore, Africa not only "provides opportunities for learning and development which simply do not exist in the West and therefore are not considered by the predominant theories" (Curran, 1984, p. 2) but also offers the cultural braid from its hybridism as an unprecedented developmental context for extending theorization and "inventing" creative methodologies. Africa's cultural braid is a product of an intermingling of earlier Islamic-Arabic influences and later Western-Christian legacies superimposed on a deeply resilient Africanity. No existing theory fittingly explains this hybridism and no antecedent evolutionary template corresponds to its triple-strand braid (Nsamenang, 2005a). As such, existing theories and research methods are not exactly fitting to contemporary African realities.

Additional emic perspectives are needed to explore and understand Africa's children and adolescents in their own right, not as imprecise copies of those of the West. Africa's contributions will be not only for Africa. Two main reasons highlight the necessity for Africa's contributions. First, Africa is a significant part of the world; rights-based concerns oblige its contributions to developmental science. Second, a holistic and pronatalist African theory of the universe and the African eco-culture prime human ontogenesis in ways that have not been imagined in developmental science.

References

Ainsworth, M. D. S. (1967). *Infancy in Uganda*. Baltimore, MD: John Hopkins University Press.

Ardila, P. (1982). International psychology. *American Psychologist*, 37(3): 323–329.

Arnett, J. J. (2007). *International encyclopedia of adolescence*. New York: Routledge.

Arnett, J. J. (2011). Emerging adulthood(s): The cultural psychology of a new life stage. In L. A. Jensen (Ed.), *Bridging cultural and developmental psychology: New syntheses in theory, research and policy* (pp. 255–275). New York: Oxford University Press.

Berry, J. W. (1976). *Human ecology and cognitive style*. New York: John Wiley.

Bradley, C., & Weisner, S. W. (1997). Introduction: Crisis in the African family. In T. S. Weisner, C. Bradley, & C. P. Kilbride (Eds.), *African families and the crisis of social change* (pp. xix–xxxii). Westport, CT: Bergin & Garvey.

Callaghan, L. (1998). Building on an African worldview. *Early Childhood Matters,* 89: 30–33.

Cameroon. (1981). *Encyclopedie de la republique unie du Cameroun [Encyclopedia of the Federal Republic of Cameroon].* Douala, Cameroon: Eddy Ness.

Cole, M., Gay, J, Glick, I. A, & Sharp, D. W. (1971). *The cultural context of learning and thinking: An exploration in experimental anthropology.* New York: Basic Books.

Curran, H. V. (1984). Introduction. In H. V. Curran (Ed.), *Nigerian children: Developmental perspectives.* London: Routledge & Kegan Paul.

Dasen, P. R. (1993). Theoretical/Conceptual issues in developmental research in Africa. *Journal of Psychology in Africa,* 1: 151–156.

Dasen, P. R. (1984). The cross-cultural study of intelligence: Piaget and the Baoule. *International Journal of Psychology,* 19: 401–434.

Dasen, P. R., R. Inhelder, M. Lavallee, & J. Retschitzi (1978). *Naissance de l'intelligence chez l'enfant Baoule de Cote d'Ivoire [Birth of intelligence among Baoule children of Ivory Coast].* Berne: Hans Huber.

Davidson, B. (1969). *The African Genius: An Introduction to African Cultural and Social History.* Boston, MA: Little, Brown & Company.

Ellis, J. (1978). *West African families in Great Britain.* London: Routledge.

Erikson, E. (1968). *Childhood and society.* Harmmondsworth, U.K.: Penguin.

Erny, P. (1968). *L'enfant dans la pensee traditionnelle d'Afrique Noire [The child in traditional African social thought].* Paris: Le Livre africain.

Erny, P. (1987). *L'enfant et son milieu en Afrique Noire [The child's environment in Black Africa].* Paris: L'Harmattan.

Fai, P. J. (1996). *Loan adaptations in Lamnso' and effects on the teaching of English.* DISPES II Memoir of Ecole Normale Superieure, University of Yaounde. Yaounde: Cameroon.

Forde, C. D. (Ed.) (1963). *African worlds: Studies in the cosmological ideas and social values of African peoples.* Oxford, UK: Oxford University Press.

Gielen, U. P., & Chunachenko, O. (2004). All the worlds children: The impact of global demographic trends and economic disparities. In U. P. Gielen & J. Roopnarine (Eds.), *Childhood and adolescence: Cross-cultural perspective and applications* (pp. 81–109). Westport, CT: Praeger.

Goldschmidt, W. (1975). Absent eyes and idle hands: Socialization for low affect among the Sebei. *Ethos,* 3: 157–163.

Goody, J. (1977). *The domestication of the savage mind.* Cambridge, UK: Cambridge University Press.

Goodnow, J. J. (2011). Merging cultural and psychological accounts of family contexts. In L. A. Jensen (Ed.), *Bridging cultural and developmental psychology: New syntheses in theory, research and policy* (pp. 73–91). New York: Oxford University Press.

Gormuyor, J. N. (1992). Early childhood education in Liberia. In Woodwill, G. A., Bernhard, J. and Prochner, L. (Eds.), *International Handbook of Childhood Education* (pp. 337–341). New York: Garland.

Gould, S. J. (1981). *The mismeasure of man.* New York: W.W Norton.

Harkness, S. & Super, C. M. (1983). The cultural construction of child development: A framework for the socialization of affect. *Ethos,* 11: 221–231.

Harkness, S. and Super, C. M. (1992). Shared child care in East Africa: Sociocultural origins and developmental consequences. In M. E. Lamb, K. J. Sternberg, C-P, Hwang and A. G. Broberg (Eds.), *Child care in context* (pp. 441–459). Hillsdale, NJ: Erlbaum.

Hounkpè, A. D. G. (2008). Education in voodoo convents in Benin. In Dasen, P. R. & A. Akkari (Eds.), *Educational theories and practices from the « majority world »* (pp. 306–325). New Delhi, India: Sage.

Ittelson, W. H. (1973). Environmental perception and contemporary perceptual theory. In *Environment and cognition*. New York: Seminar Press.

Jenks, C. (Ed.). (1982). *The Sociology of childhood-Essential Readings*. London: Batsford.

Kagitcibasi, C. (2009). Identifying features of effective interventions involving parents and children in different cultural contexts. Working Paper Discussed at the Global ECD Research Meeting of the Center on the Developing Child, Harvard University, July 14, 2009.

Kathuria, R., & Serpell, R. (1999). Standardization of the Panga Muntu Test-a non-verbal cognitive test developed in Zambia. *Journal of Negro Education,* 67: 228–241.

Kilbride, J. E. & Kilbride P. L. (1975). Sitting and smiling behavior of Baganda infants: The influence of culturally constituted experience. *Journal of Cross-Cultural Psychology,* 6: 88–107.

Kishani, B. T. (2001). On the interface of philosophy and language in Africa: Some practical and theoretical considerations. *African Studies Review,* 44(3): 27–45.

LaFontaine, J. (1986). An anthropological perspective on children in social worlds. In M. Richards, & P. Light, (Eds.), *Children's social worlds* (pp. 27–41). Cambridge, MA: Harvard University Press.

Laye, C. (1977). *The African child*. Douglas, Isle of Man: Fontana Books.

Maquet, J. (1972). *Africanity*. New York: Oxford University Press.

Mundy-Castle, A. C. (1975). Social and technological intelligence in western and non-western cultures. In Pilowsky (Ed.), *Culture in collision* (pp. 344–348). Adelaide: Australian National Association for Mental Health.

Munroe, R. L. and Munroe, R. H. (1975). *Cross-cultural human development*. Prospect Heights, IL: Waveland Press.

Munroe, R. L. and Munroe, R. H. and Whiting, B. B. (1981). *Handbook of cross-cultural human development*. New York: Garland STPM Press.

Musoke, L. K. (1975). The African child and his cultural environment. In R. Owor, V. L. Ongom, & B. G. Kirya (Eds.), *The child in the African environment: Growth, development and survival*. Nairobi, Kenya: East African Literature Bureau.

Ngaujah, D. E. (Fall, 2003). *An eco-cultural and social paradigm for understanding human development: A (West African) context*. Graduate Seminar Paper (supervised by Dr. Dennis H. Dirks), Biola University, CA.

Nsamenang, A. B. (1992a). *Human Development in Cultural Context: A Third World Perspective*. Newbury Park, CA: Sage.

Nsamenang, A. B. (1992b). Early Childhood care and education in Cameroon. In M. E. Lamb et al. (Eds.), *Day Care in Context: Socio-cultural perspectives* (pp. 419–439). Hillsdale, NJ: Erlbaum.

Nsamenang, A. B. (2002). Adolescence in sub-Saharan Africa: An Image Constructed from Africa's Triple Inheritance. In B. B. Brown, R. W. Larson, & T. S. Saraswathi (Eds.), *The World's Youth: Adolescence in Eight Regions of the Globe* (pp. 61–104). Cambridge: Cambridge University Press.

Nsamenang, A. B. (2004). *Cultures of human development and education: Challenge to growing up Africa*. New York: Nova.

Nsamenang, A. B. (2005a). Educational development and knowledge flow: Local and global forces in human development in Africa. *Higher Education Policy,* 18: 275–288.

Nsamenang, A. B. (2005b). The intersection of traditional African education with school learning. In L. Swartz, C. de la Rey, & N. Duncan (Eds.), *Psychology: An introduction* (pp. 327–337). Cape Town: Oxford University Press.

Nsamenang, A. B. (2005c). African culture, human ontogenesis within. In C. Fisher, and R. Lerner (Eds.), *Encyclopedia of Applied Developmental Science* (pp. 58–61). Thousand Oaks, CA: Sage.

Nsamenang, A. B. (2006). Human ontogenesis: An indigenous African view on development and intelligence. *International Journal of Psychology*, 41 (4): 293–297.

Nsamenang, A. B. (2008a). Agency in early childhood learning and development in Cameroon. *Contemporary Issues in Early Childhood Development*, 9(3): 211–223.

Nsamenang, A. B. (2008b). In a globalized context, local culture must be the anchor of identity. Interview on Sense of Belonging. *Early Childhood Matters*, 111: 13–17.

Nsamenang, A. B. (2009). Cultures of early childhood care and education. In M. Fleer, M. Hedegaard, & J. Tudge (Eds.), *World Yearbook of Education 2009: Childhood studies and the impact of globalization: Policies and practices at global and local levels* (pp. 23–45). New York: Routledge.

Nsamenang, A. B., Fai, P. J., Ngoran, G. N. Ngeh, M. M. Y. Forsuh, F. W. Adzemye, E. W., & Lum, G. N. (2008). Ethnotheories of developmental learning in the Western Grassfields of Cameroon. In P. R. Dasen & A. Akkari (Eds.), *Educational theories and practices from the "majority world"* (pp. 49–70). New Delhi, India: Sage.

Nsamenang, A. B. & M. E. Lamb (1995). The force of beliefs: How the parental values of the Nso of Northwest Cameroon shape children's progress towards adult models. *Journal of Applied Developmental Psychology*, 16 (4): 613–627.

Ogbimi, G. E. and Alao, J. A. (1998). Developing sustainable day care services in rural communities of Nigeria. *Early Child Development and Care*, 145: 47–58.

Ohuche, R. O. & Otaala, B. (1981). *The African child in his environment*. Oxford: Pergamon.

Olaniyan, R. (1982). African history and culture: An overview. In R. Olaniyan (Ed.), *African history and culture* (pp. 1–14). Lagos, Nigeria: Longman.

Owusu-Bempah & Moffitt (1995). How Eurocentric psychology damages Africa. *The Psychologist: Bulletin of the British Psychological Society*, October, 462–465.

Pence, A. R. & Nsamenang, A. B. (2008). *A Case for ECD in Sub-Saharan Africa*. The Hague, The Netherlands: BvLF.

Phinney & Baldelomar. (2011). Identity development in multiple cultural contexts. In L. A. Jensen (Ed.), *Bridging Cultural and Developmental Approaches to Psychology: New Syntheses in Theory, Research and Policy* (pp. 161–186). Oxford University Press.

Prout, A. & James, A. (1990). A New Paradigm for the Sociology of Childhood? Provenance, Promise and Problem. In A. James and A. Prout (Eds.), *Constructing and Reconstructing Childhood: Contemporary Issues in the Sociological Study of Childhood* (pp. 7–34). London: The Falmer Press.

Ramokgopa, M. I. (2001). *Developmental stages of the African child and their psychological implications: A comparative study*. Doctoral Thesis, Rand Afrikaans University, South Africa.

Reid, M. (2006). *From Innocents to Agents: children and children's rights in New Zealand*. Auckland: Maxim Institute.

Ricco, J. R. & Samson, K. A. (1996). *Better Together: A Report on the African Regional Conference on Men's Participation in Reproductive Health, Harare, Zimbabwe, December 1–6*. Baltimore, MD: John Hopkins Center for Communication Programs.

Richter, L. & Morrell, R. G. (2006). *Baba: men and fatherhood in South Africa*. Cape Town, South Africa: HSRC Press.

Rogoff, B. (2003). *The cultural nature of human development*. Oxford, UK: Oxford University Press.

Serpell, R. (1977). Estimatees of intelligence in a rural community in eastern Zambia. In F. M. Okatcha (Ed.), *Modern psychology and cultural adaptation* (pp. 179–216). Nairobi, Kenya: Swahili Language Consultants and Publishers.

Serpell, R. (1993). *The significance of schooling: Life-journeys into an African society.* Cambridge, UK: Cambridge University Press.

Serpell, R. (1994). An African social ontogeny: Review of A. Bame Nsamenang (1992): Human development in cultural context. *Cross-Cultural Psychology Bulletin,* 28 (1): 17–21.

Shumba, A. and Seeco, E. G. (2007). Botswana. In Arnett, J. J. (Ed.), *International Encyclopedia of Adolescence* (pp. 87–99). New York: Routledge.

Smale, J. (1998). Culturally appropriate approaches in ECD. *Early Childhood Matters,* 89: 3–5.

Shweder, R. A. (1995). The ethnographic aims of cultural psychology. ISSBD *Newsletter,* 1/95: 2–4.

Sternberg, R. J., Nokes, C., Geissler, P. W., et al. (2001). *The relationship between academic and practical intelligence: A case study in Kenya.* Unpublished manuscript.

Super, C. M. & Harkness, S. (1974). Patterns of personality in Africa: A note from the field. *Ethos,* 2: 377–381.

Super, C. M. & Harkness, S. (1986). The developmental niche: A conceptualization at the interface of child and culture. *International Journal of Behavioral Development,* 9: 545–569.

Tape, G. (1993). *Milieu africain et developpement cognitive: Une etude du raisonnement experimental chez l'adolescent Ivorien.* [Cognitive development in an African context: An experimental study of reasoning in Ivorian adolescents] Paris: L'Harmattan.

Tchombe, T. M. (2007). Cameroon. In Arnett, J. J. (Ed.), *International Encyclopedia of Adolescence* (pp. 127–139). New York: Routledge.

Townsend, N., Madhavan, S., and Garey, A. I. (2005). *Father Presence in Rural South Africa: Incorporating Social Connection and Life Course Experience.* Paper presented at the annual meeting of the American Sociological Association, Marriott Hotel, Loews Philadelphia Hotel, Philadelphia, PA. Retrieved from http://www.all academic.com/meta/p21047_index.html Accessed November 19, 2008.

UNESCO (1999). UNESCO World Conference on Science Declaration on Science and the Use of Scientific Knowledge. Available from http://www.unesco.org. Accessed April 24, 2003.

Veii, K., & Evaratt, J. (2005). Predictors of reading among Herero-English bilingual Namibian school children. *Bilingualism: Language and Cognition,* 8: 239–254.

Weisner, T. S. (1997). Support for children and the African family crisis. In T. S. Weisner, C. Bradley, & C. P. Kilbride (Eds.), *African families and the crisis of social change* (pp. 20–44). Westport, CT: Bergin & Garvey.

Whiting, B. B. & Whiting, J. W. M. (1975). *Children of six cultures: A psycho-cultural analysis.* Cambridge, MA: Harvard University Press.

Zimba, R. F. (2002). Indigenous conceptions of childhood development and social realities in southern Africa. In H. Keller, Y. P. Poortinga, & A. Scholmerish (Eds.), *Between Cultures and Biology: Perspectives on Ontogenetic Development* (pp. 89–115). Cambridge, UK: Cambridge University Press.

Zimba, R. F. & Otaala, B. (1995). *The family in transition: a study of child rearing practices and beliefs among the Nama of the Karas and Hardap regions of Namibia.* Windhoek: UNICEF Namibia and the University of Namibia.

CHAPTER 12

Emerging Adulthood(s)

The Cultural Psychology of a New Life Stage

JEFFREY JENSEN ARNETT

It has now been a decade since I proposed emerging adulthood as a new life stage in between adolescence and young adulthood, lasting from the late teens through the mid-to-late twenties (Arnett, 2000). From the beginning, emerging adulthood was proposed as a cultural theory. I emphasized that it exists only under certain cultural-demographic conditions, specifically widespread education and training beyond secondary school and entry to marriage and parenthood in the late twenties or beyond. In a book on emerging adulthood (Arnett, 2004), I proposed five features of emerging adulthood based on my research on hundreds of Americans ages 18 to 29 from diverse ethnic groups and social classes. However, I emphasized that these features applied specifically to Americans and would not necessarily be found to apply to emerging adults in other cultures.

Over the past decade, research on emerging adulthood has taken place in a wide range of cultures in many regions of the world, including Asia, North and South America, and Europe (e.g., Arnett & Tanner, 2006; Douglass, 2007; Facio & Micocci, 2007; Macek et al., 2007; Nelson & Chen, 2007). This research has added a great deal to our understanding of the cultural variations in development during emerging adulthood. However, the underlying cultural basis of emerging adulthood has not yet been delineated. As cultural psychologists have emphasized, understanding the cultural basis of development requires more than simply comparisons across different cultures (Shweder et al., 2006). It requires an illumination of the cultural beliefs that underlie normative patterns of behavior.

In this chapter I begin by giving a brief overview of the theory of emerging adulthood. I then address the ways in which "one size fits all" with respect to emerging adulthood—that is, the demographic and cultural changes that have occurred in many regions worldwide to lay the groundwork for the emerging adulthood life stage. Next, I will describe the demographic and cultural variability that exists in emerging adulthood worldwide. Finally, I will seek to bridge cultural and developmental psychology by focusing on the cultural beliefs that are at the heart of emerging adulthood, in the West and in other world regions.

Emerging Adulthood: An Overview

The theory of emerging adulthood proposes that a new life stage has arisen between adolescence and young adulthood in industrialized countries over the past half-century. Fifty years ago, most young people in these countries had entered stable adult roles in love and work by their late teens or early twenties. Relatively few people pursued education or training beyond secondary school, and consequently most young men were full-time workers by the end of their teens. Relatively few women worked in occupations outside the home, and the median age of marriage in 1960 was around age 20 for women in the United States and most other industrialized countries (Arnett & Taber, 1994; Douglass, 2005). The median marriage age for men was around 22 years, and married couples usually had their first child about 1 year after their wedding day. All told, for most young people half a century ago, their teenage adolescence led quickly and directly to stable adult roles in love and work by their late teens or early twenties. These roles would form the structure of their adult lives for decades to come.

Now all that has changed. A higher proportion of young people than ever before—more than 60% in the United States—pursue education and training beyond secondary school (National Center for Education Statistics, 2009). The early twenties are not a time of entering stable adult work but a time of immense job instability; the average number of job changes from age 20 to 29 in the United States is seven. The median age of entering marriage in the United States is now 26 for women and 28 for men (U.S. Bureau of the Census, 2009). Consequently, a new period of the life course, emerging adulthood, has been created, lasting from the late teens through the mid-twenties.

I have proposed five features that distinguish emerging adulthood from the adolescence that precedes it or the young adulthood that follows it (Arnett, 2004). Emerging adulthood is the *age of identity explorations*—that is, the period of life when people are moving toward making crucial choices in love and work, based on their judgment of their interests and preferences and how these fit into the possibilities available to them. It is the *age of instability,* because in the course of pursuing their identity explorations, emerging adults frequently change love partners, jobs, educational directions, and living arrangements. It is the *self-focused age,* because it is the period of life when people have the fewest daily role obligations and thus the greatest scope for independent decision-making. It is the *age of feeling in-between,* because emerging adulthood is when people are most likely to feel they are neither adolescents nor adults but somewhere in-between, on the way to adulthood but not there yet. Finally, it is the *age of possibilities,* because no matter what their lives are like now, nearly everyone believes in emerging adulthood that eventually life will smile on them and they will achieve the adult life they envision.

These features distinguish emerging adulthood from adolescence or young adulthood but are not unique to it. All of them begin in adolescence and continue into young adulthood, but emerging adulthood is when they reach their peak.

International Patterns: Does One Size Fit All?

The five features proposed in the theory of emerging adulthood were based originally on my research involving about 300 Americans ages 20 to 29 from various ethnic groups, social classes, and geographical regions. To what extent does the theory of emerging adulthood apply internationally?

The answer to this question depends greatly on what part of the world is considered. Demographers make a useful distinction between the "developing countries" that comprise the majority of the world's population and the economically developed countries that are part of the Organization for Economic Co-Operation and Development (OECD), including the United States, Canada, Western Europe, Japan, South Korea, Australia, and New Zealand. The current population of OECD countries is 1.2 billion, about 18% of the total world population (UNDP, 2006). The rest of the human population resides in developing countries, which have much lower median incomes, much lower median educational attainment, and much higher incidence of illness, disease, and early death. First let us consider emerging adulthood in OECD countries, then in developing countries.

Emerging Adulthood in OECD Countries: The Advantages of Affluence

The demographic changes described for the United States have taken place in other OECD countries as well. This is true of participation in postsecondary education as well as median ages of entering marriage and parenthood (e.g., Dubois-Reymond & Chisholm, 2006).

Participation in postsecondary education is driven primarily by changes in the global economy. Over the past half-century, economies in OECD countries have shifted from a manufacturing base to a base in information, technology, and services. Many manufacturing jobs have been eliminated by the increased use of machines to do jobs once performed by employees. For example, it takes far fewer workers to staff an automobile factory today than it did 50 years ago because many of the previous jobs are now mechanized. Other manufacturing jobs have been moved from OECD countries to developing countries, as companies have sought to lower their production costs by hiring cheaper workers.

Meanwhile, jobs in information, technology, and services have surged in OECD countries. Fewer automobile workers may be needed, but people are needed to design the new machines that make production more efficient and less labor-intensive. An entire industry has grown up around computer services that did not exist 50 years ago. The health services area has burgeoned as people in OECD countries live longer and need health care during their later years. As a consequence of such changes, an expanding proportion of young people have obtained postsecondary education. Table 12–1 shows current rates of participation in tertiary education in a range of OECD countries (UNESCO, 2009).

The change over recent decades is especially striking for women. At the same time as the shift from a manufacturing economy to an information/technology/services economy has taken place, a revolution in women's roles and rights has taken place, and the combination has brought young women into higher education in vast numbers. Fifty years ago, women in most OECD countries were much less likely than men to obtain postsecondary education.

Table 12.1 Gross Tertiary Enrollment, Selected OECD and Other Industrialized Countries, 2007

Country	Total	Female	Male
South Korea	96	77	114
Finland	94	104	84
United States	82	96	68
Australia	75	84	66
Spain	68	76	61
Argentina	68	82	54
Italy	67	79	56
Hungary	67	80	55
Canada	62	72	53
United Kingdom	59	69	49
Japan	58	54	61
France	55	61	48
Czech Republic	54	61	48

Source: UNESCO (2009).

Note: Gross enrollment ratio is the total enrollment in a specific level of education, regardless of age, expressed as a percentage of the eligible official school-age population corresponding to the same level of education in a given school year. For the tertiary level, the population used is that of the five-year age group following on from the secondary school leaving. Consequently, a country can have a gross enrollment ratio of over 100 if some of the participants in tertiary education are more than 5 years past leaving secondary school.

Now, in every OECD country except Japan women exceed men in post-secondary participation and achievement (Table 12–1).

Similar revolutionary changes have taken place in median ages of entering marriage and parenthood. As opportunities expanded for women in the workplace and in higher education, there was less pressure on them to marry at a young age to avoid the dreaded fate of becoming an "old maid" with a secondary role in their society, and more incentive for them to wait until they had finished a period of postsecondary education and established themselves in the workplace before entering marriage and parenthood (Cherlin, 2009). For both young women and young men, the sexual revolution of the 1960s and 1970s transformed premarital sex in many OECD countries from a rare and forbidden pleasure to a normative experience. Cohabitation, too, changed from taboo to tolerated in many countries. The combination of premarital sex and cohabitation meant that it was no longer necessary to get married in order to have a regular sex life.

The demographic changes of broader participation in postsecondary education and higher ages of entering marriage and parenthood have occurred in OECD countries worldwide, and these changes laid the foundation for the rise of the new life stage of emerging adulthood. The age period from about 18 to 25 years is no longer a period of entering and settling into stable adult roles, for most people. On the contrary, it has been transformed utterly, into a stage not of commitment but of exploration, not of stability but of exceptional instability, not of making enduring commitments to others but of self-development. In short, instead of making the transition from adolescence to young adulthood at around age 20, as young people did for most of the 20th century, today young people in OECD countries experience adolescence through most of the second decade of life, then emerging adulthood, then young adulthood beginning only by the time they approach age 30. In OECD countries, "one size fits all" in the sense that the same demographic changes have taken place and a common life stage of emerging adulthood is now normative in all of them. However, there is also substantial variability in how emerging adulthood is experienced, as we will see in the following section.

Variations Among OECD Countries

In every OECD country, young people now participate in higher education at higher rates than ever before, marry later than ever before, and have their first child later than ever before. However, this pattern of demographic changes is only the structure of emerging adulthood. The content of emerging adulthood is how the years from the late teens through the mid-twenties are experienced, and this varies widely among OECD countries.

Europe is the region where emerging adulthood is longest and most leisurely. The median ages of entering marriage and parenthood are near 30 in most European countries (Douglass, 2007). Europe today is the location of the most affluent, generous, egalitarian societies in the world—in fact, in human history (Arnett, 2007). Governments pay for tertiary education, assist young people in finding jobs, and provide generous unemployment benefits for those who cannot find one. In northern Europe, many governments also provide housing support. Emerging adults in European societies make the most of these advantages.

Abundant insights on emerging adulthood in Europe can be found in the ethnographic work of Douglass and colleagues (Douglass, 2005, 2007). Douglass and colleagues are anthropologists who set out to investigate the human experience behind the European trend of lower fertility rates. In the course of exploring the basis of lower fertility rates, they inevitably explored the larger question of how the nature of young people's lives have changed now that they no longer devote their twenties mainly to marriage and caring for young children. Consequently, they unearthed a great deal of fascinating and important information on emerging adulthood.

Douglass and colleagues described the diversity that exists across Europe, but the consistent theme across countries was that young people all over Europe want to enjoy a period of emerging adult freedom and independence beyond adolescence before they commit themselves to the enduring responsibilities of adulthood. In Norway, for example, most young people want to have children eventually, but there are many prerequisites that must first be attained: to live independently for some years, to finish education, to be settled in a job, and to have lived with a partner for some time (Ravn, 2005). There is also the expectation that the twenties will include a period devoted to travel or some other self-focused, self-developing activity. There is a clear social norm that emerging adulthood "should" be enjoyed for some years before parenthood is entered (*see also* Jensen, 2011).

Douglass's own ethnographic research in Spain provides a complementary example from southern Europe (Douglass, 2005). In recent decades the median marriage age in Spain has risen to nearly 30, and the fertility rate has plunged to among the lowest in the world despite a strong cultural tradition of large extended families. There are a variety of reasons for this change, including new opportunities for women, but the largest reason appears to be that young Spaniards in their twenties prefer to focus on enjoying the freedom and fun of emerging adulthood. Young people in their twenties repeatedly told Douglass that marriage (and especially children) would put a damper on their freedom to go out, to travel, to go skiing, and to "enjoy life." This comfortable lifestyle is made possible by remaining at home with their parents' care and support until marriage. Asked why they remained home well into their twenties, emerging adults in Spain often retorted along the lines of, "Why should we leave? We're fine here. We live in a 5-star hotel!"

Eastern Europe, after decades of oppression under communism, is rapidly headed toward the Western European model of emerging adulthood. For example, in the Czech Republic, the freedom to "work, travel, and study" during the twenties is now highly prized (Nash, 2005). Unlike in much of the rest of Europe, low birthrates are viewed by Czechs–both young and old—not as a crisis but as a happy manifestation of the new freedoms young Czechs gained with the fall of communism.

The lives of emerging adult "singles" are romanticized in Czech popular culture. "Singles" are young men and women of marriageable age who choose not to marry but to enjoy an active self-focused leisure life. They are depicted as part of a global youth culture, with lifestyles that have more in common with those of young professionals in New York and Paris than with their own parents. Rather than resenting the enjoyments of the young, parents generally support and encourage their children to enjoy the emerging adult freedoms they never had.

The lives of Asian emerging adults in OECD countries such as Japan and South Korea provide a striking contrast to the self-focused leisure lives of emerging adults in Europe. Like European emerging adults, Asian emerging adults in these countries tend to enter marriage and parenthood quite late, usually around age 30 (Jones and Ramdas, 2004). Like European emerging adults, Asian emerging adults in these countries enjoy the benefits of living in affluent societies with generous social welfare systems that provide support for them in making the transition to adulthood—for example, free university education and substantial unemployment benefits.

However, in other ways the experience of emerging adulthood in Asian OECD countries is markedly different than in Europe. Europe has a long history of individualism, dating back at least to the Reformation, and today's emerging adults carry with them that legacy in their focus on self-development and leisure during emerging adulthood. In contrast, Asian cultures have a shared cultural history emphasizing collectivism and family obligations. Although Asian cultures have become more individualistic in recent decades as a consequence of globalization, the legacy of collectivism persists in the lives of emerging adults. They pursue identity explorations and self-development during emerging adulthood, like their American and European counterparts, but within narrower boundaries set by their sense of obligations to others, especially to their parents (*see* Phinney & Baldelomar, 2011). For example, in their views of the most important criteria for becoming an adult, emerging adults in the United States and Europe consistently rank *financial independence* among the most important markers of adulthood. In contrast, emerging adults with an Asian cultural background especially emphasize becoming *capable of supporting parents financially* as among the most important criteria (Arnett, 2003; Nelson, Badger, & Wu, 2004). This sense of family obligation may curtail their identity explorations in emerging adulthood to some extent, as they pay more heed to their parents' wishes about what they should study, what job they should take, and where they should live than emerging adults do in the West. In Japan, the derisive term *parasite singles* has become a popular epithet for emerging adults who extend their individualistic identity explorations past the age of 30, and this is one way of warning emerging adults of the risk of social sanctions if they carry their individualism too far (Rosenberger, 2007).

Another notable contrast between Western and Asian emerging adults is in their sexuality. In the West, premarital sex in normative by the late teens, over a decade before most people enter marriage. In the United States and Canada, and in Northern and Eastern Europe, cohabitation is also normative;

most people have at least one cohabiting partnership before marriage. In Southern Europe, cohabiting is still taboo, but premarital sex is tolerated in emerging adulthood.

In contrast, both premarital sex and cohabitation remain rare and forbidden throughout Asia. Even dating is discouraged until the late twenties, when it would be a prelude to a serious relationship leading to marriage. Parents often provide an educational rationale for why their adolescents and emerging adults should avoid dating (Lau et al., 2009). Parents tell their children to focus on education during these years, and dating would be a distraction from this focus (*see* Tharakad, Mistry, & Dutta, 2011). This rationale fits well with the Asian cultural tradition of extolling education and learning. However, there is also a long-standing cultural tradition of sexual conservatism and female virginity at marriage in Asian cultures. It seems likely that the ban on dating, premarital sex, and cohabitation that exists today in Asian cultures is in part a legacy of this tradition. In cross-cultural comparisons, about ¾ of emerging adults in the U.S. and Europe report having had premarital sexual relations by age 20, versus less than 20% in Japan and Korea (Hatfield & Rapson, 2006).

Variation Within OECD Countries: Social Class

In addition to variations across OECD countries in the content of emerging adulthood, there is also variation within countries. One important aspect of variation within countries is social class. Social class is unquestionably an important element in the lives of emerging adults, as it is in the lives of people of other ages. Specifically, the pursuit of postsecondary education structures the lives of some emerging adults but not others, and this difference has repercussions for their lives in emerging adulthood and beyond.

For those who pursue postsecondary education, their lives are structured around going to classes and doing coursework. Many of them work at least part-time as well to support themselves and to pay educational expenses, which can make for a very busy life. Those who are not in school but working or seeking a job face the formidable challenge of finding a well-paying, enjoyable job without educational credentials at a time when such jobs are increasingly elusive. Furthermore, future prospects vary greatly for these two groups, with those pursuing postsecondary education having a higher probable social class destination than those who do not, in terms of income and occupational status.

Although social class is crucial to how the years 18 to 25 are experienced, people in this age range can be designated as emerging adults across social classes. At its core, the birth of emerging adulthood over the past half-century is a demographic phenomenon, arising from the substantial increase in median ages of marriage and parenthood in every OECD country. A half-century ago, most people entered these roles at ages 20 to 22, placing them in "young adulthood" right after adolescence, with adult responsibilities of coordinating family life with a spouse, including running the household, paying the bills, and caring for children. Now that the median ages of entering marriage and parenthood have moved into the late twenties or even the early thirties, a stage of emerging adulthood has opened between adolescence and young adulthood, during which people are more independent of their parents than they were as adolescents but have not yet entered the roles that structure adult life for most people. Young people in lower social classes may enter these roles a year or two earlier than their peers in the middle and upper classes, but for most that still leaves a period of at least 6 years between the end of secondary school and the entrance to adult roles, certainly long enough to be called a distinct life stage (Arnett et al., 2010).

My research has indicated that there are other similarities among American emerging adults across social classes, beyond the demographic similarities (Arnett, 2004). For both the lower/working class and the middle class, the years from the late teens through the twenties are a time of trying out different possibilities in love and work, and gradually making their way toward more stable commitments. For both groups, instability is common during these years as frequent changes are made in love and work. For both groups, their hopes for the future are high, although the real prospects for those with relatively low education are not favorable.

Emerging Adulthood in Developing Countries: Low But Rising

Emerging adulthood is well-established as a normative life stage in the countries described thus far, but it is growing more pervasive in developing countries. Demographically, in developing countries as in OECD countries, the median ages of entering marriage and parenthood have been rising in recent decades, and an increasing proportion of young people have obtained post-secondary education. Nevertheless, currently it is only a minority of young people in developing countries who experience anything resembling emerging adulthood. The majority of the population still marries around age 20 and has long finished education by the late teens or sooner, as illustrated in Table 12–2.

For young people in developing countries emerging adulthood exists only for the wealthier segment of society—mainly the urban middle-class—whereas the rural poor have no emerging adulthood and may even have no adolescence because they enter adult-like work at an early age and also begin marriage and parenthood relatively early. As Saraswathi and Larson (2002) observed about adolescence, "In many ways, the lives of middle-class youth in India, South East Asia, and Europe have more in common with each other than they do with those of poor youth in their own countries." However, as globalization proceeds, and economic development along with it, the proportion of young people who experience emerging adulthood is likely to increase as the middle class expands.

For young people in developing countries who do experience emerging adulthood, there are complex identity challenges. It has been proposed that many of them develop a bicultural or hybrid identity, with one aspect of themselves for participating in their local culture and a different aspect of

Table 12.2 Gross Tertiary Enrollment, Selected Developing Countries, 2007

Country	Total	Female	Male
Iran	36	39	34
Saudi Arabia	30	36	25
Brazil	30	34	26
Philippines	28	31	25
Mexico	26	26	27
China	22	22	22
Indonesia	18	18	18
India	13	11	16
Pakistan	5	5	6
Ethiopia	4	2	5
Kenya	3	3	4

Source: UNESCO (2009).

Note: Gross enrollment ratio is the total enrollment in a specific level of education, regardless of age, expressed as a percentage of the eligible official school-age population corresponding to the same level of education in a given school year. For the tertiary level, the population used is that of the 5-year age group following on from the secondary school leaving.

themselves for participating in the global economy (Arnett, 2002; Jensen, Arnett & McKenzie, 2010). One example of retaining a local identity even as a global identity is developed can be found among young people in India. India has a growing, vigorous high-tech economic sector, led largely by young people. However, even the better educated young people, who have become full-fledged members of the global economy, still mostly prefer to have an arranged marriage, in accordance with Indian tradition (Chaudhary & Sharma, 2007). They also generally expect to care for their parents in old age, again in accordance with Indian tradition. Thus they have one identity for participating in the global economy and succeeding in the fast-paced world of high technology and another identity, rooted in Indian tradition, that they maintain with respect to their families and their personal lives.

Although the demographic patterns point to the rise of emerging adulthood in developing countries, so far there is little research to shed light on who experiences emerging adulthood in these countries or how it is experienced. Here, as in other areas of psychological research, the vast majority of research is on people in OECD countries—especially the United States—and research on the developing countries that comprise more than 80% (and growing) of the world's population is relatively scarce (Arnett, 2008). This can be seen as a great challenge and a great opportunity to study the phenomenon of emerging adulthood as it spreads around the world in the course of the decades to come (Arnett, 2006).

Many Emerging Adulthoods

In sum, emerging adulthood is growing as a worldwide phenomenon, in demographic terms, yet there is a great deal of variation worldwide in how it is experienced, both across and within countries. A useful analogy can be made here to the life stage of adolescence. Cross-cultural studies, most notably Schlegel and Barry's (1991) study of 186 traditional cultures, have found that adolescence exists in nearly all human cultures as a period between the time puberty begins and the time adult roles are assumed (*see also* Schlegel, 2011). However, the length of adolescence and the nature of adolescents' experiences vary vastly among cultures. Some adolescents attend secondary school, and some drop out or never go (Lloyd, 2005). Most live in the same household as their parents, but some become "street children" and live among other adolescents in urban areas (UNICEF, 2003). Some marry by their mid-teens, especially girls in rural areas of developing countries, whereas others will not marry until after adolescence and a long emerging adulthood. Consequently, it makes sense to speak not of one adolescent experience but of *adolescences* worldwide (Larson, Wilson, & Rickman, 2010). Yet we still recognize adolescence as a life stage that exists in some form in nearly all cultures.

In the same way, we can state that there are likely to be many emerging adulthoods—that is, many forms the experience of this life stage can take depending on social class, culture, and perhaps other characteristics such as gender and religious group. Some emerging adults obtain postsecondary education and some do not. Some live with their parents during these years and some do not. Some experience a series of love relationships, whereas others live in cultures where virginity at marriage is prized and love relationships before marriage are discouraged. Yet emerging adulthood can be considered to exist wherever there is a period of at least several years between the end of adolescence—meaning the attainment of physical and sexual maturity and the completion of secondary school—and the entry into stable adult roles in marriage or love and work. The structure of emerging adulthood may be consistent in OECD countries, in the demographic patterns of widespread postsecondary education and entering marriage and parenthood in the late twenties or early thirties, whereas the content—how it is experienced, what the real range of educational and occupational opportunities is, how much premarital sex is or is not tolerated—varies greatly and may continue to do so.

At this point, emerging adulthood is not nearly as widespread as adolescence. It exists as a normative life stage in OECD countries. However, in developing countries it exists only among the small but growing urban middle class and not in the more populous rural areas, where even adolescence is often brief and adult roles and responsibilities are entered by the mid-teens for many people. Nevertheless, in developing countries around the world, the urban middle class is likely to continue to grow in the decades to come. A century from now, emerging adulthood may be a normative life stage worldwide, although it will continue to show variations within and between cultures, as adolescence does today.

The Cultural Psychology of Emerging Adulthood

The variations in emerging adulthood across and within countries are of great interest in understanding this new life stage. However, there is more to understanding the cultural psychology of emerging adulthood than merely charting national and cultural variations. Cultural psychology is fundamentally about exploring the belief systems that underlie cultural patterns of thought and behavior. What, then, are the beliefs that underlie and sustain the new life stage of emerging adulthood? I propose that there are four such beliefs: the belief that independence and self-sufficiency should be attained before entering into adult commitments; the belief that romantic love should be the basis of marriage; the belief that work should be an expression of one's identity; and the belief that the years from the late teens through at least the mid-twenties should be a time of self-focused leisure and fun.

These beliefs may not prevail in all cultures where emerging adulthood is prevalent. These four cultural beliefs are all individualistic, based on what Jensen (2011) calls an *Ethic of Autonomy*, and they are most prominent in Europe and in the English-speaking OECD countries (the United States, Canada, Australia, and New Zealand). In the Asian OECD countries of Japan and South Korea, these beliefs wrestle with more traditional collectivistic beliefs that promote the well-being and interests of the group—especially the family—over the preferences of the individual. It is an open question which beliefs will ultimately prevail in this contest, not just in Japan and South Korea but in the many developing countries that have similar traditions of collectivistic values and where emerging adulthood is expanding.

Becoming Self-Sufficient: Learning to Stand Alone

In many cultures, becoming independent and self-sufficient is seen as the central issue of the emerging adulthood life stage. Emerging adulthood is viewed by emerging adults in these cultures as a time when they need to move away from dependence on their parents and show that they can manage their lives on their own. It is important to them to demonstrate, to themselves and others, that they have learned to stand alone as self-sufficient persons (Arnett, 1998). Only after this is accomplished do they feel they are ready to enter binding long-term commitments to others, such as marriage, parenthood, and a stable occupational path.

The social and institutional structure of emerging adulthood—or rather, the lack of structure—enhance this emphasis on independence and self-sufficiency. Emerging adulthood is unique in the lifespan as the life stage that is the nadir of social and institutional control. Children and adolescents live with their parents, and their lives are structured by the rules and requirements set down by their parents and by the daily obligation to attend school. Adults (beyond emerging adulthood) mostly live with a marriage partner or other long-term partner, and most have children. Their lives are structured by their obligations in those relationships and by the daily obligation to perform work specified by an employer. However, for emerging adults, social and institutional structures are at their weakest. Most still have regular contact with their parents, but they are not bound to follow their parents' rules and wishes as they were when they were younger, even if they still live at home. Most have an employer, but they change jobs so often that they may disregard any employers' demands they consider onerous and simply move on to the next job. Many of them attend college or university, but if they occasionally decide not to attend class or do the required reading, there are few repercussions.

But the centrality of independence and self-sufficiency in the lives of emerging adults is more than just the consequence of their lack of social and institutional structure—it is a *belief* they hold among their highest values. This can be seen in the criteria they value most for becoming an adult. For more than a decade, I and many others around the world have been asking young people about the criteria they consider to be important in marking when a person has become an adult. This research has taken place among a variety of American ethnic groups (Arnett, 2003) and in countries including the Argentina (Facio & Micocci, 2003), Austria (Sirsch et al., 2009), China (Nelson, Badger, & Wu, 2004), Czech Republic (Macek, Bejček & Vaníčková, 2007)), Israel (Mayseless & Scharf, 2003), and the United Kingdom (Horowitz & Bromnick, 2007). With remarkable consistency across countries and cultures, three criteria have stood out as crucial for marking the attainment of adulthood: accepting responsibility for one's self, making independent decisions, and becoming financially independent.

All three of these criteria reflect a belief in the value of becoming independent and self-sufficient. Accepting responsibility for one's self means learning to handle life's problems and the consequences of one's actions alone, without relying on others for assistance. Making independent decisions means deciding for yourself about matters large and small, from what to have for dinner to whether to move in with your love partner. Becoming financially independent means reaching the point where you do not rely on others to provide for you. For all three criteria, interviews with emerging adults show that the independence they seek is primarily independence from parents (Arnett, 1998, 2004). Although most continue to love their parents (and in fact often they get along with them far better in emerging adulthood than they did in adolescence), by emerging adulthood they may not want their parents to be involved in their lives to a degree that would compromise or obstruct their pursuit of independence and self-sufficiency.

It is important to add that emerging adults see this emphasis on independence and self-sufficiency as unique to their current life stage (Arnett, 1998, 2004). Almost none of them want to remain unfettered indefinitely, and very few of them will remain so beyond the age of 30. They see the attainment of independence and self-sufficiency as the primary challenge of their life stage. Once they have established that they have learned to stand alone—and only then—they will be ready to commit themselves to enduring roles and long-term commitments to others in love and work.

Although I originally proposed these ideas about the importance of independence and self-sufficiency in emerging adulthood based on my interviews with Americans (Arnett, 1998, 2004), there is evidence that this is important in a variety of cultural contexts. As noted, the emphasis on criteria for adulthood that have connotations of independence and self-sufficiency has been found in many countries around the world. Also worth mentioning is a recent book by Leslie Chang on "factory girls" in China, young women in their late teens and early twenties who leave their rural villages to seek work in China's booming industrial cities (Chang, 2008). In the cities, away from their families, they quickly adopt a lifestyle that emphasizes self-focused identity development and the pursuit of independence and self-sufficiency. Yet there are also differences from the Western pattern of emerging adulthood. For example, they send money home to their families, and they often live in factory dormitories where there are many rules and restrictions on their activities that few emerging adults in the West would tolerate. Further culturally based and culturally diverse research will shed more light on the different forms that the pursuit of independence and self-sufficiency may take in different cultures.

Studies of Chinese university students (Nelson, Badger, & Wu, 2004) and Asian American emerging adults (Arnett, 2003) have found a similar balance of individualistic and collectivistic values in their views of the most important criteria for adulthood. They prize the three individualistic criteria mentioned, but they also rank highly the capability to support their parents financially, a criterion never mentioned in American interview studies (Arnett, 1998, 2004). They strive for autonomy even as they also maintain a strong sense of obligation to their parents.

Looking for Love: Finding a Soul Mate

Emerging adulthood is a life stage in which the central task is to move gradually toward making enduring commitments in love and work. With respect to both love and work, cultural beliefs of individualism often underlie emerging adults' explorations.

With regard to love, the individualism of emerging adults is evident in their descriptions of what they seek in a marriage partner. The modern ideal for marriage in Western countries is to find one's "soul mate." According to a national U.S. survey by the National Marriage Project, 94% of single 20- to 29-year-old Americans agree with the statement, "There is a special person, a soul mate, waiting for you somewhere out there" (Popenoe & Whitehead, 2001). Young Europeans share this romantic ideal in seeking a marriage partner (Douglass, 2005).

The soul mate ideal is highly individualistic. A soul mate is someone who complements your identity perfectly. This does not mean that a soul mate is a perfect person; a soul mate is a person who is perfect *for you*. All your needs, wants, and distinctive personal qualities fit snugly into the receptors your soul mate provides. You feel completely at ease with your soul mate because your soul mate views life just as you do. There is no need for conflict, because you and your soul mate want the same things out of life.

Like most ideals, the soul mate ideal is elusive. One reason for the later marriage age today than in previous decades may be that it takes a long time to find someone who resembles the soul mate ideal—or to give up this ideal and settle for a flesh and blood human being (Arnett, 2004). Until recently, finding a marriage partner may have been relatively simple (Cherlin, 2009). A woman looked for a man who would be a good provider, a decent father, and hopefully reasonably nice and attractive. A man looked for a woman who would run the household, take care of the children, and hopefully be reasonably nice and attractive. Many people within the average person's social circle would fit within these broad guidelines. However, once the expectation for a marital partner is a "special person" who is ideally and uniquely suited to you, there may be very few persons, perhaps only one, "somewhere out there," who will be deemed worthy, and finding that person is likely to take awhile.

But what about cultures in which personal choice in marriage is circumscribed and parents do much of the choosing? In most of the world there is a long tradition of arranged marriages, in which young people barely know their prospective spouse prior to the wedding (Hsu, 1985; Prakasa & Rao, 1979). Marriage was mainly a transaction between families, not individuals. Love was expected to grow after marriage, not to be the basis for entering marriage, and intimacy expectations were low. Married couples spent little time alone with each other and often did not even sleep in the same room.

However, today the tradition of arranged marriage is dead or waning everywhere, and the soul mate ideal is ascending. India is one place where arranged marriage remains the norm, but even there, nearly 40% of young Indians say they intend to choose their own mates (Chaudhary & Sharma, 2007). This still leaves the majority (60%) who expect an arranged marriage, but for 40% to choose their own spouse is a high percentage compared with any time in the past in India, when the percentage would have been close to zero. Furthermore, many arranged marriages today are in fact "semi-arranged" marriages, in which parents influence the mate selection of their children but do not simply decide it without the children's consent (Naito & Geilen, 2002). Parents may introduce a potential mate to their child. If the young person has a favorable impression of the potential mate, they date a few times. If they agree that they are compatible, they marry. Another variation of semi-arranged marriage is that young people meet a potential mate on their own but seek their parents' approval before proceeding to date the person or consider marriage. This suggests a movement toward a balance between individual choice and family considerations—that is, between individualistic values and collectivistic values.

Still, there remains little research on how emerging adults in the middle class in developing countries such as India and China view marriage, and it is a question that merits investigation. Do emerging adults in developing countries now have a soul mate ideal of marriage, much like their counterparts in the West? Or do they have less lofty expectations for marriage, seeing it in the more traditional sense as a practical arrangement for distributing duties of childcare, providing for and running a household, and the other requirements of daily life?

Looking for Identity-Based Work

Like love, the nature of work has changed in recent decades. Work has been traditionally regarded as an unpleasant but necessary requirement of life. In the Bible story that is some 3,000 years old, work is a punishment from God, the penalty inflicted on Adam and Eve for their disobedience in the Garden of Eden. Most work in the course of 10,000 years of human history has been agricultural work, which is strenuous, boring, and subject to random catastrophe. When industrialization arose, the tedium of factory work became a dubious alternative to the tedium of field work.

In the modern post-industrial economy, all this has changed. Few people in OECD countries (1%–2%) work in agriculture. More work in manufacturing, but the number is decreasing daily as manufacturing jobs are replaced by automation and companies relocate to developing countries with lower wages and weaker labor laws. Instead, there is a vast range of jobs in information, technology, and services. This economic change, along with growing individualism, has spawned a cultural belief that work should be enjoyable, not boring, and self-fulfilling, not deadening to the body or soul.

Consequently, as they enter the job market emerging adults have high expectations for the rewards of work. Unlike generations past, they do not believe that work is inherently and irremediably arduous and dreary. On the contrary, they believe that work should be enjoyable and fun, a form of self-expression (Arnett, 2004). In the same way that they believe they can find a soul mate who provides an ideal complement to their identity, they are hopeful they can find work that is an expression of their identity, an activity that allows them to use their abilities to do something they find engaging, gratifying, and self-fulfilling.

This attitude toward work can be frustrating to employers, who do not typically get up in the morning and ask themselves, "Whom can I fulfill today?" On the contrary, most ask themselves how they can get their employees to do the most work for the least amount of money, in order to maximize company profits. This disconnect between the expectations of employers and the expectations of their young employees can lead to conflict in the workplace and to high turnover. Surely one reason emerging adults change jobs so often during the decade of the twenties is that finding identity-based work is elusive, and they are quick to drop a job that does not seem to promise this possibility in favor of another job that might.

Their high expectations for work are also likely to be frustrating to emerging adults themselves, ultimately. Just as the search for a soul mate must end in a partnership with a flesh-and-blood human being, warts and all, the search for identity-based work is likely to end in a job that is not everything one would have liked it to be. Yet I have found that by the end of their twenties, most American emerging adults have made peace with their dreams, in both love and work (Arnett, 2004). They may not have quite found their soul mate ideal, but they have found someone they love and who loves them back. They may not have found self-fulfilling work that they look forward to going to every day, but they have found a job they can live with for now, as they continue to strive toward the ideal of finding a job they truly love.

Glory Days: Emerging Adulthood as a Time of Unparalleled Fun

Finally, one other key cultural belief that underlies the new life stage of emerging adulthood is that it is a time of unparalleled enjoyment of life. This is when you have the most freedom for self-focused fun. This is when you have the chance to do things you never could have done when younger and will never be able to do when older: stay out until all hours partying with friends, try unusual mind-altering substances, travel far and wide on a slender budget, or take a low-paying but adventurous job for awhile.

Europe is the cultural area where this cultural belief in emerging adulthood as a time of *joie de vivre* is most pronounced, as shown in ethnographic work by Douglass and colleagues (2005). As mentioned earlier, most European emerging adults prefer to spend the decade of their twenties enjoying travel, time with friends, and other self-focused fun.

In my research on American emerging adults I have observed similar views of emerging adulthood as a peak time of freedom to enjoy life. American emerging adults value the freedom and independence of the life stage and seek to make the most of it, realizing that once they enter adult commitments, their "glory days" will be over. They plan marriage, parenthood, and a long-term job commitment for after those days have passed. Because they enjoy their emerging adulthood freedom and leisure, they view adulthood with a great deal of ambivalence. All of them realize they will enter it eventually; virtually none of them vow to remain in their glory days forever. But, like Augustine contemplating the virtuous life—"Make me chaste, Lord, but not yet"—they are in no hurry to take on the onerous responsibilities of adult life.

Do emerging adults outside the West have a similar view of the emerging adult years as a time of peak freedom and leisure? Or are they more focused on fulfilling their duties and family obligations? There is little research yet to answer these questions, but some interesting clues come from research in Japan. Japanese secondary schools are notoriously demanding and competitive, leaving little room for leisure in adolescence (Rohlen, 1983; Stevenson & Zusho, 2002). However, once they enter college, grades matter little and standards for performance are relaxed. Instead, they have "four years of university-sanctioned leisure to think and explore" (Rohlen, 1983, p. 168). Japanese college students spend a great deal of time socializing with friends, walking around the city and hanging out together (Fackler, 2007). Average homework time for Japanese college students is half the homework time of junior high or high school students (Takahashi & Takeuchi, 2006). For most Japanese, their emerging adulthood is the only time in their lives, from childhood until retirement, that will be relatively free of pressure. Until they enter college, the exam pressures are intense, and once they leave college they enter a work environment in which the hours are notoriously long. Only during their college years are they relatively free from responsibilities and free to enjoy extensive hours of leisure.

Conclusion

The rise of emerging adulthood stems fundamentally from the demographic changes that have opened up a distinct new period between adolescence and young adulthood, most notably greater participation in tertiary education and later ages of entering marriage and parenthood. However, changes in cultural beliefs also, crucially, accompanied these demographic changes. Premarital sex became more widely acceptable in many cultures, decoupling sex from marriage and making it possible to have an active sexual life without entering marriage. The roles and opportunities available to women vastly expanded, removing the social pressure for them to marry and have children to have a legitimate place in their societies. Marriage became transformed from a practical arrangement for raising children and running a household to an arena for romantic ideals of soul mate couplehood—at least in aspiration. Work became transformed from a dreary duty to an arena for self-expression—again, at least in aspiration.

Emerging adulthood is a cultural theory, and how emerging adulthood is experienced is shaped by cultural beliefs. In many cultures these beliefs include the desirability of striving for self-sufficiency before adult responsibilities are taken on in love and work; the importance of finding a marriage partner who ideally complements your identity; the importance of finding identity-based work; and the desirability of using the freedom of the emerging adulthood life stage to pursue self-focused fun. Yet these beliefs are by no means universal, and the individualism that runs across these beliefs is tempered in cultures that emphasize obligations to others, especially to family of origin. The field of emerging adulthood is not yet a decade old, and one of its chief challenges in the years ahead will be to chart the cultural themes and variations of this new life stage.

References

Arnett, J. J. (1998). Learning to stand alone: The contemporary American transition to adulthood in cultural and historical context. *Human Development, 41*: 295–315.

Arnett, J. J. (2000). Emerging adulthood: A theory of development from the late teens through the twenties. *American Psychologist, 55*: 469–480.

Arnett, J. J. (2002). The psychology of globalization. *American Psychologist, 57*: 774–783.

Arnett, J. J. (2003). Conceptions of the transition to adulthood among emerging adults in American ethnic groups. *New Directions in Child and Adolescent Development, 100*: 63–75.

Arnett, J. J. (2004). *Emerging adulthood: The winding road from the late teens through the twenties.* New York: Oxford University Press.

Arnett, J. J. (2006). The psychology of emerging adulthood: What is known, and what remains to be known? In J. J. Arnett & J. L. Tanner (Eds.), *Emerging adults in America: Coming of age in the 21st century* (pp. 303–330). Washington, DC: APA Books.

Arnett, J. J. (2007). The long and leisurely route: Coming of age in Europe today. *Current History, 106*: 130–136.

Arnett, J. J. (2008). The neglected 95%: Why American psychology needs to become less American. *American Psychologist, 63*: 602–614.

Arnett, J. J., & Taber, S. (1994). Adolescence terminable and interminable: When does adolescence end? *Journal of Youth & Adolescence, 23*: 517–537.

Arnett, J. J., & Tanner, J. L. (Eds.) (2006). *Emerging adults in America: Coming of age in the 21st century.* Washington, DC: American Psychological Association.

Chaudhary, N., & Sharma, N. (2007). India. In J. J. Arnett (Ed.), *International encyclopedia of adolescence* (pp. 442–459). New York: Routledge.

Cherlin, A. J. (2009). *The marriage-go-round: The state of marriage and the family in American today.* New York: Knopf.

Douglass, C. B. (Ed.) (2005). *Barren states: The population "implosion" in Europe.* New York: Berg.

Douglass, C. B. (2007). From duty to desire: Emerging adulthood in Europe and its consequences. *Child Development Perspectives, 1*: 101–108.

Dubois-Reymond, M., & Chisholm, L. (2006). Effects of modernization on European youth. *New Directions for Child and Adolescent Development, 113*.

Fackler, M. (2007, June 22). As Japan ages, universities struggle to fill classrooms. *New York Times*, p. A3.

Facio, A., & Micocci, F. (2003). Emerging adulthood in Argentina. In J. J. Arnett & N. Galambos (Eds.), *New Directions in Child and Adolescent Development, 100*: 21–31.

Facio, A., Resett, S., Micocci, F., & Mistrorigo, C. (2007). Emerging adulthood in Argentina: An age of diversity and possibilities. *Child Development Perspectives, 1*: 115–118.

Hatfield, E., & Rapson, R. L. (2006). *Love and sex: Cross-cultural perspectives.* New York: University Press of America.

Horowitz, A. D., & Bromnick, R. D. (2007). "Contestable adulthood:" Variability and disparity in markers for negotiating the transition to adulthood. *Youth & Society, 39*: 209–231.

Hsu, F. L. K. (1983). *Rugged individualism reconsidered.* Knoxville, TN: University of Tennessee Press.

Jensen, L. A. (2008). Through two lenses: A cultural-developmental approach to moral psychology. *Developmental Review, 28*: 289–315.

Jensen, L. A. (2011). The cultural-developmental theory of moral psychology: A new synthesis. In L. A. Jensen (Ed.), *Bridging cultural and developmental psychology: New Syntheses in Theory, Research and Policy* (pp. 3–25). New York: Oxford University Press.

Jensen, L. A., Arnett, J. J., & McKenzie, J. (in press). Globalization and cultural identity developments in adolescence and emerging adulthood. In Schwartz, S. J.,

Luyckx, K., & Vignoles, V. L. (Eds.), *Handbook of Identity Theory and Research*. New York, NY: Springer Publishing Company.

Jones, G. W., & Ramdas, K. (2004). *Untying the knot: Ideal and reality in Asian marriage*. Singapore: Asia Research Institute.

Larson, R. W., Wilson, S., & Rickman, A. (2010). *Globalization, societal change, and adolescence across the world*. In R. Lerner & L. Steinberg (Eds.), *Handbook of Adolescent Psychology*. New York: Wiley.

Lau, M., Markham, C., Lin, H., Flores, G., & Chacko, M. R. (2009). Dating and sexual attitudes of Asian American adolescents. *Journal of Adolescent Research, 24*: 91–113.

Lloyd, C. (Ed.) (2005). *Growing up global: The changing transitions to adulthood in developing countries*. Washington, DC: National Research Council and Institute of Medicine.

Macek, P. Bejček, J., & Vaníčková, J. (2007). Contemporary Czech emerging adults: Generation growing up in the period of social changes. *Journal of Adolescent Research, 22*: 444–475.

Mayseless, O., & Scharf, M. (2003). What does it mean to be an adult? The Israeli experience. In J. J. Arnett & N. Galambos (Eds.), *New Directions in Child and Adolescent Development*, Vol. 100 (pp. 5–20). San Francisco, CA: Jossey-Bass.

Naito, T., & Gielen, U. P. (2003). The changing Japanese family: A psychological portrait. In J. L. Roopnarine & U. P. Gielen (Eds.), *Families in global perspective*. Boston, MA: Allyn & Bacon.

Nash, R. (2005). The economy of birthrates in the Czech Republic. In C. B. Douglas (Ed.), *Barren states: The population "implosion" in Europe* (pp. 93–113). New York: Berg.

National Center for Education Statistics (2009). *The condition of education, 2009*. Washington, DC: U. S. Department of Education.

Nelson, L. J., Badger, S., & Wu, B. (2004). The influence of culture in emerging adulthood: Perspectives of Chinese college students. *International Journal of Behavioral Development, 28*: 26–36.

Nelson, L. J., & Chen, X. (2007). Emerging adulthood in China: The role of social and cultural factors. *Child Development Perspectives, 1*: 86–91.

Prakasa, V. V., & Rao, V. N. (1979). Arranged marriages: An assessment of the attitudes of college students in India. In G. Kurian (Ed.), *Cross-cultural perspectives on mate selection and marriage* (pp. 11–31). Westport, CT: Greenwood Press.

Phinney, J. S., & Baldelomar, O. A. (2011). Identity development in multiple cultural contexts. In L. A. Jensen (Ed.), *Bridging cultural and developmental psychology: New syntheses in theory, research and policy* (pp. 161–186). New York: Oxford University Press.

Popenoe, D., & Whitehead, B. D. (2001). The state of our unions, 2001: The social health of marriage in America. *Report of the National Marriage Project, Rutgers, New Brunswick, NJ*. Available: http://marriage.rutgers.edu.

Ravn, M. N. (2005). A matter of free choice? Some structural and cultural influences on the decision to have or not to have children in Norway. In C. B. Douglas (Ed.), *Barren states: The population "implosion" in Europe* (pp. 29–47). New York: Berg.

Rohlen, T. P. (1983). *Japan's high schools*. Berkeley, CA: University of California Press.

Rosenberger, N. (2007). Rethinking emerging adulthood in Japan: Perspectives from long-term single women. *Child Development Perspectives, 1*: 92–95.

Saraswathi, T. S., & Larson, R. (2002). Adolescence in global perspective: An agenda for social policy. In B. B. Brown, R. Larson, & T. S. Saraswathi, (Eds.), *The world's youth: Adolescence in eight regions of the globe* (pp. 344–362). New York: Cambridge University Press.

Saraswathi, T. S., Mistry, J., & Dutta, R. (2011). Reconceptualizing lifespan development through a Hindu perspective. In L. A. Jensen (Ed.), *Bridging cultural and developmental psychology: New syntheses in theory, research and policy* (pp. 276–299). New York: Oxford University Press.

Schlegel, A., & Barry, H. (1991). *Adolescence: An anthropological inquiry*. New York: Free Press.

Schlegel, A. (2011). Adolescent ties to adult communities: the intersection of culture and development. In L. A. Jensen (Ed.), *Bridging cultural and developmental psychology: New syntheses in theory, research and policy* (pp. 138–158). New York: Oxford University Press.

Shweder, R. A., Goodnow, J., Hatano, G., Levine, R. A., Markus, H., & Miller, P. (2006). The cultural psychology of development: One mind, many mentalities. In W. Damon (Ed.), *Handbook of child development* (5th ed., Vol. 1, pp. 865–937). New York: Wiley.

Sirsch, U., Dreher, E., Mayr, E., & Willinger, U. (2009). What does it take to be an adult in Austria? Views of adulthood in Austrian adolescents, emerging adults, and adults. *Journal of Adolescent Research, 24*: 275–292.

Stevenson, H. W., & Zusho, A. (2002). Adolescence in China and Japan: Adapting to a changing environment. In B. B. Brown, R. Larson, & T. S. Saraswathi (Eds.), *The World's Youth: Adolescence in Eight Regions of the Globe* (pp. 141–170). New York: Cambridge University Press.

Takahashi, K., & Takeuchi, K. (2007). Japan. In J. J. Arnett (Ed.), *International Encyclopedia of Adolescence*. New York: Routledge.

UNESCO (2009). Tertiary indicators (Table 14). http://stats.uis.unesco.org/unesco/TableViewer/tableView.aspx?ReportId=167. Accessed September 9, 2009.

U.S. Bureau of the Census (2009). *Statistical abstract of the United States*. Washington, DC: U.S. Government Printing Office.

UNICEF (2003). *The state of the world's children*. Oxford, England: Oxford University Press.

United Nations Development Programme (2006). *Human Development Report, 2006*. New York: Author.

CHAPTER 13

Reconceptualizing Lifespan Development through a Hindu Perspective

T. S. SARASWATHI, JAYANTHI MISTRY, & RANJANA DUTTA

Our paper focuses on lifespan conceptualizations articulated in the Hindu worldview. Differing from the much more widely examined Confucian and Taoist models of the East, the Hindu worldview of lifespan development provides an alternative conceptualization of the place of humans with respect to context, the purpose and meaning of life, and ideals of successful ontological progression. We use this conceptualization to illustrate bridging developmental and cultural psychology by rephrasing the three questions posed to us by the editor of this volume as follows: *(1)* What insight can we bring from the Hindu conception of the lifespan to provide an alternative synthesis to the oppositional stance between the "one-size-fits-all" developmental perspective and the "one-theory-for-every-culture" relativistic perspective?; *(2)* Might the Hindu life-stages offer a conceptualization of the human lifespan in which both structural and content dimensions are integrated, thus arguing against characterizing the distinction between developmental and cultural psychology as one of structure versus content?; and *(3)* What is the relevance of the Hindu worldview in the current context of increased interface between cultures?

Our focus on Hindu conceptions of the lifespan is timely, not only for its potential theoretical significance but also because of its increasing relevance in the current era of globalization. Increased legitimacy and acceptance of the body–mind connection in medical and health science has led to interest in mindful and contemplative meditation practices that were methods of Hindu yoga and psychological sciences. There is increasing interest in examining the constructs of faith, spirituality, forgiveness, hope, longing, and compassion and their effect on affective, cognitive, and motivational systems, which are an integral component of the Hindu psychological worldview for optimization of mental health. In addition, India, with its young educated workforce in the global economy, is arousing interest in the psychology of its people (*see also* Arnett, 2011). In discussing the Hindu life-stages and world view as an alternate conceptualization of lifespan development, we also consider its implications for alternate stances toward life or coping strategies and techniques that are not only becoming prevalent globally but appear to have practical utility in dealing with life circumstances.

We respond to the previous questions by presenting a backdrop of the Hindu cultural milieu within which we elucidate select constructs pertinent to human development in India,[1] providing insight into the uniqueness of the Hindu perspective. We then present the Hindu life-stages with a focus on the historical ideals, rituals and purpose and relate them to contemporary manifest lifestyles. Thereafter, to illustrate bridging developmental and cultural psychology, we attempt to map and integrate Hindu conceptions within the meta-theoretical conceptual framework provided by Overton (2006). Finally, we reflect on some implications of the Hindu worldview on human development in the global context.

Hinduism in Contemporary India

Not many are aware that the term Hindu is not Indian in origin and in fact does not denote the followers of a particular religion/faith. Etymologically it means "inhabitant of the land of 'Sindhu' that is India" (Nityananda, 2000, p. i). Around the sixth century B.C. the flourishing civilization of the Indo-Gangetic plains known as the 'Sindhu Ganga Samatala' was shortened by Persians to 'Sindhus' referring to the place they lived. The syllable '*sa*' got transmuted to '*ha*' in Persian and Sindhu became Hindu henceforth for a community sharing a common heritage. Later '-ism' was added to denote the religion they followed (Nadkarni, 2003; Nityananda, 2000; Thapar, 1966). Hinduism, even today, is referred to as '*Sanatana Dharma*,' meaning 'a moral code based on the eternal sustaining values of life.' Over at least three millennia, contributions from several philosophers, common practitioners and religious reformers have led to the evolution of *Sanatana Dharma* which is seen as applicable to all people and all times. In its basic philosophy, Hinduism is a strictly monotheistic and pan theistic religion, although it is misunderstood widely (even by many Hindus) as polytheistic. Secular in its approach and tolerant of alternative paths, Hinduism now encompasses a range of belief systems, from its core monotheistic core philosophy to polytheism, and even animism and atheism (Thapar, 1966). Hinduism represents a way of life and functions as philosophical and cultural model.

Ashish Nandy (1988, cited in Nadkarni, 2003) once observed that religion should give a theory of life and a theory of transcendence and that Hinduism provides both. This may be the reason that despite the odds (abstract philosophical doctrines, written in Sanskrit language to which only the privileged few had access), Hinduism reaches the common man and woman and connects with the daily life of the Indian population. It permeates everyday life through daily rituals, celebration of festivals and storytelling of the great epics like *Mahabharata* and *Ramayana*, as well analysis and discussion of Hindu thought in newspapers, and dedicated programs on television and radio.

Erikson (1979) once commented that "faced with a traditional world image of such consistency and pervasiveness as the Hindu world, . . . we, observers and diagnosticians of today, cannot ignore or simply leave behind some fundamental questions…one such question is that of the residual power, even under conditions of rapid modernization, of the traditional world images . . ." (Erikson, 1979, p.16). We suggest that the Hindu worldview provided by these images represents the common denominator that links a vast range of individuals such as an illiterate Indian villager, a world renowned nuclear scientist, the common person on the street, or even the frequent flier at Delhi international airport (Bharati, 1985).

In the following sections, we present *(1)* core Hindu constructs about the meaning and purpose of life and their significance for lifespan development, followed by *(2)* a description of the life-stages and appropriate conduct or developmental tasks in each. We address the traditional and idealized Hindu worldview initially as the theoretical stance and later connect these ideals with contemporary practices of the Indian subcontinent when describing life-stages. In presenting core Hindu constructs about the meaning and purpose of life, we highlight the underlying dialectic of individual action and agency with duty to the structured social world within which one is embedded. This underlying coexistence and symbiosis of individuality and social embeddedness also emerges in the description of the purpose, rituals, and ideals of each stage in the Hindu life cycle (*see also* Nsamenang, 2011).

Hindu Developmental Worldview

From the Hindu perspective, the central goal of life, succinctly stated, is to use present life *ashramas*[2] (stages) to become refined so as to either take a higher-order birth or end the cycle of births and death by purification and following the tenets of *dharma*. There is no denial of this worldly life. The body is seen as the vehicle of the soul (*atman*) and has to be kept pure and healthy. "The valuable developments of Ayurveda, Natya Shastra, and Kama Sutra strongly imply the significance of worldly aspirations as genuine concerns" (G. Misra, personal communication, Aug. 1, 2009). Thus, the theme of transcendence or spirituality is not an exclusive goal but encompasses the life lived well in this world through careful observance of the *dharmas*. Common constructs that bind Hindus are the acceptance of the four life-stages (or *ashramas*), four *varnas* (classification of major occupations later distorted to caste), and four *purusharthas* (life goals)—namely, righteousness or obedience to the moral law (*dharma*), wealth or material welfare (*artha*), pleasure (*kama*), and emancipation (*moksha*). These common ideals of life provide the spirit of unity to the social and moral life of the majority of Hindus (Radhakrishnan & Moore, 1957). Many of these concepts have complex and dialectical relationships with each other. We elucidate some of these relationships that are relevant for lifespan development to make the case for the uniqueness of the Hindu worldview.

Dual View of the Individual

In the Hindu perspective, individuality is not defined by one's embodied form but by the unique nature of the individual soul or *atman*. "The notion of *atman* brings in the imagery of shared selfhood and furnishes a ground for similarity and identity, necessary for empathy, compassion, and forgiveness in this world" (G. Misra, personal communication, Aug. 1, 2009). According to the Hindu worldview, all things on earth, including one's body, are transitory. The only permanent reality is the *atman*. The body is merely a vehicle for the *atman*, and on death it will be cast away like old clothes. Hence to believe that the body is a serious substance and not a temporal existence is *maya* or illusory. The birth of the soul in a material human form is considered the highest form (albeit more limited than the spiritual form) because it affords the individual an opportunity to act with intellect, wisdom, conscience, and willpower. Individuals should search for and identify with their true and permanent spiritual self or *atman* rather than mistakenly identify with their embodied self, which is merely a transitory and perishable vehicle of the *atman*. Throughout life they are thus encouraged to rise above bodily urges and pleasures and strengthen their higher spiritual self by developing self control (e.g., control over hunger with fasts, control over mind with meditation). This identification with one's higher spiritual self sets the stage for overcoming attachments and developing a sense of individualism and personal autonomy within the collective social structure in which one is immersed (Saraswathi, 2005).

Moksha: Living Life with the Goal of Transcendence

Hindus believe that the central goal of a person is to transcend worldly life through refinement and purification of one's self. Based on belief in reincarnation, a life led with righteousness will lead to either a rebirth with greater purity or obtaining final release of the spiritual self or *atman* from the repetitive cycles of birth and death and merging with a super consciousness called *Brahma* (the ultimate soul, called *Paramatma*). This release of the soul and its merging with God consciousness is termed attainment of *moksha*. The material world is considered illusory or *maya*, in that people get distracted from their path of *moksha* by attachment to the temporal, impermanent material world (including family and friends).

The Dialectic Concepts of Karma and Dharma

Dharma refers to the moral code to live by. It is ultimately the life-governing principle and sustains righteous living. *Dharma* is interpreted in three different ways (Nadkarni, 2003), which reflect a synthesis of collectivistic and individualistic ideals that typify Hindu life. First, it refers to duty to family, society, ancestors, one's own self as well as to all living beings and nature. Second, it underscores the adoption of universal values and ethical behavior for the welfare of others and self. Third, and most important, it means to uphold and maintain the desire for knowledge, spiritual growth, and wisdom. In the third meaning of *dharma*, the core onus lies on the individual's sense of personal agency. Individuals are believed to be able to control, change, or modify their current and future *karma* or destiny through righteous practice of *dharma* in accordance with their caste, gender, stage in life, and life circumstances. The notions of *karma* and *dharma* permeate the consciousness of millions of Hindus and are part of their daily vocabulary, songs, and music. *Karma* is defined as the law of action/deed and the law of causality (Nadkarni, 2003). It is employed in three discernable ways: *(1) karma* refers to concrete actions (including thoughts and feelings) that a person does through being in this world; *(2)* it refers to the accumulated rewards and retributions one carries from past lives (most popular usage); and *(3) karma* is used to proactively change the course of one's destiny, emphasizing the "making" aspect of *karma* (Menon, 2003). *Karma* is a dialectical concept not just for explaining current situations that defy indigenous logic (accommodating to given inexplicable life events) but as a proactive concept allowing one to act in a collective world by doing what is right (*dharma*) and hence reaping rewards that can be banked and may save one from impending negative life events. "*Karma* is not just a doctrine of 'reincarnation,' 'fatalism,' or 'pre-destination'; it is a promise of hope. Given the innate tendency of the unconscious (*gunas*) towards light (*sattva*) combined with an individual's personal efforts in this direction (*dharma*), *karma* assures that the attainment of the goal of existence (*moksha*) is certain even though there are apt to be many setbacks in the process. . ."(Kakar, 1981, p.48).

The above descriptions illustrate that the Hindu developmental perspective is unique in several respects. There are many points of departure in the Hindu worldview from current views in mainstream developmental psychology. First, the "individual" is not an embodied self but rather a bodily mirage that needs to be actualized spiritually rather than in ways emphasized in current theories of self-actualization. Because the "embodied self" provides the means of actualizing the spiritual self, it has to be disciplined and kept healthy but not embellished with vanity (especially after midlife). By late life, it needs to be transcended. Second, the starting point of the individual at birth in any given "lifetime" is at a different point in their pursuit of perfection or union with the God consciousness and not comparable in its qualities (*gunas*) to any other person born. Theories of future time perspective in lifespan psychology do not adequately cover time perspective which transcends one's current lifespan. Third, the central consistent teleological goal over the lifespan is self-perfection while other goals such as material gains and legacies, which are emphasized in current lifespan theories, are underplayed. Belief in the temporal nature of life on earth as a station in the journey of the spiritual self to which one arrives with nothing and takes nothing other than the legacy of one's deeds (*karma*) has no motivational parallels. Fourth, the goal of life itself involves a dialectical way of thinking. The prescribed path is to "live" in such a way so as to transcend life itself. And fifth, there are currently no analogous dialectical constructs in psychology such as *dharma* (moral obligation to individual spiritual self as well to social collective self) and *karma* (retributive as well as proactive construct) (*see also* Jensen, 2011).

In our interpretation of the Hindu life-stages[3] presented in the following section, we extrapolate two intersecting themes: the individual as situated in the social world and the pursuit of *moksha* (which transcends social embeddeness) as the ultimate goal of life. The transformation in the final stage of life has the goal of becoming part of the cosmic universe. The mundane or worldly aspect of individual development emphasizes social adaptation. However, the ultimate goal of the life-cycle consists of a spiritual component—that of self-realization or actualization—and this, by definition, is individualistic in nature.

Herein lies the core underlying point: the Hindu life-cycle provides a third alternative to the East–West, collectivistic–individualistic prototypes that dominate thinking in cross-cultural psychology today (Kagitcibasi, 1996). Development from the Hindu perspective is characterized by both collectivism and individualism depending on the life-stage (Saraswathi, 2005; *see also* Phinney & Baldelomar, 2011). We argue that this intersection of the individual as socially situated and yet as following a path of individual self-realization represents a synthesis of individualism and collectivism that is unique to Hinduism as an alternative conception of the lifespan. Although these theoretical implications of the Hindu conceptualization of the lifespan are elaborated upon in a later section, we emphasize the simultaneous focus on individualism and collectivism that emerges in the description of the Hindu worldview and stages of life that follows.

Hindu Conceptions of the Stages of Life

The life course from birth to death is divided into four *ashramas* or stages. A brief description of these stages is provided to illustrate a perspective of human development that is a dialectic synthesis of an "individual-in-social relations focus" and an "individual pursuit of self-realization." *Ashrama* means a resting place and dharma the moral code, thus *ashramadharma* implies resting places in the forest of human life for people to achieve their liberation, that is, *moksha* (Jayaram, 2009).

The four major stages begin at the end of infancy and early childhood and are roughly translated as the stage of apprenticeship (*brahmacharya*), building family (*grahasthya*), extrication from material world (*vanaprastha*), and renouncement (*sanyasa*). Although there are substages of the infancy period, the serious observance of conduct (*dharma*) is initiated during apprenticeship or *brahmacharya*. All stages and substages are marked by samskaras (transformative rites/ceremonies) associated with the transitions that emphasize the change in social, moral, and individual obligations. These rites are aimed at "forming well or thoroughly making perfect" of the human being (Nadkarni, 2003) and involve the process of maturation and moral perfectibility and purification (Madan, 1987). Perfectibility comes from daily life customs and practices. As Pandey (1969) explained, the *samskaras* help in the refinement and purification of human life, facilitate the development of personality, impart sanctity and importance to the human body, bless all material and spiritual aspirations of man, and ultimately prepare him for an easy and happy exit from this world (pp. 277–278). Similarly, Menon (2003) emphasized that the distant goals of renunciation and *moksha* cannot be achieved without translating them into daily practices of gradual purification. Specific activities are associated with purification (e.g., bathing, fasting, meditation, prayer, almsgiving), whereas other activities are associated with impurity (such as not bathing, menstruation, death in the family, contact with a person of low caste, and negative emotions). These ideals of daily practices are instilled and reinforced culturally. It is critical to note that these practices are context specific. Characteristic of Hindu *dharma*, what is expected is governed by caste, life-stage, and context and life circumstances. "Perhaps it is this looseness of structure, this lack of emphasis on any particular set of moral obligations, that gives the Hindu moral code its resilience—a resilience that is demonstrated in that it remains a faith to live by for millions, even today" (Menon, 2003, p. 448).

Infancy and Childhood

There is acceptance of the child's individual characteristics as children are thought to be born with subconscious urges (*vasanas*) or temperament (*gunas*) as predispositions from previous lives. The rites (*see* Table 13–1) mark the gradual transition of the child as an individual into the expanding context of the collective. After the prenatal symbiotic relationship with the mother the newborn moves to a dyadic intimacy with her during early infancy. A month after birth, for the naming rite of "*namakarana*," the mother and infant emerge from a seclusion (maternal) room into the bustle of an expectant family, and the mother ceremoniously places the baby in the father's lap for a name-giving ceremony. From the family, the mother and infant move into the wider world in the third or fourth month with the performance of "*nishkramana*," the child's first outing, looking at the moon and looking at the sun. Between the sixth and ninth months, there is the important rite of "*annaprasana*," the first time the child is given solid food, initiating the process of the child's individuation or separation from the mother. This is followed by inclusion in the wider family (dyadic dissolution marked by shaving off the hair), and then into the social world of school (marked by starting of education, *vidyarambha*). Thus, the idea is that each stage goes through a cyclical process of "induct–embed–detach," which leads to the next cycle of "birth" into a new social role (first as symbiotic infant, then psychological birth as individual-but-in-social-world, then as student, then as householder, and so on.)

Socialization in infancy and childhood are characterized by indulgence and relaxed childrearing. Most parents continue to believe that it is better to let children grow at their own pace rather than rush to train them. This is witnessed often in homes where young children may fall asleep in the living room amidst adult interactions and be carried to bed rather than told "It is bed time. Go to your room." Child training comes later, after school entry. Although many factors affect employment decisions of women, conversations with educated mothers of young children who live in urban, middle-class housing societies, reveal that it is not uncommon for women to stay home (in the absence of a mother or mother-in-law as caregiver) and sacrifice their career aspirations rather than send the young children to daycare or nursery, which they believe restricts the child's freedom of expression.

Brahmacharya (Stage of Apprenticeship)

This stage starts from late childhood and extends through the period of student life (considered 8 to 18 years historically, but extended now). This stage in the life-cycle is marked by the sacred thread ceremony in males of the three upper castes of the four caste hierarchy[4]. At this stage, a person is expected to lead a strict celibate life, learn humility, and be devoted to acquisition of the knowledge necessary to lead a life useful to oneself, family, and society. "*Brahman* or consciousness is the truth of one's being. *Charya* is from "chara" to move or walk in the direction of *Brahman*. During the period of *brahmacharya*, there is high energy and it is channelized during the *gurukulavasa* or living in the teacher's house to learn the *Vedas*, *Upanishads* and other *shastras*" (Swahilya, 2009, p. 8). To concentrate on learning and avoid distractions, various austerities were prescribed in relation to food, personal comforts, and conduct (Radhakrishnan & Moore, 1957).

Although strict adherence to traditional austerities of *brahmacharya* is infrequent today, in practice, moderate expressions and expectations continue. For example, youth are expected to be celibate until attainment of educational credentials (delayed sometimes until the late twenties in the middle class). Marriage is postponed and sex outside marriage is frowned on, creating a social hiccup as the period of education keeps getting extended. Boys and girls are often sent to separate schools and/or have separate activities and seating in co-educational secondary schools. Similarly, youth are expected to postpone their indulgence in material pleasures until education is completed. Although this is changing with increasing materialism, simplicity in clothing and ornamentation is encouraged, especially during the period of apprenticeship as students.

Among *Brahmins* (highest caste), youth who are in training to become priests or *Vedic* scholars, strict adherence to the prescribed code of *brahmacharya* is still mandatory. Most school curricula include basic Indian philosophy with emphasis on tolerance and humility. Finally, respect for teachers, parents, and the elderly is a general observance even today, although not as universal as earlier. Youth today are perceived as more assertive and as challenging the views of elders, unlike their earlier cohorts. However, disagreements are rarely expressed verbally, and there is a general tolerance for the traditional views of the elderly.

Grahasthya (Stage of Family)

The order of the householder is highly lauded because "all the other *ashramas* (stages of life) depend on that of the householder, even as the living beings depend on their life for air" (Devaraja, 1994, p. 31). As Madan (1987) noted, Hinduism forbids men from renouncing worldly life (expected in the next stage) until they have discharged the traditional three debts: to the Gods, *Gurus* (teachers), and *Pitru* (ancestors). This is the stage of the life-cycle when a person marries and raises a family. This is the stage for the fulfillment of desires for *Artha* (wealth) and *Kama* (sensuous pleasures). But the primary *dharma* of the householder is to fulfill his obligations to his extended family and raise children to be good citizens. It must be noted that "Hinduism does not regard romance as the whole of married life. Husband and wife are copartners in their spiritual progress, and the family provides the training ground for the practice of unselfishness" (Nikilananda, 1998, p. 78). Even when immersed in the life of the householder, individuals are expected to develop a sense of detachment (live like water on the lotus leaf, on/in it yet separate). The householder is expected to resist becoming enslaved in bonds to such a degree that he neglects his obligation to his own self, purification, and the path of self-realization.

Contemporary norms and practices continue to reflect this traditional script. Even in nuclear families, there is emphasis on joint family functioning for major family decisions (marriage, buying property) for which the extended family is consulted. Interconnectedness in family is fostered by frequent visits and clearly prescribed roles for extended kin in weddings and other rites of passage. Despite some slackening with time, expected obligations to parents, siblings, and ancestors are fulfilled.

Marriage of the young adult is a family arrangement, and this attitude persists among the majority of youth in both urban and rural areas. The goals of marriage are security, institutionalized sex, and procreation. Duty and respect, rather than love and romance, are considered the foundation of marriage. Marriage is still considered a permanent bond, and there is social sanction only for widowers' remarriage, although exceptions are made in recent years in the case of young widows. The family system remains essentially patriarchal. Divorce is a recent phenomenon, even so, it is perhaps the lowest in the world (1.1% or 11 per 1000; www.divorcerate.org/divorce-rate-in-india.html).

Note that even in the social embeddedness and bonding necessitated by marriage and raising a family, a certain degree of detachment is expected to prevent excessive attachment that may be a deterrent for self-liberation in later stages. Fathers, in particular, are expected to remain fairly distant from their children, and open expression of affection is frowned upon. This is changing with the present generation of young fathers.

Vanaprastha (Stage of Extrication from Attachments)

The third stage (*vanaprastha*) is an antechamber to the last stage of complete renunciation (*sanyasa*). *Vanaprastha* means "forest bound," and there are a few historical accounts of kings and prosperous individuals who headed to the forest to meditate to understand the meaning of life, renouncing all worldly comforts and legacies. As a figurative expression, it involves the gradual withdrawal of the mind and from worldly material attachments to focus on the search for *atman*, the true spiritual self. It is also marked by the birth of a grandson. Individuals at this stage are expected to actively extricate themselves from all worldly activities and attachments and devote themselves to a life of contemplation. The process is not of simple disengagement, nor withdrawal from human effort and struggle, but rather the slow and painstaking development of humility and equanimity by accepting contextual influences on human goal pursuit and accomplishments and recognizing the transience of human emotional states, shifts in power, and relationships (Kakar, 1997). As Kakar explains, the middle-age crisis of renunciation versus involvement is positively resolved through the acquisition of a specific virtue—equanimity. Ideally, the Indian tradition seems to say, the contribution of middle age to human development is a sense of equanimity. This is neither a resignation from life nor a withdrawal from human effort and struggle but is that which provides a person with a wider psychological context for his actions. Equanimity implies the acceptance of the transitory nature of all relationships and emotional states. It includes awareness that human strivings are insufficient to reach desired goals unless the "surround" is also ripe for the success of these efforts (pp. 94–95)

Currently, the practice of *vanaprastha*, in principle, is evident in the thousands of senior citizens who throng to congregations where religious leaders or scholars interpret scriptures and their philosophical meanings in public forums, using epics and parables as well as contemporary life experiences to explain the laws of *karma*, *dharma*, and *moksha*. A ritualistic expression of *vanaprastha* is seen in the elderly who throng to worship at temples during early morning and late evening prayers, after domestic responsibilities have been passed on to the next generation. Temples also provide forums for explication of Hindu philosophy through scholarly analysis of the scriptures and discussions. Depending on one's intellectual orientation, the search for self-actualization may be sought through prayers (seeking Divine intervention for purifying the soul; *Bhaktiyoga*) or through the knowledge acquired from scriptures (*Gyanayoga*).

Until the recent past, upon reaching 60 years of age women would give away their ornaments to their daughters and daughters-in-law and men would transfer property to their sons, signaling the beginning of renunciation. Today, with increasing longevity and economic uncertainty, and doubts regarding whether their sons will care for them in their old age, parents do not actually transfer their jewels and property but prepare a will or let close kin know who will inherit what after their demise.

Sanyasa (Stage of Renunciation)

With the toughest of developmental tasks, the fourth stage of *Sanyasa* was a very rare attainment even in ancient times and was the prerogative of sages, ascetics, and great scholars. However, even the common man during this last stage is expected to abandon his attachment to worldly objects and focus his mind on attaining liberation from the cycle of birth and death. It is expected that prior to such renunciation one has fulfilled obligations to one's family, parents, and society and has studied the *Vedas* systematically. Death itself then becomes ". . . an encompassing cosmo-moral scheme of life" (Madan, 1987, p. 119). These notions are represented by the daily life practices of individuals (75 years and older) who withdraw from engagement in mundane household affairs, reduce food intake, consume only the amount absolutely essential for survival, reduce personal ornamentation, and end the pursuit of material wealth. Individuals at this stage spend long hours in meditation, prayers, and reading of the scriptures, even when mobility gets restricted with age and one is unable to attend discourses on scriptures by scholars in public forums. Personal self and ego are always de-emphasized. Vanity is considered a vice and usually ridiculed in people after age 60 years.

Thus far, we have described the basic Hindu worldview of development and its implications for daily life practices in the contemporary world, noting that it does not fit neatly into the individualism–collectivism continuum but rather requires a different model of individualism within collectivism. However, instead of treating it as an esoteric, obscure perspective that does not fit in the literature of developmental psychology, we now integrate the Hindu life-stages in a broader meta-theoretical framework for the study of human development offered by Overton (2006). Meta-theories are a level above theories and provide the substratum, rationale, and logic within which psychological constructs are created and integrate the methods developed to study these constructs. We suggest that at this meta-theory level we may actually find a potential way of bridging developmental and cultural psychology.

Theoretical Interpretation of *Ashramadharma*: An Alternate Conception of Human Development?

According to Overton (2006), a theory of development must address the nature of the developmental phenomena (the "what" of development) and the nature of transitions or change (the "how" of development). To address the nature of development, Overton contends that it is necessary to differentiate between two dimensions of behavior, the *expressive–constitutive* dimension of behavior (i.e., the underlying pattern or structural organization of each stage) and *instrumental–communicative dimension* (i.e., strategies and means of adapting to socio-cultural world used at each stage). To address the nature of change, Overton differentiates between *transformational change* (representing change in form, organization, or structure) and *variational change* (representing individual variations within stages).

Building upon the distinctiveness of the Hindu perspective from mainstream psychological theories and situating it within Overton's conceptual framework, we present our stance on the two questions posed in bridging developmental psychology and cultural psychology: *(1)* the one-size-fits-all question and *(2)* the structure versus content distinction as representing the focus of developmental versus cultural psychology, respectively.

In addressing the one-size-fits-all question, we contend that a universal theory of development may well be unlikely given the diversity of the human circumstances. Further, in approaches that compare cultures on dualistic linear dimensions, such as the individualism–collectivism, characterization of developmental context also seems inadequate in terms of the range of diversity that exists within and between cultural communities (Kagitcibasi, 1996). Yet, only the staunchest cultural relativist would argue for a theory for every culture. So, what is a potential solution to the debate between the universalistic ideals of developmental psychology and the cultural-specific focus of cultural psychology? We think that the answer lies in identifying a core dimension or organizing principle of human development trajectories and noting regularities in variation, as suggested by Rogoff (2003).

We propose that assumptions about the locus of developmental change in different worldviews can serve as this core dimension or organizing principle. In the models of human development typical in developmental psychology, developmental change is more often than not viewed as situated in the individual. Stage theories such as Piagetian stages of knowledge construction, Erikson's psycho-social changes, and Kohlberg's stages of moral reasoning are perhaps the best known examples. This view is often contrasted with those in which development is seen as situated in changes in the individual's relation to the social world (e.g., *see* Rogoff, 2003, for a discussion of Mayan stages of infancy and childhood). In yet another possible conception, development is viewed as situated in the individual's relation to the spiritual world— for example, Nsamenang's (1997; 2011) delineation of the stages of human development that characterizes indigenous views in West Africa. Still other potential models may be illustrated in the ethno-theories of indigenous or tribal communities, in which individual development is represented as the individual's relation to the natural world (Highwater, 1995). In terms of locus of developmental change, we extrapolate and interpret the Hindu life-stages to illustrate a model of lifespan development organized around an individual-in-social-relations focus, rather than conceptualizing lifespan development from an individual-centered focus. Menon and Shweder's (1998) analysis of life-stages, as described by *Oriya* women, is a notable illustration. They document that the phases are marked by transitions in social responsibility, family management, and moral duty, rather than by chronological age or biological markers.

Our interpretation of the Hindu developmental perspective applying Overton's (2006) criteria also addresses the second question—that is, the structure versus content distinction. Overton's discussion of the *"what"* of development, more specifically the distinction between the expressive-constitutive and the instrumental-communicative dimension has to do with the structure–function distinction. The expressive-constitutive dimension of a developmental phase/stage represents its structure, whereas the instrumental-communicative dimension represents the function (and perhaps the content) dimension. By arguing that the Hindu developmental perspective describes both the structure and function/content aspects, we take a stance against a universalistic deep structure. We assert that the contrast between "development as situated in the individual" versus "development as situated in transformations-in-individual's-relations-with-social world" is a structural contrast, not just a difference in values.

In Table 13–1, we summarize the Hindu life-stages, illustrating what develops, focusing on both the expressive-constitutive and instrumental-expressive dimensions at each developmental stage. We document the underlying organizing structure of the Hindu life-cycle in that each stage goes through a cyclical process of "induct–embed–detach" in an ever-widening social world. We argue that this organizing principle differentiates the Hindu life-cycle from more typical models in which development is viewed as situated in the individual. But that raises the next logical question: How is the Hindu conceptualization different from other discussions of "individual as situated in the social world" (e.g., Confucian models)?

We suggest that the difference lies in how the Hindu life-cycle addresses developmental transformations or the "how" question mentioned by Overton (2006). To build our argument for the Hindu stages of life as an alternative conceptual framework for development, we integrate two core underlying principles of the Hindu life-cycle to illustrate how both the *what* and *how* of development are addressed—namely, the individual as situated in the social world and the pursuit of *moksha* (which transcends social embeddedness) as the ultimate goal of life.

The "What" of Development

We propose that the expressive–constitutive dimension of the Hindu life-cycle is represented in the underlying structure or organizing principle of the Hindu stages as transformations in social relations—that is, in relations between individual and social world. The cyclical and repeating transformations (induct–embed–detach) push an individual through an ever-widening social world, with dissolution at each level leading to a birth into a higher level of synthesis with the social world, until one reaches the highest level of oneness with the universe represented in *Brahma*. For example, the child is introduced at birth to the mother, then family, then larger kinship (in some cases the village), and then through the guru to the larger peer group (*see* Table 13–1).

Table 13.1 Hindu Life-Stages: Structure and Content Dimensions

Stage Substage	Ritual marking end of period/ Transition to next	Expressive–Constitutive (Organizing principle—Central Mode of Relationship)	Instrumental–Communicative (Strategies; scripts)
Balpan Garba (Foetus)	Jatakarma (marking birth; welcome to life)	Symbiotic (dauhridya) Organizing principle: No separation between self and other.	Parents—indulge, ensure survival; Infants—express needs and have needs filled.
Ksheerda (Early infancy)	Namakarma Nishkramana Annaprasana 1–9 months (infancy)	Dyadic intimacy Dyad in family Dyad in world Organizing principle: gradual exposure and orientation to social world.	Primacy of mother–child relationship; Parents—support mother in her role; Child—to form relationship with mother or primary caretakers.
Ksheerannada	9 months to 2–3 yrs (early childhood) Chudakarana (tonsure, shaving head)	Organizing principle: self–other distinction but as embedded in dyadic social relationships; End of period: dyadic dissolution and psychological birth.	Parents—socialize child to be function in dyadic relationships Child—learning conventions of dyadic relationships
Bala	2/3 to 5/7 years (middle childhood) Vidyaramba (begin formal education)	Familial relationships are developed Organizing principle: Consolidation of familial relationships; End of period: dissolution of family relationships while transitioning to extrafamilial social world.	Parents—socialize into roles and obligations of dyadic relationships first in nuclear family, then extended, and finally in world; Children—learn to contextualize relationships and roles; be obedient, respectful, conforming.
Kumara	5–7 to 8–12 years (late childhood) Upanayana	Dissolution of familial relationships and social birth marked by Upanayana ceremony. Organizing principle: enter adult world as novitiate or inductee.	Parents—socialize to function in extra familial settings, especially formal settings; Children—learn social conventions; social responsibility; practice of religious rituals; acquire self-discipline.

(continued)

Table 13.1 Hindu Life-Stages: Structure and Content Dimensions (continued)

Stage Substage	Ritual marking end of period/ Transition to next	Expressive–Constitutive (Organizing principle—Central Mode of Relationship)	Instrumental–Communicative (Strategies; scripts)
Brahmacharya	12 years through adulthood	Organizing principle: induction into adult world, through focus on student–teacher relationships for learning. Along with skill development (usually vocational) there is considerable emphasis on overall human development—that is, on qualities or human virtues like discipline, concentration, attention, introspection, and willpower or self-control.	Emphasis on skill development: "Dhurandhar vidvaan" For example, response to hunger is trained by practicing delayed gratification through "vrattas" (fasts); Motivational appetite and self-discipline is trained by practicing celibacy and dharma or dutiful living, whether or not it felt good.
Grahasthya	Young adulthood to middle adulthood (marked by marriage)	Organizing principle: embedded in social world with responsibility for others; focus on householder responsibilities. The individual, prepared through the Brahmacharya phase, is given social sanction to enjoy all worldly pleasures of wealth, sexuality, attachment, and savor them as a connoisseur, but with a focus on the value of controlled and measured reactions to these impulses.	Principles of Dharma and Karma govern life decisions: prayer, sermon, meditation, reflective practice is used to manage desires for worldly pleasures, not by repressing or denying them but by learning to recognize these cognitions in one's psyche with meditational and reflective practice and controlling their response to them by self-adjustment, self-discipline, and regulation.

Vanaprastha	Mid-adulthood to old age	Disengage from social relationships, personal wealth directed toward caretaking at large;	Preparation for Moksha
	Stage viewed as an idealized pathway to achieve nirvana during the next stage: sanyasa	Organizing principle: dissolution of and detachment from individual relationships while becoming embedded in society at large.	The onus of truly renouncing one's egoistical strivings and engaging in generative/altruistic action for public good.
		To allow oneself to be treated as just another life form devoid of family name, fame, fortune and even basic pleasures of life was the goal of this stage, either by retiring to a forest or becoming a "bhikshuk" living on scraps donated by others.	Strategies are of self-control and spiritual development aiming toward higher spiritual and self-understanding, lowering of egoistical impulses, understanding temporality of life, and actively disengaging from worldly and bodily pleasures.
Sanyasa	Old age	Renounce all social and material relationships.	Focus on Moksha; become "nirlipta" (no bonds); merge self with cosmic energy "so-hum" (Samadhi).
		Organizing principle: dissolution of all relationships to transcend worldly relationships and become part of universe.	Transcend bodily self—asceticism. Hence, late life physical declines have less negative psychological impact.
		Aspire for salvation, having given up worldly strivings and realizing one's essence as the manifestation of the same power that governs the universe.	

Note: Descriptions of Hindu stages (columns 1 and 2 of table) taken from Kakar (1981) and Saraswathi and Ganpathy (2002) are integrated with Overton's (2006) meta-theoretical component constructs (columns 3 and 4) by Jayanthi Mistry.

Further, we suggest that the instrumental-communicative dimension and means of adapting to the socio-cultural world derive from the ideal or end-point of development. As stated earlier, in the Hindu developmental perspective, what develops is the spiritual self (*atman*), which is conceptualized differently than the embodied self. The developmental teleological goal is liberation of this spiritual self at a higher level, through self-purification, to finally merge with the *Brahman* (*moksha*). However, the significance attached to need fulfillment at each stage suggests a simultaneous attention to changes in the development of the embodied self. The developmental trajectory, therefore, is one of increasing self-control through self-discipline and purification to identify with the spiritual self rather than take pride in the fallible temporal embodied self. Throughout the stages of development, the *samskaras* (rites and rituals) marking maturation and moral growth or refinement (Madan, 1987) emphasize instrumental strategies and means of adaptation that promote self-discipline aimed at self-realization in terms of the spiritual self, going beyond merely the body. Because the body nurtures the spirit and is instrumental in performing righteous deeds, the first half of the lifespan is devoted to the development of control over body and mind, and the latter half of lifespan focuses more on mental control of desires, ego, and emotion (*see* Table 13–1, for examples of instrumental strategies at each stage). Thus, the development of reflective meta-cognition and wisdom is of prime importance to Hindu psychological ideals. We may view the *ashramadharmas* as fostering self-discipline and control by providing instrumental scripts for action from late childhood onward to support transformations in structure of relations between the individual and social world. The instrumental scripts and strategies foster setting personal goals in accordance with social norms and expectations and may facilitate use of available resources and support. Through social sanctions, as well as approval and disapproval by society, social expectations serve as an orientation or standard for development, selection, pursuit, maintenance, and disengagement of personal goals.

To summarize, we argue that the dual characterization of self as spiritual and embodied self with emphasis on purification, perfection, and transcendence from repetitive life-cycles to unite with the cosmos reflects an alternative to the dichotomy between the individual and social world. It reflects a conception of "individual-in-social-world," while also representing a dialectic fusion or synthesis of individualism and collectivism. This intersection of the individual as socially situated and yet as following a path of individual self-realization represents a fusion that is perhaps best represented as "individualism-in-collectivism" (implying inseparability of individualistic and collectivistic ideals). This synthesis is apparent in the voices of women in the study by Menon and Shweder (1998), wherein the women who might appear docile, submissive, and subject to many restrictions in fact display their culturally constructed sense of agency, power, and belief that their *karma* is in their hands.

Further, this characterization also represents a synthesis of structure and content in that the Hindu life-stages represent both dimensions of what develops (the structural organization of the stages, as well as the content dimension).

But the question remains: In what way is the synthesis of "individualism-in-collectivism" different from other models of development that focus on the individual as situated in the social world? As stated earlier, we suggest that the difference lies in the Hindu conception of developmental transformations—that is, the "how" of development.

The "How" of Development or Nature of Change

Once again we use Overton's framework to review Hindu concepts of how change occurs. Hindu constructs of change include both transformational (from one stage of life to another) as well as variational changes (individual differences in paths taken as well as the degree of progress made). As Overton suggests, from an inclusive relational meta-theoretical position, we argue that Hindu constructs offer a conceptualization of both transformational change (i.e., that drive and structure progress through the stages of life), as well as those changes that reflect individual variations in specific strategies and pathways taken.

Transformational change explains changes in the organizing principles of stages. In other words, these are changes that everyone goes through. Tied synchronously with these changes are Hindu childhood rights and ceremonial rituals shaping the child's world and initiating the child into progressively larger social circles from the symbiotic mother–infant dyad to a full-fledged member in the community. A"*samskara* refers to the forming well or thoroughly, with *sanskriti* (culture) as opposed to *prakriti* (nature). It points to the process of maturation, of moral perfectibility." (Madan, 1987, p. 99). The *samskaras* ceremoniously mark the transition points of a widening world of childhood and place the child at the center of rites that also command the intense participation of the whole family. As such, these *samskaras* heighten a sense of both belonging and personal distinctiveness—that is, they strengthen the child's budding sense of identity while embedding this budding identity in an ever-widening cycle of social inclusiveness (Kakar, 1996). The relational value of the stages following the stage of childhood is summarized succinctly by Ramanujan (1990). "If *brahmacharya* (celibate studentship) is preparation for a full relational life, *grhasthashrama* (householder stage) is a full realization of it . . . *vanaprastha* (the retiring forest dweller) loosens the bonds, and *sanyasa* (renunciation) cremates all one's past and present relations!"(p. 54).

In contrast to transformational change in a stage-like fashion that is applicable to all individuals, variational change explains individual differences in progress through the stages of development. Core constructs of the Hindu developmental perspective provide for a simultaneous focus on both transformational and variational change. The discontinuous transformational changes apply to the embodied self, and continuous variational changes apply to the individualistic spiritual self, both actualized via different paths and at different rates of progress.

In the lifelong pursuit of *moksha*, each stage of life involves progressively deeper understanding of one's nature, greater humility, and a higher level of volitional control over one's physical and mental (impulsive) self. People are encouraged to expand their capacity in executive function (ability to think, plan, reflect) to develop meta-cognition and control impulses of sexuality (*kama*), aggression (*krodha*), greed (*lobha*), and attachment (*moha*) to objects and people. These psychological strivings are thought to make people act in reactive ways for self-serving purposes. There being no end to material desires, people are advised to recognize the insatiability of material wants of the embodied self and instead identify with the spiritual self. The practice of reflection is encouraged because it can increase alertness to early signs of these cognitions, giving people the ability to control their responses to them by self-adjustment and regulation. A person in a higher state of spiritual self-control is considered wise, demonstrates equanimity, and is not easily reactive in anger or excitement but demonstrates focused intentional action and arousal.

With an inherent belief in the plasticity and malleability in human development at all stages, Hindus accept individual variation. From birth, individuals are believed to be positioned differently in their personal goal to achieve *moksha*. Their actions during life modify their advancement on this goal. Furthermore, refinement can be obtained flexibly via many paths, depending on intellect and inclination such as *karmayoga* (selfless service, as represented by Mother Theresa), *bhaktiyoga*, (complete devotion to God through prayer and meditation), and *gyanayoga* (pursuit of knowledge/enlightenment). Furthermore, the pathways noted above allow the person the flexibility to pursue the goal of *moksha* with different degrees of immersion in the collective social structure (e.g., in *bhaktiyoga* a person may renounce or walk away from worldly roles and responsibilities in pursuit of the higher pursuit of *moksha* prior to getting into *grahasthya*). Thus some individuals may not go through the stages of becoming a householder but directly progress via *bhaktiyoga* to leading the life of a saint.

Besides pursuing *moksha*, other worldly goals of the embodied selves in Hinduism depend on age, gender, caste, and chosen life paths. Attainment of these goals is achieved by actions conducted dutifully according to the moral code without awaiting reward or fearing social consequences. These Hindu notions of development represent variational change through the mechanism of "embodied action" (somewhat akin to action theory; Eckensberger, 2003). Actions involve intentional behavior toward meaningful goals and motivational processes and are accomplished via steps of planning, prioritizing, and managing oneself through accomplishment or failure of achieving outcomes.

Thus far we have focused on our response to the first two questions posed by our editor and outlined the Hindu developmental view to suggest that it is not adequately represented by current developmental theories nor does it fit into dichotomous East–West distinctions. It has its own unique teleological goal of development, distinctive structural stages and developmental tasks, and dialectic processes to accomplish these tasks, which are sufficiently distinct to warrant a third view of development. In addition, we have proposed that an examination of the locus of developmental change in different worldviews may serve as an organizing principle for theories, thus limiting the proliferation of a theory for every culture. We now turn our attention briefly to the third question—namely, what is the relevance of the Hindu worldview in the current context of increased interface between cultures?

Implications of Hindu Life Conceptions in the Global Context

In our interdependent and interconnected world, it is imperative that people become better versed with the worldview of one another. We suggest that understanding Hindu psychology and developmental perspective can certainly contribute in this regard, although it might also raise questions about the relevance of the idealized notions presented above to everyday life of Hindus and their Diasporas around the world. We do not claim that the above description fits all Hindus any more than an individualistic model fits all European Americans. As with other nations, India is undergoing rapid socio-economic change. The one unambiguous agreement among all visitors to India is its incredible diversity and coexistence of stark contrasts. We contend that the belief system we have described and analyzed cuts across region, caste, and class variations and provides a common unifying force for a very large proportion of Indians amidst all the diversity. The degree of orthodoxy of practice may well vary, but beliefs in the basic tenets (such as *karma*, *dharma*, and *moksha*) as well as the rites and rituals of stages of life continue to maintain a stronghold regardless of income, education, and residence (Bharati, 1985; Menon, 2003; Radhakrishnan & Moore, 1957; Sen, 2005). Witnessing any significant life event, such as a birth, marriage ceremony, 80th birthday, or a cremation, reveals the common shared culture of the people. Interestingly, as can be expected with a diverse society, an underlying worldview appears to pervade the psyche of non-Hindu Indians as well because of its popularization via media and practice.

This mosaic of a multicultural, gigantic society in transition offers a fertile ground for the study of dynamics between individual-level and societal-level changes. But, the contribution of the Hindu worldview can be more penetrating and pervasive if we broaden our scientific mindset to address the dialectical questions outlined in preceding sections showing the uniqueness of Indian constructs. For example, we know that cultural psychology and developmental psychology are inextricably intertwined and that people develop within the context of cultures, which are also evolving over time (Keller & Greenfield, 2000). But answers to the core question of how individuals absorb, transmit, perpetrate, and, at the same time, change cultures with their individual interpretations of it seem to elude us. These sorts of questions involve dialectical change, synthesis, and integration from which we shy away because we struggle to address them with our current theoretical and methodological tools. Instead of shying away from these dynamics of change, synthesis, and integration that characterize much of developmental psychology, we need to bring them back into focus and take bolder measures to look for answers. We claim that a balanced approach would be beneficial for psychology (*see* Hermans, 2001; Hermans & Kempen, 1998) but have limited ourselves to lip-service for over a half-century while remaining entrenched in polarizing dichotomies and debates of nature–nurture, continuous–discontinuous progression of development, active–passive view of the developing person, or, more recently, individualism–collectivism (*see* Saraswathi, 2005, on dichotomies in the study of self) as well as primary–secondary control and coping. Overton (2006) includes such reductionist theories that frame concepts as polar opposites or antinomies within one meta-theoretical perspective, which he terms, *split metatheory*.

Contrary to thinking of concepts in polarities, the Hindu developmental view challenges us to think of concepts in dialectic and contextual terms. Using the example of the "individualism–collectivism" polarity, we call for a third view to integrate the Hindu perspective because it cannot be forced to fit within such a continuum. Similar arguments can be made for many other constructs outlined in the Hindu worldview. For example, much debate has ensued related to the optimization of primary and secondary control model (OPS model; Heckhausen & Schulz, 1995; Schulz & Heckhausen, 1999) as to whether secondary control is in fact secondary (Gould, 1999) or, for that matter, if it is even control (Morling, 2006, 2007; Skinner, 2007). According to the Hindu perspective, these are not linear opposites and using one does not preclude the use of the other. In fact, acceptance (secondary control) may be what leads to changing the environment to bring it in better synchrony with oneself—that is, adapting to it. But, as Morling and Evered (2006) stated, "Western people may not wish to acknowledge that they simultaneously consider changing the environment and adapting to it, because this would acknowledge a self-contradiction that Westerners are acculturated to avoid" (p. 293).

Scientific training and articulation of psychological constructs in polar terms—especially where one pole has an advantaged position versus the other—is a formidable barrier to an inclusive developmental psychology and to efforts at integrating cultural and developmental psychology. To the extent that the Hindu psychological perspective has a high tolerance for co-existing contradictions, juxtaposed dualities, and holistic syntheses (Sinha & Tripathi, 1994), we see a consonance between the Hindu perspective and Overton's relational metatheory that involves the synthesis of opposites. In our view, developmental psychology needs to grow further in a direction that is more encompassing of complex human-environment dialectics to build bridges with cultural psychology.

Furthermore, we think such theoretical advancements will be ineffective without associated advancements in how constructs are measured, because meta-theories are closely tied to meta-methods (Overton 2006). The physical science model of an objective psychology has shut the doors to self-observation methods such as those employed in contemplative meditation in the Hindu worldview, which may, in fact, be quite fruitful in the study of adult development in particular. The recent explosion of research in mindfullness-based-stress-reduction methods in biopsychology and health sciences reveals the fertility of such methods of inquiry. When done routinely, yoga postures and breathing exercises (*pranayama*) have been found to cure and prevent physical ailments as well as mental states (stress, anxiety, depression) and offer a gold mine for further developmental psychological inquiry. Deliberate and mindful reactions to stimuli (such as those involved in acceptance, compassion, forgiveness, hope) can actually increase a sense of control and are related directly and indirectly to physiology and mental well-being (Nyklíček and Kuijpers, 2008). In our achievement-oriented stressful lifestyles, practices that nurture the spiritual self and help us regulate ourselves hold the promise of abundant balanced living. The Hindu developmental worldview was developed as a practically oriented path to afford balanced living and mental health (equanimity). Developmental science may also find it a fruitful model on how to seam the chasm between theory and practice in the art of living.

Acknowledgments

Our grateful thanks to Richard Shweder, Jaan Valsiner, Fred Rothbaum, R. C. Tripathi, Girishwar Misra, Nandita Chaudhry, & Lila Krishnan for their constructive feedback on this chapter. We incorporated as many suggestions as we could, although, perhaps, gaps still remain, and the best can always be bettered.

Notes

1. For those interested in learning more about the Hindu philosophical influence on psychology more generally we recommend other sources such as Paranjpe (1998), Chakkrath (2005), Laungauni (2007) and Rao, Paranjpe, & Dalal (2008).

2. Development of upper castes and males was anchored to these idealized life-stages as benchmarks. Our discussion reflects the focus on life-stages as applicable to males. For a more specific focus on women, *see* Menon and Shweder (1998).

3. The chapter reflects one way of approaching Hindu life-stages that we think helps bridge Hindu cultural psychology with meta-relational perspectives in developmental science. Other authors have approached life-stages in somewhat different ways (Chakkrath, 2005; Menon & Shweder, 1998) and have enumerated other core values of the Hindu worldview that extend the contribution of Indian psychology (Laungani, 2007).

4. The Hindu life-stages described here are an idealized view applicable to the three upper castes (among the fourfold division of castes) and to males in particular. However, the core concepts of *Dharma*, *Karma*, and *Moksha* color the worldview of a vast majority of Hindus, including those of the lower castes as well among those converted to other religions, with the exception of Islam.

References

Arnett, J. J. (2011). Emerging adulthood(s): The cultural psychology of a new life stage. In L. A. Jensen (Ed.), *Bridging cultural and developmental psychology: New syntheses in theory, research and policy* (pp. 255–275). New York: Oxford University Press.

Bharati, A. (1985). The self in Hindu thought and action. In A. J. Marcella, G. DeVos, & F. L. K. Hsu (Eds.), *Culture and self: Asian and Western perspectives* (pp. 185–230). New York: Tavistock.

Chakkarath, P. (2005). What can Western psychology learn from indigenous psychologies? Lessons from Hindu psychology. In W. Friedlmeier, P. Chakkarath, & B. Schwarz (Eds.), *Culture and Human Development* (pp. 31–51). New York: Psychology Press.

Devaraja, N. K. (1994). *Hinduism and the modern age.* New Delhi, India: Har-Anand Publications.

Eckensberger, L. H. (1996). Agency, action and culture: Three basic concepts for psychology in general and for cross-cultural psychology in specific. In J. Pandey, D. Sinha, & D. P. S. Bhawuk (Eds.), *Asian contributions to cross-cultural psychology* (pp. 75–102). London: Sage.

Erikson, E. H. (1979). Report to Vikram: Further perspectives on the life cycle. In S. Kakar (Ed.), *Identity and adulthood* (pp. 13–34). Delhi, India: Oxford University Press.

Heckhausen, J., & Schulz, R. (1995). A life-span theory of control. *Psychological Review, 102*: 284–304.

Hermans, H. J. M. (2001). The dialogical self: Towards a theory of personal and cultural positioning. *Culture and Psychology, 7*: 243–281.

Hermans, H. J. M. & Kempen, H. J. G. (1998). Moving cultures: A perilous problem cultural dichotomies in global society. *American Psychologist, 53*(10): 1111–1120.

Highwater, J. (1995). The intellectual savage. In N. R. Goldberger and J. B. Veroff (Eds.), *Culture and Psychology* (pp. 205–215). New York: New York University Press.

Jayaram, V. (2009). Ashram dharma—Stages in human life. Available from http://www.hinduwebsite.com/hinduism/h_ashramas.asp. Accessed May 8, 2009.

Jensen, L. A. (2011). The cultural-developmental theory of moral psychology: A new synthesis. In L. A. Jensen (Ed.), *Bridging developmental approaches to psychology: New syntheses in theory, research, and policy* (pp. 3–25). New York: Oxford University Press.

Kagitcibasi, C. (1996). The autonomous—relational self: A new synthesis. *European Psychologist, 1*: 180–186.

Kagitcibasi, C. (1997). Individualism and collectivism. In J. W. Berry, M. H. Segall, & C. Kagitcibasi (Eds.), *Handbook of cross-cultural psychology. Vol. 3: Social behavior and applications* (2nd ed., pp. 1–49). Boston, MA: Allyn & Bacon.

Kakar, S. (1981). (2nd ed) *The inner world. A psychoanalytic study of childhood in India (Second Edition).* New Delhi, India: Oxford University Press.

Kakar, S. (1996). *The Indian psyche.* New Delhi, India: Oxford University Press.

Kakar, S. (1997). *Culture and psyche.* New Delhi, India: Oxford University Press.

Keller, H. & Greenfield, P. M. (2000). History and future of development in cross-cultural psychology. [Millennium Special Issue]. *Journal of Cross Cultural Psychology, 31*: 52–62.

Laungani, P. D. (2007). *Understanding cross-cultural psychology.* London: Sage.

Madan, T. N. (1987). *Non-renunciation: Themes and interpretations of Hindu culture.* New Delhi, India: Oxford University Press.

Markus, H. R., & Kitayama, S. (1991). Culture and the self: Implications for cognition, emotion, and motivation. *Psychological Review, 98*: 224–253.

Menon, U. (2003). Morality and context: A study of Hindu understandings. In J. Valsiner & K. Connoly (Eds.), *Handbook of developmental psychology* (pp. 431–449). London: Sage.

Menon, U., & Shweder, R. (1998). The return of the "White Man's Burden": The moral discourse of anthropology and the domestic life of Hindu women. In R. Shweder (Ed.). *Welcome to Middle Age! (and other cultural fictions).* (pp. 139–188). Chicago, IL: University of Chicago Press.

Morling, B., & Evered, S. (2006). Secondary control reviewed and defined. *Psychological Bulletin, 132*: 269–296.

Nadkarni, M. V. (2003). *Hinduism: A Gandhian Perspective.* New Delhi, India: Anne Books India.

Nikhilananda, Swami. (1998). *Hinduism: Its meaning for the liberation of the spirit.* Madras: Sri Ramakrishna Math.

Nityananda, Swami. (2000). *Hinduism: That is Sanatana dharma.* Mumbai: Central Chinmaya Mission Trust.

Nsamenang, A. B. (1997). Towards an Afrocentric perspective in developmental psychology. *Ife Psychologica: An International Journal, 5*(1): 27–139.

Nsamenang, A. B. (2011). The culturalization of developmental trajectories: A perspective on african childhoods and adolescences. In L. A. Jensen (Ed.), *Bridging cultural and developmental psychology: New syntheses in theory, research and policy* (pp. 235–254). New York: Oxford University Press.

Nyklíček, I., & Kuijpers, K. F. (2008). Effects of Mindfulness-Based Stress Reduction Intervention on Psychological Well-being and Quality of Life: Is Increased Mindfulness Indeed the Mechanism? *Annals of Behavioral Medicine, 35*: 331–340.

Overton, W. F. (2006). Developmental psychology: Philosophy, concepts, methodology. In R. M. Lerner (Vol. Ed.) & W. Damon & R. M. Lerner (Eds.), *Handbook of child psychology: Vol. 1. Theoretical models of human development* (6th ed., pp. 18–88). Hoboken, NJ: John Wiley.

Pandey, R. (1969). *Hindu Samskaras. Socio-religious study of the Hindu sacraments.* Delhi, India: Motilal Banarasidas.

Paranjpe, A. C. (1998). *Self and identity in modern psychology and Indian thought.* New York: Plenum Press.

Phinney, J. S., & Baldelomar, O. A. (2011). Identity development in multiple cultural contexts. In L. A. Jensen (Ed.), *Bridging cultural and developmental psychology: New syntheses in theory, research and policy* (pp. 161–186). New York: Oxford University Press.

Radhakrishnan, S., & Moore, C. A. (1957). (Eds.). *A sourcebook in Indian philosophy.* Princeton, NJ: Princeton University Press.

Ramanujan, A. K. (1990). Is there an Indian way of thinking? An informal essay. In M. Marriott (Ed.), *India through Hindu categories* (pp. 41–58). New Delhi, India: Sage.

Rao, K. R., Paranjpe, A., & Dalal, A. K. (Eds.) *Handbook of Indian Psychology.* New Delhi, India: Cambridge University Press.

Rogoff, B. (2003). *The cultural nature of human development.* New York: Oxford University Press.

Schulz, R., & Heckhausen, J. (1999). Aging, culture, and control: Setting a new research agenda. *Journal of Gerontology: Psychological Sciences, 54B*: P139–P145.

Saraswathi, T. S. (2005) Hindu world view in the development of self ways: The "*Atman*" as the real self. In L. A. Jensen & R. W. Larson (Eds.) *New Horizons in Developmental Theory and Research/New Directions for Child and Adolescent Development, 109*: 43–50.

Saraswathi, T. S., & Ganapathy, H. (2002). Indian parents' ethnotheories as reflections of the Hindu scheme of child and human development. In H. Keller, Y. H. Poortinga, &

A. Scholmerich (Eds.), *Between culture and biology: Perspectives on ontogenetic development* (pp. 79–88). New York: Cambridge University Press.

Sen, A. (2005). *The argumentative Indian: Writings on Indian history, culture and Identity*. London: Allen Lane (Penguin Books).

Sinha, D. & Tripathi, R. C. (1994). Individualism in a collectivist culture: A case of coexistence of opposites. In U. Kim, H. C. Triandis, C. Kagitcibasi, S-C Choi, and G. Yoon, et al (Eds.) *Individualism and collectivism: Theory, method, and applications* (pp. 123–136). Cross-cultural Research Methodology Series, Vol 16, Thousand Oaks, CA: Sage.

Skinner, E. A. (2007). Secondary control critiqued: Is it secondary? Is it control? Comment on Morling and Evered (2006). *Psychological Bulletin, 133*: 911–916.

Swahilya, (2009, May 10) Indian Express, The New Sunday Express, Mind and Body, I-witness, p. 8.

Thapar, R. (1966). *A history of India.* Middlesex, England: Penguin Books.

COMMENTARY

CHAPTER 14

Commentary: Ontogenetic Cultural Psychology

RICHARD A. SHWEDER

In this brief commentary I hope to convince the reader of two points. First, this fine collection of essays aimed at synthesizing developmental and cultural psychology would be entirely unconvincing to Jean Piaget, if he were alive today. Yet this book ought to be of great interest to those who investigate the way ontogenetic changes in the mental life of individuals vary by virtue of growing up as a member of a particular group. The collection is a clarion call for the rebirth of an ontogenetic perspective on cultural psychology. Second, Jean Piaget is arguably right that it is not possible to be a developmental psychologist and a cultural psychologist at the same time, but that's no reason for despair because the developmental perspective as understood by Piaget is not the only way to understand ontogenetic change. Allow me to explain.[1]

Is It Possible to Be a Developmental Psychologist and a Cultural Psychologist at the Same Time?

By a developmental psychologist, I mean what Piaget would have meant by the designation—namely, a researcher who investigates those ontogenetic changes in the mental life of individuals that can be attributed to developmental processes *per se*. By a cultural psychologist, I mean a researcher who investigates those aspects of the mental life of individuals that are acquired (or selected for) by virtue of thick participation (typically beginning at birth) in the traditions and folkways of a particular ethical and interpretive community

303

or cultural group. So, is it possible to do developmental psychology and do cultural psychology at the same time? Piaget, as I understand the implications of his concept of development, thought the answer was "no;" and he had some good reasons for thinking so. And I, myself, speaking as an anthropologist and cultural psychologist, do not necessarily disagree with him. I certainly don't think the answer to the question is obviously "yes."

Nor do I think that the conceptual boundary or academic divide that distinguishes the study of developmental processes from the study of processes of cultural acquisition needs to be bridged, erased, or transcended for the sake of promoting interdisciplinary cooperation between psychologists interested in studying ontogenetic change and anthropologists interested in studying the mental life of "the native." Indeed, the essays in this volume attest to the fact that psychologists who study ontogenetic changes in the mental life of individuals are not necessarily studying ontogenetic change as a developmental process *per se*. Many of those psychologists would identify themselves as developmental psychologists but they are studying something else. That something else is the ontogeny of a cultural psychology. It is not only well-worth studying but is fundamental to the mental life of all human beings. Their research contributions auger well for the future of collaborative research in cultural psychology, but it is a noteworthy and significant retreat from the concept of development as understood by Piaget.

Piaget himself never retreated from the concept of development. Over time, he just restricted his research to those aspects of the mental life where he thought ontogenetic change was truly developmental. Over time, the aspects of the mental studied by Piaget became more and more remote from the aspects of the mental life studied by cultural psychologists. By the end of his career, Piaget's interest in "culture" or "society" was primarily as an enabler or inhibitor of progressive change in those areas of the mental life that were truly developmental. He cared about changes in the child's understanding of reversibility, transitivity, and logically necessary truths. He had no interest in changes in a child's conception of the stages of life, of who counts as an avoidance versus joking kinsmen, or the importance of taking a purifying ceremonial bath before entering the family prayer room, or of changes in children's attitudes to shyness in their peers, all of which he would have viewed as non-developmental changes in the mental life of the child.

What is a developmental process *per se*? What does it mean to investigate ontogenetic change in the mental life of individuals as a developmental change? As articulated by Piaget (and by other famous developmental psychologists influenced by Piaget), the very idea of a developmental process *per se* (as applied, for example, to the development of the mental life of individuals) presupposes two conditions: *(a)* the existence of some objectively desirable or ideal state of mental functioning that is understood to be a directional goal or end-state for ontogenetic changes in mental functioning (i.e., the mental end-state is not immediately or readily online at birth) and *(b)* movement in the direction of the desirable end-state must be achieved or cultivated by means of processes related to the capacity of human beings to become self-governing rational agents who are motivated to do things and believe things for good reasons and to feel justified in what they want, feel, value, know, and think. The second condition (condition "b") is what Piaget meant by self-construction.

In linking mental development to processes associated with rational self-governance (i.e., with autonomous self-construction increasingly and ultimately guided by the dictates of reason), Piaget had in mind such processes as self-reflection on ones own beliefs, the need and ability to make some kind of sense of ones picture of the world, attempts to assimilate new experiences to already-in-place interpretive frameworks, attempts to accommodate or revise already-in-place interpretive frameworks in the light of new experiences, and attempts to reason logically and eliminate inconsistencies from one's thinking. In other words, Piaget believed that the route to mental development was a temporal process (it took time to develop into a rational thinker), a progressive directional process (over time, more universally justifiable understandings superseded less justifiable understandings), and also a so-called "active process." "Active" here means that according to Piaget's idea of a developmental process *per se*, over time, more developed understandings supersede less developed understandings because individuals are self-reflective agents who try to work out and see for themselves the rational justification for their own understandings.

It was in the light of that conception of development that Piaget did not think it was possible to be a developmental psychologist and a cultural psychologist at the same time. Thus, in his research in developmental psychology, Piaget adopts the premise common to all "structural approaches"—namely, that human beings would all think the same way (reason the same way, remember the same way, make moral judgments the same way) if it weren't for differences in the content of their thought or in the social environmental contexts that either facilitate or retard the flowering of fully developed mental structures in the individual members of some group. In other words, Piaget understood the very idea of development (and its two essential conditions outlined above) to entail much more than just change over time. For Piaget, development essentially implies some rationally desirable state of mental functioning, the ultimate attainment of which is a mark of progress.

Given that focus on developmental processes *per se*, Piaget's interest in the varieties of human mentalities across cultural groups was narrow and specialized. The only point in investigating variations in mental life across cultural groups was to document the extent to which children in some societies were able to flower more than others in their mental development, and perhaps to identify the social conditions that either facilitated or retarded rational self-governance and developmental advance. In this regard, the concept of development as used by Piaget parallels the concept of development used by the grand theorists of the French Enlightenment (Voltaire, Diderot, Condorcet, and others) who imagined that there is only one ideal universal civilization, in comparison to which, over historical time, most nations fall permanently short of the ideal, whereas others become more and more civilized. In many ways, Piaget was the Condorcet of 20th-century psychology.

Not all the significant aspects of the mental life of individuals are developmental in the sense just described—for several reasons. These days many of us argue that what you think about can be decisive for how you think. Piaget, we are inclined to say, misjudged the role and importance of "mere content" and domain-specific knowledge in reasoning, judgment, and memory. Although I believe it to be true that what you think about is decisive for how you think (*see* the essay by Michelle Leichtman, Chapter 3, where this is her major conclusion) I doubt that Piaget would have disagreed. I don't think he would have denied that the mental life of both children and adults is replete with nondevelopmental thoughts, values, and ideas, but he would have associated those aspects of the mental life with "heteronomy" and viewed them as a kind of oversocialized, indoctrinated or affect-driven mental enslavement to a cultural tradition. As I understand Piaget's agenda, he was merely trying to focus research in developmental psychology on those aspects of mental life that could defensibly be examined as products of development processes *per se*, which by definition meant getting beyond local content.

Piaget's Escape from Cultural Psychology

Arguably, Piaget himself came to realize in the course of his career that his early research on Swiss children's understandings of (for example) dreams, animism, punishment, or justice might well have been about content-rich processes of cultural acquisition rather than about developmental processes *per se*. Not surprisingly, it is that early work by Piaget—*The Child's Conception of the World* (first published in 1929) or *The Moral Judgment of the Child* (first published in 1932)—that seems most congenial to cultural psychologists.

I suspect this is one reason that over time, Piaget moved away from research on nondevelopmental domains of human understanding and took up instead research focused on children's understandings of what he took to be the synthetic *a priori* (and hence universal, objective) domains identified by Immanuel Kant—namely, number, object, cause, space, time, logical necessity. In the process of rationally self-constructing his own theory of mental life, he found a way to hold onto the view that what deserves to be called a true developmental process of ontogenetic change can be characterized in terms of strictly objective ideals and standards, free of the collectively produced historically particular subjective judgments of this or that cultural group. He believed that it is precisely because the desirable mental states in those "Kantian domains" will be appealing to all rational self-governing individuals that they will be the same end-states across cultures and history.

In other words, Piaget's strategy for staying the course with his developmental agenda was to radically narrow the types of domains of knowledge (logical and experimental reasoning: yes; dream understandings and ideas about what is good: no) to which his type of developmental analysis might legitimately be applied. Looking back on his own early research informed by his subsequently constructed "structural" theory, I suspect Piaget must have viewed his own early investigations of children's ideas about dreams, word meanings, and immanent justice as somewhat misguided studies of mere content. Mere content, he might have reasoned, is not proper grist for developmental analysis. Studying the content of thought, he might have judged, is something for the cultural psychologists to do, as I myself (Jean Piaget) unwittingly did early in my career.

Of course, these days the range of application for the concept of development in the study of human mental life is at risk of being narrowed even further than Piaget would have liked. And it is not hard to understand why. In 1966, when I entered graduate school, psychology in America had long since lost its institutional connection to philosophy. So when discussing Piaget's research, no one bothered to point out to us that the core ideas ultimately examined by Piaget (number, object, cause, space, time) were the same ideas identified by Immanuel Kant as synthetic *a priori* truths. No one bothered to point out that the mastery of those ideas is a necessary precondition for empiricism, for without some *a priori* idea of number, object, cause, space, and time, the very notion of "having an experience" (the supposed source of all learning and knowledge for empiricists) makes no rational sense. Perhaps that is why no one (with the exception of, perhaps, Noam Chomsky) bothered to boggle our minds and disrupt Piaget's developmental story by asking how it is possible for a young infant to experience anything at all (including Piaget's experimental manipulations) if he or she does not already have at hand (or in its mouth or in its head) the ideas that Piaget says are not available until 18 months or 6 years of age or what have you?

I doubt we have become more philosophically sophisticated in the last 40 or 50 years. Nevertheless, for whatever reason, many are inclined to say these days that when it comes to the Kantian domains studied by Piaget (the abstract idea of an object or of number or of causation), the mental life of the child is differentiated and complex from the start and that Kant's synthetic *a priori* truths (object permanence, number, time, space, causality) are hard-wired as innate ideas. As any evolutionary psychologist will aver, the newly born already seem to know a lot from the deep past. The research literature is full of demonstrations that Piaget underestimated the intellectual sophistication and inferential capacity of infants and young children. From a structural point of view, it would appear that we come into the world old and mentally sophisticated rather than young and innocent. So even in the Kantian domains, the concept of development *per se* may not readily apply.

The relevant bottom-line message for this commentary is that it is hard to bridge the divide between developmental psychology and cultural psychology because from a conceptual or definitional point of view, there may be an ineradicable distinction between developmental processes *per se* and the processes associated with cultural acquisition. A developmental psychologist, one who honors the definition of a developmental process offered above, is honor-bound to argue like this: To the very extent that a desired mental end-state does not have a rational appeal to all self-governing agents, it does not count as a standard for development *per se*; hence, the process influencing ontogenetic change in that area of mental functioning does not count as a developmental process, at least not according the concept of development *per se* promoted by Piaget.

Plural Norms for Ontogenetic Change

The real bridge, as I see it in this collection of essays, is the one crossed by developmental psychologists and cultural psychologists walking hand-in-hand on their way to the study of plural norms for ontogenetic change, while leaving the land of developmental analysis and meandering in a variety of ways into a renewed intellectual territory where one investigates the ontogeny of some distinct type of cultural psychology. Ideally such investigations will result in a re-conceptualization of some of the ways rational and non-rational processes interact during the ontogenetic course of cultural reproduction, cultural revival, or cultural change.

Given what I have already said about the idea of development *per se*, what does it mean to speak of plural norms for ontogenetic change? Let's start with the idea of a norm, which is routinely analyzed into a descriptive sense and a prescriptive sense. A descriptive norm is a report issued by an observer about what typically or regularly is the case for some designated population—for example, a report about the typical emotions and feelings of Hopi Indian women who have made a marriage proposal to a Hopi Indian man but have not yet received a response. In contrast, a prescriptive norm is an exhortation or regulative expectation issued by a promulgator about what ought to be the case for some designated population.

Moving on to the idea of the plural, that notion of course implies "more than one." The literature in anthropology and cultural psychology is in large measure a record of the existence of plural norms in the descriptive sense. It is a standard feature of this literature to document the existence of two or more populations, each with a different historically evolved typical pattern of behavior. For example, it might be reported that unlike the vast majority of adult women living on the Upper West Side of Manhattan, the vast majority of adult Samburu women in Kenya believe that it is good and desirable for their adolescent girls to be "circumcised," or it might be reported that unlike Hindu populations in rural India, ascetic fasting is thought to be pathological by the American Psychiatric Association.

It can, of course, be eye-opening to learn (as we do from Alice Schlegel's essay in this book; *see* Chapter 7) that among the Hopi Indians, it is the women of the society who typically propose marriage to the men rather than the other way around or to learn that unlike most Western European and North American societies today among "Congo Pygmy settlements, 18- and 19th-century English, French, and German villages, and 20th-century Chinatowns" (and one is tempted to add the Taliban of Afghanistan to the list) teenage boys were allowed by the adults in the community to punish neighbors who threatened community well-being. But notice these reports are statements about the plurality of

descriptive norms on a worldwide or historical scale (and thus carry no implications about what ought to be the case or whether the described patterns of
behavior, various as they may be, are desirable or undesirable, mature or immature or should be viewed as either developed or underdeveloped in the Piagetian sense.

This brings us to the meaning of the concept of ontogenetic change in the
phrase "plural norms for ontogenetic change." In addressing the question of
bridges between developmental psychology and cultural psychology, it is
essential to recognize that the careful documentation by anthropologists and
cultural psychologists of plural norms in the descriptive sense also includes a
subclass of purely descriptive statements about the prescriptive norms (ideas
about what is right, good, desirable, mature, or highly developed) adopted by
members of different populations at different ages. These essentially descriptive positive science representations document the prescriptive norms of some
local population or people (the consensual statements from some group about
what is good or bad, desirable or undesirable, or valued or disvalued or about
how one ought—or ought not—behave). They might include, for example,
descriptions of the sort reported in the chapter by Xinyin Chen (Chapter 5) or
in the chapter by Alice Schlegel (Chapter 7). Xinyin Chen reports that in urban
elementary schools in China, the relation between shyness and peer acceptance
went from positive in 1990 to negative in 2002. Alice Schlegel reports that
whatever the prescriptive norms happen to be in a given society concerning the
socialization of sexual restraint, obedience, and responsibility, they tend to be
the same prescriptive norms for both boys and girls—on a worldwide cross-
cultural scale prescriptive socialization in those domains is not a gendered
issue.

But notice again that these are descriptive reports about the prescriptive
norms of particular groups. These types of descriptive statements do not even
begin to address the question mandated by the concept of development—
namely, whether the embrace of a new and different attitude toward shyness
among school-age children in China is a developmental gain or whether, to cite
a provocative example, the adoption or "internalization" by adolescent Samburu girls of the adult Samburu female attitude toward female "circumcision" is
a matter of progressive change with reference to objective or reason-based
standards or ideals and grounded in a process of active self-construction.

It is surely important for the world to know that there is variety in the things
that are desired or thought to be right and good by different peoples and in different times and places. But critics of the ideal of plural norms for ontogenetic
change will be quick to point out that just because there is variety in how
people behave or in what they prescriptively desire does not mean there is
diversity in what is truly desirable from a developmental point of view. Such
critics will be quick to point out that the existence of such variety in prescriptive norms does not mean that the Hopi, the Chinese, or the Samburu are anything other than the oversocialized slaves of an underdeveloped tradition.

Allow me to continue this line of attack and conclude on a mildly critical,
yet constructive, note. Speaking as an interdisciplinary research scholar, it was

stimulating and heartening to participate as a discussant in the very lively and welcome conference that resulted in this collection of bridge-building essays. However, as far as I can tell, most of the essays in this volume try to bridge the disciplines of developmental and cultural psychology by adopting the strategy of restricting one's interests to the study of plural norms in the descriptive sense, thus skirting the kinds of prescriptive questions that are in the forefront when ontogenetic change is interpreted as a development process in the strong self-constructed progressive change sense of development proposed by Piaget.

This is a terrific strategy as far as it goes, and we learn things. We learn about cross-cultural variations in conceptions of the life-course. We learn about the social, economic, and educational factors associated with the historical emergence of culturally constructed stages of life in between childhood and mature adulthood. We learn, for example, that the stage of life called "adolescence" in English has become so extended in some populations that it is becoming possible to witness the emergence of a new socially constructed stage of life in the world of cosmopolitan elites and possibly beyond, which has no culturally recognized mono-lexical label as of yet but has been dubbed "Emerging Adulthood" by Jeff Arnett and others. We learn about the costs and benefits of being "normal" or fitting in with the consensus as judged by ones peers and other significant others who share one's particular social location within a society. We learn about the ontogenetic patterns of children's reliance on different types of moral concepts (autonomy promoting concepts, community promoting concepts, and divinity promoting concepts), patterns that are not uniform across moral concepts and may in some instances (e.g., with regard to divinity promoting concepts) vary across cultural groups. The bridge I would propose for the future is to try to wed Jean Piaget's idea of rational self-governance and active self-construction to the very process of cultural acquisition; so as to make it more apparent that cultural psychology is not just the study of "the despotism of tradition"; and to show that it is possible for equally rational human beings to diverge in their ontogenetic mental trajectories, in their understandings of what is true, good, and valuable and in their conceptions of self, society, and nature.

Note

1. This commentary carries forward, revises, and partially draws on formulations in two earlier essays: Richard A. Shweder, "True Ethnography: The Lore, the Law, and the Lure," In R. Jessor, A. Colby & R.A. Shweder (Eds.), *Ethnography and Human Development*, Chicago: University of Chicago Press, 1996; and R.A. Shweder, "Culture and Development in Our Post-Structural Age," In R.A. Shweder (Ed.), *Why Do Men Barbecue?: Recipes for Cultural Psychology* Cambridge, MA: Harvard University Press, 2003. I wish to thank Elliot Turiel for his helpful commentary on my commentary. I also wish to thank the Institute for Advanced Study in Princeton, New Jersey (where I was a Rosanna and Charles Jaffin Founders' Circle Member during the time of the conference on "Bridging Cultural and Developmental Approaches to Psychology") for their generous support of my writing and academic work.

Index

Note: Page numbers followed by "*f*" and "*t*" denote figures and tables, respectively.

A

Aaker, J. L., 193
Abstracting generalization, 225
Acceptance. *See also* Socialization,
　　and childrearing
　cultural differences in, 187–88.
　　See also Cultural differences,
　　in acceptance
　defined, 187
　integrating claims regarding, 195–96
　non-evaluative vs. positive, 193–95
　policy implications, 202–4
　self. *See* Self acceptance
　world. *See* World acceptance
Achievement goals, 36. *See also*
　　Learning purposes
Activities, 75–76. *See also* Contexts;
　　Practices
Adolescence
　in Africa, 244–48
　in Catholicism, 10
　Ethic of Autonomy in, 8
　Ethic of Community in, 8–9
　Ethic of Divinity in, 9–10
　in Judaism, 10
Adolescent-adult relationship, 140–41.
　　See also Adolescent socialization

in modern societies, 150–52
　resources provided by adults, 152–53
Adolescent socialization
　aggressiveness and, 144
　antisocial behavior and, 143–44
　competitiveness and, 144
　cross cultural study of, 142–46
　cultural approaches to, 153–55
　extended-family household, 144–45
　household forms and, 144–46
　nuclear-family household and, 144
　overview, 138–40
　sex-differences in, 146
　in significant social groups, 146–50
　stem-family household and, 145
Adulthood
　Ethic of Autonomy in, 8
　Ethic of Community in, 9
　Ethic of Divinity in, 10
Adults, adolescents' relationship with,
　　140–41. *See also* Adolescent
　　socialization
　in modern societies, 150–52
　resources provided by adults, 152–53
Africa
　childbearing in, 240–42
　childrearing in, 240–42

Africa (*Cont'd*)
  developmental research in, 237–40
  geographical structure, 236
  marriage in, 240–41
  overview, 235–37
  pedagogies in, 246
  policy research, 248–49
  psychology in, 247–48
  social ecology, 240–42
African Child, The, 245
Africentric developmental trajectory,
   242–44. *See also* Social selfhood
Aggression, 78, 100, 101, 143
  disruption, 104
Aggressive behavior, and peer
  rejection, 101
Aggressiveness, and adolescent
  socialization, 144
Ahadi, S., 194
Ainsworth, M. D. S., 187, 238
Alao, J. A., 241
Alipura, L., 170, 173
Allen, J. J. B., 56
Almond, G. A., 114
Alvarez, J., 79
Amadeo, J., 118
Ambady, N., 56
Anagnost, A., 117, 124
Anker, A. L., 99
Annaprasana, Hindu concept, 282.
   See also Hindu life conception
Anthropology, xxii, 139, 238, 308
Anticipation vs. responsiveness, 199–200
Antisocial behavior, and adolescent
  socialization, 143–44
Antisocial groups, 100
Antisocial-deviant friends, 93
Apostoleris, N. H., 99
Apprenticeship, 150–51, 152, 243, 244
  in Hindu life conception, 283–84
Ardila, P., 236
Argentina
  emerging adults, 267
  postsecondary participation, 258
Argyle, M., 99
Ariel, S., 95
Armer, M., 96, 101
Arnett, J. J., xxii, 3, 5, 16, 124, 154, 163,
   167, 240, 255, 256, 259, 261, 263,
   264, 266, 267, 268, 269, 270, 271

Arranged marriages, 169, 269
Asakawa, K., 194
Asendorpf, J. B., 96
Asher, S., 101
Asian OECD countries, emerging
   adults in, 261–62
Atkinson, R. C., 53
Attachment, 198–99
Attachment–autonomy link, 199
Attili, G., 98
Australia, 120, 174
  individual responsibility, 121
  in OECD, 257
  postsecondary participation, 258
Autobiographical memories, 57, 58.
   See also Memory systems
  socio-cultural perspectives, 62, 63
Autonoetic consciousness, 53. *See also*
   Episodic memory
Autonomy, 103, 119, 173, 196–97,
   199, 200, 268
  assertiveness and, 101, 106
  in peer group, 99
Autonomy, ethic of, 5, 11. *See also*
   cultural-developmental template
  in adolescence, 8
  in adulthood, 8
  in children, 7
  degree and type of use, 7, 8
Avlar, B., 60
Azmitia, M., 99, 105, 178
Azuma, H., 28, 197, 198
Azuma, M., 28

B

Baddley, A. D., 52
Badger, S., 261, 267, 268
Baker, Sir Samuel, 237
Baldelomar, O. A., 165, 167, 168,
   182, 229
Baldi, S., 117
Baldwin, A. L., 187
Baldwin, J. M., 212
Banaszynski, T. L., 5, 8
Bandura, A., 128
Baran, B., 60
Barber, B., 202
Barber, B. K., 115
Barber, C. H., 129
Barkley, R. A., 56

Bar Mitzvah, 10
Barrett, M., 114, 115, 121, 175
Barrionuevo, A., xxii
Barry, H. III., 9, 140, 141, 142, 143, 147, 155, 197, 265
Bartholomew, K., 192, 199
Bartsch, K., 33
Batchelder, E. H., 76
Baumeister, R., 162
Baumrind, D., 187, 201
Beaty, E., 32
Beck, U., 77
Bedolla, L. G., 127
Behavioral characteristics, in peer acceptance/rejection, 100–102. *See also* Peer relationship social change and, 102
Behavioral dimensions, 286–87
Bejček, J., 267
Bempechat, J., 37
Benenson, J. F., 99
Berger, P., 76
Berndt, T. J., 93
Berntsen, D., 60
Berry, J. W., 105, 118, 174, 175, 238
Bersoff, D. M., 8
Bertalanffy, L. von, 214
Best, D., 177
Beyers, W., 163
Bhaktiyoga, 294. *See also* Hindu life conception
Bharati, A., 278, 295
Bhatia, S., 171
Bhogle, S., 58
Bidell, T. R., 221
Bjorklund, D., 52
Blackburn, T. C., 191
Blasi, A., 14
Blehar, M. C., 187
Boehnke, K., 123
Boesch, E. E., 215, 223
Bond, M., 99
Bosma, H. A., 77, 162, 172, 182
Botcheva, L., 122
Botswana, 127, 244
Bourdieu, P., 82
Bowker, A., 100
Boys. *See also* Adolescent-adult relationship

and adults, 146, 149–50
aggressive behavior, 143–44
competitiveness and aggressiveness, 144, 145–46
economic pressures, 179
in peer relations, 99, 101
socialization, 142
Bradley, C., 240
Brainerd, C. J., 4
Brazil, 5, 264
loneliness in, 106
play behaviors of children in, 96
Breese, F. H., 187
Brendgen, M., 95
Brewer, M. B., 126
Brickman, P., 39
Bridges, L. J., 200
Bridging, 18, 35, 93, 276
cultural and developmental psychology, xxii–xxiii, 113
Bromnick, R. D., 267
Bronfenbrenner, U., 51, 52, 79, 81, 162
Brown, A., 61
Brown, B. B., 94, 99, 147
Brown, J., 103
Brown, M., 93
Bruck, M., 51
Bruner, J. S., 29
Buchanan, T., 5, 8, 11, 14
Buchanan-Barrow, E., 114
Bucher, A., 9
Buckley, J. J., 172
Buckner, R. L., 50
Buddhism, 4, 118, 188
Bugental, D. B., 80
Buitelaar, M. W., 77, 172
Bukowski, W., 9, 92, 99
Bulgaria, 118, 120, 121–22
Bulman, R. J., 39
Burbank, V. K., 140
Burton, Richard, 237
Butler, E. A., 194
Byrnes, J., 73

C
Cairns, B. D., 94
Cairns, R. B., 94, 213
Caldwell, K., 28
Callaghan, L., 248

Cameroon, 237, 242
 family, 241
 peer culture in, 246
Camazine, S,., 215
Cameroon., 246
Campbell, B., 115, 122
Campos, J., 197, 198
Canada
 cohabitation, 261
 in OECD, 257, 266
 peer interaction in, 97
 postsecondary participation, 259
Cao, H. T., 82
Caregivers, 187, 188. *See also*
  Socialization, and childrearing
 acceptance of children
  (*see* Acceptance)
 East Asian, 189
 European American, 192–93
Caregiving. *See* Socialization, and
 childrearing
Cariglia-Bull, T., 51
Carranza, M. E., 82
Casiglia, A. C., 100, 101
Cassidy, J., 199
Catell, R. B., 53, 54, 55, 56
Cauffman, E., 16
CBOs. *See* Community-based
 organizations (CBOs)
Ceci, S. J., 49, 51, 52, 130
Cen, G., 102
Chae, Y. J., 130
Chaffee, C., 128
Chagnon, N. A., 101
Chakkarath, P., 297n1
Chan, C., 27, 32
Chang, E. C., 194
Chang, L., xxii, 99, 100, 102, 204
Chao, R. K., 28, 40, 201, 202
Chaudhary, N., 223, 264, 269
Chavajay, P., 51, 63
Chen, H., 96, 102
Chen, J., 191
Chen, L., 82
Chen, S., 198
Chen, X., 3, 96, 97, 98, 99, 100, 101,
 102, 103, 104, 105, 106, 197, 255
Cherlin, A. J., 259, 269
Cherney, I. D., 118
Cheung, F. M., 191

Chi, M. T. H., 52
Chiaravalloti, N. D., 50
Childbearing in Africa, 240–42
Childhood, African developmental
  principles and processes in, 244–48
 developmental learning, 245
 family and community, 245–46
 immaturity, 244–45
 individuation of, 247
 peer cultures, 246
Childhood memories, studies on,
  57–60
Childrearing
 in Africa, 240–42
 socialization and. *See* Socialization,
  and childrearing
Children
 acceptance of self and world.
   See Acceptance; Self acceptance;
   Socialization, and childrearing;
   World acceptance
 Ethic of Autonomy in, 7
 Ethic of Community in, 8–9, 11
 Ethic of Divinity in, 9, 10
 learning beliefs of. *See* Learning;
   Learning beliefs (BL)
Chile, 115, 130
 citizenship, 117
 groupways in civic identity, 118
 during military rule, 114
 Penguin Revolution, 117, 125
 urban teenagers in, xxi–xxii
China, 102, 117, 124, 180, 188, 194,
  264, 267, 268, 269, 309
 childhood memory, 58, 59, 60
 children's learning in, 29
 factory girls in, xxii
 friendship functions, 98
 one-child policy in, 64
 peer interactions in, 96–97
 play in, 95
Chinese learning model, 30–32, 30t.
   See also Cultural learning models;
   Learning beliefs (BL)
 components and dimensions of, 30
Christianity, 14, 118, 250
Chisholm, L., 257
Chiu, C. Y., 190, 191, 200
Cho, G. E., 98, 196
Choi, I., 190, 191

Choi, S. H., 197, 199
Chunachenko, O., 235
Cillessen, A. H., 101
Citizens
    obligations of, 116–19
    prerogatives of, 116–19
    rights of, 116–19
Citizenship. *See* Citizens
Civic identity. *See also* Civil societies
    as collective identity, 126–27
    peer relations and, 127–29
Civil societies
    citizens. *See* Citizens
    civic identity. *See* Civic identity
    defined, 113
    as economic and political systems,
        113–115
    in globalization, 131–132
    groupways, 115–116
    mediating institutions. *See* Mediating
        institutions
    politics, 121–123
    routine practices, 114
    values, 121–123
    and younger generations. *See* Younger
        generations
Clancy, P. M., 202
Clark, K., 174
Clark, M., 174
Closeness, 197–99. *See also*
    Socialization, and childrearing
Coding system, 6
Cognitive development, 4, 14, 32, 57, 75,
    79, 93, 238, 239
    Cohabitation, in OECD countries, 259
    Western vs. Asian emerging adults,
        261–62
Cohen, D., xxii, 31, 193, 201
Coie, J. D., 92, 94
Colby, A., 4, 7, 14
Cole, E., 170, 178
Cole, M., xxii, 238
Cole, P. M., 194, 196, 200
Coleman, C. C., 93
Collective identity, civic identity as,
    126–27. *See also* Civil societies
Collectivism, 165–66
Collectivistic cultures, 165
Community, ethic of, 5. *See also*
    cultural-developmental template

in adolescence, 8–9
in adulthood, 9
in children, 8–9, 11
    degree and type of use, 8–9
Community-based organizations
    (CBOs), 119–21
    as free spaces, 129–30
    practices of, 120
Competitiveness, and adolescent
    socialization, 144
Condon, R. G., 140
Confucianism, 98
Connolly, K. J., 212
Constellations of ethics thesis, 14–15
Contarello, A., 99
Content, 75
Contexts
    activities and, 75–76
    interconnections and, 78–83. *See also*
        Interconnections
    overview, 73–75
    practices and, 75–76
    shared views, 76–78
    social policies, 83–87
    unshared views, 76–78
Contextual differences, in memory
    development, 51–52
Contextualizing specification, 225
Conway, A. R., 55
Conway, M. A., 58, 60
Conzen, K. N., 105
Coon, H. M., 118
Cooper, C. R., 85, 99, 105
Coplan, R. J., 96, 101
Coppotelli, H., 94
Corriveau, K., 33, 34, 35
Corsaro, W. A., 105, 106
Costa Rica, 98, 173
Cote, J., 162
Criticism, 200–201. *See also*
    Socialization, and childrearing
Crockett, L. J., 180
Cross-cultural identity status model,
    167–70, 168*f*
    between-culture variability, 169
    domains, 168–69
    identity exploration, 168
    identity options, 167–68
    independent identity
        achievement, 167

Cross-cultural identity status
    model *(Cont'd)*
  interdependent identity
      achievement, 167
  within-culture variability, 169–70
Cross cultural study, of adolescent
    socialization, 142–46
Crouter, A. C., 82
Crystallized intelligence, 54
Csapo, B., 122
Csikszentmihalyi, M., 10
Cultural approaches, to adolescent
    socialization, 153–55
Cultural change and identity
    formation, 179–80
  globalization in, 180
  historical events in, 180
  immigration in, 179
Cultural context, identity formation in,
    162–64
  characteristics, 163–64
  concepts and theories, 162–63
  conceptualizing culture, 164–66
  cultural goals, 164
  identity options, 163
  personhood and identity, 163–64
  social relations, 163
Cultural-developmental template, 3, 6,
    7f, 10–12
  constellations of ethics, 14–15
  cultural variations and, 16–17
  developmental changes and, 13
  in developmental contexts, 16–17
  developmental patterns, 7
  lifespan changes and, 13
  moral emotions, 15
  and morality thesis, 13–14
  and policy considerations, 17–19
  in religious liberals, 11, 11f
  in religiously conservative, 11, 12, 12f
  and social policies, 17–19
  thesis, 13
Cultural differences, in acceptance,
    187–88
  non-evaluative vs. positive acceptance,
    193–95
  of self. *See* Self acceptance
  of world. *See* World acceptance
Cultural effects, on memory, 57–62.
    See also Episodic memory

Cultural learning models, 27–40
  Chinese learning model, 30–32, 30t
  defined, 28
  European American model,
      29, 30, 30t
  learning beliefs (BL), 32–38. *See also*
      Learning beliefs (BL)
  peers and, 38–40
Cultural psychologist, 303–4
Cultural psychology, 223–24
  ● meaning-making, 224–25
Cultural variations
  and developmental contexts, 16–17
  in life-course, 16
Culture, defined, 4
Culture wars, 19
Cumsille, P., 115, 125, 129
Curran, H. V., 250
Cury, F., 36
Czech Republic, 120, 121–22, 258,
    260, 267

D
D'Andrade, R. G., 28, 81
D'Hondt, W., 99
Dalal, A. K., 297n1
Dall'Alba, G., 32
Damon, W., xxii, 4, 14, 31
Dasen, P. R., 28, 118, 239
Dating, 169, 176, 262
Davidson, A. L., 82
Davidson, B., 237
Davies, K., 60
Davis, D. A., 140
Davis, S. S., 140
Dayan, J., 98
Deal, J. E., 76
Deane, S., 51
Deci, E. L., 29, 198
De Kort, G., 99
Dekovic, M., 99
Delli Carpini, M., 124
Deluca, J., 50
Dennis, T. A., 194, 196, 200
DeRosier, M. E., 92, 98
Deschamps, J. C., 118
Desgranges, B., 52, 53, 64
DeSouza, A., 96
De Tocqueville, A., 114
Devaraja, N. K., 284

Developing countries, emerging
  adulthood in, 263–64
age of parenthood, 263
education, 263, 264
identity challenges, 263, 264
marital age, 263
Development, defined, 4. *See also*
  Developmental processes
Developmental processes,
  218–21
developmental psychology, 219
functional time unit, 218
hierarchical organization of,
  219–20, 220*f*
multilevel nature of, 218–21
novelty as, 212–14
TEM, 217–18
as unfolding of uniqueness,
  214–18. *See also* Open systems
as unity of disappearance and
  emergence, 212–14
ZEPD, 216–17
Developmental psychologist, 303
Developmental psychology,
  214, 219
Developmental systems theory, 162
Deviation-amplifying processes, 221
Devich-Navarro, M., 175, 177
DeVos, G. A., 197
Dias, M. G., 5
Dickson, R., 60
Dien, D. S., 4, 15
Diener, C., 194
Diener, E., 193, 194
Diener, M., 194
Dishion, T. J., 93
Divinity, ethic of, 5. *See also*
  cultural-developmental template
in adolescence, 9–10
in adulthood, 10
age pattern for, 9–10
in children, 9, 10
degree and type of use, 9–10
religious cultures and, 10
Dodge, K. A., 93, 94, 204
Domedel, A., 117
Dominquez, E., 85
Douglass, C. B., 255, 256, 259, 260,
  268, 271
Doyle, A. B., 98

Dubas, J. S., 199
Du Bois-Reymond, M., 77, 257
Duffy, S., 61, 63
Durham, D., 126, 127
Durkheim, E., 114
Dutta, R., 162
Duty, 6, 116, 118, 280, 284
Duval, T. S., 192
Dweck, C. S., 36, 189, 190, 191, 192, 200
Dzokoto, V., 193, 194

E
Easton, D., 121, 131
Ebbinghaus, H., 50
Ebenbach, D. H., 5, 8
Eccles, J. S., 73
Edwards, C. P., 4, 9, 95, 103, 104, 106,
  197, 198
Ehrenfels, C., 219
Eichenbaum, H., 50
Eid, M., 194
Eisenberg, N., 7, 8, 9, 15, 100, 101
Eisenberg, R., 39
Elliot, A. J., 36
Ellis, J., 237, 242, 244, 247
Elloitt, J., 27, 28
Elwin, V., 139, 148
Emerging adulthood
age of feeling in-between, 257
age of identity explorations, 256
age of instability, 256
age of possibilities, 257
cultural psychology of, 266–72
independence and, 266–68
marriage and, 268–70
overview, 256–57
research on, 255
self-focused age, 256–57
self-sufficiency and, 266–68
soul mate and, 268–70
as time of unparalleled enjoyment
  of life, 271–72
work and, 270–71
Emmeche, C., 220
Engels, R. C. M. E., 99
Engle, R. W., 55
Episodic memory. *See also*
  Memory systems
adults' earliest childhood memories,
  studies on, 57–60

Episodic memory *(Cont'd)*
  autonoetic consciousness, 53
  concept of, 53
  memory tasks, 54
  and research across cultures,
    57–60
Erdogan, A., 60
Erikson, E. H., 115, 124, 161, 162,
    247, 278
Erny, P., 245, 247
Espelage, D. L., 94
Estes, D., 33
Ethic of Autonomy, 5, 11. *See also*
    Cultural-developmental template
  in adolescence, 8
  in adulthood, 8
  in children, 7
  degree and type of use, 7, 8
Ethic of Community, 5. *See also*
    Cultural-developmental template
  in adolescence, 8–9
  in adulthood, 9
  in children, 8–9, 11
  degree and type of use, 8–9
Ethic of Divinity, 5. *See also*
    Cultural-developmental template
  in adolescence, 9–10
  in adulthood, 10
  age pattern for, 9–10
  in children, 9, 10
  degree and type of use, 9–10
  religious cultures and, 10
Ethnic identity, 173–75
  and cultural context, 174–75
  defined, 173
  and dominant majority, 173–74
  ethnicity and, 174
  in immigrants, 174
  and non-dominant minorities, 174
  vs. national identity, 173
Ethiopia, 264
Europe, emerging adults in, 259–61
European American model,
    of learning, 29, 30, 30t.
    See also Cultural learning models;
    Learning beliefs (BL)
  components and dimensions of, 30
Eustache, F., 52, 53, 64
Evaratt, J., 239
Evered, S., 296

Expressive–constitutive dimension,
    of behavior, 286
Extended-family household, adolescent
    socialization, 144–45
Extrication from attachments.
    See Vanaprastha, Hindu life-stages

F
Facio, A., 267
Fackler, M., 271
Fagan, J. F., 55
Fai, P. J., 239
Families. *See also* Contexts
  children in, 82
  and outside world, 82–83
  parents in, 82
Farmer, T. W., 101
Farver, J. M., 95, 96, 102
Feeney, B. C., 199
Feldman, S. S., 16
Fenko, A., 124
Ferguson, L. R., 98
Fiese, B., 75
Filial piety, 4, 197
Finland, 5, 258
Fischer, K. W., 221
Fiske, A. P., 57, 80, 163, 190, 191
Fivush, R., 60, 62
Fixed qualities, 189
Fixed vs. malleable views
  of self acceptance, 189–90
  of world aceeptance, 190–92
Fixed world, 190
Flanagan, C. A., 17, 115, 120, 122, 123,
    125, 126, 127, 129, 131
Flavell, E. R., 33
Flavell, J. H., 33
Fluid intelligence, 53–54
Fonzi, A., 101
Forde, C. D., 237
Forster, K. I., 56
Fortin, N. J., 50
France, 116, 245, 258
Fraser, C., 114
French, D. C., 3, 97, 98, 99,
    103, 104
Freud, S., 49
Friedlmeier, W., 199, 200
Friendship, 93. *See also*
    Peer relationship

instrumental aid and, 98
  quality of, 98–99
  self-worth and, 98
Fu, H., 191
Fuligni, A. J., 79, 81, 105, 166, 167, 176
Fülöp, M., 39
Fun, meaning of, 225–26. *See also*
  Promoter signs
Fung, H., 6, 38, 40, 196, 201, 202
Furstenberg, F. F., 82

G
Gaertner, L., 193
Gallay, L., 122, 129
Gallimore, R., 27
Ganapathy, H., 291*t*
Gardner, H., 204
Gardner, W. L., 126, 193
Garey, A. I., 249
Gaskell, G., 114
Gaskins, S., 95, 104
Gauvain, M., 81
Gazelle, H., 101
Gell, S. M. S., 148
Gender identity, 177–78
  at cultural group level, 178
Generational replacement,
  political change and, 123–25
  younger generation, 124–25
Gerber, D. A., 105
Germany, 123, 131, 150–51
Gerris, J. R., 199
Gibson, E., Jr., 94
Gielen, U. P., 235
Gill, S., 129
Gilligan, C. F., 4, 7, 8
Gimpel, J. G., 130
Girls, 143–44, 151, 309
  and adults, 146, 167
  Moroccan, 77
  Muslim, 172
  peer pressure, 99
  in rural areas of developing
    countries, 265
  secondary educational institutions, 17
  in separate schools, 283
  socialization, 142, 143
  socio-economic status and, 179
Gledhill C., 77
Global citizen, 131

Globalization, 43–44, 106, 131,
  179–80, 261, 263
Gold, A., 52
Goldenberg, C., 27
Goldschmidt, W., 238
Goldsmith, L. R., 58
Goldstein, W. M., 75, 197
Goncu, A., 95
Gonzalez, Y., 98
Goodnow, J. J., 75, 77, 81, 84, 87, 103
Goody, J., 237
Goossens, L., 163, 169
Gormuyor, J. N., 244
Gosso, Y., 96
Gottlieb, G., 213, 219
Gould, S. J., 235
Graham, S., 49
Gramsci, A., 77
Green, E., 118
Green, F. L., 33
Greenfield, P. M., 164, 166, 167
Gross, J. J., 194
Groupways, concept of, 115–16
Gruper, H., 52
Gunz, A., 31
Guzman, M. R. T., 103
Gyanayoga, 294. *See also* Hindu
  life conception

H
Habermas, J., 153
Haden, C. A., 60, 62
Hagan, J., 123
Haidt, J., 5, 7, 8, 15
Haight, W. L., 81
Hallahan, M., 191
Hallin, D. C., 77
Halvorson, C. F., 76
Hamamura, T., 193
Hamedani, M. G., 164, 165
Hammack, P., 162, 165
Hamilton, M. A., 150
Hamilton, S. F., 150
Han, J. J., 57, 59, 60, 62, 63
Hanyu, K., 60
Haque, S., 60
Harach, L., 80
Harackiewicz, J. M., 36
Harkness, S., 28, 55, 63, 95, 103, 104,
  197, 238, 244

Harris, J. R., 92, 103
Hart, B., 40
Hart, C. H., 102
Hartup, W. W., 92, 93, 100, 101
Harwood, R. L., 8
Haslam, N., 80
Hatano, G., 79, 132
Hatfield, E., 262
Hau, K. T., 28
Hayes, S. A., 187, 195, 223
Hayne, H., 59
He, Y., 99, 100, 102
Heckhausen, J., 296
Hefler, G., 123
Heine, S. J., 31, 32, 190, 193, 194, 195,
    201, 204
Heingartner, D., xxii
Henderlong, J., 201
Henderson, M., 99
Henkel, R. R., 94
Herdt, G. H., xxii
Herman, H., 51
Hermans, H. J. M., 171, 296
Hernández, A. C., 117, 126
Herzog, T., 191
Hess, R. D., 28
Heyman, G. D., 40
Hidi, S., 29
Higgins, E. T., 39
Hildebrandt, N., 202
Hinde, R. A., 92, 103
Hindu. *See also* Hindu life conception
    common constructs of, 278–79
    dharma, 280
    Ethic of Divinity and, 10
    individuality in, 279
    karma, 280
    moksha, 279, 293–94
    religious devotion in, 10
Hinduism, in India, 277–78
    Sanatana Dharma, 277
    Sindhus, 277
Hindu life conception
    brahmacharya, 283–84
    childhood, 282–83
    grahasthya, 284–85
    implications in global context,
        295–97
    infancy, 282–83
    major stages, 281–82

meta-theoretical framework, 288–95
    samskaras, 282
    sanyasa, 286
    structure and content dimensions,
        289–91*t*
    transformational change, 293–95
    vanaprastha, 285–86
Hobeika, D., 58
Hoff -Ginsberg, E., 54
Hofstede, G., 165
Holland, C. R., 55
Holland, D., 28
Hollnsteiner, M. R., 98
Hollos, M., 140
Holt, M. K., 94
Hong, Y., 190, 191
Horowitz, A. D., 267
Horvath, K., 33
Hoshino-Browne, E., 193, 201
Hou, Y., 58
Hounkpè, A. D. G., 244
Household forms, and adolescent
    socialization, 144–46
Hsu, F. L. K., 195
Huddy, L., 18
Hufton, N., 27, 28
Hughes, D., 82
Human development
    alternate conception of, 286–88.
        See also Hindu life conception
    and peer relationship, 93–94. *See also*
        Peer relationship
Hungary, 120, 121, 122, 258
Hunter, J. D., 19
Huntsinger, C., 200
Hurrelmann, K., 9
Huston, A. C., 83, 86
Huttunen, A., 99
Hwang, K. K., 105
Hyman, C., 92
Hyman, I., 51, 52
Hymel, S., 101

I
I/C distinction. *See* Individualism and
    collectivism (I/C) distinction
Identity domains, 168–69
    ascribed, 169
    chosen, 169
    interaction of, 178–79

Identity formation
  commitment in, 166
  cultural change and, 179–80
  in cultural context. *See* Cultural
    context, identity formation in
  domains in. *See* Identity domains
  exploration in, 166
  overview, 161–62
  research and policy implications,
    180–81
  socio-economic status and,
    178–79
Identity status model, 166–67
  achievement status, 166
  commitments and, 166
  development of, 166
  diffusion status, 166
  exploration and, 166
  foreclosure status, 166
  moratorium status, 166
IEA. *See* International Association
    for the Evaluation of Educational
    Achievement (IEA)
Iizuka, Y., 99
Imada, S., 5
Imada, T., 188
Immigrants
  civic involvement of, 18
  ethnic identity, 174
  occupational identity, 171
  and social policies, 18
Independence, and emerging adulthood,
    266–68
India, 8, 9, 11, 16, 58–60, 264, 269.
    See also Hinduism, Hindu, Hindu
    life conception
Individual autonomy, in peer group, 99.
    See also Peer group
Individualism and collectivism (I/C)
    distinction, 165–66
  concept, 165
  critics on, 165
  self-constructs in, 165
  theoretical positions, 165
Indonesia, 98, 101, 264
Instrumental aid and friendship, 98
Instrumental–communicative dimension,
    of behavior, 286–87
Intelligence, 28, 29, 37, 39,
    53–56, 190

Interconnections, 78–83
  across contexts, 81–83
  among people, 79–81
Interdependence, 126, 161, 165, 167, 171
International Association for the
    Evaluation of Educational
    Achievement (IEA), 117
*International Encyclopedia of
    Adolescence,* 240
Internet, 131
Iran, 264
Ishii, K., 188
Israel, 9, 148, 178, 267
Italy, 150, 152, 258
Ittelson, W. H., 236
Iyengar, S. S., 37

J
Japan, 27, 28, 61, 198, 199, 200
  acceptance, 197
  children's learning in, 37, 39, 40, 43
  cultural contexts, 164
  emerging adults in, 261, 262, 266
  life satisfaction, 194
  Morita, 197
  national identities, 173
  in OECD, 257
  parasite singles, 261
  play in, 95
  postsecondary participation, 258
  views of self, 190, 191, 192
James, A., 244
Jansen, E. A., 98
Jayaram, V., 281
Jenks, C., 244
Jensen, L. A., xxii, 3, 4, 5, 6, 8, 9, 10, 11,
    12, 13, 14, 15, 16, 17, 18, 75, 127,
    164, 197, 264
Ji, L., 191
Jones, G. W., 261
Jose, P. E., 200
Juang, L. P., 123
Judaism, 10

K
Kabat-Zinn, J., 188
Kagan, J., 15
Kagitcibasi, C., 119, 126, 247, 281, 287
Kahne, J. E., 115
Kakar, S., 280, 285, 291*t*, 293

Kakinuma, M., 197, 198, 199
Kalhorn, J., 187
Kamins, M. L., 200
Karmayoga, 294. *See also* Hindu
    life conception
Kashima, Y., 177
Kashiwagi, K., 28
Kaspar, V., 98
Kassimir, R., 131
Kathuria, R., 239
Keating, D., 9
Keller, H., 166, 167, 198, 200
Keltner, D., 5, 8
Kemmelmeier, M., 57, 118
Kempen, H. J. G., 171, 296
Kenya, 95, 238, 239, 244, 264, 309
Kessel, F., 75
Ketner, S. L., 77, 172
Khatib, N., 18
Kiesner, J., 99
Kilbride, J. E., 238
Kilbride, P. L., 238
Killen, M., 8
Kim, H. S., 29
Kim, U., 27, 38
Kim, Y. K., 95
Kim-Gervey, C., 174
Kim-Jo, T., 171, 176
Kinderman, T. A., 94
Kirshner, B., 126
Kishani, B. T., 248
Kitayama, S., xxii, 57, 61, 63, 165, 167,
    188, 189, 190, 191, 194, 195, 200
Klatzky, R. L., 50
Klemfuss, J. Z., 51
Klineberg, O., 194
Klute, C., 94
Kochenderfer, B. J., 93
Koh, S. F., 99
Kohlberg, L., 4, 7, 8, 9, 16
Koller, S. H., 5
Køppe, S., 220
Koreishi, A., 62
Kostron, L., 122
Krappmann, L., 95
Krieg, D. B., 200
Kristel, O. V., 80
Kroger, J., 163, 166, 177
Kuczynski, L., 80, 202
Kuhn, H. M., 57

Kuijpers, K. F., 297
Kulkofsky, S., 51
Kumru, A., 103
Kunnen, S., 162, 182
Kupersmidt, J., 92
Kupersmidt, J. B., 98
Kuscynski, L
Kwak, K., 199

L

Labissirere, Y., 18
Ladd, G. W., 92, 93, 101
LaFontaine, J., 245
Lagerspetz, K., 99
Lai, C.-Y., 31
Laible, D., 80
Lam, M., 176
Lamb, M. E., 246
Lapsley, D. K., 14
Larson, J., 147
Larson, R. W., xxii, 17, 95, 104, 121,
    126, 263, 265
Latin America, 95, 130
Latz, S., 197
Lau, M., 262
Laughlin, J. E., 55
Laungani, P. D., 297n3
Lave, J., 52
Learning
    children's beliefs of. *See* Learning
        beliefs (BL)
    Chinese approach to, 26–27
    cultural learning models. *See* Cultural
        learning models
    intelligence and, 28
    non-negotiable sense of, 38
    non-questionable sense of, 38
    peers and, 38–40
    process, 33–36
    purposes. *See* Learning purposes
    research on, 27–28
Learning beliefs (BL), 32–36
    of achievement goals. *See* Learning
        purposes
    attentiveness, 35
    capacity notion, 34
    socialization and, 40–42
    structure vs. content, 34
    theory of mind (ToM) and, 33, 34
    understanding notion of learning, 33

Learning purposes, 36–38
Lebra, T. S., 139
Lee, A. Y., 193
Lee, F., 191
Lee, O., 104
Lee, T. L., 194
Lee, Y., 95
Leekam, S. R., 34
Lehman, D. R., 31, 190, 194
Leichtman, M. D., 3, 49, 51, 53, 56, 57, 58, 59, 60, 62, 63, 64
Leis, P. E., 140
Lenox, K., 92
Lepper, M. R., 37, 201
Lerner, M., 122
Lerner, R. M., xxii, 10, 73, 162
Leung, A. K.-Y., 193, 201
Levine, C., 162
Levine, M., 51
LeVine, R. A., 103, 198
Lewis, C. C., 28, 201
Li, B., 100
Li, D., 100, 102
Li, J., 28, 29, 31, 33, 34, 35, 36, 37, 38, 39, 40
Li, Z., 100, 101
Liang, C.-H., 38, 40, 196, 201
Liang, S., 96
Liebkind, K., 175
Liew, J., 100
Life conception, of Hindu. *See* Hindu life conception
Lightfoot, C., 124
Lima, M. D., 96
Little, T. D., 95
Liu, H., 100
Liu, M., 98, 100
Liu-Constant, Y., 202
Lloyd, C., 265
Lochman, J., 92
Lo Coco, A., 100
Lonner, W. J., 223
Lopez, M. H., 18
Love, E. D., 75
Lowe, S. R., 153
Lowery, L., 5
Lozano, A., 56
Lozoff, B., 197
Luo, L., 38, 40

Luo, Z., 200
Luthar, S., 8

M
Ma, H. K., 4
Maccoby, E. E., 105
MacDonald, S., 59
Macek, P., 122, 255, 267
Mac Iver, D., 39
Madan, T. N., 282, 284, 286, 292, 293
Madden, T., 176
Madhavan, S., 249
Maehr, M. L., 36
Mahoney, A., 10
Maier-Bruckner, W., 52
Maisel, S., 172
Malinowski, B., 140, 155
Malleable qualities, 189
Malleable vs. fixed views
    of self acceptance, 189–90
    of world aceeptance, 190–92
Mangelsdorf, S. C., 81
Mani, A., 169
Maquet, J., 236
Marcelo, K. B., 18
Marcia, J. E., 161, 166
Markiewicz, D., 98
Markle, F. A., 130
Markus, H. R., 57, 164, 165, 167, 188, 189, 190, 194, 195, 200
Marriage and emerging adulthood, 268–70
Marriage in Africa, 240–41
Martínez, M. L., 115, 117, 125, 126
Marton, F., 32
Maruyama, M., 221
Masten, A. S., 100
Mastery, 31, 36, 37–38, 54, 200
Masuda, T., 61
Matsumoto, D., 194
Maynard, A., 166, 167
Mayseless, O., 16, 267
McBride-Chang, C., 204
McClaskey, C. L., 93
McCollom, T. L., 94
McDermott, C., 125
McDevitt, M., 128
McDougall, P., 100
McGough, L., 51
McGraw, A. P., 80

McKenzie, J., xxii, 3, 9, 10, 14, 264
McKinnon, J., 100
McWhorter, J., 180
Mead, G. H., 99
Mead, M., 139
Mebert, C., 59, 63
Mediating institutions, 113, 114.
    See also Civil societies
  CBOs, 119–21, 129–30
  in political incorporation of younger
    generations, 119–21, 130–31
  practices, 119–21, 130–31
Memory development. *See also* Memory
  systems
  contextual differences in, 51–52
  future directions, 64
  individual differences in, 51
  overview, 49–50
  socio-cultural perspectives of, 62–64
  structure vs. content in, 65
  traditional perspective on, 50
Memory systems, 52–56
  cultural effects on, 57–62
  episodic memory. *See* Episodic
    memory
  intellectual functioning and, 53–54
  procedural memory, 55–56
  PRS, 56
  semantic memory, 54–55
  working memory, 53
Menon, T., 191
Menon, U., 280, 282, 287, 297n3
Mental life, ontogenetic changes in.
    See Ontogenetic changes,
    as developmental process
Merrill, B. D., 128
Mesogenesis, 218
Meta-theoretical framework, Hindu life
  conception, 288–95
Mexico, 95, 164, 264
Michell, J., 219, 221
Micocci, F., 267
Microgenesis, 218
Middaugh, E., 115
Miller, J. G., xxii, 4, 6, 7, 8, 114
Miller, P. J., 75, 81, 98, 120, 196,
  201, 202
Mistry, J., 51, 64, 95, 162
Miyake, K., 198
Miyamoto, Y., 190, 191

Mizuta, I., 196, 200
Moffitt, T., 248
Moksha, Hindu concept, 279, 293–94
Molenaar, P. C. M., 214, 215
Montessori, M., 49
Moore, C. A., 279, 283, 295
Morais, S. E., 96
Moral. *See* Morality; Moral reasoning
Morality, 13–14. *See also*
    Cultural-developmental template;
    Three ethics approach
  and cultural variations, 16–17
  and social policies, 17–19
Moral reasoning. *See also*
    Cultural-developmental template
  coding system for, 6
  subcategories, 6
  three ethics approach to. *See* Three
    ethics approach
Moran, T. J., 15
Morawska, E., 105
Morelli, G., 200, 202
Moreno, D. S., 98
Moreno, J. L., 94
Morling, B., 191, 192, 296
Morris, M. W., 190, 191
Moscovici, S., 114
Mosier, C., 95
Mullen, M. K., 57, 58, 59, 62
Mumme, D. L., 197
Munroe, R. H., 239
Munroe, R. L., 238, 239
Muramoto, Y., 201
Muraven, M., 162
Muslim identity, 172
Musoke, L. K., 240

N
Nadkarni, M. V., 277, 280, 282
Nagaoka, R., 197, 198, 199
Namakarana (naming rite),
    Hindu concept, 282
Narvaez, D., 14
Nash, R., 260
National identity, 175–77
  defined, 173
  in multicultural settings,
    175–77
  study on, 175–76
  vs. ethnic identity, 173

Nations, and citizens, 116–19. *See also*
    Civil societies
Nature of change, 287
Nature of development, 286–87
Neisser, U., 51, 52
Nelson, E., 105, 106
Nelson, K., 62, 63
Nelson, L. J., 16, 255, 261,
    267, 268
Nelson, S. S., 180
Netherlands, 77, 172
New Zealand, 59, 257, 266
Ngaujah, D. E., 239
Ngomane, T., 123, 125
Nicotra, E., 99
Nikhilananda, Swami, 284
Nisan, M., 4, 9
Nisbett, R. E., 61, 190, 191
Nishkramana, Hindu concept, 282
Nityananda, Swami, 277
Niwa, E., 174
Non-governmental organizations
    (NGOs), 129–30
Norenzayan, A., 190, 191
Norway, 260
Novelty, 212–14. *See also*
    Developmental processes
Nsamenang, A. B., 3, 236, 239, 240, 241,
    242, 243, 244, 245, 246, 247, 248,
    249, 250, 287
Nucci, L. P., 165
Nuclear-family household, and
    adolescent socialization, 144
Nyklíček, I., 297

O
O'Neil, K., 101
Obama, Barack, 180
Obeid, A., 172
Oberg, G., 56
Obligations, of citizens, 116–19
Occupational identity, 170–72
    in collectivistic cultures, 171
    diverse societies and, 171–72
    immigrants and, 171
    independent pathway in, 170
    and religious identity, 178
OECD. *See* Organization for Economic
    Co-Operation and Development
    (OECD)

OECD countries, emerging adulthood in
    age of parenthood, 259, 261
    cohabitation in, 259, 261–62
    demographic changes, 259
    economic change, 257–58
    marital age, 259, 260, 261
    premarital sex in, 259, 261–62
    social class, 262–63
    tertiary education in, 258
    variations, 259–63
    women's roles and rights, 258, 259
Ogbimi, G. E., 241
Ohuche, R. O., 238
Oishi, S., 193, 194
Olaniyan, R., 236
Oliveira, Z. M. R., 224
One-size-fits-all, xxiii, xxv, 3, 4, 188,
    228, 276, 287
One-theory-for-every culture, xxv, 4, 276
Ong, A., 174, 176
Ontogenetic changes,
        as developmental process
    cultural psychology of, 305–8
    developmental psychology of, 304–5
    plural norms for, 308–10
Ontogeny, 218
Open systems
    concept of, 214
    construct of, 215
    non-ergodicity of, 214–15
Opwis, K., 52
Organization for Economic Co-Operation
        and Development (OECD), 257
Orren, G., 121
Oser, F. K., 9
Osorio, S., 171, 176
Ostrosky-Solis, F., 56
Otaala, B., 238, 242
Otta, E., 96
Overton, W. F., 162, 277, 286, 288,
    291*t*, 296
Owusu-Bempah, 248
Oyserman, D., 57, 118
Ozawa-de Silva, C., 197

P
Páez, D., 118
Paine, L. W., 31
Pakistan, 264
Pandey, R., 282

Panga Muntu Test, 239
Panter, A. T., 58
Paranjpe, A. C., 297n1
Parasite singles, 261
Parenting, 75, 76, 77, 83, 84
    authoritarian, 201–2
    peer group prosocial–antisocial
        norms, 100
    shared, 248
    social class differences in, 124
Parents, 60, 62–63, 82, 83–85, 86, 125.
        See also Adolescent-adult
        relationship
    differences with children, 76–78
Park, Y. S., 27, 38
Parker, J. G., 9, 92, 99
Parkhurst, J. T., 101
Parkin, C. M., 78
Parmar, P., 95
Parnass, J., 99
Passeron, C., 82
Patterson, C., 92
Pearce, N. J., 126
Pearl, R., 101
Pearson-Merkowitz, S., 130
Pedagogies, in Africa, 246
Peer acceptance, 94. *See also*
        Peer relationship
    behavioral characteristics and,
        100–102
    prosocial–cooperative behavior and,
        100–101
    shyness and, 101, 102
    social change and, 102
Peer culture, in Africa, 246
Peer group, 94. *See also*
        Peer relationship
    individual autonomy in, 99
    social relationships in, 99–100
Peer interaction, 93. *See also*
        Peer relationship
    play in, 94–95
    social evaluations and responses in,
        96–97
    socio-dramatic behaviors, 95–96
Peer rejection. *See also*
        Peer relationship
    aggressive behavior and, 101
    shyness and, 101, 102
    social change and, 102

Peer relationship
    aspects of, 93–94
    in civic identify formation,
        127–29
    contextual–developmental perspective,
        103–5
    culture and, 103–5
    future directions, 105–6
    and human development, 93–94
    overview, 92–93
    socialization and, 103–5
Peers, and children's learning, 38–40
Penay Lillo, M., 117
Pence, A. R., 246, 247, 249
Peng, K., 190, 191
Penguin Revolution, 117
Perceptual representation system (PRS),
        56. *See also* Memory systems
Perez, S. M., 81
Perner, J., 34
Petit, G. S., 93
Phelan, P., 82
Philippines, 5, 98, 264
Phillips, D. A., 83, 86
Phinney, J. S., 3, 105, 170, 171, 173,
        174, 175, 176, 177, 229
Phylogeny, 218
Physical proximity. *See* Closeness
Piaget, J., 8, 9, 16, 92, 303. *See also*
        Ontogenetic changes,
        as developmental process
Pidada, S., 98, 100, 104
Pillemer, D. B., 51, 52, 53, 56,
        57, 58, 60, 62
Pinquart, M., 123
Pittinsky, T. L., 56
Pizarroso, N., 222
Play in peer interaction, 94–95
    cross-cultural differences in, 95
    in pre-industrialized societies, 95
Policy, 17–19, 180–81, 202–4,
        248–49
Political change, and generational
        replacement, 123–25
    younger generation, 124–25
Political incorporation, of younger
        generations, 119–21
Politics, values and, 121–23
    hegemonic world views, 122–23
Ponte, I., 199

Poortinga, Y. H., 118
Popenoe, D., 268
Porter, T., 221
Pott, G., 202
Potter, S. H., 194
Poulin, F., 99
Pozzetta, G. E., 105
Practices, 75–76. *See also* Contexts
  analysis, 85
  evaluative judgments, 76
Praise, 200–201. *See also* Socialization,
  and childrearing
Prakasa, V. V., 269
Prakash, K., 101
Pratt, D. D., 31
Premarital sex, in OECD countries, 259
  Western vs. Asian emerging adults,
  261–62
Prerogatives, of citizens, 116–19
Pressley, M., 51, 53
Procedural memory. *See also*
  Memory systems
  concept of, 55
  as implicit memory, 55
  memory tasks, 55–56
Promoter signs
  feed-forward function, 227
  meaning making and, 226–28
  semiotic mediator as, 226–27
Prosocial–cooperative behavior, and peer
  acceptance, 100–101
Prout, A., 244
PRS. *See* Perceptual representation
  system (PRS)
Purusharthas (life goals),
  Hindu perspective, 279

Q
Quinn, N., 28

R
Radhakrishnan, P., 194
Radhakrishnan, S., 279, 283, 295
Radmacher, K., 178
Raeff, C., 165, 198
Raffaelli, M., 82
Rakoczy, H., 34
Ram, A., 77, 78
Ramanujan, A. K., 293
Ramaswamy, J., 188

Ramdas, K., 261
Ramokgopa, M. I., 242
Ramos, K. D., 5
Rao, K. R., 297n1
Rao, N., 27
Rao, V. N., 269
Rappaport, J., 125
Rapson, R. L., 262
Ravenhill, P. L., 224
Ravn, M. N., 260
Reese, E., 59, 60, 62
Reid, M., 248
Relativism, xxiii
Religious identity, 172
Renninger, K. A., 29
Renunciation, stage of. *See* Sanyasa,
  Hindu life-stages
Resch, J., 38, 40
Responsibility, in peer group, 99–100
Responsiveness, anticipation vs.,
  199–200
Rhodes, J. E., 140
Riansari, M., 98
Richardson, W. K., 129
Richter, L., 249
Rickman, A., 265
Rights, 116–19. *See also* Civil societies
Risley, T. R., 40
Rituals. *See* Routines
Roazzi, A., 52, 63
Rodkin, P. C., 101
Rogers, C. R., 187
Rogoff, B., xxii, 51, 63, 75, 95, 147,
  164, 169, 197, 198, 245, 287
Rohlen, T. P., 271
Rohner, R. P., 187
Romney, K. A., 76
Rosa, A., 222
Rosas, S., 85
Rosemont, H., 118
Rosenbaum, P. J., 219
Rosenberg, M., 194
Rosenberger, N., 261
Ross, H ., 77, 78
Ross, M., 63
Rothbaum, F. M., 3, 191, 196, 197,
  198, 199, 200, 202
Routines, 75
Rozin, P., 5, 15
Rubin, D. C., 60

Rubin, K. H., 9, 92, 93, 94, 99, 100, 101
Ruble, D. N., 39, 79
Rudden, D., 200
Rudolph, L., 218, 221
Russell, B., 26
Ryan, R. M., 29, 198

S
Saarni, C., 197
Sacks, J., 32
Sahin, B., 59, 63
Salili, F., 28
Salmivalli, C., 99
Sam, D. L., 105, 174
Sanatana Dharma, 277
Sanchez-Jankowski, M., 115
Sandel, T. L., 98, 196
Sandhu, K. S., 169
Sankaranarayanan, A., 58
Santos, C., 174
Sanyasa, Hindu life-stages, 286
Saraswathi, T. S., 10, 16, 179, 263, 279, 281, 291t, 296
Sato, T., 217
Saudi Arabia, 264
Scarlett, G., 9
Schachter, E., 162, 165, 178, 182
Schacter, D. L., 50, 54, 55, 56
Scharf, M., 16, 267
Schatz, M., 54
Schimmack, U., 194
Schlegel, A., 9, 140, 141, 142, 143, 146, 147, 155, 156, 164, 166, 197, 265
Schneider, B. H., 3, 98, 101
Schneider, W., 51, 52, 53, 63
Schnyer, D. M., 56
Schulz, R., 296
Schwartz, D., 204
Schwille, J., 118
Scollon, C. K. N., 193
Sedikides, C., 193, 204
Seeco, E. G., 244
Segal, Z. V., 195
Segall, M. H., 118
Seif, H., 127
Self. See specific entries of self
Self acceptance
    fixed things and, 192–93
    malleable vs. fixed views of, 189–90

notion of, 189
Self-esteem, 196, 199, 200, 201, 203, 204
Self-expression, in peer interactions, 95–96. See also Peer interaction
Selfhood, 242–44
    concept, 242–43
    infancy stage, 244
    newborn period, 243–44
    puberty, 244
    social apprenticeship, 244
    stages of, 243–44
Self-improvement, vs. self-regard, 200–201
Self-regard, self-improvement vs., 200–201
Self-sufficiency, and emerging adulthood, 266–68
Self-worth and friendship, 98
Semantic memory, 54–55. See also Memory systems
    concept of, 54
Semi-arranged marriages, 169
Semiotic mediation. See Cultural psychology
Sen, A., 295
Sense of structure, 75
Sensitive caregiving, 199–200. See also Socialization, and childrearing
Separatist" perspectives, 74
Serpell, R., 27, 28, 75, 239, 242
Setiono, K., 98
Sever, I., 95
Sharabany, R., 97, 99, 104
Shared views
    and contexts, 76–78
    social policies, 85–87
Sharma, N., 264, 269
Shaver, P. R., 192, 199
Shiffrin, R. M., 53
Shih, M., 56
Shin, Y. L., 96
Shing, U. L., 118
Shirai, T., 99
Shonkoff, J. P., 83, 86
Shore, B., xxii
Shumba, A., 244
Shweder, R. A., xxii, 3, 4, 5, 8, 10, 28, 31, 74, 75, 114, 161, 197, 223, 245, 255, 287, 297n3

Shyness, and peer acceptance/rejection, 101, 102
Significant social groups, adolescent socialization in, 146–50
Silbereisen, R. K., 123, 180
Silva, C., 117, 126
Silva, E., 117
Silvia, P. J., 192
Sim, T. N., 99
Simon, J., 128
Sindhus, 277
Singapore, 27
Sinha, D., 296
Sirsch, U., 267
Sita, L., 10
Six Cultures Study of Childrearing, 238
Skinner, E. A., 296
Skowronek, J. S., 51, 56
Smale, J., 249
Smart, A., 98
Smetana, J. G., 17, 95, 199
Smith, B., 215
Smollar, J., 9
Snarey, J. R., 7, 8
Snibbe, A. C., 188
Snyder, M., 126
Sobel, D. M., 33, 34, 35
Social change and peer acceptance, 102
Social class, and emerging adulthood in OECD countries, 262–63
Social evaluations/responses, in peer interactions, 96–97. See also Peer interaction
Social groups, adolescent socialization in, 146–50
Socialization, and childrearing
  closeness, 197–99
  criticism, 200–201
  exercise of control, 201–2
  fostering of values, 196–97
  praise, 200–201
  sensitive caregiving, 199–200
Socialization, and children's learning beliefs, 40–42
Social policies, 83–87
  analyses of practices, 85
  cultural-developmental approach to morality and, 17–19
  differences in, 83–84
  identification of problems, 84

moral development and, 17–19
  shared views, 85–87
  state and, 83–84
Social relationships, in peer group, 99–100. See also Peer group
Social selfhood, 242–44
  concept, 242–43
  infancy stage, 244
  newborn period, 243–44
  puberty, 244
  social apprenticeship, 244
  stages of, 243–44
Socio-cultural perspectives, of memory development, 62–64
Socio-cultural theory, 103
Socio-dramatic behaviors, in peer interaction, 95–96
  cultural differences, 96
South Korea, 188
  emerging adults in, 261, 266
  instrumental assistance in, 98
  in OECD, 257
  postsecondary participation, 258
Squire, L. R., 50
Staff, J., 141
State and social policies, 83–84
Stateless citizen, 131
Steinberg, L., 147
Stem-family household, and adolescent socialization, 145
Stepick, A., 18
Stepick, C. D., 18
Sternberg, R. J., 3, 28, 204, 239
Stevens, N., 93
Stevenson, H. W., 27, 28, 95, 101, 190, 196, 271
Stewart, A. J., 125
Stewart, S. M., 202
Stigler, J. W., xxii, 27, 28, 196
Stipek, D., 39
Stjernfeldt, F., 220
Stout, M., 126
Strauss, C., 28, 77
Strauss, S., 33
Strosahl, K., 187
Structure, 4, 34, 65, 74–75
  Hindu life-stages, 289–91
Sugimura, K., 163, 165
Suh, E. M., 193, 194

Sullivan, H. S., 92, 98, 100, 104
Sullivan, H. W., 194
Sullivan, M. A., 223
Sun, S. L., 100
Super, C. M., 28, 55, 63, 95, 103, 104, 197, 238, 244
Supranational entities, 131
Sutin, A. R., 51
Swahilya, 283
Swanson, H. L., 53, 54, 55, 66
Sweden, 120, 122
Sweeney, C. D., 51
Syed, M., 178
Syvertsen, A. B., 127

T
Taber, S., 256
Taiwan, 27, 40–41, 196
Tajfel, H., 79
Takahashi, K., 132
Takemura, K., 188
Tamis-LeMonda, C. S., 106
Tanner, J. L., 255
Taoism, 276
Tape, G., 239
Tas, A. C., 60
Tchombe, T. M., 244
Tekcan, A. I., 60
TEM. See Trajectory Equifinality Model (TEM)
Terry, R., 92
Test for Tacit Knowledge for Natural Herbs, 239
Tetlock, P., 80
Thapar, R., 277
Tharakad, S., 162
Theory of mind (ToM), 33
Thompson, R. A., 80
Thomson, J., 120
Three ethics approach, 4–6. See also Cultural-developmental template
degree of use of, 6–10
development and, 7–10
Ethic of Autonomy. See Ethic of Autonomy
Ethic of Community. See Ethic of Community
Ethic of Divinity. See Ethic of Community
subcategories, 6

type of use of, 6–10
Tieszen, H. R., 96
Tietjen, A., 97, 98
ToM. See Theory of mind (ToM)
Tomasello, M., 27, 34
Tong, Y., 191
Torney-Purta, J., 118, 129
Townsend, N., 249
Trajectory Equifinality Model (TEM), 217–18
Transformational change, hindu life conception, 293–95
Triandis, H. C., 95, 165, 194, 195
Tripathi, R. C., 296
Trommsdorff, G., 199, 200
Troop-Gordon, W., 92
Tse, H. C., 105
Tseng, V., 176, 201, 202
Tu, W. M., 31
Tuholski, S. W., 55
Tulving, E., 52, 53, 54, 55, 56
Turiel, E., 4, 7, 8, 16, 165
Turkey, 59, 60, 116–17
Tweed, R. G., 31

U
U.N. Convention on the Rights of the Child (UNCRC), 118, 248–49
UNCRC. See U.N. Convention on the Rights of the Child (UNCRC)
United Kingdom, 60, 258, 267
United States, 5–6, 11, 16, 39, 95, 96, 173, 174, 175, 188, 190, 191, 199, 256, 257, 258, 261, 264, 266
childhood memory, 58
civil societies and, 115, 117–18, 127, 129
immigrants in, 18
individual responsibility, 121
memory development in, 58, 59, 61, 63, 64
religious liberals and conservatives in, 19
youth activists in, 126
Units of analysis, 222
developmental units, 222–23
Universalist perspectives, 74, 188
Unshared views, and contexts, 76–78
Urdan, T. C., 36
Uzgiris, I. C., 198

V

Vainio, A., 5, 6, 11
Valsiner, J., xxii, xxiv, 3, 124, 212, 213, 215, 216, 218, 219, 219*f*, 221, 222, 223, 224, 226, 227, 228
Values, and politics, 121–23
hegemonic world views, 122–23
van Acker, R., 101
Vanaprastha, Hindu life-stages, 285–86
van der Veer, R., 216
Vandewiele, M., 99
van Geert, P., 221
Van Horn, B., 120
Vaníčková, J., 267
van Ijzendoorn, H. W., 101
van Lieshout, C. F., 101
Vasquez, K., 5, 8
Vecoli, R. J., 105
Vedder, P., 105, 174, 175
Veii, K., 239
Ventura, J., 182
Verba, S., 114, 121
Verma, S., 95, 104, 121
Vermigli, P., 98
Vevea, J. L., 193
Victor, A., 98
Vidyarambha, Hindu concept, 282.
See also Hindu life conception
Vilhjalmsdottir, P., 171, 176
Vogel, S. M., 224
Vygotsky, L. S., 51, 103, 115, 119, 216, 217, 222, 229

W

Wagner, A. D., 50
WAIS. *See* Wechsler Adult Intelligence Scale (WAIS)
Walker, L. J., 7, 8, 9, 10, 14, 15, 17
Wall, S., 187
Walzer, M., 118
Wampler, K. S., 76
Wang, L., 96, 98
Wang, Q., 39, 40, 53, 57, 58, 59, 60, 62, 63, 64
Wang, S., 98, 196
Wang, Y., 200, 201
Wanner, B., 95
Warneken, F., 34
Waters, E., 187
Waters, M., 173, 174

Way, N., 98, 105, 174
Weaving, 164
Webley, P., 124
Wechsler Adult Intelligence Scale (WAIS), 54–55
Weisner, S. W., 240
Weisner, T. S., 82, 202, 241, 248
Weisz, J. R., 191, 195
Weller, S. C., 76
Wellman, H. M., 33, 34, 36
Wentzel, K. R., 28, 93
Wertsch, J. V., 79, 115, 131
White, S. H., 58, 64
Whitehead, B. D., 268
Whiting, B.B., 238
Whiting, B. B., 9, 95, 104, 198, 238
Whiting, J. W. M., 79, 238
Wigfield, A., 73
Wiley, A. R., 196, 200, 201
Wilk, R., 229
Williams, G. A., 101
Williams, J., 177
Wilson, J. Q., 14
Wilson, K., 187
Wilson, M., 139, 149
Wilson, S., 265
Wimmer, H., 34
Wittgenstein, L., 213
Wolf, A. W., 197
Wong, D. B., 118
Working memory, 53. *See also* Memory systems
World acceptance
fixed things, 192–93
malleable vs. fixed views of, 190–92
notion of, 189
Worldview, Hindu development, 278–79
Wray-Lake, L., 127
Wu, B., 261, 267, 268
Wu, D. Y. H., 194
Wu, P.202, 212
Wu, S.-P., 31

X

Xu, Y., 102

Y

Yates, M., 14, 17
Yi, S., 59, 62
Young, H. B., 98

Younger generations
  in political change, 124–25
  political incorporation of, 119–21
Youniss, J., 9, 14, 17
Yu, L., 102
Yu, R., 102

Z
Zahn-Waxler, C., 196, 200
Zambia, 8, 9, 239
Zappulla, C., 100
Zhang, Y., 98

Zhang, Z., 102
Zheng, S., 98
Zimba, R. F., 4, 8, 9, 241,
  242, 247
Zittoun, T., 224
Zone of proximal development (ZPD),
  216–17
  empirical use of, 217
  and intelligence tests, 217
ZPD. *See* Zone of proximal
  development (ZPD)
Zusho, A., 271